The British Monarchy Miscellany

A Collection of Royal Facts, Lists and Trivia

By Alex David

First Edition Published Independently through Amazon KDP 2017.
This Updated Edition Published Independently through Amazon KDP 2019.

London, United Kingdom

Author's contacts and web presence:
Website: www.alex-david.com
Twitter: @alexdavidwriter
Email: alexdavidwriter@yahoo.co.uk

Cover image: '*Charles II*' by John Michael Wright, c.1676.
Reproduced by kind permission of Royal Collection Trust.

This book is respectfully
and humbly dedicated
to His Royal Highness
The Prince of Wales.

CONTENTS

Introduction

This book was written for two reasons. The first one is that I am an insatiably curious person. Who was the first king of England? Which monarch and consort had the longest marriage? What happened to illegitimate children of kings? How many royal statues are in London? As I kept exploring the subject of the British monarchy, questions like these arose in my mind, and for each of them I was often forced to look up the answer in different places, or sometimes research the answer from scratch myself when it was not clearly available anywhere. I certainly could not find any single reference work containing answers to all my curious questions, so, to paraphrase politician and writer Benjamin Disraeli (a monarchy expert himself), since I could not find the book I needed, I wrote it.

The second reason was to show the many ways in which the British monarchy is inextricably connected to the political, social and cultural life of the country. The *Monarchs Facts Sheets* illustrate how the lives of individual monarchs influenced the history of England and then Britain. Chapters on royal ceremonies and on the National Anthem show how the monarchy has shaped the formation of national traditions. The sections on the monarchy and government, the monarchy and the church, and the monarchy and the Armed Forces show how these social and political institutions are all chained together through the monarch, the almost invisible but ever-present link bringing the whole state together under one crown. Even chapters on royal writers, artists and patrons of the arts are meant to spotlight the individual contributions of Royal Family members to British cultural life. The monarchy is not just members of the Royal Family waving from a balcony on important occasions. It is an institution with roots and branches reaching into every part of life in the UK, which is one of the reasons why this book has been structured into different sections highlighting different areas.

This however is not a manual. To write a complete manual or encyclopaedia on all the subjects associated with the British monarchy would take an extremely lengthy and superhuman effort. I know. I initially undertook research to write exactly such a British monarchy manual, and it resulted in a rough first draft of over 200,000 words (over 700 pages)—before even completing half the project! Hence, this is instead a miscellany, a collection of the most valuable and interesting information on the British Monarchy. Do not let the words 'miscellany' and 'trivia' mislead you, however, on the quality of the information contained herein. All the information in this book has been scrupulously researched and checked for accuracy: a full list of sources can be found at the end. Because of the many areas covered, I have tried to be accurate, yes, but also as concise as possible, so that what is written in here might serve not as a complete account of things but as a basic guide, a springboard to learn more. I have also, for the sake of conciseness and a strict focus, concentrated solely on the English/British monarchy starting at the Norman Conquest of 1066. More information on the Anglo-Saxon monarchy and Scottish monarchy might be included in a second book, together with the rest of the extra research which did not found its way here. I have striven to be fair and objective in compiling lists and presenting information, though in some cases I found it necessary to be guided by my personal judgement where it mattered. For example, few historians consider Eadred to be a candidate for the first king of England, but I do; I do not consider Lady Jane Grey to have a been a legitimate monarch (see my explanation in *Monarchs Facts Sheets*); and the 'Great Gems of State' category in *The Crown Jewels* chapter is entirely my own creation as I do believe that those particular, incredible gemstones deserve to be known in a class of their own. Generally though, be assured that the royal information you find here is right and true.

I hope you enjoy reading this book as I enjoyed writing it. As all reference and trivia books, it is not necessary to start at the beginning and read orderly until the end. Dip in and out at your leisure. Surf where your interest takes you. And be surprised, fascinated and perplexed at what you read. The institution of the British monarchy and its 1,000-year history are like an inextinguishable well, always springing up new surprises. It is a national saga with a dozen incarnations, hundreds of traditions, and a cast of thousands. What you will find in here is just a sketch of it. To paraphrase Marco Polo's introduction to his account of travels to wonders-full medieval China, what you read in this book is not even half of what I learned...

Alex David
London, June 2017.

MONARCHS

The First King of England

It can be difficult to determine exactly who was the first King of England. Unlike other countries, England's unification was achieved in stages, and the English monarchy developed by degrees, between the 8th and 11th centuries. There are several Anglo-Saxon monarchs who can be said to have been the first to reign over a unified country, or a unified English people, between the 790s and 970s. They include:

Offa, 790s

Offa, King of Mercia, (c.730- 796) is sometimes called the first king of England because he established lordship over most of the English territories towards the end of his reign in the 790s. He never ruled over Northumbria however, and his dominions were broken up after his death.

Alfred the Great, 880s

Alfred (849-899) was the first monarch to be given the title 'King of the English'. Originally King of Wessex (roughly Southern England) from 871, the Anglo-Saxon Chronicle recorded that after he led the English against Viking invaders in the 880s "all of the English people not subject to the Danes submitted themselves to King Alfred." He is therefore traditionally acknowledged as the first king who ruled over the English people, however his dominions excluded most of Eastern and Northern England.

Aethelstan, 920s

The grandson of Alfred of the Great, Aethelstan (c.895-939) was the first king who, after conquering Northern England, ruled over the whole modern English territory. On 12 July 927 he was recognized 'King of England and Overlord of Britain' by the other rulers of the island, and this day is taken by some as the foundation date of England. After his death however York and Northumbria escaped royal control and became independent again.

Eadred, 950s

Half brother of Aethelstan, Eadred (923-955) was the English king under whom the kingdoms of York and Northumbria permanently lost their independence and became part of the Kingdom of England around the year 952. The permanent unification of England under one crown therefore dates back from his reign. Sadly, Eadred died shortly of illness after this unification and is almost forgotten today, overshadowed in importance by the other monarchs in this list.

Edgar the Peaceful, 959-975

The nephew of Eadred, Edgar (c.943-975) was the last great unifier of the English nation. After pacifying the country from the internal divisions that had arisen under Eadred's successor, Edgar centralised the state, the church and the currency, and divided the country into the familiar counties of today. Most significantly, his achievements were recognised when he became the first monarch to receive an official coronation as King of the English in 973. No local kingdoms or internal divisions arose again in England after his death.

Royal Dynasties

Listed below are the 10 dynastic Royal Houses that have ruled in England/Britain since the Kingdom of England began to be unified by Alfred the Great in the 880s.

House of Wessex

Named after the local kingdom in Southern England from which the first Anglo-Saxon kings of a unified Kingdom of England emerged.

RULED: 880s to 1013, 1014 to 1016, 1042 to 1066
MONARCHS: 11
Alfred the Great, Edward the Elder, Aethelstan, Edmund the Elder, Eadred, Eadwig, Edgar the Peaceful, Edmund the Martyr, Aethelred the Unready, Edmund Ironside, Edward the Confessor

House of Denmark

Named after the Danish invader kings who ruled the country briefly in the 11th century.

RULED: 1013 to 1014, 1016 to 1042
MONARCHS: 4
Sweyn Forkbeard, Cnut, Harold Harefoot, Hartacnut

House of Godwin

Named after Harold Godwinson (meaning 'son of Godwin'), an Anglo-Saxon earl who reigned as king in 1066 after the rule of the House of Wessex came to an end, and before the Norman Conquest.

RULED: 1066
MONARCHS: 1
Harold Godwinson

House of Normandy

Named after the place of origin of William the Conqueror, Duke of Normandy, who conquered England in 1066.

RULED: 1066 to 1154
MONARCHS: 4
William I, William II, Henry I, Stephen

House of Plantagenet

Named after Geoffrey Plantagenet, the father of the first Plantagenet King, Henry II. The name itself refers to the *Planta Genista*, a broom flower Geoffrey adopted as his personal emblem.

RULED: 1154 to 1485

MONARCHS: 14

Henry II, Richard I, John, Henry III, Edward I, Edward II, Edward III, Richard II, Henry IV, Henry V, Henry VI, Edward IV, Edward V, Richard III

In the 15th century, the House of Plantagenet split in the following two branches that ruled England separately over an 85-year period:

House of Plantagenet—Lancaster Branch

Named after John of Gaunt, Duke of Lancaster,
father of the first Lancastrian King.

Ruled: 1399 to 1461, 1470 to 1471

Monarchs: 3

Henry IV, Henry V, Henry VI

House of Plantagenet—York Branch

Named after Richard, Duke of York,
father of the first Yorkist King.

Ruled: 1461 to 1470, 1471 to 1485

Monarchs: 3

Edward IV, Edward V, Richard III

House of Tudor

Named after Owen Tudor, the Welsh paternal grandfather of the first Tudor King, Henry VII. Henry himself was known as Henry Tudor before his accession.

RULED: 1485 to 1603

MONARCHS: 5

Henry VII, Henry VIII, Edward VI, Jane (disputed), Mary I, Elizabeth I

House of Stuart

Named after the Scottish royal dynasty, called Stewart in Scotland, that inherited the English throne after the death of the last Tudor monarch because of their descent from Henry VII. The name was changed from Stewart to Stuart by Mary Queen of Scots and Lord Darnley, parents of James I, the first Stuart monarch of England.

RULED: 1603 to 1714
MONARCHS: 7
James I, Charles I, Charles II, James II, William III and Mary II, Anne

House of Hanover

Named after the Electorate of Hanover, the German state whose Protestant ruling family inherited the British throne after the death of the last Stuart monarch, because of their descent from James I. Although the Electorate was formally known as the Electorate of Brunswick-Luneburg, it was more commonly referred to by the name of its capital city, Hanover.

RULED: 1714 to 1901
MONARCHS: 6
George I, George II, George III, George IV, William IV, Victoria

House of Saxe-Coburg-Gotha

Named after the German duchy of Saxe-Coburg-Gotha, to whose ducal family Prince Albert, husband to Queen Victoria, belonged. With Queen Victoria's approval, Albert passed on his family name to their children and descendants.

RULED: 1901 to 1917
MONARCHS: 2
Edward VII, George V

House of Windsor

Named after the town of Windsor, Berkshire that is the location of Windsor Castle, the oldest inhabited royal castle in Britain. King George V, who belonged to the House of Saxe-Coburg-Gotha, officially changed the German-sounding name of his dynasty to the more acceptable English name of Windsor in 1917, during the First World War.

RULED: 1917 to present
MONARCHS: 4
George V, Edward VIII, George VI, Elizabeth II

Note: *George V is listed in two different dynasties as he was both a member of the House of Saxe-Coburg-Gotha (1910-1917) and the House of Windsor (1917-1936).*

The Monarchs of Anglo-Saxon England From Alfred the Great to 1066

Listed below are the monarchs who reigned in Anglo-Saxon England from Alfred the Great, the first king to be acknowledged King of the English, to Harold Godwinson, the last king to reign before the Norman Conquest.

Monarch *(Date of Birth/Death)*	*Reigned:*

House of Wessex

Monarch	Reigned
Alfred the Great (849-899)	880s-899
Edward the Elder (c.874/77-924)	899-924
Aethelstan (895-939)	924-939
Edmund The Elder (c.921-946)	939-946
Eadred (c.923-955)	946-955
Eadwig (c.940-959)	955-959

Edgar the Peaceful
(c.943-975) 959-975

Edmund the Martyr
(c.962-978) 975-978

Aethelred the Unready
(c.968-1016) 978-1013, 1014-1016

House of Denmark

Sweyn Forkbeard
(c.960-1014) 1013-1014

House of Wessex

Edmund Ironside
(c.993-1016) 1016

House of Denmark

Cnut
(c.995-1035) 1016-1035

Harold Harefoot
(c.1016-1040) 1035-1040

Harthacnut
(1018-1042) 1040-1042

House of Wessex

Edward the Confessor
(c.1003-1066) 1042-1066

House of Godwin

Harold Godwinson
(c.1020-1066) 1066

The Monarchs of Scotland From Kenneth MacAlpin to 1707

Listed below are the monarchs who reigned in Scotland from Kenneth MacAlpin, the traditional first King of Scots in the 9th century, to Queen Anne, the last monarch of an independent Scotland before the Act of Union with England was passed in 1707.

Note: exact dates of birth for many monarchs of the House of Alpin are not known.

Monarch *(Date of Birth/Death)*	***Reigned:***

House of Alpin

Kenneth I MacAlpin (c.810-858)	c.843-858
Donald I (c.812-862)	858-862
Constantine I (?- 877)	862-877
Aedh (c.850s-878)	877-878
Giric (?-889)	878-889

Donald II	
(?-900)	889-900
Constantine II	
(c.870s-952)	900-943
Malcolm I	
(c.900-954)	943-954
Indulf	
(?-962)	954-962
Duff	
(?-967)	962-967
Colin	
(?-971)	967-971
Amlaib	
(?-977)	971-977
Kenneth II	
(c.950s-995)	971-995
Constantine III	
(c.960s-997)	995-997
Kenneth III	
(c.960s-1005)	997-1005
Malcolm II	
(c.954-1034)	1005-1034

House of Dunkeld

Duncan I (c.1001-1040)	1034-1040
Macbeth (c.1005-1057)	1040-1057
Lulach (c.1030-1058)	1057-1058
Malcolm III (c.1031-1093)	1058-1093
Donald III (c.1033-1099)	1093-1094, 1094-1097
Duncan II (c.1060-1094)	1094
Edgar (c.1074-1107)	1097-1107
Alexander I (c.1078-1124)	1107-1124
David I (1084-1153)	1124-1153
Malcolm IV (1141-1165)	1153-1165
William I (c.1143-1214)	1165-1214

Alexander II
(1198-1249) 1214-1249

Alexander III
(1241-1286) 1249-1286

House of Norway (Disputed)

Margaret
(1283-1290) 1286-1290

First Interregnum 1290-1292

Scotland is administered by the Guardians of Scotland whilst Edward I of England arbitrates between different claimants to the Scottish throne.

House of Balliol

John Balliol
(c.1249-1314) 1292-1296

Second Interregnum 1296-1306

Scotland is administered again by the Guardians of Scotland after John Balliol is deposed and the Scots fight against Edward I of England who wishes to conquer the country. Between 1304-1306 Scotland is occupied militarily by Edward I's English forces.

House of Bruce

Robert I, the Bruce
(1274-1329) 1306-1329

David II
(1324-1371) 1329-1371

House of Balliol (Disputed)

Edward Balliol
(c.1283-1367) 1332-1336

House of Stewart

Robert II
(1316-1390) 1371-1390

Robert III
(1337-1406) 1390-1406

James I
(1394-1437) 1406-1437

James II
(1430-1460) 1437-1460

James III
(1451-1488) 1460-1488

James IV
(1473-1513) 1488-1513

James V
(1512-1542) 1513-1542

Mary I
(1542-1587) 1542-1567

James VI
(1566-1625) 1567-1625

In 1603 Scottish monarchs also become monarchs of England. The crowns of the two monarchies were kept separate.

Charles I
(1600-1649) 1625-1649

Charles II
(1630-1685) 1649-1651

Third Interregnum 1651-1660

Scotland is incorporated by Oliver Cromwell into the Republican Commonwealth of England.

House of Stewart

Charles II
(re-instated) 1660-1685

James VII
(1633-1701) 1685-1688

Mary II
(1662-1694) 1689-1694
&
William II
(1650-1702) 1689-1702

Anne
(1665-1714) 1702-1707

Scotland and England ceased to have separate monarchies in 1707 after the Act of Union was passed establishing the Kingdom of Great Britain.

The Monarchs of England/ Great Britain/United Kingdom Since 1066

Listed below are the monarchs who have reigned in England, and later Great Britain and the United Kingdom, from the Norman Conquest of 1066 until our own day. For more information about each monarch refer to the *Monarchs Fact Sheets*.

Monarch *(Date of Birth/Death)*	***Reigned:***

House of Normandy

William I (c.1027/28-1087)	1066-1087
William II (c.1056/60-1100)	1087-1100
Henry I (c.1068/69-1135)	1100-1135
Stephen (c.1092/96-1154)	1135-1154

House of Plantagenet

Henry II (1133-1189)	1154-1189

Richard I (1157-1199)	1189-1199
John (1166-1216)	1199-1216
Henry III (1207-1272)	1216-1272
Edward I (1239-1307)	1272-1307
Edward II (1284-1327)	1307-1327
Edward III (1312-1377)	1327-1377
Richard II (1367-1400)	1377-1399

House of Plantagenet—Lancaster Branch

Henry IV (1366-1413)	1399-1413
Henry V (1386-1422)	1413-1422
Henry VI (1421-1471)	1422-1461, 1470-1471

House of Plantagenet—York Branch

Edward IV (1442-1483)	1461-1470, 1471-1483
Edward V (1470-1483)	1483
Richard III (1452-1485)	1483-1485

House of Tudor

Henry VII (1457-1509)	1485-1509
Henry VIII (1491-1547)	1509-1547
Edward VI (1537-1553)	1547-1553
Jane (Disputed) (c.1536/7-1554)	1553
Mary I (1516-1558)	1553-1558
Elizabeth I (1533-1603)	1558-1603

House of Stuart

James I
(1566-1625) 1603-1625

Charles I
(1600-1649) 1625-1649

Interregnum 1649-1660

In 1649 the monarchy was abolished and England was governed as a Republican Commonwealth. From 1653 to 1658 Oliver Cromwell ruled as king in all but name, using the title of Lord Protector.

Charles II
(1630-1685) 1660-1685

James II
(1633-1701) 1685-1688

Mary II
(1662-1694) 1689-1694
&
William III
(1650-1702) 1689-1702

Anne
(1665-1714) 1702-1714

House of Hanover

George I
(1660-1727) 1714-1727

George II
(1683-1760) 1727-1760

George III
(1738-1820) 1760-1820

George IV
(1762-1830) 1820-1830

William IV
(1765-1837) 1830-1837

Victoria
(1819-1901) 1837-1901

House of Saxe-Coburg-Gotha

Edward VII
(1841-1910) 1901-1910

House of Windsor

George V
(1865-1936) 1910-1936
(House of Saxe-Coburg-Gotha until 1917)

Edward VIII
(1894-1972) 1936

George VI
(1895-1952) 1936-1952

Elizabeth II
(1926-) 1952-present

MONARCHS FACTS SHEETS

William I

Reign: 25 December 1066 – 9 September 1087

Birth: Circa 1027-28 (exact date unknown). Illegitimate son of Robert I, Duke of Normandy, and a woman named Herleva of Falaise. Through his great-aunt, Queen Emma, first wife of King Aethelred the Unready, William was first cousin once removed to King Edward the Confessor.

Queen: Matilda of Flanders (c.1031-1083), daughter of Count Baldwin V of Flanders, and granddaughter of King Robert II of France.

Death: 9 September 1087, in Rouen, Normandy, France.

Key Facts:

He ruled Normandy as Duke during the first part of his life, proving himself to be politically astute, ruthless, and a skilled warrior. In 1051 he was chosen by his cousin, the childless king Edward the Confessor, to succeed him on the English throne after his death. Despite this, at Edward's death the English crown was offered to Harold Godwinson instead, prompting William to take action to defend his claim to the throne.

In 1066, he invaded England to claim the English crown in what is called the Norman Conquest. After landing in Sussex with an army, William defeated and killed King Harold Godwinson at the Battle of Hastings on 14 October 1066. He then marched onto London where he was crowned king in Westminster Abbey on

Christmas Day. His remarkable conquest of England in only a few weeks earned him the name of William the Conqueror.

After the Conquest, William redistributed Saxon lands to Norman nobles, creating a new ruling class. He also introduced French laws and concepts into England leading to the establishment of feudalism. The variant of the French language spoken by William and his court became the language of royal administration in England for over 350 years, and brought many new words into English. William also replaced Anglo-Saxon bishops and officials with continental prelates, in the process reshaping the English Church.

In order to control the local Anglo-Saxon population William introduced castles to England, which had previously been unknown in the country. By the end of his reign in 1087 over 70 castles were erected across the land, including the White Tower in London and castles at Dover, York and Nottingham. Small Saxon cathedrals were also replaced with much more imposing, massive Norman buildings. Among the cathedrals started in William's reign were Canterbury, Winchester, Ely, and York Minster.

He fought several Anglo-Saxon rebellions during his reign, the most serious of which was an uprising in the North of England in 1068-1069. In response to it, William led a major punitive campaign to the area in 1069-1070 later called 'The Harrying of the North'. Many people were slaughtered, food and livestock were destroyed, and fertile land was laid waste to make sure nothing could grow on it again. It is said that over 100,000 people perished as a result of the destruction and subsequent winter starvation. The North of England did not recover its prosperity for centuries.

In 1085-86 he ordered the compilation of the Domesday Book, an extensive census of people and their property across England done primarily for taxing purposes. One the most remarkable administrative surveys in Western history, Domesday remained unmatched in completeness in Europe until the 19th century. People called it Domesday because they said the facts therein were as accurate and inescapable as the judgments on Domesday (the Day of Judgment). It remains the oldest public record in England.

William's conquest of England was the most significant event in English history. By imposing Norman laws, culture and feudalism he severed England's previous political and cultural ties to Scandinavia and re-oriented the country towards continental Europe, particularly France. The social and political reorganization of the country under him was so complete, and the changes he introduced so lasting, that the history of England as a unified nation is considered to have begun with his conquest. The current numbering of British monarchs had its start in his reign.

Peculiar Fact:

William was very sensitive about his illegitimate birth. Once when some citizens in Alencon, France, mocked him about his bastard origins, William retaliated by having their hands and feet cut off. He also, unusually for his time, never took up a mistress himself.

William II

Reign: 9 September 1087 – 2 August 1100

Birth: Circa 1056-1060 (exact date unknown), in Normandy. Third son of King William I and Queen Matilda of Flanders.

Queen: None.

Death: 2 August 1100, in the New Forest, Hampshire.

Key Facts:

Called Rufus because of his red complexion, William resembled his father William the Conqueror in military skills and courage in battle, ensuring that he was picked as his father's successor even though he was not a firstborn son. Early in his reign he successfully fought an attempt by his elder brother Robert to capture the throne, during which he also fought and exiled his uncle, the powerful Archbishop Odo of Bayeux. Afterwards he went on to rule England with a firm hand.

He had a troubled relationship with the Church. Among other things, after the Archbishop of Canterbury died in 1089 William kept the position vacant for 4 years in order to cash in its revenues. He was accused of despoiling Church wealth, and angry ecclesiastical chroniclers retaliated by claiming that William led a debauched life and that under him sodomy and adultery had increased in the kingdom

He caused much resentment among both nobles and commoners by imposing heavy taxes and adopting harsh punishments for lawbreakers, including mutilation and dispossessing people of their property. He eventually died in suspicious circumstances whilst hunting in the New Forest when an arrow hit him in the heart. His only long-lasting legacy was the building of Westminster Hall, at the time the largest medieval hall in Europe, and still standing today as part of the Palace of Westminster in London.

Peculiar Fact:

William encouraged a new men's fashion at court which included sporting long hair, wearing shoes with long curled up tips, and dressing in revealing clothes. This contributed to him being accused by chroniclers of homosexuality and debauchery, however the fashion might actually have been aimed at seducing women.

Henry I

Reign: 2 August 1100 – 1 December 1135

Birth: Circa 1068-69 (exact date unknown), most probably in Yorkshire. Fourth son and youngest child of King William I and Queen Matilda of Flanders.

Queens:
1. *(1100-1118)* Matilda of Scotland (c.1080 – 1 May 1118), daughter of King Malcolm III of Scotland and of Margaret of Wessex.
2. *(1121-1135)* Adeliza of Louvain (c.1103 – 23 Apr 1151), daughter of Godfrey the Great, Count of Louvain.

Death: 1 December 1135 in Saint-Denis-en-Lyons, Normandy, France.

Key Facts:

An unexpected king of England, Henry healed the rift between the Anglo-Saxon population and its Norman foreign rulers by repealing many of the unfair, unpopular laws passed by the previous two kings against the native-born. He also gained popularity by marrying Matilda of Scotland, a descendant of the House of Wessex, and so uniting the Norman and Anglo-Saxon royal blood lines.

He established state bureaucracy in Medieval England and made it the most efficient in Europe in several ways: he founded the Exchequer as the centre of a new revenue system; he centralised the existing justice system inherited from the Saxon state and promoted fair and just laws for everyone, earning him the nickname of 'Lion of Justice'; and he created a new class of professional clerics based on merit alone who administered state business on his behalf. Under Henry, the Royal Court became firmly established as the centre of English government.

In 1120 he lost his only son and heir, William Adelin, in the White Ship shipwreck disaster. Henry immediately remarried, in his early 50s, to produce more male heirs but was he not successful, despite the fact that ironically he had already produced over a dozen illegitimate children. In the end, he tried to solve the succession problem by naming his daughter Matilda heir to the throne instead, making his barons swear allegiance to her as a future monarch during his own lifetime.

Peculiar Fact:

A just but ruthless man, Henry allowed two of his own illegitimate granddaughters to be blinded in retaliation for a similar act their parents had performed on a young boy. The enraged girls' mother, Henry's own illegitimate daughter, then tried to kill Henry by shooting him with a crossbow arrow as he entered her castle, barely missing him.

Stephen

Reign: 22 December 1135 – 25 October 1154

Birth: Between 1092 and 1097 (exact date unknown). Son of Stephen-Henry, Count of Blois, and of Adela, daughter of William the Conqueror.

Queen: Matilda of Boulogne (c.1103/5-1152), daughter of Count Eustace III of Boulogne.

Death: 25 October 1154, in Dover, Kent.

Key Facts:

He seized the English crown after the death of his uncle, Henry I, despite having previously sworn an oath that he would support the succession of Henry's daughter, Matilda, who was abroad when her father died. When Matilda arrived in England in 1139 to claim the throne a 15-year civil war ensued between her and Stephen, later called The Anarchy. Lawlessness and fighting ravaged England, with medieval chroniclers describing the period as a time 'when Christ and his saints slept'.

England was split in two for most of his reign, with Stephen controlling most of the east of the country and Matilda controlling the west. Their armies gained the upper hand at different times throughout the civil war. Stephen was captured in Lincoln in February 1141, then he was released in September of the same year after his wife personally led an army against Matilda's forces in Winchester. Then Matilda was kept under siege in Oxford in 1142 and forced to flee the town. After fighting eventually came to a stalemate in the late 1140s, Stephen agreed that Matilda's son would succeed him on the throne after he died, instead of his own son.

Known for his personal qualities including courtesy and chivalry, Stephen was a good commander on the battlefield. However he lacked the political skills necessary to rule which caused him to lose followers during the civil war and prolonged the conflict. Besides England, he also lost control of Wales during his reign.

Peculiar Fact:

In an odd twist during the military fighting, Stephen in 1147 bailed out his adversary, Matilda's son, the future Henry II, when he could not pay for the mercenary troops he had brought to England to fight with him. Stephen paid the troops himself and allowed Henry to leave the country to regroup, before he could come back to England and fight Stephen again.

Henry II

Reign: 25 October 1154 – 6 July 1189

Birth: 5 March 1133, in Le Mans, France. First son of Geoffrey, Count of Anjou, and of Matilda, former Empress of Germany and daughter of King Henry I.

Queen: Eleanor of Aquitaine (c.1122/24-1204), daughter of Duke William X of Aquitaine.

Death: 6 July 1189 at Chinon Castle, Touraine, France.

Key Facts:

The son of Henry I's daughter Matilda, Henry inherited the crown as a compromise to end the fighting between his mother and King Stephen. As king he re-established order in England after the Anarchy, brought renegade nobles under control, and reformed the currency. He also instituted landmark legal reforms like trial by jury and documentation of legal precedent, and is generally considered the father of English Common Law.

Before he became king he married the greatest land heiress of the age, Eleanor of Aquitaine, which gave him control of her vast lands of Aquitaine in southwest France. These, together with England, the French lands he inherited from his father and later conquests gave Henry the largest empire in Medieval Europe, stretching from Scotland in the north to the Pyrenees in the south, including half of France.

♔ He clashed repeatedly with the Archbishop of Canterbury, Thomas Becket, a former friend, over control of the English Church. He famously caused Becket's death by wishing aloud to be rid of him, after which four knights murdered the Archbishop in Canterbury Cathedral in 1170. Henry was later forced to do public penance at Becket's tomb.

♔ His reign was famously marred by family squabbles over power. His wife Eleanor and his three eldest sons rebelled against him in 1173-74, and after defeating them Henry imprisoned Eleanor on house arrests for the rest of his reign. Although he reconciled with his sons, his unwillingness to share power with them caused more rebellions later in his reign. The last family revolt was led by his son Richard the Lionheart in 1189, in the midst of which Henry died a broken and defeated man.

♔ His most troublesome foreign legacy was the invasion of Ireland he launched in 1171, inaugurating 700 years of English domination in Irish affairs. Henry encouraged English settlement of the island, built castles, and imposed his own allies as chiefs upon the population. The most poisonous dynamics of Anglo-Irish relationships, like dispossession of local rulers and English disdain towards the Irish population, began during his reign.

Peculiar Fact:

Henry had an explosive temper and his fits of anger were legendary. On one occasion people saw him tear off his clothes in a fit of rage and roll naked on the floor chewing straw (medieval house floors were strewn with straw for cleanliness). It was during one of these uncontrollable rages that he wished aloud for the death of Becket.

Richard I

Reign: 6 July 1189 – 6 April 1199

Birth: 8 September 1157 at Oxford. Second son of King Henry II and Queen Eleanor of Aquitaine.

Queen: Berengaria of Navarre (c.1163/65-1230), daughter of King Sancho VI of Navarre.

Death: 6 April 1199, in Chalus, Limousin, France.

Key Facts:

Richard was one of greatest knights of his age, known for his military skills and courage in battle. However he spent only six months of his 10-year reign in England, preferring instead to travel through in his French domains. He treated his English kingdom primarily as a source of revenue for his foreign military enterprises, including a crusade to the Holy Land and the defence of his French possessions against King Philip II of France.

His greatest achievement was his leadership of the Third Crusade between 1191-92 during which he achieved renown by defeating the Muslim leader Saladin in battle and won Christian pilgrims access to Jerusalem. Coming back to Europe, he was taken prisoner by one of his enemies in Austria and had to be ransomed with 34 tonnes of gold, raised primarily through high taxes and confiscations in England.

♔ He died during a minor military siege in France after getting struck by an arrow as he carelessly exposed himself to the enemy. Despite the fact that as a monarch he both neglected and exploited his English kingdom, his fame as the greatest knight of his generation meant that he is instead remembered as one of England's greatest kings.

Peculiar Fact:

Richard was a patron of French troubadours, played music, and composed songs himself. Whilst kept prisoner in Austria in 1192-93 he composed a troubadour lament entitled *Ja Nus Hons Pris Ne Dira* (No man who is prisoner can tell) which became a popular medieval song and is still performed today.

John

Reign: 6 April 1199 – 19 October 1216

Birth: 24 December 1166, at Oxford. Fourth son and youngest child of King Henry II and Queen Eleanor of Aquitaine.

Queen: Isabella of Angouleme (c.1187-1246), daughter of Aymer Taillefer, Count of Angouleme.

Death: 19 October 1216, in Newark Castle, Nottinghamshire.

Key Facts:

Reputed to have had some of the worst qualities of any monarch, John is said to have been cruel, greedy and lustful. As a young prince he rebelled against his father Henry II, and during his brother Richard I's reign he usurped royal power whilst Richard was fighting abroad. After he became king he murdered his nephew, Arthur of Brittany, who had a better claim than him to the English throne.

He lost most of the vast French domains amassed by his father Henry II through poor leadership and poor political judgements. By 1204 Normandy, joined to the English crown since 1066, had been lost permanently to France, and by 1206 only Aquitaine remained in English possession. Although he spent the rest of his reign trying to re-capture territories from the French King Philip II, his efforts came to nothing and culminated in a disastrous defeat at the Battle of Bouvines in 1214.

He quarrelled with Pope Innocent III over the English Church's rights to appoint bishops and to own property. The quarrel led to the pope excommunicating John in 1209 and placing England under an interdict, forbidding administration of the holy sacraments. The English population was denied Mass and other church rites for three and a half years until the dispute was finally resolved in 1213 after John submitted to the pope's authority.

He abused many English barons through extortionate fining, imprisonment and personal humiliations. After the barons rebelled, John was forced to sign Magna Carta in 1215, a new contract between the king and his subjects guaranteeing baronial rights, individual rights, and the freedom of the Church. John repudiated Magna Carta shortly after signing it however, and a civil war broke out between the parties which was later called The First Barons War.

John died in the midst of the war, right after the barons invited Prince Louis of France to invade England and take over the English throne. Shortly before his death, he famously lost most of his jewels whilst travelling in the sea marshes of East Anglia. He left the country in complete chaos with royal, baronial and French armies all marching across the land.

Peculiar Fact:

John was made Lord of Ireland by his father at the age of 10. Initially an absentee Lord, he finally visited Ireland at the age of 19 and caused great offense by making fun of the local chieftains' long beards, even going as far as pulling them for laughs. This damaged royal alliances and the expedition turned out a failure.

Henry III

Reign: 19 October 1216 – 16 November 1272

Birth: 1 October 1207, at Winchester Castle. First child of King John and Queen Isabella of Angouleme.

Queen: Eleanor of Provence (c.1223-1291), daughter of Count Raymond-Berengar IV of Provence.

Death: 16 November 1272, at the Palace of Westminster, London.

Key Facts:

Henry was only nine years old when he ascended the throne, at the height of the First Barons War. A regency of knights and lords ruled the country in his name during the first ten years of his reign. These capable regents ended the First Barons War, expelled the invading French army, and rebuilt England after the chaos of John's reign.

After he assumed personal rule at his majority he provoked much resentment among English nobles by favouring foreign relatives, and the foreign relatives of his wife. His poor leadership at home, poor foreign policy and high taxation caused a new rebellion among the barons called the Second Barons War, with opposition led by Henry's own brother-in-law Simon de Montford.

He was taken prisoner by Simon De Montford at the height of the Second Barons War after losing the Battle of Lewes in 1264. De

Montford and his allies then governed the country briefly in place of Henry, and during that time they presided over the first Parliament in English history in 1265. Henry regained power shortly after when his son, Prince Edward, defeated and killed De Montford at the Battle of Evesham in 1265. Henry however acknowledged the emergence of Parliament and continued to call it into session for the rest of his reign.

A deeply pious man, Henry rebuilt Westminster Abbey in the new gothic style, and rebuilt a new shrine to Saint Edward the Confessor to whom he was strongly devoted. His reign of 56 years was the longest of any English monarch until the 19th century, and saw the settling of national government in London around Henry's favourite area of Westminster.

Peculiar Fact:

Henry was the only monarch in English history to be crowned twice. The first coronation was a rushed affair in Gloucester Abbey to proclaim him king immediately after his father died, since French invading forces were in control of London. There were no proper crown jewels available and he was crowned with one of his mother's gold circlets. He was later re-crowned in Westminster Abbey after London was freed from French forces.

Edward I

Reign: 16 November 1272 – 7 July 1307

Birth: 17 June 1239, at the Palace of Westminster, London. First son of King Henry III and Queen Eleanor of Provence.

Queens:
1. *(1272-1290)* Eleanor of Castile (1241-1290), daughter of King Ferdinand III of Castile.
2. *(1299-1307)* Margaret of France (c.1279-1318), daughter of King Philip III of France.

Death: 7 July 1307, at Burgh by Sands, Cumberland.

Key Facts:

As a young prince, Edward led his father's army in the Second Barons War and restored his father to the throne after defeating Simon de Montford at the Battle of Evesham in 1265. Before his accession he went on Crusade to the Holy Land where he was the subject of an assassination attempt in Acre that failed when Edward wrestled the assassin and killed him.

As king, he conquered Wales by defeating local rulers and subduing the area militarily. Afterwards he made the country a principality of England in 1283, encouraged English settlement of the land, and made his son Edward the first Prince of Wales. To keep the most rebellious part of the country in the north under control he built numerous castles which loomed over the land.

He tried to bring Scotland under English control by numerous means in an effort to unite the whole island of Britain under one crown. First, in 1292, after he was asked to act as arbiter on a disputed Scottish royal succession, he favoured one candidate, John Balliol, whom he tried to make a puppet king. Then when the Scots rebelled against Balliol in 1295 he tried to impose direct control over the country by invading Scotland and installing English officials in power. In an attempt to humiliate the Scots he also took the Stone of Scone to England and set it in the English coronation chair.

Domestically, he reformed English laws and strengthened the administration of justice. He also made the calling of Parliament more frequent and granted it permanent rights, like the right to approve taxation. His worst domestic legacy was the expulsion of all Jews from England in 1290 after he had taxed them and exploited them to exhaustion. They would not be admitted back into England until 1656.

The last part of his reign was dominated by a renewed attempt to make himself direct ruler of Scotland, this time authorising destructive raids and acts of brutality against the Scots. The Scottish people however defied Edward, first by rebelling under William Wallace in 1297-1298, and then by uniting behind Robert the Bruce who made himself King of Scots in 1306. Edward died while travelling to Scotland to fight Robert the Bruce, his dream of conquering the country remaining unfulfilled. The legacy of enmity he established between Scotland and England persists to this day.

Peculiar Fact:

Tradition says that one of Edward's last wishes before he died was that his bones be boiled, cleaned and carried in procession in any future military campaign against Scotland. His wishes were not carried out.

Edward II

Reign: 7 July 1307 – 25 January 1327

Birth: 25 April 1284, at Caernarfon Castle, Wales. Tenth-surviving child and only surviving son of King Edward I and Queen Eleanor of Castile.

Queen: Isabella of France (c.1295-1358), daughter of King Philip IV of France.

Death: 21 September 1327, in Berkeley Castle, Gloucestershire.

Key Facts:

A very different man from his father, Edward II had no liking for war preferring instead leisurely pursuits. He was profoundly stubborn yet also easily led by others, and at times highly vindictive. He is considered by many to have been the worst monarch England ever had, leaving no positive legacies to his name.

His over-reliance on self-seeking favourites, including Piers Gaveston, caused great resentment among the English nobility who begrudged the many favours Edward showered on them. The nobility eventually ousted and executed Gaveston in 1312, however Edward continued to alienate nobles by focusing his attention on a new favourite, the young English noble Hugh Despenser.

To great national consternation, he lost control of Scotland after he led an English army to disastrous defeat at the Battle of Bannockburn in 1314, allowing the Scots to proclaim complete independence from England. He also caused discontent across the country by executing nobles opposed to his policies, including his own cousin Thomas, Earl of Lancaster. General discontent was further fuelled by the Great Famine of 1315-1317 which affected England into the 1320s.

His continued relationship with Hugh Despenser (possibly a romantic/sexual one) alienated Edward's wife Isabella, who took refuge abroad in her native France and began openly opposing Edward. After planning an invasion of the country together with her new lover, Roger Mortimer, Isabella landed in England in 1326 at the head of a small army and deposed Edward, whose support quickly melted away. She also executed Hugh Despenser.

The first English King to be officially deposed, Edward was forced to relinquish the throne in January 1327 to his teenage son, Edward III, and his ousting set a legal precedent for future royal depositions. Initially allowed to live out his days in seclusion, he later died in mysterious circumstances whilst imprisoned at Berkeley Castle, some say murdered on the orders of Isabella's lover, Roger Mortimer. Other contemporary rumours claimed however that he was allowed to escape and live in obscurity abroad.

Peculiar Fact:

Unusually for his time, Edward enjoyed unroyal past-times like digging, hedging and rowing, activities that were usually associated with labourers. This prompted speculation that he was not the great Edward I's son but a changeling that had been switched with the real prince at birth. No real claimant however ever came forward proving that he was the real Edward II.

Edward III

Reign: 25 January 1327 – 21 June 1377

Birth: 13 November 1312, at Windsor Castle. First son of King Edward II and Queen Isabella of France.

Queen: Philippa of Hainault (c.1311/15-1369), daughter of Count William I of Hainault (Flanders).

Death: 21 June 1377, in Sheen Palace, near London.

Key Facts:

After inheriting the crown at age 14 at the forced deposition of his father, Edward spent the first years of his reign under the control of his mother's lover, Roger Mortimer, who acted as king in all but name. At the age of 17, in 1330, he finally overthrew Mortimer, had him executed, and began to rule directly.

In 1337 he claimed the French throne as the grandson of King Philip IV of France, through his mother Isabella, beginning to style himself King of France. When his claim was rejected by the French Parliement, he took up arms against France starting the Hundred Years War. He won initial resounding victories including the Battle of Crecy in 1346 where Edward's archers famously decimate the French nobility. In 1347 he captured the town of Calais after an 11-month siege, following which the town remained in English hands for 200 years.

He won control of a third of the French kingdom after his son, Edward the Black Prince, won the Battle of Poitiers in 1356. At the Treaty of Bretigny in 1360 Edward agreed to abandon his claims to the French throne in exchange for sovereignty over the territory England had gained up until that point. However by the end of his reign in 1377 the French had regrouped and had conquered back almost all the lands Edward had won in the war.

An able commander in the field and an innovative strategist, Edward turned the English army into one of the most formidable military machines in Europe, adopting the longbow in battle as well as artillery. A natural leader of men, in 1348 he founded the Order of the Garter, the oldest order of chivalry in England, as a group of knights bound together in honour and service to the king.

His rule was marked by almost 50 years of domestic peace, due largely to his personal and political abilities as ruler. Among his achievements he fostered national identity at home by beginning to use the English language in government, and he promoted English literature and architecture. In the following centuries his reign came to be seen as a golden age for England and the English monarchy.

Peculiar Fact:
In 1363 Edward issued a decree banning football, handball, hockey and other 'idle games' so that people could spend their free time practicing archery instead. The long bow arch was the key to English success on the battlefield during the Hundred Years War, so the ban was meant to promote archery training and pass down skills.

Richard II

Reign: 21 June 1377 – 30 September 1399

Birth: 6 January 1367, in Bordeaux, France. Second son of Edward the Black Prince and of Joan of Kent; grandson of King Edward III.

Queens:
1. *(1382-1394)* Anne of Bohemia (1366-1394), daughter of Holy Roman Emperor Charles IV.
2. *(1396-1399)* Isabella of Valois (1389-1409), daughter of King Charles VI of France.

Death: Around 14 February 1400, at Pontefract Castle, Yorkshire.

Key Facts:

Richard inherited the crown at age 10 because his father, Edward the Black Prince, had predeceased Edward III. A regency council was in place during his minority but real power was wielded by Richard's uncle John of Gaunt, Duke of Lancaster. In 1381, at the age of 14, Richard showed great courage during the Peasants Revolt when he met with rebel crowds in London to listen to their demands and prevented a mob riot during a scuffle. After the danger passed however he approved severe punishments for the rebel leaders.

After he begun to exercise direct power in his late teens he was accused of misgovernment and of giving too much power to favourites. In 1387 he was forced to accept the supervision of a group of nobles called the Lords Appellant, who executed or exiled people from Richard's circle and forced him to accept Parliament's advice. Later in his reign Richard took revenge on the Lords Appellant and their supporters by executing or punishing many of them.

He tried to adopt an early form of absolute monarchy by refusing to work with Parliament and the nobility, punishing people for what he perceived to be slights to his person, and creating a court culture centred on utter submission to the monarch. He is said to have developed a narcissistic personality and was the first monarch to adopt the title 'Your Majesty'.

His rule became increasingly unpopular after he agreed a 28-year-truce with France in the Hundred Years War in 1396. He also began dispossessing nobles of their estates including his cousin Henry Bolingbroke, the richest noble in England, who was exiled on a pretext in 1398. Richard's actions caused alarm among the nobility who began to complain of his tyranny.

Abandoned by most of his supporters, he was deposed in 1399 by his cousin Henry Bolingbroke after he came back from exile to lead a rebellion against Richard. Henry became King in his place, and Richard was imprisoned in Pontefract Castle in Yorkshire where he later died in mysterious circumstances, most likely murdered on Henry's orders.

Despite his failings Richard was a great patron of the arts, and under him the English court became one of the most refined in Europe. His contributions included the rebuilding of Westminster Hall, the commissioning of paintings and illuminated manuscripts, and the invention of the handkerchief. He was also a patron of writers Geoffrey Chaucer and John Gower.

Peculiar Fact:

Although their marriage was childless, Richard was deeply attached to his first wife Anne of Bohemia. After she died of plague at Sheen Manor, near London, in 1394 a distraught Richard had that palace, where they had shared many good memories, razed to the ground.

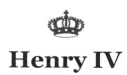

Henry IV

Reign: 30 September 1399 – 20 March 1413

Birth: 15 April 1367, at Bolingbroke Castle, Lincolnshire. First son of John of Gaunt, Duke of Lancaster; grandson of King Edward III.

Queen: Joanne of Navarre (c.1368/70-1437), daughter of King Charles II of Navarre, Dowager Duchess of Brittany.

Death: 20 March 1413, in the lodgings of Westminster Abbey, London.

Key Facts:

Heir to the Lancastrian inheritance, one of largest fortunes in England, Henry had a distinguished career before he became king. He was one of most famous European jousters of his generation, he fought crusades with Teutonic knights in Lithuania, and travelled to the Holy Land in pilgrimage where in 1393 he became the first English king to enter the city of Jerusalem.

One of the Lords Appellant who forced Richard II to reform his government in 1387, he was initially spared from Richard's vengeful reprisals in 1397. A year later however Richard exiled him to France and confiscated his vast Lancastrian inheritance, leaving him as a penniless exile in France.

In 1399, after it became clear that an increasingly tyrannical Richard II had lost the support of the country, Henry came back to

England, deposed Richard with popular support, and was crowned king in his place. He was not next in the line of succession to the throne however, and his usurpation of the crown from Richard II and his legitimate heirs set off a ticking time bomb that would later explode in the Wars of the Roses.

He spent most of his reign putting down rebellions by disaffected nobles and former supporters of Richard II. The largest rebellion, by the Percy family of Northern England, was put down in 1403 when Henry defeated their army at the Battle of Shrewsbury. Two more Percy rebellions followed later, during one of which Henry was forced to execute the Archbishop of York who had risen against him. Henry also fought repeatedly against Owain Glyn Dwr, the Welsh leader who had proclaimed himself Prince of Wales.

In 1401 he became the first English king to pass harsh laws against Christian heresy, including death penalties for preaching heretical ideas. The laws were aimed at the followers of John Wycliffe, called 'Lollards', some of whom became in Henry's reign the first English people to be burned at the stake for heresy.

He became afflicted from the middle of his reign with a mysterious disease that affected his skin and nervous system, and died in the Jerusalem Chamber of Westminster Abbey in 1413, fulfilling a previous prophecy that he would 'die in Jerusalem'. Many people, including Henry himself, considered the painful manner of his death to be God's punishment for his usurpation of the crown from Richard II.

Peculiar Fact:

Obsessed with health for most of his life, Henry put great faith in uroscopy, a medieval method used to diagnose someone's diseases and prescribe cures by looking into urine samples, even commissioning a medical treatise on it.

Henry V

Reign: 20 March 1413 – 31 August 1422

Birth: 9 August 1387, in Monmouth Castle, Wales. First son of King Henry IV and his first wife, Mary de Bohun.

Queen: Catherine of Valois (1401-1437), daughter of King Charles VI of France.

Death: 31 August 1422, in the Chateau de Vincennes, near Paris, France.

Key Facts:

A valiant soldier since his teens, Henry was permanently disfigured at the age of 16 whilst fighting with his father at the Battle of Shrewsbury when an arrow struck the right side of his face. He later became a strong military commander capable of inspiring troops through his bravery, as well as a model of medieval chivalry and honour.

As king he mended the divisions that had damaged his father's reign, pardoning former rebels and including everyone in his government. He adopted English as the official language of government records, and was the first king to leave written correspondence in English since before the Norman Conquest.

In 1415 he re-started the Hundred Years War with France by claiming the French throne like his great-grandfather Edward III had done. He led a great army across the Channel to France that same year winning a famous victory against the odds at Agincourt in October. He then went on to re-conquer Normandy in 1419.

♔ Taking advantage of internal struggles at the French court, he overpowered his opponents and occupied most of Northern France by 1420. After forcing the Treaty of Troyes in 1420 he became Regent of France as well as heir to the French throne. The treaty was sealed by his marriage to the French king's daughter, Catherine. Henry however died of dysentery soon afterwards at the height of his triumphs before he could consolidate English power in France.

Peculiar Fact:

In 1419 Henry accused his stepmother, Queen Dowager Joan of Navarre, of using witchcraft to poison him and imprisoned her for three years. It is thought the accusations were spurious, caused by a family argument and Henry's wish to confiscate her large wealth. He finally dropped the charges and released her from prison on his deathbed.

Henry VI

Reign:
31 August 1422 – 4 March 1461;
3 October 1470 – 11 April 1471

Birth: 6 December 1421, at Windsor Castle. Only child of King Henry V and Queen Catherine of Valois.

Queen: Margaret of Anjou (1430-1482), daughter of Rene', Duke of Anjou, and niece of Charles VII, King of France.

Death: 21 May 1471, in the Tower of London.

Key Facts:

The youngest ever king of England, Henry ascended the throne at the age of 9 months after the sudden death of his father Henry V. Meek by nature, indecisive and easily led by others, he grew up ill-suited to be king in the medieval age.

A regency council governed the kingdom successfully during his minority, but when Henry assumed power at his majority he began to make poor choices. These included a controversial marriage to French princess Margaret of Anjou, and poor leadership in the Hundred Years War which resulted in the loss of all the territories the English had won in France under his father.

In 1453, following the loss of the last English lands in France, he lost his sanity and sank into a catatonic state for 18 months when he was unable to recognise people or surroundings. After his recovery in 1454 he never completely regained his sanity, so royal leadership began to be exercised by his wife Margaret instead.

Henry's lack of leadership, inability to keep magnates under control and subsequent madness led directly to the Wars of the Roses between his own dynasty, the Lancastrians, and those opposed to them, the Yorkists, led by Richard Duke of York who had himself a claim to the throne and who challenged Henry's fitness to be king.

After the Wars of the Roses erupted in 1455 he only acted as a figurehead for the Lancastrians as his sanity began to slip away permanently. His wife Margaret assumed leadership of their faction to protect the rights of their young son, the Prince of Wales. Following five years of battles, Henry was deposed in 1461 by Richard Duke of York's son, Edward, who became king in his place as Edward IV. Henry was then imprisoned in the Tower of London.

He was briefly restored to the throne as a Lancastrian figurehead king for seven months between 1470-1471, after Richard Neville, Earl of Warwick, the most powerful noble in the realm, rebelled against Edward IV and forced him to flee abroad. After Edward IV came back to England and regained the throne by battle in 1471 Henry was deposed once again and was murdered shortly afterwards in the Tower of London in April 1471.

A deeply pious man, his greatest legacies were the religious and educational buildings he founded at Eton College, Windsor; All Souls' College, Oxford; and King's College, Cambridge with its magnificent chapel. After his death a short-lived cult developed at his tomb and he was briefly considered for sainthood, but without success.

Peculiar Fact:

Once at Christmas, when he was a teenager, one of Henry's lords arranged for a group of young women to dance before him showing bare breasts. Presented with this sight, Henry covered his eyes with a mixture of anger and shame and left the room saying "Fie, fie, for shame! Forsooth, you are to blame!"

Edward IV

Reign:
4 March 1461 – 3 October 1470;
11 April 1471 – 9 April 1483

Birth: 28 April 1442, in Rouen, France. First son of Richard, Duke of York, and of Cecily Neville.

Queen: Elizabeth Woodville (c.1437-1492), daughter of Richard Woodville, Earl Rivers, and of Jacquetta of Luxembourg.

Death: 9 April 1483, in the Palace of Westminster, London.

Key Facts:

The leader of the Yorkist faction during the Wars of the Roses from 1460, Edward became king in 1461 after defeating Henry VI's Lancastrians at the Battle of Towton, the largest, bloodiest battle ever fought on English soil. An imposing yet affable figure, as a military commander he was never defeated on the field of battle.

As king he created resentment among nobles and allies by secretly marrying, in 1464, Elizabeth Woodville, a Lancastrian widow who was considered unsuitable as a royal bride. The marriage, and the preferential treatment Edward showed to her relatives, led to a rebellion by Edward's allies in 1469 led by Richard Neville, Earl of Warwick, the most powerful noble in the realm.

♔ He was deposed from the throne for a 7 month-period in 1470-1471 after Richard Neville forced him to go into exile. During this time Neville arranged for the Lancastrian King Henry VI to be reinstated to the throne. After gathering forces abroad, Edward came back to England in March 1471 and regained the throne by defeating Neville at the Battle of Barnet, and later by crushing the Lancastrians once and for all at the Battle of Tewkesbury in May 1471.

♔ After his restoration he spent the last 12 years of his reign re-establishing peace and order in the kingdom following the upheavals of the Wars of the Roses. He created prosperity through trade and commerce, and greatly enriched the royal estates by confiscating Lancastrian properties. He became a great patron of the arts and of writers, and is widely considered England's first Renaissance prince.

♔ Although he made the House of York secure by eliminating all its Lancastrian enemies except one (Henry Tudor), his sudden death in 1483 at the age of 41 ignited a power struggle between the Yorkists themselves that would eventually lead to the self-destruction of their dynasty, and to the rise of the House of Tudor.

Peculiar Fact:

Edward was the tallest king in English history. When his tomb was opened in 1789 his skeleton was measured at roughly 6'4". He was also one of the fairest-looking, with one chronicle describing him as 'a person of most elegant appearance and remarkable beyond all others for the attractions of his person.'

Edward V

Reign: 9 April – 26 June 1483

Birth: 2 November 1470, in the precincts of Westminster Abbey, London. First son of King Edward IV and Queen Elizabeth Woodville. Born during the short period in 1470-1471 when his father was deposed from the throne.

Queen: None

Death: Presumed to be sometime between August and October 1483, in the Tower of London.

Key Facts:

The shortest-reigning monarch in English history since 1066, Edward became king at the age of 12 after the sudden death of his father. He was deposed two and a half months later by his uncle, Richard Duke of Gloucester (later Richard III) who had been appointed as his protector, and who claimed Edward was not a rightful king because he had been born illegitimate.

He disappeared in mysterious circumstances shortly after his deposition together with his younger brother and heir, Prince Richard, whilst the two were being kept prisoners in the Tower of London. The two, commonly called the Princes in The Tower, are generally presumed to have been murdered under the orders, or with the complicity, of their uncle Richard III.

Peculiar Fact:

Despite his short life, Edward was made Prince of Wales at the age of 8 months and Knight of the Garter at 5-years-old. At the age of 10 he was married to Anne, heiress of the Duchy of Brittany in France, who was 4-years-old at the time. Their marriage was to be legally consummated later once they both became of age.

Richard III

Reign: 26 June 1483 – 22 August 1485

Birth: 2 October 1452, at Fotheringhay Castle, Northamptonshire. Fourth son of Richard, Duke of York, and Cecily Neville.

Queen: Anne Neville (1456-1485), daughter of Richard Neville, Earl of Warwick.

Death: 22 August 1485, at Bosworth Field, Leicestershire.

Key Facts:

Richard was a loyal brother to King Edward IV who during his reign entrusted him with many tasks and missions including administration of the entire North of England. He also fought valiantly on the Yorkist side at the Battle of Barnet and Battle of Tewkesbury during the Wars of the Roses.

Declared Lord Protector during the short reign of his nephew Edward V, he seized power claiming that he was trying to prevent a coup by the family of the Queen Dowager Elizabeth Woodville. After confining Edward V to the Tower of London, Richard usurped his crown by convincing Parliament to depose the young king for being illegitimate (he claimed his brother Edward had married another woman before he married Elizabeth Woodville), and having Parliament proclaim him king instead as Richard III.

♔ He is presumed responsible for the disappearance, and possible murders, of Edward V and his younger brother Richard who was next in line to the throne. The boys, known as the Princes in the Tower, were last seen in 1483 in the Tower of London where they were kept prisoners on Richard's orders. No irrefutable evidence has yet been found however proving him directly guilty of their deaths.

♔ He was defeated and killed at the Battle of Bosworth in 1485 by Henry Tudor, the last Lancastrian claimant to the throne who became King Henry VII in his place. Richard was the last English king to die in battle, the last Plantagenet king to rule England, and his death marked the definite end of the Wars of the Roses.

♔ Demonized by the Tudor dynasty as an evil king, he was famously turned by William Shakespeare into a scheming hunchbacked monster in his play *Richard III*. He was partly rehabilitated in the 21st century after the rediscovery of his remains in Leicester in 2012, which proved among other things that he suffered from scoliosis but was not a hunchback.

Peculiar Fact:
Extensive DNA analysis carried out on Richard's bones showed that his diet as king included lots of shellfish; that he ate bird meat like heron, crane and swan; and that he drank about a bottle of wine a day. It also showed that he had a roundworm infection when he died.

Henry VII

Reign: 22 August 1485 – 21 April 1509

Birth: 28 January 1457, at Pembroke Castle, Wales. Only child of Edmund Tudor, Earl of Richmond, and of Margaret Beaufort, a descendant of King Edward III.

Queen: Elizabeth of York (1466-1503), daughter of King Edward IV and Elizabeth Woodville.

Death: 21 April 1509, at Richmond Palace, near London.

Key Facts:

The founder of the Tudor dynasty, Henry finally brought peace to England after decades of political chaos caused by the Wars of the Roses between Yorkists and Lancastrians. He won the crown at the Battle of Bosworth in 1485 as the last Lancastrian claimant to the throne after defeating the Yorkist Richard III. By marrying Elizabeth of York, daughter of the Yorkist Edward IV, he united the two warring dynasties.

Throughout his reign he had to put down several rebellions fomented by remaining Yorkists factions. These included uprisings led by two fake pretenders to the throne: Lambert Simnel in 1487 and Perkin Warbeck in 1495/97. Although initially merciful towards the house of York, these uprisings forced him later in his reign to execute some of the last Yorkist royal claimants.

♔ He strengthened the institution of the monarchy by breaking the power of the English nobility, which had been one of the causes of factional fighting during the Wars of the Roses. He accumulated much wealth by annexing former Yorkist and Lancastrian lands and by imposing taxes and fines.

♔ Because of the many taxes he imposed across the land he gained the reputation of a miser among the people. Increasing financial burdens on all classes provoked popular resentment, and a rebellion eventually erupted in Cornwall in 1497 which marched across southern England and was put down only on the outskirts of London.

♔ He sponsored trips of exploration to the newly discovered American lands, particularly the voyages of John and Sebastian Cabot. The two Italian explorers claimed the first lands in North America for the English Crown in the 1490s, in present-day Newfoundland.

Peculiar Fact:
After marrying Elizabeth of York Henry created the Tudor rose emblem, a symbol that combined the red rose of the house of Lancaster and the white rose of the House of York. The Tudor rose has since become one of the national symbols of England, shown on many English government buildings and included in the insignia of many military regiments. It is also shown on British coins and on the shirts of the England national football team.

Henry VIII

Reign: 21 April 1509 – 28 January 1547

Birth: 28 June 1491, at Greenwich Palace, near London. Second son of King Henry VII and Queen Elizabeth of York.

Queens:
1. *(1509-1533)* Catherine of Aragon (1485-1536), daughter of King Ferdinand II of Aragon and Queen Isabella I of Castile.
2. *(1533-1536)* Anne Boleyn (c.1500/01-1536), daughter of Thomas Boleyn, Earl of Wiltshire.
3. *(1536-1537)* Jane Seymour (c.1507/09-1537), daughter of Sir John Seymour.
4. *(1540)* Anne of Cleves (1515-1557), daughter of Duke John III of Cleves.
5. *(1540-1541)* Catherine Howard (c.1522/25-1542), daughter of Lord Edmund Howard.
6. *(1543-1547)* Catherine Parr (c.1512-1548), daughter of Sir Thomas Parr.

Death:
28 January 1547, at Whitehall Palace, London.

Key Facts:

A larger than life personality, Henry was a true Renaissance Prince with a humanist education. He was a skilled musician, dancer, jouster, writer and poet. He created one of the most refined courts in Europe and patronised artists and musicians.

♔ He increased England's status in Europe through diplomacy, alliances and short wars. His meeting with King Francis I of France at the Field of the Cloth of Gold in France in 1520 was one of the most grandiose occasions of the century. He competed for glory and renown with both Francis I and Holy Roman Emperor Charles V.

♔ His famous search for a male heir drove him to divorce his first wife, Catherine of Aragon, and marry Anne Boleyn, whom he also divorced and executed later before marrying a third time to Jane Seymour. His subsequent three marriages were driven more by political alliances and the need for companionship.

♔ In order to divorce Catherine of Aragon he split England away from the Roman Catholic Church, created the Church of England in its place and proclaimed independence from the pope. He then made himself Supreme Head of the English Church. At heart however he remained a Catholic when it came to religious doctrine.

♔ His religious reforms saw the Dissolution of the English Monasteries, the dispersal of monks and nuns, and the re-distribution of church lands to the Crown and English nobility. He also ordered the destruction of sacred relics and shrines. All these upheavals caused a popular rebellion in 1536 called the Pilgrimage of Grace which was put down with much difficulty.

♔ He officially united Wales into the kingdom of England, making English the official language, creating new counties, and including Welsh representation in Parliament. He also made himself the first English King of Ireland.

♔ He became increasingly obese, illness-ridden and paranoid as he grew older. The last 10 years of his reign were marked by court intrigues and multiple executions, including those of Thomas

Cromwell, Catherine Howard, Margaret de la Pole and Henry Howard, Earl of Surrey.

Peculiar Fact:

Although Henry VIII's court in his last years was a dangerous place where mere words could bring disgrace and even death, there was one person who was allowed to say anything he wanted: Henry's jester Will Somers. For over 20 years Somers made Henry laugh while making fun of people at court. Only once he caused displeasure to his master, in 1535 when he insulted Anne Boleyn and their daughter Elizabeth. He was forgiven however and lived on to survive both Anne and Henry.

Edward VI

Reign: 28 January 1547 – 6 July 1553

Birth: 12 October 1537, at Hampton Court Palace, near London. Only son of King Henry VIII by his third wife Jane Seymour.

Queen: None

Death: 6 July 1553, at Greenwich Palace, near London.

Key Facts:

The long-awaited male heir of King Henry VIII, Edward succeeded his father at the age of 9. A regency council was initially appointed to rule in his name but power was soon usurped, first by Edward's uncle the Duke of Somerset in 1547, then by John Dudley, Duke of Northumberland in 1550. Edward never ruled directly in his own name.

He was raised as a committed Protestant and anti-Catholic from a very early age, and even as a minor he strongly supported the sweeping Protestant reforms in the Church of England introduced by his councillors. His reign saw the introduction in 1549 of the Act of Uniformity outlawing all Catholic and idolatrous practices, and the adoption of Thomas Cranmer's *Book of Common Prayer* which was made compulsory for church services.

A sickly child, his health became worse as a teenager and he died of a respiratory illness at the age of 16. In the last weeks of his life he tried to change the succession by nominating his Protestant cousin Lady Jane Grey as his heir, in place of his half-sister Mary who was a Catholic.

Peculiar Fact:

Edward was reportedly much smarter than children of his own age and often grew angry and frustrated at the way his regency councillors tried to use him for their own ends. On one famous occasion he stormed back to his bedchamber after a meeting, grabbed his favourite falcon, plucked out his feathers in frustration and then killed it by tearing it apart, saying that one day he would do the same to those who were trying to abuse him.

Jane Grey: Monarch or Not?

Disputed Reign: 10 - 19 July 1553

Birth: Circa 1536-1537, exact birth location unknown. Oldest child of Henry Grey, Duke of Suffolk, and of Frances Brandon, niece of King Henry VIII.

Spouse: Guilford Dudley (c.1535-1554), son of John Dudley, Duke of Northumberland.

Death: 12 February 1554, on the execution scaffold at the Tower of London.

The Succession:

The case of whether Jane Grey was a legitimate monarch or not is a grey area indeed. Jane was chosen by Edward VI as his successor as he was slowly dying in the summer of 1553, in spite of the existing Act of Succession of 1544 and Henry VIII's last will, both of which specifically stipulated that should Edward die without heirs the crown would pass to his oldest half-sister Mary, Henry VIII's daughter by Catherine Aragon; that if then Mary died with no children the crown would pass to their half-sister Elizabeth, Henry's daughter by Anne Boleyn; and that if Elizabeth died with no children, then finally the crown would be passed to the descendants of Henry VIII's sister Mary Tudor, which included her eldest granddaughter Jane Grey.

Edward's motives for cutting his half-sister Mary from the succession were both religious and political: Mary was a confirmed

Catholic who was certain to undo the Protestant reforms instituted by Edward's council. His reasons for excluding his half-sister Elizabeth, who was also a Protestant, are not as clear, but it was likely due to political machinations at Edward's court. Jane Grey was married to the son of Edward's chief minister, the Duke of Northumberland, who had more power to gain if Jane Grey were to be proclaimed Queen instead of Elizabeth.

The Events:

In June 1553 Edward VI issued letters patent officially altering the succession, stating that at his death the crown would pass to Lady Jane Grey and her heirs. The king died before the changes to the succession could be confirmed by Parliament, but the plans were implemented nevertheless. On 10 July 1553, four days after Edward VI died, the Privy Council proclaimed Jane Grey Queen, and she was installed in the Tower of London in preparation for her coronation as per the traditional custom.

Edward's half-sister Mary however also asserted her right to the crown, and after writing to the Privy Council demanding that they proclaim her Queen she travelled to East Anglia to gather followers and prepare troops for a possible showdown against the Duke of Northumberland, Jane's father-in-law and real power behind the throne.

As Mary's support grew in London and elsewhere, the Privy Council changed their allegiance and on 19 July they proclaimed Mary Queen in place of Jane. The Duke of Northumberland, who had left for East Anglia in the hope of capturing Mary, was arrested and later executed. Jane was officially arrested on 19 July and imprisoned in the Tower, and two weeks later Mary entered London in triumphal procession as Queen acknowledged by all.

Jane and her husband Guilford Dudley were later tried and convicted of treason, but Mary decided initially to spare their lives as there was evidence they both had been victims of

Northumberland's political ambition. It was noted that Jane had been reluctant to receive the crown and was only convinced to accept it when her parents forced her, and that later she did not resist her uncrowning. Mary's initial pardon was revoked however after an armed revolt in January 1554 called Wyatt's rebellion, in which Jane's father took part. Although Jane had not been involved in it, she, her husband and her father were all executed in February 1554.

The Case For Jane's Legitimacy as a Monarch:

Edward VI's change to the succession was not a one-sided affair forced upon the country. His letter patents of 21 June 1553 proclaiming Jane his heir was signed by over 100 notable persons in the realm, including the entire Privy Council, peers, bishops, judges and officials of the City of London. It can be argued that this group of people represented the unofficial collective will of the realm, and that if Edward had not died so quickly the new succession would most likely have been approved a few months later by Parliament, the body representing the official will of the realm, which had already been convoked by Edward for September 1553.

There was a genuine case to be made against the legitimacy of both Mary and Elizabeth as heirs to the throne, caused by a legal quirk in the previous Succession Acts passed by Henry VIII. The First Succession Act of 1533, passed after Catherine of Aragon was divorced, had disinherited Mary and proclaimed her illegitimate. The Second Succession Act of 1536, passed after Anne Boleyn had been divorced, had disinherited Elizabeth and also proclaimed her illegitimate. The Third Succession Act of 1544, passed after the birth of the future Edward VI, had reinstated Mary and Elizabeth in the line of succession, but had not revoked their illegitimate status. It had only enabled their capacity to succeed to the throne but curiously had not made them legitimate heirs of Henry's body once again, as indeed it could not do as Henry's marriage to their mothers had been declared void. Furthermore, the Third Succession Act also gave Henry VIII power to alter the succession at his pleasure simply by issuing letters patent or last wills, and this power could arguably be said to have been inherited by Edward as his successor—which he had therefore exercised legally through precedent when he disinherited his half-sisters by letters patent in 1553. It is said that Edward himself had grave doubts about his half-sisters' suitability as monarchs exactly because of their confirmed illegitimacy.

♛ Jane was not proclaimed Queen as a rival claimant against an existing monarch, as for example happened in 1487 when the pretender Lambert Simnel was illegally proclaimed king against Henry VII, or as it would later happen with the Jacobite pretenders in the 18th century. Her accession was proclaimed legally by the country's Privy Council and was confirmed by the City of London as per tradition. She was installed in the Tower of London as all new monarchs awaiting their coronation were supposed to be, and she did issue legitimate legal documents signed 'Jane the Queen'. One could make the case that Jane began to reign as a legitimate monarch but was quickly deposed after a legal nine-day reign.

The Case Against Jane's Legitimacy as a Monarch:

♛ Regardless of how many notable people put their signatures to Edward VI's letters patent altering the succession, the new line of succession was never approved by Act of Parliament, which left the existing Third Succession Act of 1544 in place naming Mary as heir to Edward VI. This Act was also re-enforced by Henry VIII's last will of 1547 restating his wish that Mary inherit the crown should Edward die without issue. Furthermore, it is not clear if the provisions of the Third Succession Act authorising the king to alter the succession at will through letters patent or last wills applied to any monarch except Henry VIII with whom the Act was solely concerned. Also, Edward VI died at the age of 15 before achieving his legal majority, making his letters patent legally questionable and any decision regarding the succession subject to Parliament's legal approval, which was not granted because it had not convened yet by the time Edward died.

In the absence of Parliament passing a new succession act, not only did the Third Succession Act of 1544 naming Mary as heir to a childless Edward remain in place: the Treason Act of 1547 made altering the existing succession as established by Parliament a crime punishable by death. This treason act was in force when the Privy Council proclaimed Jane Queen, making her proclamation therefore illegal and a crime.

It is significant that the same Privy Council who had proclaimed Jane Queen on 10 July switched their allegiance soon afterwards to proclaim Mary Queen on 19 July. This change of heart occurred after the Duke of Northumberland left London on 14 July to fight Mary in East Anglia. This suggests that the Council's initial proclamation of Jane might have been forced upon them by the Duke and his party, making Jane's proclamation an act of usurpation of the crown. This was confirmed in September by Parliament, the ultimate legal authority in the kingdom, who confirmed Mary as the legitimate monarch and proclaimed Jane to have been a usurper.

Conclusion:

The issue of Jane Grey's legitimacy as a monarch has never been fully resolved. This is shown in the way she is often referred to in popular culture as 'the nine-day Queen', though the title by which she is also known is not Queen Jane, but 'Lady' Jane Grey. Ultimately, her legitimacy rests on personal interpretations of her historical case and legal standing as monarch. In this writer's opinion, the fact that Parliament—the ultimate legal authority in England—was never consulted on the changes to the succession and later refused to recognise Jane's accession means that Jane Grey cannot be considered a legitimate monarch. She is therefore excluded from many relevant sections and lists in this book.

Mary I

Reign: 6 July 1553 – 17 November 1558

Birth: 18 February 1516, at Greenwich Palace, near London. Only surviving child of King Henry VIII and his first wife Catherine of Aragon.

King Consort: Prince Philip, later King Philip II, of Spain (1527-1598), son of Charles V, King of Spain and Holy Roman Emperor.

Death: 17 November 1558, at St James's Palace, London.

Key Facts:

The first Queen Regnant in English history, Mary's path to the throne was fraught with difficulty. As the daughter of Catherine of Aragon she was first removed from the line of succession in 1533 after her father divorced her mother, and was only reinstated as heir during the last years of Henry VIII's life. Her half-brother Edward also tried to disinherit her as his own heir in 1553 because she was a Catholic, and after his death Mary had to fight an attempt to make her cousin Jane Grey Queen in her place.

She tried to restore Catholicism in England by reversing the changes instituted by the two previous monarchs. She famously sanctioned the burning of some Protestants as heretics including Thomas Cranmer, the former Protestant Archbishop of Canterbury, earning for herself the nickname of Bloody Mary for posterity.

In 1554 she married her cousin, the Catholic Philip of Spain who was made King Consort, but she retained sole constitutional power as monarch, setting a precedent for future Queens Regnant. The marriage was deeply unpopular in England and led to an uprising against Mary in the south called Wyatt's Rebellion.

Following Wyatt's Rebellion in 1554 she was forced to execute Lady Jane Grey along with her husband and father. She also had a strained relationship with her Protestant half-sister Elizabeth, who many wished to see Queen in place of Mary, and in 1554 she briefly imprisoned Elizabeth in the Tower of London under suspicion of plotting to take her throne. She only accepted Elizabeth as her heir in 1558 when it became clear that her marriage to Philip of Spain would remain childless.

During her reign the territory of Calais, the last English possession in mainland France, was permanently recaptured by the French in 1558, leaving Mary to famously utter the words "When I am dead and opened, you shall find 'Calais' lying on my heart!"

Peculiar Fact:
Although it might not have been initially named after her, the cocktail drink 'Bloody Mary' is today associated with Mary I and her persecution of Protestants. The drink was created in the 1920s and, deliberately or not, was given the same name given to Mary in John Foxe's Protestant *Book of Martyrs* of 1563. The drink is made with vodka and tomato juice, the red of the tomato juice recalling the blood spilled by Mary's executions (even though most of her victims were burned).

Elizabeth I

Reign: 17 November 1558 – 24 March 1603

Birth: 7 September 1533, at Greenwich Palace, near London. Only surviving child of King Henry VIII and his second wife Anne Boleyn.

Consort: None

Death: 24 March 1603, at Richmond Palace, near London.

Key Facts:

Widely regarded as the greatest monarch in English history, Elizabeth presided over England's Golden Age when the country enjoyed domestic peace, prosperity, and grew in international status. She encouraged the cult of herself as Gloriana, the glorious personification of England itself.

Intelligent and extensively educated at a young age, she was skilled in languages and wrote her own public speeches. She wisely surrounded herself with capable advisers and administrators which formed perhaps the best royal council in English history. These included William Cecil, Francis Walsingham, Robert Dudley, Thomas Gresham, Robert Cecil and Francis Bacon.

She famously refused to marry despite many offers from foreign princes, but she used offers of betrothal as diplomatic tools to shape European alliances. Although when young she enjoyed a romantic—but most likely unconsummated—affair with Robert Dudley, Earl of Leicester, she later opted to remain unmarried, claiming that she was a Virgin Queen married to her country.

♔ She presided over a new religious settlement in England that struck a balance between Protestant doctrine and Catholic tradition, the results of which survive to this day. She opposed Protestant extremism and quietly tolerated private Catholic worship, famously saying that she did not wish to make windows into people's souls.

♔ Excommunicated by the pope in 1570, she was subject to several assassination attempts by some Catholics who wished to see her replaced on the throne by her Catholic cousin, Mary Queen of Scots. Her secretary and chief spymaster, Francis Walsingham, established the first secret service in England to protect her from plots and threats.

♔ She had a strained relationship with her Catholic cousin, and presumed heir, Mary Queen Scots, whom she welcomed in England in 1568 after Mary lost her Scottish throne. After keeping Mary on house arrests for 18 years and finally finding proof that she had conspired with others to murder her, Elizabeth reluctantly approved her execution for treason in 1587.

♔ During her reign England had a long-running enmity with Spain which was fought by military proxy in the Netherlands, and at sea through piracy. After Mary Queen of Scots' execution in 1587 King Philip II of Spain sent his Spanish Armada to invade England in 1588 and dethrone Elizabeth. She however led the country to defend itself, and on that occasion she gave a famous, rousing speech on the English shore at Tilbury to stir courage into her troops. The Armada was defeated.

- She encouraged and sponsored English maritime exploration abroad. Her reign saw the first English circumnavigation of the globe by Francis Drake in 1577-80; the exploration of South America by Walter Raleigh in 1595; the first English colony established in North America in 1584; and trading posts established in Africa and Asia in the 1580s-1590s.

- Among the legacies of her age are the works of William Shakespeare, whom she supported in the 1590s; the establishment of the first Royal Exchange in the 1560s; the empowering of the House of Commons; and the eventual union of England and Scotland into one crown after her death.

Peculiar Fact:

One of the reasons Elizabeth I wore elaborate make-up and wigs was to cover the effects of a near-fatal case of smallpox she suffered in 1562 that left her face scarred and her hair thinned. Her obsession with her appearance grew worse with the years, and in her old age she refused to have mirrors hung in any rooms she used.

James I

Reign: 24 March 1603 – 27 March 1625

Birth: 19 June 1566 at Edinburgh Castle, Scotland. Only son of Mary Queen of Scots and of Henry Stuart, Lord Darnley.

Queen: Anne of Denmark (1574-1619), daughter of King Frederick II of Denmark.

Death: 27 March 1625, at Theobalds House, Hertfordshire.

Key Facts:

The first Scottish and first Stuart king of England, James was a king for almost his entire life after he acceded to the throne of Scotland at the age of one year in 1567, 36 years before assuming the English crown. His claim to the English throne derived from both his parents, Mary Queen of Scots and Henry Stuart, Lord Darnley, who were great-grandchildren of King Henry VII. James never met either of his parents.

He was the first monarch to join England and Scotland into one crown and to call himself King of Great Britain. He tried to unite England and Scotland into one single nation, without success, however he did succeed in introducing a new flag for the two joined countries in 1606, the Union Flag, combining the flags of England and Scotland.

Perhaps the most learned of all English monarchs, he was an accomplished writer, philosopher and linguist. He wrote two political treatises, *The True Law of Free Monarchies* and *Basilikon Doron*, in which he articulated his theory of the divine right of kings. Yet he was also hard-drinking, slothful and lecherous towards young men, famously earning for himself the nickname of 'the wisest fool in Christendom'.

He famously escaped the Gunpowder Plot in 1605, an attempt by Catholic extremists to blow up the Houses of Parliament whilst James and the country's government assembled in it for the State Opening. The occasion is remembered in England today every November 5th in Guy Fawkes Night, named after one of the conspirators.

In 1604, to standardise the many Bible versions that were being used at the time, he commissioned a group of scholars to produce a new translation of the Bible into English, the writing of which he personally supervised. The work was later named after him as the King James Bible. A great literary patron, he also supported Shakespeare, Ben Jonson and John Donne.

In 1609 he initiated the settlement of Protestants in Northern Ireland on lands confiscated from local Catholics chiefs, and in so doing he sowed the seeds of a conflict that persists to this day. His reign also saw the establishment of the first permanent colonies in North America from 1607.

Peculiar Fact:

James was a strong opponent of tobacco after it was first introduced to England from America, and ordered an exorbitant import tax on it to reduce its consumption. He even wrote a treatise in 1604 called *A Counterblaste to Tobacco* where he described smoking as 'loathsome to the eye, hateful to the nose, harmful to the brain, dangerous to the lungs'.

Charles I

Reign: 27 March 1625 – 30 January 1649

Birth: 19 November 1600, in Dunfermline Palace, Fife, Scotland. Second son of King James VI of Scotland, later James I of England, and of Queen Anne of Denmark.

Queen: Henrietta Maria of France (1609-1669), daughter of King Henri IV of France.

Death: 30 January 1649, on the execution scaffold in Whitehall, London.

Key Facts:

Charles is considered by many to be one of worst monarchs in English history. His belief in the divine right of kings, his inflexibility, and his untrustworthy personality made him unsuited to deal with the growing religious tensions in England and Scotland, and the growing power of Parliament.

He married Henrietta Maria of France, one of the most influential but also most pernicious royal consorts in British history. Said to be even more inflexible than Charles on the subject of royal power, she encouraged him to fight against Parliament and supported him during the Civil War by selling off royal jewels abroad. She also introduced Catholic worship in the royal family, sowing the seeds of future troubles for the Stuart dynasty

A committed Anglican, Charles alienated both English Puritans and Scottish Presbyterians by trying to impose elaborate Anglican worship in churches. His attempts to impose the Book of Common Prayer in Scotland in 1637 caused a rebellion and a short civil war which Charles lost.

He ruled without parliament for 11 years from 1629 to 1640, and tried to usurp its power to raise taxes. After finally being forced to call Parliament into session in 1640 Charles tried in 1642 to arrest members who had raised grievances against him. A heightened feeling of untrustworthiness between Charles and Parliament led directly to civil war.

In 1642 he was the first to raise the standard of war against Parliament, starting the English Civil War. He won initial royalist victories but the tide of war turned against him after Parliament, led by Oliver Cromwell and Thomas Fairfax, created the groundbreaking New Model Army. This army won resounding victories at Marston Moor in 1644 and Naseby in 1645, after which Charles lost the war and was taken prisoner.

After he was taken prisoner in 1646 Charles tried to play different Parliamentary factions against each other to his own advantage, but with no success. After a Puritan army faction gained control of Parliament he was put on trial in 1649 for treason against the people, and was sentenced to death during a great show trial in Westminster.

The only British king to be publicly executed, he was beheaded with an axe on a scaffold in Whitehall, London, in January 1649. The courage and dignity he showed in death gained him wide public sympathy, and he was hailed as a martyr immediately after his execution.

♔ Despite his political failings and personal flaws, he was one of the greatest patrons of the arts in British history. He personally employed Antony Van Dyck and Peter Paul Rubens as painters, and Bernini as a sculptor. He also amassed the most valuable painting collection in all of Europe, containing works by Leonardo, Raphael and Titian. The collection was sold after his execution and only partly recovered after the restoration of the monarchy in 1660.

Peculiar Fact:
Born a sickly and weak child, Charles could still not walk nor speak properly by the age of four. His walk was impaired by weak ankle joints and his speech was affected by a tongue deformity. He managed to overcome both defects by the age of 8 by sheer determination and with the help of a caring governess, though he retained a slight stammer for the rest of his life.

The Interregnum

Duration: 30 January 1649 – 29 May 1660

After the execution of Charles I in 1649, the Puritan army faction that had taken control of Parliament proceeded to abolish the monarchy, the House of Lords, the Episcopal Church, and proclaimed England to be a free republican Commonwealth.

Although power was nominally vested in parliaments and councils, from 1651 onwards true power was exercised by the army's most capable and forceful general, Oliver Cromwell, who in 1653 was declared Lord Protector and ruled as king in all but name until his death in 1658.

Greatly unpopular among the people, the rule of the Commonwealth slowly descended into chaos after Cromwell's death in 1658. Finally in 1660 a select group of leaders decided to restore political stability to the country by recalling Charles I's heir from exile and re-establish the monarchy.

Charles II

Reign: 29 May 1660 – 6 February 1685

Birth: 29 May 1630, in St James's Palace, London. First surviving son of King Charles I and Queen Henrietta Maria of France.

Queen: Catherine of Braganza (1638-1705), daughter of King John IV of Portugal.

Death: 6 February 1685, at Whitehall Palace, London.

Key Facts:

Stripped of the crown of England in 1649 after the execution of his father and the abolition of the monarchy, Charles was briefly crowned King of Scots in 1650, before the monarchy was abolished in Scotland also. He led royalist troops in the last great clash of the Civil War, the Battle of Worcester in 1650, and following that defeat he escaped into exile, wandering the courts of Europe for the next 10 years. He was finally restored to the throne in 1660 when the monarchy was re-established in England.

He successfully healed the wounds of the Civil War by being merciful towards all former enemies, famously refusing to take revenge on Parlamentarians except those who had signed his father's death warrant. He included both royalists and parliamentarians in his government, and whilst he re-established monarchical power he remained pragmatic in his dealings with Parliament.

♔ He was famously nicknamed the 'Merry Monarch' because of his love affairs with many mistresses. He fathered over a dozen illegitimate children from whom descended several British noble families today. He was however unable to father legitimate children with his wife, Catherine of Braganza, which made his brother James the next in line to the throne.

♔ During the Great Fire of London of 1666 he took part in rescue efforts by personally turning out in the streets to help fire-fighters and distributing money to homeless Londoners. He later supported the rebuilding of many London buildings, naming Sir Christopher Wren as the main architect.

♔ A patron of sciences, sports and entertainment, he founded the Royal Society for scientists and philosophers; he authorised the building of new theatres and supported acting companies; he introduced yachting to England; and he was the first monarch to patronise horse racing.

♔ In 1678 he achieved a significant political victory against Parliament during the great Exclusion Crisis, when a parliamentary faction tried to pass a law excluding Charles' heir, his brother James, from the succession because he was Catholic. Charles successfully prevented the law to be passed, preserving the principle of inherited royal succession which persists to this day. The event saw the birth of the two-party political system in Britain, with those supporting Charles and James forming together as Tories, and those opposed to them grouping as Whigs.

♔ Always an ambiguous Protestant, Charles signed the Secret Treaty of Dover with Louis XIV of France in 1670 which stipulated that Charles would receive large amounts of money from Louis in exchange for a promise to publicly convert to Catholicism at some point in the future. Although most of the money was paid, the promise was never fulfilled, however Charles did secretly convert to Catholicism on his deathbed in 1685.

Peculiar Fact:

One of Charles' nicknames during his lifetime was Old Rowley, after a racing horse he owned who was also a breeding stallion, a tongue-and-cheek reference to his own womanising. The nickname was first given to him in the racing town of Newmarket, Suffolk, where there still exists a racetrack called The Rowley Mile (named after both the king and the horse).

James II

Reign: 6 February 1685 – 11 December 1688

Birth: 14 October 1633, in St James's Palace, London. Second son of King Charles I and Queen Henrietta Maria of France.

Queen: Mary of Modena (1658-1718), daughter of Duke Alfonso IV of Modena, Italy.

Death: 16 September 1701, at the Chateau of St Germain-en-Laye, near Paris, France.

Key Facts:

The second son of Charles I, James inherited his father's inflexibility of character and belief in absolute monarchy. He accompanied his brother Charles into exile after the Civil War and became his heir in 1660, remaining so after Charles failed to father legitimate sons.

A capable naval commander and Lord High Admiral during his brother's reign, he was forced to resign his posts in 1672 after his conversion to Catholicism. He still remained his brother's heir after his conversion however and, despite fierce opposition from some quarters, succeeded his brother to the throne.

Soon after his accession in 1685 he defeated a Protestant rebellion seeking to depose him led by Charles II's eldest illegitimate son, the Duke of Monmouth. James refused mercy to Monmouth, his own nephew, after his capture and had him executed. He also authorised fierce reprisals towards those who had supported the Monmouth Rebellion in the west of England.

♔ In 1687 he issued a Declaration of Indulgence granting freedom of worship to all Christian denominations, and ending the requirement to be in communion with the Church of England to take up public office. Although welcomed by many, the Declaration raised fears that James was planning to impose Catholicism in England.

♔ He provoked general alarm among the people when he began to adopt despotic tendencies and started to appoint Catholics to positions of power in the Privy Council, the army and the courts. Fears that James would establish a new Catholic absolutist dynasty in England modelled on France were heightened in June 1688 after his wife finally gave birth to a son after several miscarriages and child deaths.

♔ He finally lost his throne after William of Orange, James' son-in-law, was invited to invade England by a group of Protestant political leaders to free the country from James' increasing despotism. After William landed in England in November 1688 James was deserted by many and fled the country instead of fighting, leaving the throne vacant. He later tried to regain his crown by invading Ireland with an army but was defeated at the Battle of the Boyne in 1690. He lived out the rest of his life in exile in France.

Peculiar Fact:

When he was 13-years-old James was taken prisoner by Parliamentarians during the English Civil War and put under house arrests at St James's Palace. He eventually escaped during a game of hide-and-seek in the palace gardens, slipped secretly into the adjacent St James's Park, then donned a girl's clothes and sailed down the Thames to board a ship to Holland.

William III & Mary II

Reign:
William and Mary: 13 February 1689 – 28 December 1694
William alone: 28 December 1694 – 8 March 1702

Note: *There was a gap of two months between the date when James II was considered to have vacated the English throne by fleeing the country, 11 December 1688, and the date when William and Mary were officially offered the crown by Parliament, 13 February 1689. During that time, whilst constitutional arrangements were being debated, England was governed by a committee composed of Lords, Commons and William himself as unofficial Regent. Some chronologies eliminate this gap by backdating the start of William and Mary's reign to 11 December 1688 however the actual chronology has been retained here since no monarch officially reigned during that time.*

Birth:
William III: 4 November 1650, in Binnenhof Palace, The Hague, The Netherlands. Only child of William II, Prince of Orange, and of Mary, daughter of King Charles I and sister to Kings Charles II and James II.
Mary II: 30 April 1662, in St James's Palace, London. Oldest surviving child of King James II and Anne Hyde (when Duke and Duchess of York). She and William were first cousins.

Consort: William and Mary were married to each other.

Death:
Mary II: 28 December 1694, in Kensington Palace, London.
William III: 8 March 1702, in Kensington Palace, London.

Key Facts:

♔ William and Mary were the first and only joint monarchs in British history, equal in status and constitutional power. In practice however William exercised power alone. Mary happily confined herself to a passive role, except when acting as regent when William was abroad. Mary's popularity as a vivacious English princess compensated for William's foreign origins and dour personality.

♔ They gained their throne through the Glorious Revolution of 1688-89 by replacing the unpopular James II who fled the country after William landed in England at the invitation of English political leaders. As part of the Glorious Revolution settlement that offered them their crowns, William and Mary agreed to restrictions on the power of the monarchy which effectively placed it under the authority of Parliament. This and other constitutional changes during their reign gave birth to constitutional monarchy in Britain.

♔ William personally led troops to victory against James II at the Battle of the Boyne in Ireland in 1690, fought by James to regain his throne. This battle, and the subsequent Battle of Aughrim in 1691, confirmed the Glorious Revolution and the Protestant succession in England, Scotland and Ireland. The Battle of the Boyne's commemoration as a victory for the Protestant succession later became a contentious issue in Northern Ireland.

♔ William authorised—some say unwittingly—the 1692 Glencoe Massacre in Scotland when dozens of members of the MacDonald clan were killed for failing to swear an oath of allegiance to William and Mary before the appointed deadline of 1 January 1692. The event increased William's unpopularity as a foreigner.

♔ William laid the foundations of British military influence in Europe by involving England in a European coalition war against

Louis XIV of France between 1689-1701. He spent regular periods on military campaigns in Europe and personally led troops into a battle, proving himself to be a capable, respected commander. His wars against France continued into the next reign.

♔ Besides the birth of constitutional monarchy, William and Mary's reign also saw the adoption of the Bill of Rights in 1689, the establishment of the Bank of England in 1694, and the start of modern financial and banking practices imported from the Netherlands. Mary founded the Royal Naval Hospital at Greenwich in 1692 for the care of seamen injured in William's wars.

♔ Mary died suddenly in 1694 of smallpox, leaving William personally heartbroken and ruling alone until 1702. As William and Mary had no children and their successor, Anne, was also childless by 1700, Parliament adopted the Act of Settlement in the last year of William's reign, passing the crown to the most suitable Protestant relative: William and Anne's first cousin once removed, Sophia of Hanover, and her successors.

Peculiar Fact:

William III: William's father, mother and wife all died suddenly of smallpox at different times in his life. Even in an age when the disease was rife, the chances of this happening to very close family members in succession were rare.

Mary II: When Mary was first told at the age of 15 that she was arranged to be married to William she wept uncontrollably for a day and a half. Their personalities were very different and William was notoriously plain, not to mention 4 inches shorter than Mary. With time however their relationship blossomed.

Anne

Reign: 8 March 1702 – 1 August 1714

Birth: 6 February 1665, in St James's Palace, London. Second surviving child of King James II and Anne Hyde (when Duke and Duchess of York).

Prince Consort: Prince George of Denmark (1653-1708), son of King Frederick III of Denmark.

Death: 1 August 1714, in Kensington Palace, London.

Key Facts:

The last monarch of the House of Stuart, Anne was unable to provide for the succession after 18 pregnancies led to 17 miscarriages, stillbirths or children who died in infancy. Her only surviving child, William, died at age 11 before she became Queen.

She became the first monarch of a united Great Britain after the Act of Union, formally uniting England and Scotland into one nation, was passed in 1707. Her reign saw the continuing development of constitutional monarchy as cabinet ministers gained more power over policy making. She became the last monarch to exercise a veto over a Parliamentary bill in 1708, when she vetoed a bill that would have established a separate militia for Scotland after the Act of Union.

♛ Although grossly overweight and almost infirm from gout and rheumatisms by the time she became Queen, Anne reigned with great diligence and conscientiousness. She famously attended more council meetings during her reign than all the previous Stuart monarchs combined.

♛ She had a close friendship with Sarah Churchill, Duchess of Marlborough, who was her chief confidante and adviser for most of her life. The friendship caused a rift between Anne and her sister, Queen Mary II, which was not mended before Mary's death. Anne's friendship with Sarah Churchill eventually also ended acrimoniously in 1711 when the two women fell out over politics and personal friendships.

♛ She presided over the War of the Spanish Succession, fought by Britain and its allies against France between 1702-1713 to prevent Louis XIV's grandson becoming king of Spain. British armies, led by the gifted general John Churchill, Duke of Marlborough (Sarah Churchill's husband), won great victories against the French including the Battle of Blenheim in 1704. The war established Great Britain as a major world power for the first time in its history, and gained it new territories in Nova Scotia, Newfoundland and Gibraltar.

Peculiar Fact:

Anne kept a 19-year-long correspondence with her close friend Sarah Churchill, but they never signed their letters with their own names. On Anne's suggestion they used the names of Mrs Morley for Anne, and Mrs Freeman for Sarah, both to promote equality in their conversations and to preserve anonymity should the letters fall in the wrong hands.

George I

Reign: 1 August 1714 – 11 June 1727

Birth: 28 May 1660, in Hanover, Germany. First son of Ernest Augustus, Elector of Hanover, and of Sophia, Electress of Hanover, who was a granddaughter of King James I. George was a second cousin to Queen Anne, King William III and Queen Mary II.

Queen: None. He divorced his wife, Sophia Dorothea of Celle, before he ascended the British throne.

Death: 11 June 1727, at Osnabruck Palace, Osnabruck, Germany.

Key Facts:

George I was the first Hanoverian and first German king of Great Britain. His family line was chosen to succeed the last Stuart monarch because of their descent from James I, and because of their solid Protestantism. He spoke little English, communicating instead through French and Latin whilst in Britain. At the time that he became king he was the oldest monarch on accession in English history, at the age of 54.

He had a difficult temper that caused strains within the Royal Family. Before he came to Britain George had divorced his wife and imprisoned her for life after she had had an affair, and had banned their children from seeing her. This caused a permanent rift between him and his eldest son and heir, George, who ended up setting up a rival court in London as Prince of Wales in 1717.

♔ As king he showed more interest in his possessions in Hanover than in Britain. This, combined with his inability to communicate in English, meant that he delegated much of British political decision-making to his council of ministers. This led to the establishment of the cabinet system and the rise of the first Prime Minister, Robert Walpole, in the 1720s.

♔ Several Jacobite rebellions and plots took place during his reign, organised by those who aimed to restore the Catholic heirs of James II to the throne. These included the Jacobite Rebellion of 1715 in Scotland, led by James the Old Pretender, which was defeated; and the Atterbury Plot of 1722, a conspiracy to seize the government in London that was foiled in its planning stages.

♔ He was involved in the South Sea Bubble Crash of 1720, one of the first financial market crashes of modern times, caused by inflated share prices and company corruption. George had invested in the company's shares with other members of the Royal Family and was saved from disgrace only by the shrewd political management of the Prime Minister, Robert Walpole.

♔ A great patron on music, he supported musicians and opera composers in Britain and Hanover. His most famous contribution was bringing Georg F. Handel to Britain from Hanover, who later composed his famous *Water Music* suite of 1717 specifically for one of George's summer fetes.

Peculiar Fact:

Before his death George promised the Duchess of Kendal, one of his mistresses, that he would pay her a visit from the other world. The Duchess recorded that soon after he died a large black bird flew into her room. She was convinced that it was him so she treated it with the utmost respect until finally it flew away.

George II

Reign: 11 June 1727 – 25 October 1760

Birth: 30 October 1683, in Hanover, Germany. First son of King George I (then Prince of Brunswick-Lüneburg), and of Sophia Dorothea of Celle.

Queen: Caroline of Ansbach (1683-1737), daughter of Margrave John Frederick of Brandenburg-Ansbach, Germany.

Death: 25 October 1760, in Kensington Palace, London.

Key Facts:

The last king to be born outside Great Britain, George only arrived in the country at the age of 30 but differently from his father he learned to speak English and to appreciate Britain. A great enthusiast of all military things, he was the last monarch to lead troops into battle, in 1743 at the Battle of Dettingen, Germany, won against the French during the War of the Austrian Succession.

In 1745 he survived the last Jacobite rebellion against Hanoverian rule in Britain, led by Bonnie Prince Charlie, son of the Stuart Old Pretender. The Prince marched from Scotland as far south as Derby, but turned back north without fighting when faced with a larger army. George II's son, William Duke of Cumberland, destroyed Bonnie Prince Charlie's forces in the Scottish Highlands at the Battle of Culloden in 1746, the last pitched battle fought on British soil.

♔ George fostered constitutional monarchy by supporting the cabinet system and by abiding to limitations imposed by the Glorious Revolution. His largely supervisory approach to government throughout his long reign ensured that much royal power was permanently devolved to Parliament and the Prime Minister.

♔ His reign witnessed the growth of Great Britain as a major world power, with the country imposing dominance upon the seas and growing in military strength. Thanks to wars and trade, by George's death in 1760 Britain had also become the world's most prosperous nation and held a growing Empire stretching from the colonies of North America to trading outposts in Asia and Africa.

♔ At the end of his reign George also presided over the Seven Years' War, fought by Britain and France between 1756-1763 over colonial possessions abroad, and considered to be the first truly global conflict. Britain fought France in Europe, North America, Africa, India, and won resounding victories thanks partly to the superiority of its navy. The war gained Britain control of India and new territories in Canada and the Caribbeans.

♔ His reign saw the beginning of several royal traditions including the Trooping the Colour ceremony for the Monarch's official birthday; the adoption of *God Save the King* as the national anthem; and the use of *Zadok The Priest* during the coronation ceremony.

Peculiar Fact:

Royal family tradition holds that George II was once robbed while walking in the gardens of Kensington Palace. He was taking a stroll one morning when a man jumped over the wall, approached the king, and respectfully asked him to hand over his money, his watch, and the buckles of his shoes. After George handed over the items the robber climbed back up the wall and disappeared.

George III

Reign: 25 October 1760 – 29 January 1820

Birth: 4 June 1738, at Norfolk House, St James' Square, London. First son of Frederick, Prince of Wales, and of Princess Augusta of Saxe-Gotha. Grandson of King George II.

Queen: Charlotte of Mecklenburg-Strelitz (1744-1818), daughter of Duke Charles Louis Frederick of Mecklenburg-Strelitz, Germany.

Death: 29 January 1820, at Windsor Castle.

Key Facts:

The first Hanoverian king to be born in Great Britain, George was also at the age of 22 the youngest king to ascend the throne since 1547. Differently from his German predecessors, English was his first language and he never travelled outside Britain.

He tried to re-assert the monarchy's influence in government, previously eroded under George I and George II, by appointing favourites as ministers and directly influencing policy. His attempts however made him unpopular and were ultimately unsuccessful. By the end of his reign the political power of the monarchy had greatly diminished.

He lost the American Colonies through the American War of Independence in 1775-83 and was personally held responsible by the colonists for bringing about the conflict. Much of the criticism levelled by Americans against George III was unfair—they did not acknowledge Parliament's role in bringing about the crisis—however the popular reputation of George as a tyrant in America has persisted to this day.

Despite the loss of the American Colonies his reign saw a great expansion of the British Empire in Canada, India, Southeast Asia, South Africa, Australia and the Caribbeans. His reign also saw the abolition of the slave trade in British possessions in 1807.

In 1801 he became the first king of the United Kingdom of Great Britain and Ireland after full political union was established between the two islands. George however was against Catholic emancipation—the repeal of laws against Catholics—and his opposition set back the cause of Catholic relief in both islands by 30 years, causing lasting resentment in Ireland.

In the second part his reign Britain witnessed the French Revolution in 1789 and British military intervention against Napoleon from 1803, including Nelson's famous victory at the Battle of Trafalgar in 1805. A feeling of patriotism in Britain at this time meant that George's popularity surged to great heights for the first time since his accession.

A great patron of arts, he was one of the founders of the Royal Academy of Arts in 1768 and bought many works of arts for the Royal Collection. He was also a patron of scientists and a supporter of astronomer William Herschel, the discoverer of the planet Uranus. His reign saw the beginning of the Industrial Revolution in Britain as well advances in science and literature.

He famously suffered from bouts of madness which are now thought to have been the effects of porphyria. His first and most famous attack took place in 1788-89, and was followed by shorter attacks in 1801 and 1804. His final attack of madness in 1810 proved to be permanent and he spent the last ten years of his life under medical seclusion at Windsor Castle. His functions as monarch from 1811 onwards were taken over by his heir, Prince George, as Prince Regent.

Peculiar Fact:

George had a great interest in farming and in 1787 wrote a series of letters to the *Annals of Agriculture* magazine under the pseudonym of Ralph Robinson. In them, he praised a system of husbandry which had greatly impressed him practiced by a certain Mr Ducket at Petersham, near London, not far from one of the royal residences at Kew.

George IV

Reign: 29 January 1820 – 26 June 1830

Birth: 12 August 1762, in St James' Palace, London. First son of King George III and Queen Charlotte of Mecklenburg-Strelitz.

Queen: Caroline of Brunswick (1768-1821), daughter of Duke Charles II of Brunswick-Wolfenbuttel, and of Princess Augusta of Great Britain, sister of King George III. George IV and Caroline were first cousins.

Death: 26 June 1830, at Windsor Castle.

Key Facts:

Before he became king, George acted as Prince Regent during his father's last period of madness from 1811 to 1820, bringing the actual length of his rule to 19 years. In contrast to his father, his rule as Regent and King was characterised largely by non-interference, leaving the business of governing in the hands of Prime Ministers and Parliament. The most important events of his time were Napoleon's final defeat at Waterloo in 1815 and the Catholic Emancipation Bill of 1829.

His first secret marriage to Maria Fitzherbert, when Prince of Wales in 1785, was declared illegal because she was Catholic and they had not sought his father's consent as required by law. His second marriage to his cousin, Caroline of Brunswick, in 1795 quickly deteriorated into mutual hate and in both leading separate lives. George publicly ostracised Caroline, unsuccessfully tried to have her convicted of adultery once he became king in 1820, and excluded her from his coronation in Westminster Abbey in 1821.

♔ He was one of the greatest art patrons in British history, and a hoarder of treasures for the Royal Collection. Renowned for his good taste, George's choices of dress and architecture influenced the Regency style, named after his period as Regent. His architectural projects included the building of Buckingham Palace and the Brighton Pavilion, the creation of Regent Street, and the rebuilding of Windsor Castle.

♔ In 1822 he carried out a very successful visit to Scotland, the first by a reigning monarch since 1650. The visit, which included an enthusiastic George wearing tartan kilt and meeting with Highland clan chiefs, bound Scotland closer to the monarchy and the Union, whilst at the same time reviving the country's interest in its history and traditions.

♔ His and Caroline of Brunswick's only daughter and heir to the throne, Princess Charlotte, died while giving birth in 1817, leaving George with no descendants and causing his childless brothers to rush into marriages to produce heirs.

♔ Despite his achievements in the arts and Britain's increase in world power during his reign, George died as one of the most unpopular monarchs in English history, due largely to his troubled marriage, his affairs with married women, and his extravagant lifestyle. Even *The Times* proclaimed at his death in 1830: "There never was an individual less regretted by his fellow-creatures than this deceased king."

Peculiar Fact:

After Napoleon was defeated at the Battle of Waterloo during his tenure as Prince Regent, George—who had not been there—began to tell stories at dinner parties that he had fought in the battle himself disguised as a German general and that he had led the charge to victory. Some thought he was going mad until people realised that he always told these stories in the presence of the Duke of Wellington, who had led the British army at Waterloo and whom George personally disliked, as a way to annoy him.

William IV

Reign: 26 June 1830 – 20 June 1837

Birth: 21 August 1765, at Buckingham House, London. Third son of King George III and Queen Charlotte of Mecklenburg-Strelitz.

Queen: Adelaide of Saxe-Meinengen (1792-1849), daughter of Duke George I of Saxe-Meinengen, Germany.

Death: 20 June 1837, at Windsor Castle.

Key Facts:

An unexpected king, William became the oldest monarch to ever ascend the throne at the age of 64, a record he currently retains. He did not become heir to the childless George IV until 1827, three years before he became king.

Before he became king he lived with his mistress, actress Dorothy Jordan, for 20 years in a common law marriage, producing ten illegitimate children whom William ennobled and provided for after he became king. He left his mistress in 1811 and finally married in 1818 at the age of 54, but failed to produce any legitimate heirs.

Commonly called the Sailor King because of his earlier service in the Navy, his previous naval life caused him to retain a sense of informality as king which made him very popular after the extravagant reign of his brother George IV. Famously modest, William abolished the lavish coronation banquet that had previously followed the coronation ceremony. When in London he lived in modest residences at Clarence House, named after his previous title of Duke of Clarence, from which he sometimes emerged to take walks in the St James's neighbourhood.

He was instrumental in helping to pass the Reform Act of 1832 which widened the voting franchise and produced a more representative Parliament. Other reforms passed during his reign included the abolition of child labour in Britain and the abolition of slavery in the British Empire. In 1834 he became the last monarch to personally dismiss a Prime Minister.

Peculiar Fact:

In 1782, during the American War of Independence, George Washington approved a plan to kidnap William while he was visiting New York City as part of his service in the Royal Navy. The idea of kidnapping one of the sons of King George III was highly thought of as a way to improve the American position at the negotiating table, however plans soon leaked out and security was increased around the young prince.

Victoria

Reign: 20 June 1837 – 22 January 1901

Birth: 24 May 1819, in Kensington Palace, London. Only child of Prince Edward Duke of Kent and Princess Victoire of Saxe-Coburg-Saalfeld. Granddaughter of King George III.

Prince Consort: Prince Albert of Saxe-Coburg-Gotha (1819-1861), second son of Duke Ernest of Saxe-Coburg-Gotha, Germany, who was an uncle of Victoria. She and Prince Albert were first cousins.

Death: 22 January 1901, at Osborne House, Isle of Wight.

Key Facts:

Victoria was born specifically to provide for the royal succession after the premature death of George IV's daughter and heir, Princess Charlotte. She was prepared for her future role as Queen from an early age by her mother, after her father died when she was 8 months old. She ascended the throne four weeks after her 18th birthday.

In 1840 she married Prince Albert, a German first cousin, whose greatest accomplishments was the Great Exhibition in London in 1851. After his premature death in 1861 Victoria retreated into seclusion and plunged herself into a deep mourning that lasted 15 years. She commemorated her husband's memory in many ways, including the erection of the Albert Memorial and the Royal Albert Hall in London.

♔ She and Prince Albert were the creators of the modern monarchy, founded not on political power but on national symbolism, moral example and patronage of public causes. Victoria was the first truly constitutional monarch in British history, setting precedents for the crown's political impartiality, its deference to Parliament, as well as the monarch's right to be consulted and to advise.

♔ Over her long reign she presided over the largest expansion of the British Empire in its history, including new territories in Australia, New Zealand, the Pacific, India, Asia, Africa, Canada and the Americas. Under Victoria the British Crown's possessions covered 20% of the world's surface and included a quarter of the world population. She was the first British monarch to be proclaimed Empress of India in 1876.

♔ Her reign, rechristened the Victorian age, saw the greatest social and economic transformation Britain had ever seen, with great advances in technology, science and transportation. By her death, Victoria had become the personification of Britain itself, and of British power around the world.

♔ She was the first monarch to be photographed, to use the railways, to use a telephone, to use electricity, and to be captured on film. She was the first monarch to live in Buckingham Palace, and after the construction of Balmoral she also became the first monarch to start spending part of the year in Scotland. She popularised the use of anaesthesia in childbirth after she used it to deliver her eight child, Leopold. Together with Prince Albert they also popularised the use of Christmas trees in Britain.

♔ Known as the 'Grandmother of Europe', her children and grandchildren married into European royal families including the royal dynasties of Germany, Russia, Spain, Sweden, Norway, Greece and Romania. Her descendants sit on five European thrones today.

In 1896 she became the longest reigning monarch in British history, a title she retained until 2015. A year later, she became the first monarch to hold a Diamond Jubilee celebrating 60 years on the throne. At her death in 1901 she was also the longest-lived monarch in British history, a title she retained until 2007.

Peculiar Fact:
In her seventies Victoria learned how to speak and write Urdu, one of the languages spoken by her subjects in India. She was given regular lessons by her Indian private secretary and kept up an Urdu journal until shortly before her death.

Edward VII

Reign: 22 January 1901 – 6 May 1910

Birth: 9 November 1841, in Buckingham Palace, London. First son of Queen Victoria and Prince Albert.

Queen: Alexandra of Denmark (1844-1925), daughter of King Christian IX of Denmark.

Death: 6 May 1910, in Buckingham Palace, London.

Key Facts:

One of the longest-serving Princes of Wales in history, Edward spent most of his life in the shadow of his mother, Queen Victoria, who refused to let him participate in royal constitutional duties. As a result, he spent most of his time engaging in pleasurable social activities including gambling, horse racing, parties and frequenting mistresses. As Prince of Wales he was involved in both a public divorce case and a gambling scandal which undermined his reputation.

He almost died when Prince of Wales in 1871 when he contracted typhoid but miraculously recovered to great popular relief. He also escaped an assassination attempt whilst visiting Brussels in 1900, and an early death as king in 1902 when he had to have an emergency operation for appendicitis before his coronation.

♔ He proved to be a popular and conscientious king, working within and refining the limits of constitutional monarchy. His governments used his social skills and royal connections by sending him on state visits to France, Italy and Russia, where he successfully laid down the foundations of new alliances. His successful visit to France in 1903 led to the Entente Cordiale, the first successful alliance between England and France for centuries.

♔ After the long-term seclusion of his mother, Edward instituted changes to make the monarchy more visible. A lover of spectacle, he revived and adapted many royal ceremonies for the modern age, including the Trooping the Colour ceremony, the state opening of parliament, and the coronation festivities.

♔ He bought Sandringham House in Norfolk, which later became a royal winter retreat for his successors. He was the first modern monarch to own a horse racing stable, and was the first monarch to own and ride in an automobile.

Peculiar Fact:
In 1901 Edward instituted a separate time zone for his royal estate at Sandringham by moving clocks half hour forward of Greenwich Mean Time. This was done initially to allow the king extra time for hunting on the estate on winter evenings, however the practice was later extended to the whole year and was continued by his successor George V. It was finally abolished in 1936 by Edward VIII.

George V

Reign: 6 May 1910 – 20 January 1936

Birth: 3 June 1865, at Marlborough House, London. Second son of King Edward VII and Queen Alexandra (then Prince and Princess of Wales).

Queen: Mary of Teck (1867-1953), daughter of Francis, Duke of Teck, and of Princess Mary Adelaide of Cambridge, who was a granddaughter of King George III.

Death: 20 January 1936, at Sandringham House, Norfolk.

Key Facts:

A career naval officer in his youth, George became heir to the throne unexpectedly after his elder brother Albert Victor died in 1892. He then married his dead brother's fiancée, Mary of Teck, who later proved to be a formidable Queen. A quiet family man and a conscientious king, George came to symbolize the values of upright, middle class Britain in the early 20th century.

In 1911 he became the only reigning Emperor of India to visit the country when he was enthroned in an elaborate ceremony at the Delhi Durbar. He was also the first monarch to ever see Australia, New Zealand and South Africa, in 1901 before he became King.

He provided guidance and unity during the First World War, and led by example by imposing rations in Buckingham Palace and having members of the Royal Family involved in the war effort. He visited British troops at the French front numerous times, on one of those times breaking his pelvis when he was thrown off a spooked horse.

In 1917, during the First World War, he changed the name of the Royal Family from the German-sounding Saxe-Coburg-Gotha to Windsor, and ordered all family members to abandon German titles. He also limited the number of Royal Family members who could call themselves Prince or Princess, restricting the privilege to the immediate relatives of the monarch.

George presided over the greatest extent the British Empire ever reached, in the early 1920s, and was deeply devoted to the idea of a diverse empire community united under one crown. He was the first monarch to address the peoples of his dominions directly by radio, and instituted the Christmas Message broadcast in 1932. He also oversaw the granting of self-governance, under the British Crown, to Canada, Australia, New Zealand and South Africa.

He acted as constitutional arbiter during the great national and political crises of his reign, including the constitutional reforms of 1911 which took power away from the House of Lords; the demand for Irish Home rule in 1914; the General Strike of 1926; and the Great Depression crisis of the 1930s.

Peculiar Fact:
Despite his upright, middle class public image, George had a large tattoo of red and blue dragon on his arm. It was done in Japan in 1881 before he became heir to the throne while he was serving in the Royal Navy as a midshipman. The tattoo was never shown in public after he came back to England and became a full time royal.

Edward VIII

Reign: 20 January – 11 December 1936

Birth: 23 June 1894, at White Lodge, Richmond, London. First son of King George V and Queen Mary of Teck (when Duke and Duchess of York).

Queen: None

Death: 28 May 1972, 35 years after his abdication, in his private villa in the Bois de Boulogne, Paris, France.

Key Facts:

As a very popular Prince of Wales, Edward travelled extensively throughout the British Empire to acquaint himself with the countries over which he would reign one day. These royal tours, taken between 1919 and 1925, made him at the time the most widely travelled British royal in history, as well as a world celebrity.

Widely considered by many, including his father, as unfit to be king because of his lack of interest in royal duties and questionable morals, he preferred the pleasures of society life instead, including affairs with married women. His doubters' fears were confirmed after he became king when he neglected state affairs, indulging instead in parties and foreign holidays. He also showed a worrying sympathy for Adolf Hitler's Nazi party.

♔ In 1934 he began an affair with Wallis Simpson, an American married woman who was previously divorced, and later fell in love with her. His determination to marry her and make her his Queen brought about a constitutional crisis. Edward, as Head of the Church of England, could not marry a previously divorced woman since the Church did not allow divorced people to remarry. Although his government warned him about the impossibility of such marriage, Edward continued in his determination to marry Wallis Simpson after she divorced her second husband in 1936.

♔ He finally abdicated the throne to marry Wallis Simpson on 11 December 1936 after losing the support of his government, explaining to the nation afterwards that he could not carry out his duties as king without the support of the woman he loved. His voluntary abdication of the throne was the first in English history, with the crown passing to his brother Prince Albert. Edward's reign of 10 months stands as the second shortest since the Norman Conquest of 1066 (after Edward V's reign in 1483).

♔ After his abdication he went into voluntary exile and married Wallis Simpson in 1937 in France. Reverting back to the rank of Royal Prince, he was given the title of Duke of Windsor. He continued to enjoy the pleasures of society life until his death in his seventies, residing mostly in France.

Peculiar Fact:

In 1927, at the height of Edward's popularity as Prince of Wales, a song was released entitled "I Have Danced With a Man Who's Danced With a Girl Who's Danced With the Prince of Wales". It included lines such as "It was simply grand—he said 'Topping band'—and she said 'Delightful, Sir'".

George VI

Reign: 11 December 1936 – 6 February 1952

Birth: 14 December 1895, at York Cottage, Sandringham, Norfolk. Second son of King George V and Queen Mary of Teck (when Duke and Duchess of York).

Queen: Elizabeth Bowes-Lyon (1900-2002), ninth child and youngest daughter of Claude Bowes-Lyon, Earl of Strathmore and Kinghorne.

Death: Night of 5-6 February 1952, at Sandringham House, Norfolk.

Key Facts:

Christened as Albert and known as Bertie in the family, he came to throne unexpectedly after the abdication of his brother Edward VIII in 1936. Shy, nervous and suffering from a stammer, he was totally unprepared to be king as he had never been trained in state business. He nevertheless rose to the enormous challenge, supported by his strong wife Queen Elizabeth.

His strong sense of duty and exemplary family life restored dignity and stability to the monarchy after the abdication of Edward VIII. His choice of George as a regnal name was meant to provide continuity with the reign of his father, George V. Finding it difficult to make public speeches because of his stammer, he worked with a speech therapist to overcome his difficulties.

♔ He led the country through the Second World War and provided inspiration to the people, as for example when he and Queen Elizabeth refused to leave London during the Blitz raids so they could share the dangers of war with their people. He also made surprise visits to British troops fighting abroad, delivered messages of support on the radio, and together with Queen Elizabeth toured bombed areas throughout Britain.

♔ He was the last Emperor of India before the country declared independence in 1947, and he presided over the birth of the British Commonwealth in 1949. He was also the last British king to reign over a united Ireland before Southern Ireland became a republic in 1949. In 1939 he became the first reigning monarch to visit Canada.

♔ The strains of kingship, the stress of the Second World War, and his lifelong smoking addiction drastically impaired his health by the time he was 50. Following a series of operations, including the removal of part of one lung in 1951, more and more duties were taken over by his daughter, Princess Elizabeth, until George finally died in his sleep at the age of 56.

Peculiar Fact:
One of George VI's pastimes was needlework, a hobby he inherited from his mother Queen Mary and which he to relax during his stressful years as king. Some of the seat covers he embroidered are still used on chairs in some of the private royal residences.

Elizabeth II

Reign: 6 February 1952- present

Birth: 21 April 1926, at 17 Bruton Street, Mayfair, London. First child of King George VI and Queen Elizabeth Bowes-Lyon (then Duke and Duchess of York).

Prince Consort: Prince Philip of Greece, later Philip Mountbatten (1921-), fifth child and only son of Prince Andrew of Greece and Princess Alice of Battenberg.

Death: Still living.

Key Facts:

Elizabeth became monarch whilst outside of Europe while she was visiting Kenya in February 1952, following the sudden death of her father in Britain. Her coronation in 1953 was followed in Britain by almost 70% of the population either on TV or through radio, and was the first global TV event,.

She has provided stability to the monarchy and led the institution through a period of great social and technological change in Britain. She adapted the monarchy first to the television age during the first part of her reign, and then to the digital age in the 21st century.

Her long reign saw the initial decline of Great Britain as a world power and the introduction of socialist policies in the 1950s-1970s;

the dismantling of the socialist state in the 1980s; and the rebirth of the country into a 21st century's world financial power. Her reign also witnessed Britain's transformation into a multi-ethnic, multi-cultural country.

After presiding over the slow dismantling of the British Empire during the 1950s and 1960, Elizabeth greatly contributed to the creation of the Commonwealth. She strengthened the monarchy's ties to the Commonwealth through personal involvement in its affairs and personal visits to Commonwealth countries by herself and members of her family.

The failed marriages of her children and associated scandals damaged the monarchy's popularity in the 1990s, culminating in hostility towards the Royal Family following the death of Diana, Princess of Wales in 1997. The popularity of the monarchy was restored following Elizabeth's Golden Jubilee in 2002, and greatly increased after the wedding of Prince William in 2011 and Elizabeth's Diamond Jubilee in 2012. As of 2017, Elizabeth II reigns as one of the most popular monarchs in British history.

She has become the most widely travelled monarch in British history after visiting 115 countries on official visits as Queen. She has visited all Commonwealth Realms, almost all other Commonwealth Countries, and was the first reigning monarch to visit Australia and New Zealand in 1953-54. She was also the first reigning monarch to visit the Irish Republic in 2011.

The innovations introduced to the monarchy during her reign include equal primogeniture, giving equality to men and women in the line of succession; the weekly audience between the monarch and the Prime Minister; the royal walkabout; the televised Christmas Day message; the introduction of the monarch's likeness on banknotes; and the opening of Buckingham Palace to the public.

♛ In 2015, she became the longest-reigning monarch in British history, surpassing Queen Victoria's record, as well as the longest-reigning female monarch in recorded world history. She is also the longest-lived monarch in British history, and the first to reach the age of 90. In 2017 she also became the world's oldest and longest-serving head of state in the world.

Peculiar Fact:

The Queen trained as an auto mechanic during the Second World War when she joined the Women's Auxiliary Territorial Service in London as a honorary Subaltern. She learned how to change tires, fix engines, change oil, and how to drive military trucks, passing her final exam with flying colours. She continues to drive large cars on the Windsor and Balmoral estates well into her 90s.

MONARCHS' RECORDS

The 5 Longest Reigns

Listed below are the five monarchs who have had the longest reigns since the Norman Conquest of 1066, updated as of June 2019.

Note: the longest-reigning Scottish monarch, James VI of Scotland and I of England, reigned in Scotland for 57 years, 8 months, 3 days; but only reigned in England for 22 years and 2 days.

	Length of Reign
1. Elizabeth II *6 Feb 1952 to present*	**67+ years**
2. Victoria *20 Jun 1837 to 22 Jan 1901*	**63 years, 7 months, 2 days**
3. George III *25 Oct 1760 to 29 Jan 1820*	**59 years, 3 months, 4 days**
4. Henry III *18 Oct 1216 to 16 Nov 1272*	**56 years, 29 days**
5. Edward III *25 Jan 1327 to 21 Jun 1377*	**50 years, 4 months, 27 days**

The 5 Shortest Reigns

Listed below are the five monarchs who have had the shortest reigns since the Norman Conquest of 1066, updated as of June 2019.

Note: if the disputed reign of Jane Grey were to be included, she would rank first on the list with a reign of 9 days (10 to 19 July 1553).

	Length of Reign
1. Edward V *9 Apr to 26 Jun 1483*	**2 months, 17 days**
2. Edward VIII *20 Jan to 11 Dec 1936*	**10 months, 21 days**
3. Richard III *26 Jun 1483 to 22 Aug 1485*	**2 years, 1 month, 26 days**
4. James II *6 Feb 1685 to 11 Dec 1688*	**3 years, 10 months, 5 days**
5. Mary I *6 Jul 1553 to 17 Nov 1558*	**5 years, 4 months, 11 days**

The 5 Longest-Lived Monarchs

Listed below are the five monarchs with the longest life-spans since the Norman Conquest of 1066, as of June 2019.

Note: Edward VIII (born 23 Jun 1894 – died 28 May 1972) lived to 77 years, 11 months and 6 days. However, since he spent the last 35 ½ years of his life living as Duke of Windsor and not as monarch after his abdication, he is not included in this list.

	Age
1. Elizabeth II *21 Apr 1926-present*	**93+ years**
2. Victoria *24 May 1819-22 Jan 1901*	**81 years, 7 months, 29 days**
3. George III *4 Jun 1738-29 Jan 1820*	**81 years, 7 months, 14 days***
4. George II *30 Oct 1683-25 Oct 1760*	**76 years, 11 months, 14 days***
5. William IV *21 Aug 1765-20 Jun 1837*	**71 years, 9 months, 30 days**

* *Note: During George II's and George III's lifetimes both Hanover and Great Britain switched from the Old Julian Calendar to the New Gregorian Calendar (in 1700 and 1752 respectively). The switch involved bringing the calendar forward by 11 days, therefore the final number of days in George II and George III's life spans above is shorter than it should be.*

The 5 Shortest-Lived Monarchs

Listed below are the five monarchs with the shortest life-spans since the Norman Conquest of 1066, updated as of June 2019.

Note: If Jane Grey were to be included on this list she would rank in third place with a life-span of approximately 17 years (her exact date of birth is unknown).

	Age
1. Edward V *2 Nov 1470-c.September 1483*	**12 years, c.10 months**
2. Edward VI *12 Oct 1537-6 Jul 1553*	**15 years, 8 months, 24 days**
3. Mary II *30 Apr 1662-28 Dec 1694*	**32 years, 7 months, 29 days**
4. Richard III *2 Oct 1452-22 Aug 1485*	**32 yrs, 10 months, 20 days**
5. Richard II *6 Jan 1367-c.February 1400*	**33 years, c.1 month**

The 5 Oldest Monarchs at Accession

Listed below are the five oldest monarchs at the time of their accession since the Norman Conquest of 1066, updated as on June 2019.

Note: If Prince Charles were to become king he would immediately rank in first place with an age of 70+ years as of June 2019.

	<u>**Age at Accession**</u>
1. William IV *Born: 21 Aug 1765.* *Accession date: 26 Jun 1830*	**64 yrs, 10 months, 5 days**
2. Edward VII *Born: 9 Nov 1841.* *Accession date: 22 Jan 1901*	**59 years, 2 months, 13 days**
3. George IV *Born: 12 Aug 1762.* *Accession date: 29 Jan 1820*	**57 years, 5 months, 17 days**
4. George I *Born: 28 May 1660.* *Accession date: 1 Aug 1714*	**54 years, 2 months, 4 days**
5. James II *Born: 14 October 1633.* *Accession date: 6 Feb 1685*	**51 years, 3 months, 23 days**

The 5 Youngest Monarchs at Accession

Listed below are the five youngest monarchs at the time of their accession since the Norman Conquest of 1066, updated as on June 2019. All of these monarchs had regency councils governing on their behalf after their accession because of their minority.

	Age at Accession
1. Henry VI *Born: 6 Dec 1421.* *Accession date: 31 Aug 1422*	**8 months, 25 days**
2. Henry III *Born: 1 Oct 1207.* *Accession date: 19 Oct 1216*	**9 years, 18 days**
3. Edward VI *Born: 12 Oct 1537.* *Accession date: 28 Jan 1547*	**9 years, 3 months, 16 days**
4. Richard II *Born: 6 Jan 1367.* *Accession date: 21 Jun 1377*	**10 years, 5 months, 15 days**
5. Edward V *Born: 2 Nov 1470.* *Accession date: 9 Apr 1483*	**12 years, 5 months, 7 days**

Breakdown of Male-to-Female Monarchs in England/Britain since 1066

Listed below and on the next page is a comparison table showing the breakdown of male-to-female monarchs on the English/British throne for different eras: the 951 years from 1066 to 2019; the two hundred years from 1819 to 2019; and the breakdown for each royal dynasty.

Note: Years are rounded up for all reigns. Also, the sums for 1066 to 2019 and for the Stuart dynasty do not add up to an equivalent number of years because of the shared reign of William III and Mary II between 1689 and 1694.

	Male	**Female**
From 1066 to 2019	759 years	199 years
From 1819 to 2019	72 years	128 years

Breakdown by dynasty:

	Male	**Female**
Norman	88 years	0 years
Plantagenet (including Lancaster & York)	331 years	0 years

	Male	Female
Tudor	68 years	50 years
Stuart	87 years	17 years
Hanover	123 years	64 years
Saxe-Coburg-Gotha	16 years	0 years
Windsor	35 years	67 years

English/British Monarchs Born Outside England

Of the 41 monarchs who have sat on the English/British throne since 1066, 14 were born outside England. These monarchs are listed below with their places of birth grouped by country in chronological order.

Monarch	*Place of Birth*

Born in France:

William I *Born c.1027/28*	Falaise, Normandy
William II *Born c.1056/60*	Normandy (exact location unknown)
Stephen *Born c.1092/96*	Blois, Loire Valley
Henry II *Born 5 Mar 1133*	Le Mans, Loire Valley
Richard II *Born 6 Jan 1367*	Bordeaux, Aquitaine
Edward IV *Born 28 Apr 1442*	Rouen, Normandy

Born in Wales:

Edward II Caernarfon, Gwynedd
Born 25 Apr 1284

Henry V Monmouth, Monmouthshire
Born 9 Aug 1386

Henry VII Pembroke, Pembrokeshire
Born 28 Jan 1457

Born in Scotland:

James I Edinburgh, Lothian
Born 19 Jun 1566

Charles I Dunfermline, Fife
Born 19 Nov 1600

Born in The Netherlands:

William III The Hague
Born 16 Nov 1650

Born in Germany:

George I Hanover, Lower Saxony
Born 28 May 1660

George II Hanover, Lower Saxony
Born 30 Oct 1683

English/British Monarchs Born in the Modern Greater London Area

Of the 41 monarchs who have sat on the English/British throne since 1066, 18 were born in the modern Greater London area (defined as the 32 modern London Boroughs plus the City of London). The list below gives the location of each monarch's birth within the capital.

Monarch	*London Location*
Edward I *Born 17 Jun 1239*	Palace of Westminster
Edward V *Born 2 Nov 1470*	Westminster Abbey precincts
Henry VIII *Born 28 Jun 1491*	Greenwich Palace, Greenwich
Edward VI *Born 12 Oct 1537*	Hampton Court Palace, Hampton Court
Mary I *Born 18 Feb 1516*	Greenwich Palace, Greenwich
Elizabeth I *Born 7 Sep 1533*	Greenwich Palace, Greenwich
Charles II *Born 29 May 1630*	St James's Palace, St James's

James II *Born 14 Oct 1633*	St James's Palace, St James's
Mary II *Born 30 Apr 1662*	St James's Palace, St James's
Anne *Born 6 Feb 1665*	St James's Palace, St James's
George III *Born 4 Jun 1738*	Norfolk House, St James's Square
George IV *Born 12 Aug 1762*	St James's Palace, St James's
William IV *Born 21 Aug 1765*	Buckingham House (later rebuilt into Buckingham Palace)
Victoria *Born 24 May 1819*	Kensington Palace, Kensington
Edward VII *Born 9 Nov 1841*	Buckingham Palace
George V *Born 3 Jun 1865*	Marlborough House, St James's
Edward VIII *Born 23 Jun 1894*	White Lodge, Richmond Park
Elizabeth II *Born 21 Apr 1926*	17 Bruton Street, Mayfair

Causes of Death of Monarchs

Listed below are the causes of death of each English/British monarch since William the Conqueror's in 1087. The list has been compiled from historical records, biographical accounts, and in some cases educated guesses and/or interpretation since not every monarch's exact cause of death is known.

William I
Date of death: 9 Sep 1087
Age at death: c.59-60
Cause: Internal injuries received while riding a horse during a military siege in France.

William II
Date of death: 2 Aug 1100
Age at death: c.44-46
Cause: Arrow shot in the heart as an accident during hunting. There is some reason to believe that the accident was part of a murder conspiracy.

Henry I
Date of death: 1 Dec 1135
Age at death: c.66-67
Cause: Food poisoning caused by a surfeit of lampreys, a favourite dish Henry had been specifically advised not to eat.

Stephen
Date of death: 25 Oct 1154
Age at death: c.58-61
Cause: Stomach/intestinal illness, probably cancer.

Henry II
Date of death: 6 Jul 1189
Age at death: 56
Cause: Unidentified long-term illness aggravated by physical and emotional stress. Henry died shortly after fighting a rebellion led against him by his sons Richard and John.

Richard I
Date of death: 6 Apr 1199
Age at death: 41
Cause: Gangrene caused by an arrow in the shoulder received during a castle siege in France.

John
Date of death: 19 Oct 1216
Age at death: 49
Cause: Dysentery caught whilst campaigning against his barons in the First Barons' War. A spurious legend later arose that he was poisoned by a monk.

Henry III
Date of death: 16 Nov 1272
Age at death: 65
Cause: Old age

Edward I
Date of death: 7 Jul 1307
Age at death: 68
Cause: Dysentery caught whilst travelling on military campaign to Scotland.

Edward II
Date of death: 21 Sep 1327
Age at death: 43

Cause: Murdered after his deposition from the throne, most likely by smothering. The notorious story that he died by having a red-hot poker inserted in his anus only started as a rumour decades after his death.

Edward III
Date of death: 21 Jun 1377
Age at death: 64
Cause: A series of strokes which progressively weakened him in the last years of his life, the last of which proved fatal.

Richard II
Date of death: around 14 Feb 1400
Age at death: 33
Cause: Either murdered, likely by smothering, or starved to death after his deposition from the throne.

Henry IV
Date of death: 20 Mar 1413
Age at death: 46
Cause: Unidentified chronic illnesses, the symptoms of which included a disfiguring skin condition, lower limbs weakness and seizures.

Henry V
Date of death: 31 Aug 1422
Age at death: 36
Cause: Dysentery caught whilst campaigning in France during the Hundred Years' War.

Henry VI
Date of death: 21 May 1471
Age at death: 49
Cause: Murdered in the Tower of London, likely by a blow to the head, after his second deposition from the throne.

Edward IV
Date of death: 9 Apr 1483
Age at death: 40
Cause: Unidentified sudden illness. Chroniclers report this illness was made worse by years of overindulgence in food and drink.

Edward V
Date of death: unknown, likely between Aug-Oct 1483
Age at death: 12
Cause: Unknown. He was most probably murdered by smothering, in the Tower of London.

Richard III
Date of death: 22 Aug 1485
Age at death: 32
Cause: Fatal injuries received in battle against his rival claimant to the throne, Henry Tudor, who became Henry VII.

Henry VII
Date of death: 21 Apr 1509
Age at death: 52
Cause: Unidentified recurrent respiratory illness, perhaps tuberculosis.

Henry VIII
Date of death: 28 Jan 1547
Age at death: 55
Cause: Multiple ailments including morbid obesity, blood poisoning from infectious ulcers, and chronic injuries from a jousting accident in 1536. Other suggested medical conditions for what caused his death include Type II Diabetes, syphilis, and MacLeod Syndrome.

Edward VI
Date of death: 6 Jul 1553
Age at death: 15

Cause: Unidentified respiratory illness, most likely tuberculosis.

Mary I
Date of death: 17 Nov 1558
Age at death: 42
Cause: Influenza. Although Mary I suffered from what is thought to have been a form of gynaecological cancer this was not the direct cause of her death. Chroniclers report that Mary died of an influenza epidemic that swept through London in the autumn of 1558.

Elizabeth I
Date of death: 24 Mar 1603
Age at death: 69
Cause: Old age. A bout of depression brought on by the death of old friends caused her health to sink fast in the last few months of her life.

James I
Date of death: 27 Mar 1625
Age at death: 58
Cause: Multiple ailments including kidney disease, gout, and what seem to have been a series of strokes.

Charles I
Date of death: 30 Jan 1649
Age at death: 48
Cause: Execution by beheading with an axe, after being found guilty of treason against the people in a Parliamentary trial.

Charles II
Date of death: 6 Feb 1685
Age at death: 54
Cause: Apoplexy brought on by kidney failure. Some attribute the kidney failure to have been the result of the advanced stages of syphilis infection. In any case, it is very likely that the direct cause of

his death was the intensive medical treatment Charles received following his apoplectic fit, which included massive bloodletting, extensive purging, and blistering on much of his body.

James II
Date of death: 16 Sep 1701
Age at death: 67
Cause: A series of fainting fits and strokes brought on by extreme penitential practices whilst in exile after he lost his throne.

Mary II
Date of death: 28 Dec 1694
Age at death: 32
Cause: Smallpox

William III
Date of death: 8 Mar 1702
Age at death: 51
Cause: Pulmonary fever aggravated by a broken collarbone after a fall off a horse two weeks earlier. Contrary to popular legend, the fall was not the direct cause of William's death but rather it weakened his chronic poor respiratory condition that had been present since childhood.

Anne
Date of death: 1 Aug 1714
Age at death: 49
Cause: Stroke, caused or aggravated by gout, obesity and stress.

George I
Date of death: 11 Jun 1727
Age at death: 67
Cause: Stroke whilst travelling by carriage from Britain to Hanover, Germany. George died in the palace of his brother, the Prince-Bishop

of Osnabruck, in Hanover, and legends says that he departed life in the very bed in which he was born.

George II
Date of death: 25 Oct 1760
Age at death: 77
Cause: Massive heart attack whilst emptying his bowels after waking up in the morning.

George III
Date of death: 29 Jan 1820
Age at death: 81
Cause: Old age aggravated by insanity and dementia.

George IV
Date of death: 26 Jun 1830
Age at death: 67
Cause: Multiple ailments caused by years of overindulgence in food and drink. These included morbid obesity, arteriosclerosis, gout, bladder disease, and overdependence on medical drugs.

William IV
Date of death: 20 Jun 1837
Age at death: 71
Cause: Heart failure brought on by chronic pulmonary disease.

Victoria
Date of death: 22 Jan 1901
Age at death: 81
Cause: Old age, aggravated by an inability to sleep and poor appetite in the last weeks of her life.

Edward VII
Date of death: 6 May 1910
Age at death: 68

Cause: Cardiovascular attack and chronic bronchitis caused by a lifetime of smoking and overindulgence in food and drink.

George V

Date of death: 20 Jan 1936

Age at death: 70

Cause: Chronic obstructive pulmonary disease caused by life-long smoking. George's direct cause of death however was a fatal dose of mixed cocaine and morphine given to shorten his suffering and hasten his death.

Edward VIII

Date of death: 28 May 1972

Age at death: 77

Cause: Throat cancer caused by life-long smoking.

George VI

Date of death: 5 or 6 Feb 1952

Age at death: 56

Cause: Severe arteriosclerosis and lung disease caused by excessive smoking and stress. George's direct cause of death was a coronary thrombosis heart attack, likely during his sleep. His exact time of death during the night of 5/6 February 1952 is not known as he died alone.

Burial Places of Monarchs

Listed below are the burial locations of each monarch since William the Conqueror's death in 1087. Except where noted, these are current burial locations.

William I
Burial: Abbaye aux Homes, Caen, Normandy, France.
Note: William I's original tomb and remains were destroyed in 1562 during the French Wars of Religion. A new grave today only contains a thighbone said to have survived destruction.

William II
Burial: Winchester Cathedral.
Note: During the English Civil War the remains of William II were desecrated and mixed with those of older Anglo-Saxon kings who were also buried in the cathedral. They remain mixed today and are kept in mortuary chests in the sanctuary.

Henry I
Burial: Reading Abbey, Berkshire
Note: Reading Abbey was destroyed during the English Dissolution of the Monasteries in the 1530s. The fate of Henry I's remains is not known.

Stephen
Burial: Faversham Abbey, Kent
Note: Faversham Abbey was destroyed during the English Dissolution of the Monasteries in the 1530s. The fate of Stephen's remains is not known.

Henry II
Burial: Fontevraud Abbey, Loire Valley, France.
Note: The remains are lost, likely destroyed during the French Revolution. Only the sculpted tomb survives.

Richard I
Burial: Fontevraud Abbey, Loire Valley, France.
Note: The remains are lost, likely destroyed during the French Revolution. Only the sculpted tomb survives.

John
Burial: Worcester Cathedral, Worcestershire

Henry III
Burial: Westminster Abbey, London

Edward I
Burial: Westminster Abbey, London

Edward II
Burial: Gloucester Cathedral, Gloucestershire

Edward III
Burial: Westminster Abbey, London

Richard II
Burial: Westminster Abbey, London
Note: Originally buried in All Saints Church, Kings Langley, Hertfordshire.

Henry IV
Burial: Canterbury Cathedral, Kent

Henry V
Burial: Westminster Abbey, London

Henry VI
Burial: St George's Chapel, Windsor Castle, Berkshire
Note: Originally buried in Chertsey Abbey, Surrey.

Edward IV
Burial: St George's Chapel, Windsor Castle, Berkshire

Edward V
Burial: Unknown, perhaps Westminster Abbey, London

Richard III
Burial: Leicester Cathedral, Leicestershire.
Note: Originally buried in Greyfriars Priory, Leicester.

Henry VII
Burial: Westminster Abbey, London

Henry VIII
Burial: St George's Chapel, Windsor Castle, Berkshire

Edward VI
Burial: Westminster Abbey, London

Mary I
Burial: Westminster Abbey, London

Elizabeth I
Burial: Westminster Abbey, London

James I
Burial: Westminster Abbey, London

Charles I
Burial: St George's Chapel, Windsor Castle, Berkshire

Charles II
Burial: Westminster Abbey, London

James II
Burial: Church of St Germain en Laye, near Paris, France
Note: After he died in exile James II's body was laid to rest in the Church of the English Benedictines in Paris in 1701. His remains there were destroyed in 1793 during the French Revolution. His current funerary monument in St Germain en Laye only contains a small part of his chest entrails that had been set apart for separate burial, as per French royal custom.

Mary II
Burial: Westminster Abbey, London

William III
Burial: Westminster Abbey, London

Anne
Burial: Westminster Abbey, London

George I
Burial: Herrenhausen Palace, Hanover, Germany
Note: George I was originally buried in Leine Castle, Hanover. After the castle was destroyed in the Second World War his remains, which had miraculously survived, were moved to a chapel in the grounds of Herrenhausen Palace.

George II
Burial: Westminster Abbey, London

George III
Burial: St George's Chapel, Windsor Castle, Berkshire

George IV
Burial: St George's Chapel, Windsor Castle, Berkshire

William IV
Burial: St George's Chapel, Windsor Castle, Berkshire

Victoria
Burial: Frogmore Royal Mausoleum, Windsor Home Park, Berkshire

Edward VII
Burial: St George's Chapel, Windsor Castle, Berkshire

George V
Burial: St George's Chapel, Windsor Castle, Berkshire

Edward VIII
Burial: Frogmore Royal Burial Grounds, Windsor Home Park, Berkshire

George VI
Burial: St George's Chapel, Windsor Castle, Berkshire

FAMILY

Queens and Royal Consorts Since 1066

Listed in this chapter are all the English/British royal consorts who reigned since the Norman Conquest 1066. Each entry includes basic biographical data and notable facts from each consort's life, plus their burial places. Note that, following the practice followed elsewhere in this book, Guilford Dudley, the husband of Lady Jane Grey, is not included. George I's wife, Sophia Dorothea of Celle, is also not included on the list as she never reigned as Queen of Great Britain because of her divorce from George in 1694, prior to his accession as king.

Matilda of Flanders

(c.1031 – 2 Nov 1083)

Spouse: William I
Tenure as Queen: 25 Dec 1066 – 2 Nov 1083
Marriage: c.1050-52 to 2 Nov 1083.
Parents: Count Baldwin V of Flanders and Adele of France.

Notable Facts:

• Granddaughter of the King of France and a descendant of Charlemagne.
• Legend says she was unwilling to marry William because of his illegitimate birth and that he convinced her by rough wooing her.
• Their marriage was a happy one with no evidence of William keeping mistresses.
• She was often a peacemaker in the family between William and his sons.

• She acted as regent for the Duchy of Normandy when her husband was in England.
• At about 4-5 feet, she is reputed to have been the shortest queen in English history.

Burial: Abbaye aux Dames church, Caen, Normandy, France.

Matilda of Scotland

(c.1080 – 1 May 1118)

Spouse: Henry I
Tenure as Queen / Marriage: 11 Nov 1100 – 1 May 1118
Parents: King Malcolm III of Scotland and Margaret of Wessex

Notable Facts:
• Before her marriage she spent time in a convent and had to obtain a church dispensation to marry Henry.
• Originally named Edith, she changed it to the Norman name Matilda upon marriage.
• A descendant of the royal House of Wessex, her marriage united the Norman and Anglo-Saxon royal dynasties.
• She was a full political partner to Henry, often advising him and chairing council meetings in his absence.
• Known for her piety and religious works, she founded two leper hospitals.
• She was also a patron of the arts, commissioning literary works and architectural projects.

Burial: Westminster Abbey, London.

Adeliza of Louvain

(c.1103 – 23 Apr 1151)

Spouse: Henry I
Tenure as Queen / Marriage: 24 Jan 1121 – 1 Dec 1135
Parents: Count Godfrey I of Louvain and Ide of Namur

Notable Facts:
• Thirty-five years younger than her husband, she was married to Henry to produce more heirs to the throne, however their 14-year marriage was barren.
• After Henry died she remarried to one of his Norman vassal earls and eventually produced seven children.
• Later in life she entered a convent in her native Flanders.

Burial: Presumed to be at Affligem Abbey, Belgium, where she retired before dying.

Matilda of Boulogne

(c.1105 – 3 May 1152)

Spouse: Stephen
Tenure as Queen: 22 Dec 1135 – 3 May 1152
Marriage: c.1125 – 3 May 1152
Parents: Count Eustace III of Boulogne and Mary of Scotland

Notable Facts:
• One of the richest heiresses of her time, she was Countess of Boulogne in her own right. He marriage to Stephen was arranged by King Henry I.
• A niece of Queen Matilda of Scotland (see above), like her she was also descended from the Anglo-Saxon House of Wessex.

• She supported her husband's seizure of the crown and gained allies for him in England and abroad.
• She personally led armies during the Anarchy, capturing Dover Castle and winning the Battle of Winchester.
• Said to be wiser and more politically astute than her husband, her death finally crippled his cause.

Burial: Faversham Abbey, Kent, which was destroyed at the Dissolution of the Monasteries in the 1530s. Her remains are lost.

Eleanor of Aquitaine

(c.1122/24 – 1 Apr 1204)

Spouse: Henry II
Tenure as Queen: 25 Oct 1154 – 6 Jul 1189
Marriage: 18 May 1152 – 6 Jul 1189
Parents: Duke William X of Aquitaine and Aenor of Chatellerault

Notable Facts:
• One of the most remarkable women of the Middle Ages, Eleanor was the only woman to have been separately both Queen of France and Queen of England.
• The richest heiress in Europe, she was ruler of the vast Duchy of Aquitaine, France, in her own right.
• While Queen of France she travelled to the Holy Land on Crusade leading an 'army of ladies'.
• She was a patroness of poets and troubadours, many of whom congregated at her court in Poitiers.
• Her marriage to Henry was passionate and stormy, and often damaged by his philandering.
• She encouraged her sons to rebel against Henry and as a punishment she was kept prisoner by her husband for 15 years until his death.

• Freed from her imprisonment when she was in her 60s, she acted as an energetic regent of England during her son Richard I's absences, and travelled widely around Europe.
• She lived into her 80s to advise her son John at the beginning of his reign.

Burial: Fontevraud Abbey, Loire Valley, France. Her remains are lost, only the effigy remains.

Berengaria of Navarre

(c.1163/65 – 23 Dec 1230)

Spouse: Richard I
Tenure as Queen / Marriage: 12 May 1191 – 6 Apr 1199
Parents: King Sancho VI of Navarre and Sancha of Castile

Notable Facts:
• She married Richard in Cyprus whilst he was travelling on Crusade and accompanied him to the Holy Land.
• The marriage was arranged for political reasons. She was neglected by Richard and failed to produce heirs.
• She was overshadowed in her role as queen by her mother-in-law Eleanor of Aquitaine who acted as Richard's regent in England during his reign.
• Said to have never visited England when she was Queen, she may however have visited the country afterwards.
• After Richard's death she spent the rest of her life as a widow in France doing charitable works.

Burial: L'Epau Abbey, Le Mans, France.

Isabella of Angouleme

(c.1187 – 31 May 1246)

Spouse: John
Tenure as Queen / Marriage: 24 Aug 1200 – 19 Oct 1216
Parents: Count Aymer of Angouleme and Alice of Courtenay

Notable Facts:

- Twenty years younger than her husband, she was only 12 years of age when John stole her from her intended husband, Count Hugh of Lusignan in France.
- Said to be vain and fickle, she did not play a part in government.
- After John died she arranged the crowning of their 9-year-old son, Henry, but then went back to France leaving most of her children behind.
- She later married the son of her first intended husband and had at least 10 more children from him.

Burial: Fontevraud Abbey, Loire Valley, France. Her remains are lost, only the effigy remains.

Eleanor of Provence

(c.1223 – 24 Jun 1291)

Spouse: Henry III
Tenure as Queen / Marriage: 14 Jan 1236 – 16 Nov 1272
Parents: Count Ramon Berenguer IV of Provence and Beatrice of Savoy

Notable Facts:

- She was one of four sisters, each of whom married a European king.
- Known to be cultured, intelligent, and skilled in poetry.

• She enjoyed a close, loving marriage with Henry, but was unpopular in the country because of her favouritism to foreign relatives.
• She supported Henry during the Second Barons' War by raising funds abroad.
• After Henry died she became a nun but continued to exercise influence in the family as Queen Mother.

Burial: Amesbury Abbey, now the parish church of St Mary and St Melor, Amesbury, Wiltshire.

Eleanor of Castile

(1241 – 28 Nov 1290)

Spouse: Edward I
Tenure as Queen: 16 Nov 1272 – 28 Nov 1290
Marriage: 1 Nov 1254 – 28 Nov 1290
Parents: King Ferdinand III of Castile and Joan of Dammartin

Notable Facts:
• Her marriage to Edward started as a diplomatic arrangement but developed into a true love match.
• She accompanied Edward on Crusade to the Holy Land and on military campaigns in Wales.
• A patron of literature and architecture, she introduced water gardens and Spanish carpets to England.
• She was not however popular with the English people who resented her for the wealth she amassed and thought her greedy.
• After 36 years of marriage she predeceased Edward. Her death greatly affected him and he built a series of 'Eleanor Crosses' in England to commemorate her passing.

Burial: Westminster Abbey, London.

Margaret of France

(c.1279 – 14 Feb 1317)

Spouse: Edward I
Tenure as Queen / Marriage: 8 Sep 1299 – 7 Jul 1307
Parents: King Philip III of France and Marie of Brabant

Notable Facts:
• Forty years younger than her husband, like Edward's first marriage they were married for diplomatic reasons but developed a true loving relationship.
• She often accompanied Edward on military campaigns.
• She acted as a peacemaker between her husband and his wayward son Prince Edward.
• After her husband died she never remarried.

Burial: Greyfriars Church, London, now destroyed. Her remains are lost.

Isabella of France

(c.1295 – 22 Aug 1358)

Spouse: Edward II
Tenure as Queen: 25 Jan 1308 – 20 Jan 1327
Marriage: 25 Jan 1308 – 21 Sep 1327
Parents: King Philip IV of France and Joan I of Navarre

Notable Facts:
• Famous for her great beauty and intelligence, she also was one of the most controversial royal consorts in British history.
• Her marriage was unhappy as Edward, who preferred his male favourites, often spurned her and marginalised her. She finally left Edward during a visit abroad to France, and after gathering support

she came back to England to lead her husband's deposition after he had become unpopular in the country.
• She had a love affair with the man who helped her depose Edward, Roger Mortimer, whom she allowed to rule the country after Edward died, in place of her young son King Edward III.
• After Roger Mortimer was executed she became repentant of her actions and was allowed to live to old age in peace.

Burial: Greyfriars Church, London, now destroyed. Her remains are lost.

Philippa of Hainault

(c.1311/15 – 15 Aug 1369)

Spouse: Edward III
Tenure as Queen / Marriage: 24 Jan 1328 – 15 Aug 1369
Parents: Count William I of Hainault and Joan of Valois

Notable Facts:
• One of the best-loved queens of medieval England, she became popular among the people for her charity and her intercessions on behalf of condemned men.
• Her marriage to Edward was a successful one, and she was responsible for creating harmony in their large, ambitious family.
• She often accompanied her husband on military campaign during the Hundred Years War.
• She famously convinced Edward to spare the lives of the Burghers of Calais after the city was conquered in 1347.

Burial: Westminster Abbey, London.

Anne of Bohemia

(11 May 1366 – 7 Jun 1394)

Spouse: Richard II
Tenure as Queen / Marriage: 20 Jan 1382 – 7 Jun 1394
Parents: Holy Roman Emperor Charles IV and Elizabeth of Pomerania

Notable Facts:
• Unpopular on her arrival to England, she eventually became well loved by the people because of her kindness.
• Well educated, she spoke three languages and was a patron of learning and religious institutions.
• She was the first to introduce to England the custom of riding side saddle for ladies.
• A good influence of Richard, she tempered his worst character flaws. He was greatly traumatised by her early death from the plague.

Burial: Westminster Abbey, London.

Isabella of Valois

(9 Nov 1389 – 13 Sep 1409)

Spouse: Richard II
Tenure as Queen: c.1 Nov 1396 – 30 Sep 1399
Marriage: c.1 Nov 1396– c.14 Feb 1400
Parents: King Charles VI of France and Isabeau of Bavaria

Notable Facts:
• Only seven years old at her wedding, and 21 years younger than Richard, Isabella was the youngest Queen England has had since 1066.

• Her marriage was arranged as part of a diplomatic peace treaty with France during the Hundred Years War and was unpopular in the country.
• She and Richard developed a brother/sister relationship which was affectionate but chaste.
• After Richard's deposition and death she went back to France where she re-married and died in childbirth at the age of 19.

Burial: Abbey of St Laumer, Blois, France, initially. Her remains were later transferred to the Church of the Celestines in Paris which was destroyed at the French Revolution. Her remains are now lost.

Joan of Navarre

(c.1368/70 – 10 Jun 1437)

Spouse: Henry IV
Tenure as Queen / Marriage: 7 Feb 1403 – 20 Mar 1413
Parents: King Charles II of Navarre and Joan of Valois

Notable Facts:
• Previously the widow of Duke John IV of Brittany, by whom she had seven children, she was proposed marriage by Henry during both their widowhoods after they developed a genuine friendship.
• She had a good relationship with Henry's children by his previous marriage, to Mary de Bohun, before he became king.
• After Henry died however she was unjustly accused by her stepson Henry V of being a witch and placed under house arrests, though she was later cleared of all charges (see Henry V in *Monarchs Fact Sheets*).
• She lived out her final days quietly into the reign of Henry VI.

Burial: Canterbury Cathedral, Kent.

Catherine of Valois

(27 Oct 1401 – 3 Jan 1437)

Spouse: Henry V
Tenure as Queen / Marriage: 2 Jun 1420 – 31 Aug 1422
Parents: King Charles VI of France and Isabeau of Bavaria

Notable Facts:

- Younger sister of Isabella of Valois who was Queen of Richard II (see above).
- Her marriage to Henry was arranged as part of victorious English negotiations during the Hundred Years War.
- Widowed at the age of 20 after only 2 years of marriage, she decided to stay in England.
- She later re-married secretly to a squire in her household, Owen Tudor, and had at least 4 children with him. Through one of them she became grandmother to King Henry VII.
- She is said to have transmitted a form of madness to her son Henry VI inherited from her father, Charles VI of France, who had also become mad.

Burial: Westminster Abbey, London.

Margaret of Anjou

(23 Mar 1430 – 25 Aug 1482)

Spouse: Henry VI
Tenure as Queen: 23 Apr 1445 – 4 March 1461; 3 October 1470 – 11 April 1471
Marriage: 23 Apr 1445 – 21 May 1471
Parents: Duke Rene' of Anjou and Isabella of Lorraine

Notable Facts:

• A niece of French king Charles VII, her diplomatic marriage to Henry VI was unpopular in England.

• Passionate and strong-willed, she was virtual ruler of England after her husband lost his sanity in the 1450s.

• She became the leader of the Lancastrian faction during the Wars of the Roses and was present at two major battles.

• She was deposed as Queen together with her husband in 1461, but was briefly reinstated in 1470 after her husband was made king again, following negotiations she herself had led with Richard Neville, Earl of Warwick. (see Henry VI in *Monarchs Fact Sheets*)

• After the Lancastrians' final defeat in 1471 she was sent back to France to live quietly until her death.

Burial: Angers Cathedral, Anjou, France. Her remains are now lost.

Elizabeth Woodville

(c.1437 – 8 Jun 1492)

Spouse: Edward IV

Tenure as Queen: 1 May 1464 – 3 October 1470; 11 April 1471 – 9 April 1483

Marriage: 1 May 1464 – 9 April 1483

Parents: Richard Woodville, Earl Rivers, and Jacquetta of Luxembourg

Notable Facts:

• Previous to her marriage Elizabeth had been the widow of a Lancastrian knight by whom she had had two children.

• Edward became struck with her and determined to marry her despite her low rank. They were married in secret 6 months before the marriage was made public.

• Their union caused resentment at court for political reasons and because of the many Edward favours bestowed to her relatives.
• The controversial marriage eventually caused a rebellion among Edward's allies which led to his temporary deposition from the throne. They were both restored to their thrones in 1471. (see Edward IV in *Monarchs Fact Sheets*)
• Her marriage was later declared invalid under Richard III, but was recognised again by Henry VII.
• An enigmatic personality, she retired to a nunnery in the last years of her life.

Burial: St George's Chapel, Windsor Castle, Berkshire.

Anne Neville

(11 Jun 1456 – 16 Mar 1485)

Spouse: Richard III
Tenure as Queen: 26 Jun 1483 – 16 Mar 1485
Marriage: 12 Jul 1472 – 16 Mar 1485
Parents: Richard Neville, Earl of Warwick, and Anne Beauchamp

Notable Facts:
• A daughter of Richard Neville, Earl of Warwick, the most powerful noble during the Wars of the Roses, Anne was used as a pawn in dynastic politics and alliances from an early age.
• Her first marriage in 1470 was to Edward Prince of Wales, son of the Lancastrian King Henry VI, which made her briefly Princess of Wales before he was killed at the Battle of Tewkesbury in 1471.
• Her second marriage to the Yorkist Richard, when he was Duke of Gloucester, was also arranged as part of a dynastic alliance, however they seemed to have developed a loving relationship.

• A timid and unhealthy woman, she was heartbroken at the death of her only son in 1484. She died a year later after one of the briefest tenures as Queen in English history.

Burial: Westminster Abbey, London.

Elizabeth of York

(11 Feb 1466 – 11 Feb 1503)

Spouse: Henry VII
Tenure as Queen / Marriage: 18 Jan 1486 – 11 Feb 1503
Parents: King Edward IV and Queen Elizabeth Woodville

Notable Facts:

• Elizabeth was the only woman to have been daughter, sister, niece, wife, and mother to five different English kings (respectively Edward IV, Edward V, Richard III, Henry VII and Henry VIII).
• A Yorkist claimant to the throne herself, her marriage to Henry was meant to unite the houses of Lancaster and York. Despite its political beginnings however the marriage grew into a true loving relationship.
• She chose not to be involved in politics and dedicated herself instead to charity and family life, including the education of her children.
• Her death in childbirth left Henry and her children in deep grief.

Burial: Westminster Abbey, London.

Catherine of Aragon

(16 Dec 1485 – 07 Jan 1536)

Spouse: Henry VIII
Tenure as Queen / Marriage: 11 Jun 1509 – 23 May 1533
Parents: King Ferdinand II of Aragon and Queen Isabella I of Castile

Notable Facts:

• First married to Henry's brother, Prince Arthur, who died shortly after their wedding, Catherine was then married to Henry. She was the longest-married of his wives at over 23 years of marriage.
• Despite several pregnancies and one daughter she failed to produce male sons which led Henry to want to divorce her. He used as a pretext the biblical injunction against marrying a brother's wife.
• Catherine refused to agree to a divorce, forcing Henry to appeal to the pope in Rome. When the pope refused to grant a divorce, Henry broke the English church away from Rome and divorced Catherine on his own terms.
• She ended her divorced years in poverty, under house arrest, still claiming to be married to Henry.

Burial: Peterborough Cathedral, Peterborough, Cambridgeshire.

Anne Boleyn

(c.1500/1501 – 19 May 1536)

Spouse: Henry VIII
Tenure as Queen / Marriage: 28 May 1533 – 17 May 1536
Parents: Thomas Boleyn, Earl of Wiltshire and Elizabeth Howard

Notable Facts:

• A maid of honour to Catherine of Aragon, she was pursued by Henry as a mistress but she refused to submit to him unless he married her.

• Henry sought to divorce Catherine of Aragon, but when divorce was refused from the pope he separated the English Church from Rome to divorce Catherine and marry Anne.
• A patron of Protestant reformers, she provided the very impetus for the break from Rome, and for religious reform in England.
• She had a stormy, intense relationship with Henry that broke down after a few years. She also failed produce a son, giving birth to only one daughter instead.
• Finally spurned by Henry, she was tried on trumped charges of adultery and treason, and executed by beheading.

Burial: Chapel of St Peter ad Vincula, Tower of London.

Jane Seymour

(c.1507/1509 – 24 Oct 1537)

Spouse: Henry VIII
Tenure as Queen / Marriage: 30 May 1536 – 24 Oct 1537
Parents: Sir John Seymour and Margery Wentworth

Notable Facts:
• Maid of honour to both Catherine of Aragon and Anne Boleyn, Jane was pursued by Henry during the last months of his previous marriage and was married to him 11 days after Anne Boleyn's execution.
• A kind and compassionate woman, she reconciled Henry with his estranged daughter by Catherine of Aragon, Princess Mary.
• She gave Henry his much longed-for son, Edward, but she died of childbirth complications shortly afterwards.
• Said to be Henry's favourite wife, at his death he chose to be buried by her side.

Burial: St George's Chapel, Windsor Castle, Berkshire.

Anne of Cleves

(22 Sep 1515– 16 Jul 1557)

Spouse: Henry VIII
Tenure as Queen / Marriage: 6 Jan – 9 Jul 1540
Parents: Duke John III of Cleves and Maria of Julich-Berg

Notable Facts:

• Anne's marriage to Henry was arranged for diplomatic reasons by Henry's chief minister, Thomas Cromwell. Henry is said to have been very unhappy with her looks as they did not match portraits he had seen of her.
• The shortest reigning English consort since the Norman Conquest, Henry divorced her after only six months based on his inability to consummate the marriage.
• After the divorce, she was allowed to stay in England honourably in wealth and status as the 'King's Sister'.
• She was the last of Henry's wives to die, during Mary I's reign.

Burial: Westminster Abbey, London.

Catherine Howard

(c.1522/25 – 13 Feb 1542)

Spouse: Henry VIII
Tenure as Queen / Marriage: 28 Jul 1540 – 23 Nov 1541
Parents: Lord Edmund Howard and Joyce Culpeper
Notable Facts:

• A first cousin of Anne Boleyn and maid of honour to Anne of Cleves, Catherine was at least 30 years younger than Henry, and may have been as young as 15 when she married him.
• Henry became infatuated with her during his previous marriage and married her only three weeks after divorcing Anne of Cleves.

The marriage was encouraged by her powerful family, the Howards, for political reasons.

• She had however dangerously concealed a previous sexual relation, and had a reckless affair with one of Henry's courtiers during her marriage, bringing about her own downfall.

• Accused of adultery and treason, she was tried and executed by beheading, dying as the shortest-lived English queen since 1066.

Burial: Chapel of St Peter ad Vincula, Tower of London.

Catherine Parr

(c.1512 – 5 Sep 1548)

Spouse: Henry VIII
Tenure as Queen / Marriage: 12 Jul 1543 – 28 Jan 1547
Parents: Sir Thomas Parr and Maud Green

Notable Facts:

• Before marrying Henry she had been twice married and twice widowed, but with no children.

• Her marriage to Henry was motivated by his need for companionship, but she became a very capable queen.

• She convinced Henry to bring all three of his children from his previous marriages at court and acted as a loving mother to them.

• She served as Regent of the kingdom whilst Henry was away fighting in France, issuing royal proclamations and organising provisions for Henry's troops abroad.

• A committed protestant, she was the first Queen to publish a book in England—a religious treatise—but she caused some tension in her marriage because of her religious views.

• After Henry died she re-married a fourth time to Thomas Seymour, a brother of Jane Seymour, and died in childbirth shortly afterwards during her first pregnancy.

Burial: Sudeley Castle, Winchcombe, Gloucestershire.

Philip of Spain

(21 May 1527 – 13 Sep 1598)

Spouse: Mary I
Tenure as Consort / Marriage: 25 Jul 1554 – 17 Nov 1558
Parents: Charles V, Holy Roman Emperor and King of Spain, and Isabella of Portugal

Notable Facts:
• Philip was a first cousin once removed of Mary and the son of the most powerful man in Europe at the time.
• The first male royal consort in English history, he was created King Consort without real political power, setting the precedent for all future male consorts of Queens Regnant.
• The marriage, his second, was purely political and was meant to bring England back to Catholicism. Mary however developed great affection for him which was not returned.
• In 1556 he became King of Spain and spent most of his following years as English King Consort abroad.
• After Mary's death he proposed to her half-sister Elizabeth with no success. Later in Elizabeth's reign he famously sent the Spanish Armada against her in an effort to conquer England.

Burial: El Escorial Palace, near Madrid, Spain.

Anne of Denmark

(12 Dec 1574 – 4 Mar 1619)

Spouse: James I
Tenure as Queen: 24 Mar 1603 – 4 Mar 1619
Marriage: 23 Nov 1589 – 4 Mar 1619
Parents: King Frederick II of Denmark and Sophie of Mecklenburg-Gustrow

Notable Facts:

- Anne married James when he was King of Scotland before his accession to the English throne, and so is the only woman to have been separately both Queen of Scotland and Queen of England.
- Their relationship was loving at first, but they drifted apart over the years as James adopted male favourites.
- She became a patron of artists in England, including Inigo Jones who created the Queen's House at Greenwich for her. She also commissioned and took part in lavish masques performances at court.
- She was rumoured to have converted secretly to Catholicism in her later years, the first of the Stuarts to do so in the 17th century.

Burial: Westminster Abbey, London.

Henrietta Maria of France

(25 Nov 1609 – 10 Sep 1669)

Spouse: Charles I
Tenure as Queen / Marriage: 13 Jun 1625 – 30 Jan 1649
Parents: King Henry IV of France and Marie de Medici

Notable Facts:

- One of the most troublesome royal consorts in English history, she was vivacious yet stubborn and proud, with a famous hot temper.

• Despite initial problems she and Charles enjoyed a successful, loving marriage, with no evidence of Charles ever taking a mistress.
• A passionate Catholic, she refused to convert to Anglicanism and openly promoted Catholicism in England, becoming unpopular with the people because of her faith and personality.
• She encouraged Charles to resist Parliament's demands and to rule alone instead, worsening the tensions that contributed to the English Civil War.
• During the English Civil War she moved abroad, raising money and allies for the Royalist cause, yet still counselled Charles by letters.
• She later saw the monarchy restored and her son Charles II crowned but, complaining about the English weather, she lived out her last years in France.

Burial: Basilica of St Denis, Paris, France. Her remains were lost during the French Revolution.

Catherine of Braganza

(25 Nov 1638 – 30 Nov 1705)

Spouse: Charles II
Tenure as Queen / Marriage: 21 May 1662 – 6 Feb 1685
Parents: King John IV of Portugal and Luisa de Guzman

Notable Facts:
• Her marriage was arranged for diplomatic reasons and to provide for an heir however she failed to produce any offsprings.
• She was initially shocked by Charles' determination to keep mistresses after his marriage but the two came to an understanding, and had a true loving relationship despite the lack of children.

• Privately Catholic, she was often the target of anti-Catholic resentment and was accused of treason during the Popish Plot of 1678, however Charles defender her against all accusations.
• After Charles' death she went back to Portugal where she lived actively into her 60s, including serving as Regent for her young brother.
• She is widely credited with popularising tea drinking in England which she introduced from her native Portugal.

Burial: Monastery of Sao Vicente de Fora, Lisbon, Portugal.

Mary of Modena

(5 Oct 1658 – 7 May 1718)

Spouse: James II
Tenure as Queen: 6 Feb 1685 – 11 Dec 1688
Marriage: 30 Sep 1673 – 16 Sep 1701
Parents: Duke Alfonso IV d'Este of Modena and Laura Martinozzi

Notable Facts:
• Married when she was only 15-years-old, she was 25 years younger than her husband. Despite her age she became a good stepmother to James' two daughters from his first marriage who later both became Queens Regnant.
• Most of her pregnancies ended in miscarriages or infant deaths. When she finally gave birth to a healthy son in 1688 a rumour spread that the child was a changeling who had been smuggled into her bedchamber in a warming pan.
• The changeling rumour was later disproved, however fears that the baby would establish a Catholic dynasty in England sparked the Glorious Revolution of 1688-89, forcing James and Mary to flee to France (see James II in *Monarchs Fact Sheets*).

• After James' death she remained in France and became a popular member of the French royal court.

Burial: Convent of Chaillot, Paris, France, destroyed during the French Revolution. Her remains are lost.

George of Denmark

(2 Apr 1653 – 28 Oct 1708)

Spouse: Anne
Tenure as Prince Consort: 8 Mar 1702 – 28 Oct 1708
Marriage: 28 Jul 1683 – 28 Oct 1708
Parents: King Frederick III of Denmark and Sophie Amalie of Brunswick-Luneburg

Notable Facts:
• The first true Prince Consort in English/British history, George was also a Prince of Denmark in his own right, and a second cousin once removed to Anne.
• Famously modest and effacing, he acquired a reputation for dullness. Said to be interested mostly in eating and drinking, he took little part in politics.
• He was nevertheless deeply devoted to Anne, and his early death of chronic respiratory problems devastated her.
• His passive role as Prince Consort reinforced the notion that Queens Regnant were full monarchs in their own right.

Burial: Westminster Abbey, London.

Caroline of Ansbach

(1 Mar 1683 – 20 Nov 1737)

Spouse: George II
Tenure as Queen: 11 Jun 1727 – 20 Nov 1737
Marriage: 22 Aug 1705 – 20 Nov 1737
Parents: Margrave John Frederick of Brandenburg-Ansbach and Princess Eleanore Erdmuthe of Saxe-Eisenach

Notable Facts:

• One of the most capable royal consorts in British history, Caroline was well-educated and interested in the arts, philosophy and science.
• Politically liberal and wise, she was an ally and supporter of the first Prime Minister, Robert Walpole, and a Regent of the kingdom when George travelled occasionally to Hanover.
• She had a successful marriage and knew how to handle her husband's famous bad temper. However she had a contentious relationship with her firstborn son, Frederick Prince of Wales, whom she abhorred.
• She was the first German royal family member to be popular with the people and made the Hanoverian dynasty acceptable to the British.

Burial: Westminster Abbey, London.

Charlotte of Mecklenburg-Strelitz

(19 May 1744 – 17 Nov 1818)

Spouse: George III
Tenure as Queen / Marriage: 8 Sep 1761 – 17 Nov 1818
Parents: Duke Charles Louis Frederick of Mecklenburg and Princess Elisabeth Albertine of Saxe-Hildburghausen

Notable Facts:

• Charlotte was the longest-serving Queen Consort in English/British history, with a 57-year tenure. She also had the most children of any English/British queen with 15 offsprings.

• She did not involve herself in politics, leading instead a domestic life raising children and looking after household matters. She became especially attached to her daughters, many of whom she forced to live with her, unmarried, until her death.

• She was greatly interested in botany and created new gardens at Kew, Frogmore and other royal residences.

• During her husband's bouts of madness she often served as his legal guardian, including during his final long period of permanent illness when she found it difficult to deal with his mental condition.

Burial: St George's Chapel, Windsor Castle, Berkshire.

Caroline of Brunswick

(17 May 1768 – 7 Aug 1821)

Spouse: George IV
Tenure as Queen: 29 Jan 1820 – 7 Aug 1821
Marriage: 8 Apr 1795 –7 Aug 1821
Parents: Duke Charles William Ferdinand of Brunswick-Wolfenbuttel and Princess Augusta of Great Britain

Notable Facts:

• One of the most colourful Princesses of Wales and Queens in British history, she was generous, spirited but poorly educated and ill-prepared for a royal marriage.

• Her nature as a tomboy and poor personal appearance clashed with George's refined tastes. Their relationship broke down immediately after their marriage and they lived apart afterwards.

• She engaged in a scandalous life as Princess of Wales, supposedly having affairs with politicians and questionable characters. Many however saw her as a victim of George's selfish behaviour and she became a focus of popular opposition to him.
• She moved abroad for six years when she was Princess of Wales, engaging in more scandalous behaviour before coming back to England in 1820 on George's accession as King. She was then tried in the House of Lords for her alleged adultery but was acquitted.
• George refused to admit her to his own coronation in Westminster Abbey in 1821, and she died shortly afterwards of illness. Her last wish was to be buried away from England in her native Brunswick.

Burial: Brunswick Cathedral, Brunswick, Germany.

Adelaide of Saxe-Meiningen

(13 Aug 1792 – 2 Dec 1849)

Spouse: William IV
Tenure as Queen: 26 Jun 1830 – 20 Jun 1837
Marriage: 13 Jul 1818 –20 Jun 1837
Parents: Duke George I of Saxe-Meiningen and Princess Louise Eleanore of Hohenloe-Langenburg

Notable Facts:
• Twenty six years younger than her husband, their marriage was meant to provide for the royal succession but resulted only in miscarriages and infant deaths.
• A gentle and caring woman, their marriage was a loving one and she was tolerant of William's many illegitimate children.
• She was generally conservative and was criticised as Queen for her opposition to political and electoral reform which was the central issue of William's reign.

• After William died she became a popular Queen Dowager, doing charitable work and providing guidance to the young Queen Victoria.

Burial: St George's Chapel, Windsor Castle, Berkshire.

Albert of Saxe-Coburg-Gotha

(26 Aug 1819 – 14 Dec 1861)

Spouse: Victoria
Tenure as Prince Consort / Marriage: 10 Feb 1840 – 14 Dec 1861
Parents: Duke Ernest I of Saxe-Coburg-Gotha and Princess Louise of Saxe-Gotha-Altenburg

Notable Facts:
• One of the most influential royal consorts in British history, together with Victoria he was the creator of the modern monarchy.
• Incredibly multitalented, he was skilled in politics, architecture, music, painting, and designing. He was a patron and supporter of innumerable causes in the sciences, arts, social charities and reforms.
• He organised the Great Exhibition of 1851 which showcased Britain's progress in the world, the proceeds of which went to build museums in London.
• Albert bought and rebuilt Osborne House on the Isle of Wight and Balmoral in Scotland, to be used as new royal residences.
• A full political partner to Victoria, she came to greatly rely on him in government matters. His premature death at the age of 42 left her devastated, and in mourning for the rest of her life.
• Originally unloved in the country because of his foreign origins, he came to be appreciated after his death.

Burial: Frogmore Royal Mausoleum, Windsor Home Park, Berkshire.

Alexandra of Denmark

(1 Dec 1844 – 20 Nov 1925)

Spouse: Edward VII
Tenure as Queen: 22 Jan 1901 – 6 May 1910
Marriage: 10 Mar 1863 – 6 May 1910
Parents: King Christian IX of Denmark and Princess Louise of Hesse-Kassel

Notable Facts:

• Kind, considerate and good-natured, Alexandra was also one of the great royal beauties of her day, setting fashion trends in society.
• She had a testing but loving relationship with Edward because of his mistresses, some of whom she came to accept as social companions.
• As Princess of Wales she took over many social duties from Queen Victoria during her mourning period and became greatly loved by the people. She remained the most popular member of the Royal Family until her death.
• She was devoted to nursing, founding several corps and assisting in the formation of the British Red Cross.
• Although her tenure as Queen was short, she remains the longest-serving Princess of Wales in history.

Burial: St George's Chapel, Windsor Castle, Berkshire.

Mary of Teck

(26 May 1867 – 24 Mar 1953)

Spouse: George V
Tenure as Queen: 6 May 1910 – 20 Jan 1936
Marriage: 6 Jul 1893 – 20 Jan 1936

Parents: Duke Francis of Teck and Princess Mary Adelaide of Cambridge

Notable Facts:
- Mary was originally engaged to George's older brother Albert Victor. After his premature death in 1892 George proposed and they were married. Although both reserved, their marriage was happy with Mary providing steadfast support to George when he became king.
- She was the first royal consort to visit Commonwealth dominions and colonies. During World War One she visited hospitals, and supported nurses and troops.
- She became known popularly for her great regal bearing and monumental use of jewels. A passionate art collector, she increased and catalogued the holdings in the Royal Collection.
- After George V's death, she supported her son George VI during and after the Abdication Crisis of 1936.
- A great believer in duty and service, she passed on her beliefs to her granddaughter Elizabeth II.

Burial: St George's Chapel, Windsor Castle, Berkshire.

Elizabeth Bowes-Lyon

(4 Aug 1900 – 30 Apr 2002)

Spouse: George VI
Tenure as Queen: 11 Dec 1936 – 6 Feb 1952
Marriage: 26 Apr 1923 – 6 Feb 1952
Parents: Claude Bowes-Lyon, Earl of Strathmore and Kinghorne, and Cecilia Cavendish-Bentinck

Notable Facts:

• The first British commoner Queen (i.e. of non-royal lineage) since Catherine Parr in 1543, Elizabeth was known for her charms, wit and ability to relate to everyone.

• She provided crucial support to her husband George VI, and helped him restore the standing of the monarchy after the Abdication Crisis of 1936.

• She became an icon of British resistance during World War Two when she refused to leave her husband's side in London and toured bombed out areas and hospitals.

• After George's death she became a popular Queen Mother, continuing to support charities and the military.

• She continued to carry out hundreds of engagements into her 90s as the respected matriarch of the Royal Family. She died aged 101 as the oldest royal consort in British history.

Burial: St George's Chapel, Windsor Castle, Berkshire.

Philip of Greece

(10 Jun 1921 – present)

Spouse: Elizabeth II
Tenure as Prince Consort: 6 Feb 1952 – present
Marriage: 20 Nov 1947 – present
Parents: Prince Andrew of Greece and Princess Alice of Battenberg

Notable Facts:

• A grandson and nephew of two Kings of Greece, Philip officially changed his name to Mountbatten, borne by his mother's family, after becoming a British citizen in 1947.

• He served in combat in World War Two and had a successful naval career before becoming a full time royal consort.

- He has provided constant support to his wife for over 65 years, and has supported over 800 organisations and causes as a royal consort.
- He helped modernise the monarchy by introducing the use of TV filming during royal occasion and documentaries, and by opening up the Royal Collection. His most successful contribution has been the Duke of Edinburgh Award providing leadership training to thousands of young people.
- His tenure as Royal Consort is the longest in English/British history, and his marriage to Elizabeth is the longest for any English/British monarch.

ROYAL CONSORTS RECORDS

The 5 Longest-Lived Royal Consorts

Listed below are the five longest-lived consorts married to English/British monarchs since the Norman Conquest of 1066, updated as of June 2019.

Royal Consort	*Age at Death*
1. Elizabeth Bowes-Lyon *(4 Aug 1900-30 Mar 2002)* Consort of King George VI	**101 yrs, 7 months, 26 days**
2. Philip of Greece *(10 Jun 1921-present)* Consort of Queen Elizabeth II	**98+ years**
3. Mary of Teck *(26 May 1867-24 Mar 1953)* Consort of King George V	**85 years, 9 months, 26 days**
4. Alexandra of Denmark *(1 Dec 1844-20 Nov 1925)* Consort of King Edward VII	**80 years, 11 months, 19 days**
5. Eleanor of Aquitaine *(c.1122/1124-1 Apr 1204)* Consort of King Henry II	**c.80-82 years**

The 5 Shortest-Lived Royal Consorts

Listed below are the five shortest-lived consorts married to English/British monarchs since the Norman Conquest of 1066, updated as of June 2019.
Note: If Lady Jane Grey were considered a legitimate monarch her husband, Guilford Dudley (c.1535-1554), would rank in second place at approximately 19 years of age at death.

Royal Consort	*Age at Death*
1. Catherine Howard *(c.1522/1525-13 Feb 1542)* Fifth consort of King Henry VIII	**c.17 to 20 years**
2. Isabella of Valois *(9 Nov 1389-13 Sep 1409)* Second Consort of King Richard II	**19 years, 10 months, 4 days**
3. Anne of Bohemia *(11 May 1366-7 Jun 1394)* First Consort of King Richard II	**28 years, 27 days**
4. Anne Neville *(11 Jun 1456-16 Mar 1485)* Consort of King Richard III	**28 years, 9 months, 5 days**
5. Jane Seymour *(c.1507/1509-24 Oct 1537)* Third consort of King Henry VIII	**c.28-30 years**

The 5 Longest-Serving Royal Consorts

Listed below are the five longest-serving consorts married to English/British monarchs since the Norman Conquest of 1066, updated as of June 2019. Length of service is defined as time spent married to a living monarch.

Royal Consort *(Tenure)*	*Length of Tenure*
1. Philip of Greece *(6 Feb 1952-present)* Consort of Queen Elizabeth II	**67+ years**
2. Charlotte of Mecklenburg-Strelitz *(8 Sep 1761-17 Nov 1818)* Consort of King George III	**57 years, 2 months, 9 days**
3. Philippa of Hainault *(24 Jan 1328-15 Aug 1369)* Consort of King Edward III	**41 years, 6 months, 22 days**
4. Eleanor of Provence *(14 Jan 1236-16 Nov 1272)* Consort of King Henry III	**36 years, 10 months, 2 days**
5. Eleanor of Aquitaine *(25 Oct 1154-6 Jul 1189)* Consort of King Henry II	**34 years, 8 months, 11 days**

The 5 Shortest-Serving Royal Consorts

Listed below are the five shortest-serving consorts married to English/British monarchs since the Norman Conquest of 1066, updated as of June 2019. Length of service is defined as time spent married to a living monarch.

Note: If Lady Jane Grey were considered a legitimate monarch her husband, Guilford Dudley, would rank first on this list with a 9-day tenure.

Royal Consort (*Tenure*)	*Length of Tenure*
1. Anne of Cleves *(6 Jan to 9 Jul 1540)* Fourth Consort of King Henry VIII	**6 months, 3 days**
2. Catherine Howard *(28 Jul 1540-23 Nov 1541)* Fifth Consort of King Henry VIII	**1 year, 3 months, 26 days**
3. Jane Seymour *(30 May 1536-24 Oct 1537)* Third Consort of King Henry VIII	**1 year, 4 months, 24 days**
4. Caroline of Brunswick *(29 Jan 1820-7 Aug 1821)* Consort of King George IV	**1 year, 6 months, 9 days**
5. Anne Neville *(26 Jun 1483-16 Mar 1485)* Consort of King Richard III	**1 year, 8 months, 18 days**

The 5 Longest Marriages of Monarchs and Consorts

Listed below are the five longest marriages of English/British monarchs and their consorts since the Norman Conquest of 1066, updated as of June 2019.

Monarch & Consort	*Length of Marriage*
1. Elizabeth II & Philip of Greece	**71+ years** *(20 Nov 1947 to present)*
2. George III & Charlotte of Mecklenburg-Strelitz	**57 years, 2 months, 9 days** *(8 Sep 1761-17 Nov 1818)*
3. Edward VII & Alexandra of Denmark	**47 years, 1 month, 26 days** *(10 Mar 1863-6 May 1910)*
4. George V & Mary of Teck	**42 years, 6 months, 14 days** *(6 Jul 1893-20 Jan 1936)*
5. Edward III & Philippa of Hainault	**41 years, 6 months, 22 days** *24 Jan 1328-15 Aug 1369*

The 5 Shortest Marriages of Monarchs and Consorts

Listed below are the five shortest marriages of English/British monarchs and their consorts since the Norman Conquest of 1066, updated as of June 2019.
Note: If Lady Jane Grey were considered a legitimate monarch, her marriage to Guilford Dudley of 8 months and 22 days would rank in second place.

Monarch & Consort	*Length of Marriage*
1. Henry VIII & Anne of Cleves	**6 months, 3 days** *(6 Jan to 9 Jul 1540)*
2. Henry VIII & Catherine Howard	**1 year, 3 months, 26 days** *(28 Jul 1540-23 Nov 1541)*
3. Henry VIII & Jane Seymour	**1 year, 4 months, 24 days** *(30 May 1536-24 Oct 1537)*
4. Henry V & Catherine of Valois	**2 years, 2 months, 19 days** *(2 Jun 1420-21 Aug 1422)*
5. Henry VIII & Anne Boleyn	**2 years, 11 months, 19 days** *(28 May 1533-17 May 1536)*

◆

◆

Monarchs Who Never Married

Listed below are the English/British monarchs who never married, either before or during their reigns, since the Norman Conquest of 1066. *Note: Edward VIII (1894-1972) remained a bachelor before and during his reign, marrying only after his abdication. He is therefore excluded from this list.*

William II *(c. 1056/60-1100)*
He died at about 40 years of age without marrying and without fathering any illegitimate children. Contemporary church chroniclers suggested he was homosexual though there is no firm evidence for this.

Edward V *(1470-1483)*
He died at 12 years of age. At the time of his death he was betrothed to six-year-old Anne, heiress to the Duchy of Brittany, with the marriage to take place after both reached their majorities.

Edward VI *(1537-1553)*
He died at 15 years of age. At the time of his death he was betrothed to 8-year-old Elizabeth of Valois, daughter of French King Henry II, with the marriage to take place at a later date. Before then he had been briefly betrothed to the infant Mary Queen of Scots.

Elizabeth I *(1533-1603)*
She famously died at age 69 without ever having married, and supposedly having remained a virgin her entire life. The closer she came to marriage was during negotiations in the 1570s to marry Francois, Duke of Anjou, a son of Catherine de Medici and brother to three kings of France.

Some Monarchs Who Married Their Cousins

Because of the constant intermarriage between the royal houses of Europe throughout history it is not unusual to find English/British monarchs and consorts who were related as cousins in the third, fourth or fifth degree. Occasionally however monarchs married much more closely related cousins. The list below includes English/British monarchs who married cousins they were related to in the first to the second degrees.

Edward I and Margaret of France
Married on 8 Sep 1299
First cousins once removed
Edward's mother, Eleanor of Provence, and Margaret's paternal grandmother, Margaret of Provence, were sisters.

Edward III and Philippa of Hainault
Married on 24 Jan 1328
Second cousins
Edward's maternal grandfather, King Philip IV of France, and Philippa's maternal grandfather, Charles Count of Valois, were brothers.

Richard III and Anne Neville
Married on 12 Jul 1472
First cousins once removed
Richard's mother, Cecily Neville, Duchess of York, and Anne's paternal grandfather, Richard Neville, Earl of Salisbury, were brother and sister.

Mary I and Philip of Spain
Married on 25 Jul 1554
First cousins once removed
Mary's mother, Queen Catherine of Aragon, and Philip's paternal grandmother, Queen Joanna of Castile, were sisters.

William III and Mary II
Married on 4 Nov 1677
First cousins
William's mother, Mary Princess of Orange, and Mary's father, King James II, were brother and sister.

George I and Sophia Dorothea of Celle
Married on 21 Nov 1682
First cousins
George's father, Ernest Augustus, Elector of Hanover, and Sophia's father, George William, Duke of Brunswick-Luneburg, were brothers.

George IV and Caroline of Brunswick
Married on 8 Apr 1795
First cousins
George's father, King George III, and Caroline's mother, Augusta, Duchess of Brunswick, were brother and sister.

Queen Victoria and Prince Albert
Married on 10 Feb 1840
First cousins
Victoria's mother, Victoire of Saxe-Coburg-Saalfeld, and Albert's father, Duke Ernest of Saxe-Coburg-Gotha, were brother and sister.

Royal Children

Listed below and in the following pages are all the children born to English/British monarchs since King William I, based on available historical records. Each entry includes royal and noble titles, spouses, and other important brief information where appropriate. No miscarriages or stillbirths are included, but children who died shortly after birth are, provided they received a name. Children whose existence is uncertain are marked by the symbol ≠ and not officially counted. Monarchs who were childless are not included.

William I

(c.1027/28-1087)

By Matilda of Flanders (c.1031-1083):

1. Robert Curthose (c.1052/54-1134), Duke of Normandy
Married Sybilla of Conversano. Had issue.
Claimant to the English throne against his brothers William II and Henry I.

2. Richard (c.1054/56-c.1069-81)
Died unmarried in a hunting accident in the New Forest, like his brother King William II later on.

3. Adelida (c.1055-before 1113)
Became a nun.

4. King William II (c.1056/60-1100)
Died unmarried.

5. Cecilia (c.1056/65-1126)
Became a nun and rose to be Abbess.

6. Constance (c.1057/61-1090), Duchess of Brittany
Married Duke Alan IV of Brittany. No issue.

7. Matilda (?1061-before 1112)
Died unmarried.

8. Adela (c.1062/67-1137), Countess of Blois
Married Count Stephen-Henry of Blois. Had issue.
Mother of King Stephen, and of Henry of Blois, Bishop of Winchester.

***≠. Agatha** (c.1064-before 1080)*
Died unmarried.

9. King Henry I (c.1068/69-1135)
Married Matilda of Scotland. Had issue. (See below)
Married Adeliza of Louvain. No issue.

Henry I

(c.1068/69-1135)

By Matilda of Scotland (c.1080-1118):

1. Matilda (1102- 1167), Holy Roman Empress, Countess of Anjou, Lady of the English
Married Holy Roman Emperor Henry V. Widowed. No issue.
Married Count Geoffrey V of Anjou. Had issue.
Nominated heir to the English throne by her father, but passed over by the English barons after his death in favour of King Stephen. Her

efforts to wrestle the English crown from King Stephen led to the Anarchy (see Stephen in *Monarchs Fact Sheets*).

2. William Atheling (1103-1120), Heir to the Throne
Married Matilda of Anjou. No issue.
Heir to the throne, died before his father.

Stephen

(c.1092/97-1154)

By Matilda of Boulogne (c.1105-1152):

1. Baldwin (c.1026-before 1135)
Died unmarried.

2. Eustace (c.1130/35-1153), Count of Boulogne
Married Constance of France, daughter of King Louis VI of France.
No issue.
Heir to the throne, died before his father.

3. William (c.1132/37- 1159), Count of Boulogne, Earl of Surrey
Married Isabelle de Warenne, Countess of Surrey. No issue.

4. Matilda (c.1033-c.1037/41)
Married Waleran de Beaumont, Count of Meulan, Earl of Worcester.
No issue.

5. Marie (c.1136-1182), Countess of Boulogne
Married Matthew of Alsace. Marriage annulled. Had issue.
She was a nun before her marriage, and became a nun again after her marriage ended.

Henry II

(1133-1189)

By Eleanor of Aquitaine (c.1122/24-1204):

1. William (1153-1156), Count of Poitiers
Died in childhood.

2. Henry 'The Young King' (1155-1183)
Married Margaret of France, daughter of King Louis VII of France.
No surviving issue.
Crowned future King of England in his father's lifetime but died before him.

3. Matilda (1156-1189), Duchess of Saxony and of Bavaria
Married Henry the Lion, Duke of Saxony and Bavaria. Had issue.
Mother of Holy Roman Emperor Otto IV.

4. King Richard I (1157-1199)
Married Berengaria of Navarre. No issue

5. Geoffrey (1158-1186), Duke of Brittany
Married Constance, Duchess of Brittany. Had issue.
Father of Arthur of Brittany, claimant of the throne in King John's reign.

6. Eleanor (1161-1214), Queen of Castile
Married King Alfonso VIII of Castile. Had issue.
Mother of four European queens.
Great-grandmother of Eleanor of Castile, queen of Edward I.

7. Joan (1165-1199), Queen of Sicily, Countess of Toulouse
Married King William II of Sicily. Widowed. No issue.
Married Count Raymond VI of Toulouse. Had issue.

8. King John (1166-1216)
Married Isabella of Angouleme. Had issue. (See below)

John

(1166-1216)

By Isabella of Angouleme (c.1187-1246):

1. King Henry III (1207-1272)
Married Eleanor of Provence. Had issue. (See below)

2. Richard (1209-1272), Earl of Cornwall, King of the Romans (i.e. King of Germany)
Married Isabella Marshal. Widowed. Had issue.
Married Sanchia of Provence. Widowed. Had issue.
Married Beatrice of Falkenburg. No issue.

3. Joan (1210-1238), Queen of Scotland
Married King Alexander II of Scotland. No issue.

4. Isabella (1214-1241), Holy Roman Empress, Queen of Sicily
Married Frederick II, Holy Roman Emperor and King of Sicily. Had issue.

5. Eleanor (1215-1275), Countess of Pembroke, Countess of Leicester
Married William Marshal, Earl of Pembroke. Widowed. No issue.
Married Simon de Montford, Earl of Leicester, leader of the baronial revolt against Henry III in the Second Barons War (see Henry III in *Monarchs Fact Sheets*). Had issue.

Henry III

(1207-1272)

By Eleanor of Provence (c.1223-1291):

1. King Edward I (1239-1307)
Married Eleanor of Castile. Had issue.
Married Margaret of France. Had issue.
(See below)

2. Margaret (1240-1275), Queen of Scotland
Married King Alexander III of Scotland. Had issue.

3. Beatrice (1242-1275), Countess of Richmond
Married John, heir to the Dukedom of Brittany and Earl of Richmond. Had issue.

4. Edmund Crouchback (1245-1296), Earl of Leicester, Earl of Lancaster
Married Aveline de Forz. Widowed. No issue.
Married Blanche of Artois. Had issue.
First person to bear the title of Earl or Duke of Lancaster.
Father of Thomas of Lancaster, who was executed by King Edward II (see Edward II in *Monarchs Facts Sheet*).

5. Katherine (1253-1257)
Died in childhood.

Edward I

(1239-1307)

By Eleanor of Castile (1241-1290):

1. Eleanor (c.1264/69-1298), Countess of Bar
Married Count Henry III of Bar. Had issue.

2. Joan (1265)
Died in infancy.

3. John (1266-1271)
Died in childhood.
First heir to the throne of Edward I. Died before his father.

4. Henry (c.1267/68-1274)
Died in childhood.
Second heir to the throne of Edward I. Died before his father.

5. Juliana (1271)
Died in infancy.

6. Joan of Acre (1272-1307), Countess of Gloucester and Hertford
Married Gilbert de Clare, Earl of Gloucester and Hertford. Had issue.
Married Sir Ralph de Monthermer. Had issue
Two of her daughters from her first marriage married favourites of Edward II, Piers Gaveston and Hugh Despenser the Younger (see Edward II in *Monarchs Facts Sheets*).

7. Alfonso (1273- 1284), Earl of Chester
Died in childhood.
Third heir to the throne of Edward I. Died before his father.

8. Margaret (1275-1318), Duchess of Brabant
Married Duke John II of Brabant. Had issue.

9. Berengaria (1276-c.1276/79)
Died in childhood.

10. Mary (1278-c.1332)
Became a nun.

≠. Isabella *(c.1279)*
Died in infancy.

11. Elizabeth (1282-1316), Countess of Hereford
Married Count John I of Holland. No issue.
Married Humphrey de Bohun, Earl of Hereford. Had issue.
Great-grandmother of Mary de Bohun, first wife of King Henry IV.

12. King Edward II (1284-1327)
Married Isabella of France. Had issue. (See below)
Fourth and final heir to the throne of Edward I.

By Margaret of France (c.1279-1317):

1. Thomas (1300-1338), Earl of Norfolk
Married Alice de Hales. Had issue.
Married Mary de Braose. No issue.

2. Edmund (1301-1330), Earl of Kent
Married Margaret Wake. Had issue.
Father of Joan, Countess of Kent, who married Edward the Black Prince (see below)
Grandfather of King Richard II.
Executed by Roger Mortimer during the minority of Edward III (See Edward III in *Monarchs Fact Sheets*)

3. Eleanor (1306-1311)
Died in childhood.

Edward II

(1284-1327)

By Isabella of France (c.1295-1358):

1. King Edward III (1312-1377)
Married Philippa of Hainault. Had issue. (See below)

2. John of Eltham (1316-1336), Earl of Cornwall
Died unmarried.

3. Eleanor (1318-1355), Countess of Guelders
Married Duke Reginald II of Guelders. Had issue.

4. Joan of the Tower (1321-1362), Queen of Scotland
Married King David II of Scotland. No issue.
At 33 years and three months she was the longest-serving Queen Consort in Scottish history before the crowns of England and Scotland were united in 1707.

Edward III

(1312-1377)

By Philippa of Hainault (c.1311/15-1369):

1. Edward, the Black Prince (1330-1376), Prince of Wales
Married Joan, Countess of Kent. Had issue.
Heir to the throne, died before his father.
Hero of the Hundred Years War.
Father of King Richard II.

2. Isabella (1332-c.1382), Countess of Bedford
Married Enguerrand de Coucy, Earl of Bedford. Had issue.

3. Joan (c.1333/35-1348)
Died unmarried in the Black Plague.

4. William (c.1336/37-1337)
Died in childhood.

5. Lionel of Antwerp (1338-1368), Duke of Clarence,
Married Elizabeth de Burgh, Countess of Ulster. Widowed. Had issue.
Married Violante Visconti of Milan. No issue.
First person to bear the title of Duke of Clarence.
Ancestor of the House of York.

6. John of Gaunt (1340-1399), Duke of Lancaster
Married Blanche of Lancaster. Had issue (the Lancaster line).
Married Constance of Castile. Had issue (the Castile line).
Married Katherine Swynford (his former mistress). Had issue (the Beaufort line).
Father of King Henry IV.
Progenitor of the House of Lancaster.
Ancestor of House of Tudor.

7. Edmund of Langley (1341- 1402), Duke of York
Married Isabella of Castile. Had issue.
Married Joan Holland, granddaughter of Joan, Countess of Kent (see above) from a previous marriage. No issue.
First person to bear the title of Duke of York.
Ancestor of the House of York.
Great-grandfather of King Edward IV.

8. Blanche (1342)
Died in infancy.

9. Mary (1344-1361), Duchess of Brittany
Married Duke John IV of Brittany. No issue.

10. Margaret (1346-1361), Countess of Pembroke
Married John Hastings, Earl of Pembroke. No issue.

11. Thomas (c.1347-1348)
Died in childhood.

12. William (1348)
Died in infancy.

13. Thomas of Woodstock (1355-1397), Duke of Gloucester
Married Eleanor de Bohun, sister of Mary de Bohun, first wife of King Henry IV (see below). Had issue.
First person to bear the title of Duke of Gloucester.
One of the Lords Appellants during Richard II's reign (see Richard II in *Monarchs Fact Sheets*).
Murdered on the orders of Richard II.

Henry IV

(1367-1413)

By Mary de Bohun (c.1369-1394):

1. King Henry V (1386-1422)
Married Catherine of Valois. Had issue. (See below)

2. Thomas (1387- 1421), Duke of Clarence
Married Margaret Holland, granddaughter of Joan, Countess of Kent (see above) from a previous marriage. No issue.
Died in battle during the Hundred Years War.

3. John (1389-1435), Duke of Bedford
Married Anne of Burgundy. Widowed. No issue.
Married Jacquetta of Luxembourg. No issue.

(Jacquetta of Luxembourg later re-married and became the mother of Elizabeth Woodville, Queen of Edward IV)
Regent of France in 1422-1435 for the English territories gained in the Hundred Years War.

4. Humphrey (1390-1447), Duke of Gloucester
Married Jacqueline, Countess of Hainault and Holland. Marriage annulled. No issue.
Married Eleanor Cobham. No issue.
Lord Protector of England during the minority of King Henry VI.

5. Blanche (1392-1409), Countess Palatine of the Rhine
Married Louis III, Count Palatine of the Rhine. Had issue.

6. Philippa (1394-1430), Queen of Denmark, Norway and Sweden
Married Eric of Pomerania, King of Denmark, Norway and Sweden. No issue.

Henry V

(1386-1422)

By Catherine of Valois (1401-1437):

1. King Henry VI (1421-1471)
Married Margaret of Anjou. Had issue. (See below)

Henry VI

(1421-1471)

By Margaret of Anjou (1430-1482):

1. Edward of Westminster (1453-1471), Prince of Wales
Married Anne Neville. No issue.
Killed at the Battle of Tewkesbury during the Wars of the Roses.

Edward IV

(1442-1483)

By Elizabeth Woodville (c.1437-1492):

1. Elizabeth (1466-1503), Queen Consort of England
Married King Henry VII. Had issue. (See below)

2. Mary (1467-1482)
Died unmarried.

3. Cecily (1469-1507), Viscountess Welles
Married John, Viscount Welles. Had issue.
Married Thomas Kyme. Had issue.

4. King Edward V (1470-1483)
Died unmarried.
Assumed to have been murdered in the Tower of London.

5. Margaret (1472)
Died in childhood

6. Richard (1473-1483), Duke of York
Married Anne de Mowbray, Countess of Norfolk. Marriage was unconsummated. Widowed.
Assumed to have been murdered in the Tower of London.

7. Anne (1475- 1511)
Married Thomas Howard, later Duke of Norfolk. Had issue.

8. George (1477-1479), Duke of Bedford
Died in childhood.

9. Katherine (1479-1527), Countess of Devon
Married William Courtenay, Earl of Devon. Had issue.

10. Bridget (1480-c.1513/17)
Became a nun.

Richard III

(1452-1485)

By Anne Neville (1456-1485):

1. Edward of Middleham (c.1473/76-1484), Prince of Wales
Died in childhood.
Heir to the throne, died before his father.

Henry VII

(1457-1509)

By Elizabeth of York (1466-1503):

1. Arthur (1486-1502), Prince of Wales
Married Catherine of Aragon. No issue. Marriage said to be unconsummated. Catherine of Aragon's first marriage to Arthur later became the main issue affecting the validity of Henry VIII's own marriage to Catherine.
Heir to the throne, died before his father.

2. Margaret (1489-1541), Queen of Scotland
Married King James IV of Scotland. Widowed. Had issue.
Married Archibald Douglas, Earl of Angus. Divorced. Had issue.
Married Henry Stewart, Lord Methven. No issue.
Grandmother of both Mary Queen of Scots, via her first marriage, and of Mary's husband Henry Stuart, Lord Darnley, via her second marriage.
Link of succession line to the English Crown from the House of Tudor to the House of Stuart.

3. King Henry VIII (1491-1547)
Married Catherine of Aragon. Had issue.
Married Anne Boleyn. Had issue.
Married Jane Seymour. Had issue.
Married Anne of Cleves. No issue.
Married Catherine Howard. No issue.
Married Catherine Parr. No issue.
(See below)

4. Elizabeth (1492-1495)
Died in childhood.

5. Mary (1496-1533), Queen of France, Duchess of Suffolk
Married King Louis XII of France. Widowed. No issue.
Married Charles Brandon, Duke of Suffolk. Had issue.
Grandmother of Lady Jane Grey.

6. Edmund (1499-1500), Duke of Somerset
Died in childhood.

*≠. **Edward** (c.1498/99-c.1499/1501)*
Died in childhood.

7. Katherine (1503)
Died shortly after birth.

Henry VIII

(1491-1547)

By Catherine of Aragon (1485-1536):

1. Henry (1511), Duke of Cornwall
Died in infancy.

2. Queen Mary I (1516-1558)
Married Philip of Spain. No issue.

By Anne Boleyn (c.1500/01-1536):

1. Queen Elizabeth I (1533-1603)
Died unmarried.

By Jane Seymour (c.1507/09-1537):

1. King Edward VI (1537-1553)
Died unmarried.

James I

(1566-1625)

By Anne of Denmark (1574-1619):

1. Henry Frederick (1594-1612), Prince of Wales
Died unmarried.
Heir to the throne, died before his father.

2. Elizabeth (1596-1662), Electress Palatine, Queen of Bohemia
Married Frederick V, Elector Palatine, King of Bohemia. Had issue.
Mother of Prince Rupert, famous Royalist Commander in the English Civil War.
Grandmother of King George I.
Link of succession line to the English/British Crown from the House of Stuart to the House of Hanover.

3. Margaret (1598-1600)
Died in childhood.

4. King Charles I (1600-1649)
Married Henrietta Maria of France. Had issue. (See below)

5. Robert (1602), Duke of Kintyre
Died in infancy.

6. Mary (1605-1607)
Died in childhood.

7. Sophia (1606)
Died shortly after birth.

Charles I

(1600-1649)

By Henrietta Maria of France (1609-1669):

1. Charles (1629), Duke of Cornwall and Rothesay
Died on the same day of his birth.

2. King Charles II (1630-1685)
Married Catherine of Braganza. No issue.

3. Mary (1631-1660), Princess Royal, Princess of Orange
Married William II, Prince of Orange, Stadtholder of the Netherlands. Had issue.
Mother of King William III.
First woman to hold the title of Princess Royal.

4. King James II (1633-1701)
Married Anne Hyde. Had issue.
Married Mary of Modena. Had issue.
(See below)

5. Elizabeth (1635-1650)
Died unmarried of illness while kept prisoner by Parliament in the English Civil War.

6. Anne (1637-1640)
Died in childhood.

7. Catherine (1639)
Died on the same day of her birth.

8. Henry (1640-1660), Duke of Gloucester
Died unmarried of illness shortly after returning to England from exile at the Restoration.

9. Henrietta Anne (1640-1670), Duchess of Orleans
Married Philippe, Duke of Orleans, brother of King Louis XIV of France. Had issue.
Acted as ambassador between Charles II and Louis XIV of France.
Ancestress of Kings Louis XV and Louis XVI of France.

James II

(1633-1701)

By Anne Hyde (1637-1671):

1. Charles (1660-1661), Duke of Cambridge
Died in infancy.

2. Queen Mary II (1662-1694)
Married William III. No issue.

3. James (1663-1667), Duke of Cambridge
Died in childhood.

4. Queen Anne (1665-1714)
Married Prince George of Denmark. Had issue. (see below)

5. Charles (1663-1667), Duke of Kendal
Died in childhood.

6. Edgar (1667-1671), Duke of Cambridge
Died in childhood.

7. Henrietta (1669)
Died in infancy.

8. Catherine (1671)
Died in infancy.

By Mary of Modena (1658-1718):

1. Catherine Laura (1675)
Died in infancy.

2. Isabel (1676-1681)
Died in childhood.

3. Charles (1677), Duke of Cambridge
Died in infancy.

4. Elizabeth (1678)
Died in infancy.

5. Charlotte Maria (1682)
Died in infancy.

6. James (1688-1766), Prince of Wales, 'The Old Pretender'
Married Clementina Sobieska. Had issue.
First Jacobite Pretender to the English/British throne.
Father of Bonnie Prince Charlie.

7. Louisa Maria (1692-1712)
Died unmarried.
Born in exile after her father lost the English throne.

Anne

(1665-1714)

From George of Denmark (1653-1708):

1. Mary (1685-1687)
Died in childhood.

2. Anne Sophia (1686)
Died in infancy.

3. William (1689-1700), Duke of Gloucester
Died in childhood.
His early death caused the succession to the throne to pass to the House of Hanover, via its descent from Elizabeth of Bohemia (see above).

4. Mary (1690)
Died on the same day of her birth.

5. George (1692)
Died on the same day of his birth.

Note: All other pregnancies by Anne ended either in stillbirths or miscarriages.

George I
(1660-1727)

By Sophia Dorothea of Celle (1666-1726):

1. King George II (1683-1760)
Married Caroline of Ansbach. Had issue. (See below)

2. Sophia Dorothea (1687-1757), Queen in Prussia
Married Frederick William I, King in Prussia. Had issue.
Mother of King Frederick the Great of Prussia.
Mother of Queen Louisa Ulrika of Sweden.

George II

(1683-1760)

By Caroline of Ansbach (1683-1737):

1. Frederick Louis (1707-1751), Prince of Wales
Married Princess Augusta of Saxe-Gotha. Had issue.
Heir to the throne, died before his father.
Father of King George III.

2. Anne (1709-1759), Princess Royal, Princess of Orange
Married William IV, Prince of Orange, Stadtholder of the Netherlands. Had issue.
Regent of the Netherlands during the minority of her son William V, Prince of Orange.

3. Amelia (1711-1786)
Died unmarried.

4. Caroline (1713-1757)
Died unmarried.

5. George William (1717-1718)
Died in infancy.

6. William Augustus (1721-1765), Duke of Cumberland
Died unmarried.
Chief General of the British forces during the Jacobite Rebellion of 1745. Controversial victor of the Battle of Culloden.
Commander-in-Chief of the Forces, 1745-1757.

7. Mary (1723-1772), Landgravine of Hesse-Cassel
Married Landgrave Frederick II of Hesse-Cassel. Had issue.
Grandmother of Princess Augusta of Hesse-Cassel, wife of Adolphus, Duke of Cambridge, son of King George III (see below).

8. Louisa (1724-1751), Queen of Denmark and Norway
Married King Frederick V of Denmark and Norway. Had issue.

George III
(1738-1820)

By Charlotte of Mecklenburg-Strelitz (1744-1818):

1. King George IV (1762-1830)
Married Caroline of Brunswick. Had issue. (See below)

2. Frederick (1763-1827), Duke of York and Albany
Married Princess Frederica of Prussia. No issue.
Commander-in-Chief of the Forces 1795-1809, and 1811-1827
Heir to the throne from 1820 to 1827 after the accession of his brother George IV.

3. King William IV (1765-1837)
Married Adelaide of Saxe-Meiningen. Had issue. (See below)

4. Charlotte (1766-1828), Princess Royal, Queen of Wurttemberg
Married King Frederick of Wurttemberg. No issue.

5. Edward (1767-1820), Duke of Kent and Strathearn
Married Princess Victoire of Saxe-Coburg-Saalfeld. Had issue.
Father of Queen Victoria.
First member of the Royal Family to live in North America. Often called 'Father of the Canadian Crown'.

6. Augusta Sophia (1768-1840)
Died unmarried.

7. Elizabeth (1770-1840), Landgravine of Hesse-Homburg
Married Landgrave Frederick VI of Hesse-Homburg. No issue.

8. Ernest Augustus (1771-1851), Duke of Cumberland, King of Hanover
Married Princess Frederica of Mecklenburg-Strelitz, his first cousin, niece of his mother, Queen Charlotte. Had issue.
Inherited the crown of Hanover in 1837 on the death of William IV as the next male heir.
Heir to the British throne from 1837 to 1840 after the accession of Queen Victoria.

9. Augustus Frederick (1773-1843), Duke of Sussex
Married Lady Augusta Murray. Had issue.
Married Lady Cecilia Buggin. No issue.
Both his marriages were contracted against the Royal Marriages Act of 1772.

10. Adolphus (1770-1840), Duke of Cambridge
Married Princess Augusta of Hesse-Cassel. Had issue.
Grandfather of Queen Mary of Teck, consort of King George V.
Viceroy of Hanover from 1811 to 1837.

11. Mary (1776-1857), Duchess of Gloucester and Edinburgh
Married Prince William Frederick, Duke of Gloucester and Edinburgh, her first cousin, son of a brother of George III. No issue.

12. Sophia (1777-1848)
Died unmarried.
Rumoured to have had an illegitimate child by one of her father's equerries.

13. Octavius (1779-1783)
Died in childhood from a smallpox inoculation.

14. Alfred (1780-1782)
Died in childhood from a smallpox inoculation.

15. Amelia (1783-1810)
Died unmarried of illness.

George IV

(1762-1820)

By Caroline of Brunswick (1768-1821):

1. Charlotte (1796-1817) Heir Apparent
Married Prince Leopold of Saxe-Coburg-Saalfeld (uncle of Queen Victoria). No issue.
(Prince Leopold later became the first King of the Belgians in 1831.)
Heir to the throne, died before her father.

William IV

(1765-1837)

By Adelaide of Saxe-Meiningen (1792-1849):

1. Charlotte Augusta Louise (1819)
Died shortly after birth.

2. Elizabeth Georgina Adelaide (1820-1821)
Died in infancy.

Victoria

(1819-1901)

From Albert of Saxe-Coburg-Gotha (1819-1861):

1. Victoria (1840-1901), Princess Royal, Empress Consort of Germany
Married Emperor Frederick III of Germany. Had issue.
Mother of Emperor William II of Germany.
Mother of Sophia, Queen Consort of Greece.

2. King Edward VII (1841-1910)
Married Alexandra of Denmark. Had issue. (See below)

3. Alice (1843-1878), Grand Duchess of Hesse-Darmstadt and the Rhine
Married Grand Duke Louis IV of Hesse-Darmstadt and the Rhine. Had issue.
Mother of Empress Alexandra of Russia.
Great-grandmother of Prince Philip of Greece.

4. Alfred (1844-1900), Duke of Edinburgh, Duke of Saxe-Coburg-Gotha
Married Grand Duchess Maria Alexandrovna of Russia. Had issue.
Father of Marie, Queen of Romania.
Inherited the title of Duke of Saxe-Coburg-Gotha from his uncle, Prince Albert's brother.

5. Helena (1846-1923), Princess Christian of Schleswig-Holstein
Married Prince Christian of Schleswig-Holstein. Had issue.

6. Louise (1848-1939), Duchess of Argyll
Married John Campbell, Duke of Argyll, Governor General of Canada. No issue.
Vice-Regal Consort of Canada from 1878 to 1883.

7. Arthur (1850-1942), Duke of Connaught and Strathearn
Married Princess Louise Margaret of Prussia. Had issue.
Governor General of Canada from 1911 to 1916.

Great-grandfather of King Carl XVI Gustaf of Sweden and Queen Margrethe II of Denmark.

8. Leopold (1853-1884), Duke of Albany
Married Princess Helena of Waldeck-Pyrmont. Had issue.
First member of the Royal Family to be diagnosed with haemophilia, died of the disease aged 30.
Great-grandfather of King Carl XVI Gustaf of Sweden.

9. Beatrice (1857-1944), Princess Henry of Battenberg
Married Prince Henry of Battenberg. Had issue.
Mother of Victoria Eugenie, Queen of Spain.

Edward VII

(1841-1910)

By Alexandra of Denmark (1844-1925):

1. Albert Victor (1864-1892), Duke of Clarence and Avondale
Died unmarried. Betrothed to Mary of Teck before his death (who later married King George V, see below).
Heir to the throne, died before his father.

2. King George V (1865-1936)
Married Mary of Teck. Had issue. (See below)

3. Louise (1867-1931), Princess Royal, Duchess of Fife
Married Alexander Duff, Duke of Fife. Had issue.

4. Victoria (1868-1935)
Died unmarried.

5. Maud (1869-1938), Queen of Norway
Married King Haakon VII of Norway (originally Prince Carl of Denmark), her first cousin, son of Alexandra of Denmark's brother. Had issue.
First Queen Consort of modern Norway, grandmother of King Harald V.

6. Alexander John (1871)
Died shortly after his birth.

George V

(1865-1936)

By Mary of Teck (1867-1953):

1. King Edward VIII (1894-1972), later Duke of Windsor
Married Wallis Simpson when Duke of Windsor. No issue.

2. King George VI (1895-1952)
Married Elizabeth Bowes-Lyon. Had issue. (See below)

3. Mary (1897-1965), Princess Royal, Countess of Harewood
Married Henry Lascelles, Earl of Harewood. Had issue.

4. Henry (1900-1974), Duke of Gloucester
Married Alice Montagu Douglas Scott. Had issue.
Governor-General of Australia from 1945 to 1947

5. George (1902-1942), Duke of Kent
Married Princess Marina of Greece, first cousin of Prince Philip. Had issue.
Was the last Royal Family member to marry a foreign princess.
Died during World War II.

6. John (1905-1919)
Died when a teenager of epilepsy.

George VI

(1895-1952)

By Elizabeth Bowes-Lyon (1900-2002):

1. Queen Elizabeth II (1926-)
Married Philip of Greece. Had issue. (See below)

2. Margaret Rose (1930-2002), Countess of Snowdon
Married Antony Armstrong-Jones, Earl of Snowdon. Divorced. Had issue.
First child of a monarch to divorce in modern times, in 1978.

Elizabeth II

(1926-)

By Philip of Greece (1921-):

1. Charles (1948-), Prince of Wales
Married Lady Diana Spencer. Divorced. Had issue.
Married Camilla Parker-Bowles. No issue.
First Prince of Wales to divorce.

2. Anne (1950-), Princess Royal
Married Captain Mark Phillips. Divorced. Had issue.
Married Vice-Admiral Timothy Laurence. No issue.

3. Andrew (1960-), Duke of York
Married Sarah Ferguson. Divorced. Had issue.

4. Edward (1964-), Earl of Wessex
Married Sophie Rhys Jones. Had issue.

Monarchs With the Most Children

Listed below are the three monarchs who since the Norman Conquest of 1066 have had the largest number of legitimate children from their wives, each of them counting 15 children as their progeny. Each monarch's list includes children who died in infancy or childhood, but not stillbirths of miscarriages. Illegitimate children are also not included.

EDWARD I: 15 children

By Eleanor of Castile: Eleanor (c.1264/69); Joan (1265); John (1266); Henry (c.1267/68); Juliana (1271); Joan (1272); Alfonso (1273); Margaret (1275); Berengaria (1276); Mary (1278); Elizabeth (1282); Edward (1284).
By Margaret of France: Thomas (1300); Edmund (1301); Eleanor (1306).

JAMES II: 15 children

By Anne Hyde: Charles (1660), Mary (1662), James (1663), Anne (1665), Charles (1663), Edgar (1667), Henrietta (1669), Catherine (1671).
By Mary of Modena: Catherine Laura (1675), Isabel (1676), Charles (1677), Elizabeth (1678), Charlotte Maria (1682), James (1688), Louisa Maria (1692).

GEORGE III: 15 children

By Charlotte of Mecklenburg-Strelitz: George (1762), Frederick (1763), William (1765), Charlotte (1766), Edward (1767), Augusta Sophia (1768), Elizabeth (1770), Ernest Augustus (1771), Augustus Frederick (1773), Adolphus (1774), Mary (1776), Sophia (1777), Octavius (1779), Alfred (1780), Amelia (1783).

A FEW NOTES:

Although each of the monarchs above counts 15 children, **George III** had the largest numbers of children who survived into adulthood (defined as over 18 years of age): 13 children. After excluding infant and childhood deaths, Edward I only had 8 children who survived into adulthood, while James II only had 4.

Queen Charlotte of Mecklenburg-Strelitz, who gave birth to all of George III's 15 children, holds the record for the most children born by a Queen Consort.

Queen Anne had at least 17 pregnancies between 1684-1700 but gave birth to only 3 healthy children, the rest of the pregnancies ending in miscarriages, stillbirths or children dying within hours of birth. Of her three healthy children, two died in childhood and one at the age of 11. She left no descendants.

Edward I holds the record for the longest child-producing span in royal history, either for legitimate or illegitimate children: about 40 years between his first children born around 1264-69 and his last child born in 1306.

Monarchs Who Died Childless

Listed below are the English/British monarchs since the Norman Conquest of 1066 who are recorded to have had no children, either legitimate or illegitimate. It does not include therefore Richard I and Charles II, both of whom had illegitimate offspring. Also, if Lady Jane Grey were considered a legitimate monarch she would be listed after Edward VI as married but with no children.

William II (c.1056/60-1100)
Never married. There are no records indicating he ever fathered illegitimate children. Church chroniclers suggested that he was homosexual.

Richard II (1367-1400)
Married twice, but both unions were childless. His first wife Anne of Bohemia is not recorded to ever have been pregnant. His second wife Isabella of Valois was only six years old when they were wed and their marriage remained unconsummated at Richard's death.

Edward V (1470-1483)
Died unmarried at 12 years of age.

Edward VI (1537-1553)
Died unmarried at 15 years of age.

Mary I (1516-1558)
Married but the union was childless. Although she believed herself pregnant at the age of 38, during her first year of marriage to Philip of Spain, this turned out to be a false pregnancy.

Elizabeth I (1533-1603)
Never married. There are no reliable records indicating she was ever pregnant.

William III (1650-1702) **& Mary II** (1662-1694)
The only joint monarchs in British history were married to each other but their union was childless. After early pregnancies that ended in miscarriage Mary never conceived again.

Edward VIII (1894-1972)
Married Wallis Simpson as Duke of Windsor after his abdication but the marriage was childless. There have been rumours over the years that he fathered at least one illegitimate child before he became king, however there is no reliable evidence for this.

Monarchs With Confirmed Illegitimate Children

Listed below are the English/British monarchs who are confirmed to have fathered illegitimate children. The monarchs are ranked by the number of children fathered. Note that starting from Queen Victoria's reign illegitimate children ceased to be acknowledged publicly, so no firm evidence exists to confirm royal illegitimate children for the last 150 years.

1. Henry I *(c.1068/69-1135)*
At least 17 children from at least 8 mistresses.
The children were born both before and during his first marriage to Matilda of Scotland, but before his second marriage to Adeliza of Louvain. The children were born both before and after his accession to the throne. The exact number of children is unclear and is presumed to be even higher.

2. Charles II *(1630-1685)*
13 children from 7 mistresses.
The first five children were born before his marriage to Catherine of Braganza, the remaining eight during the marriage. The first four children were born before his accession to the throne, the remaining nine during his time as monarch.

3. William IV *(1765-1837)*
11 children from 2 mistresses.
All the children were born before his marriage to Adelaide of Saxe-Meiningen, ten of them borne by his long-term mistress Dorothy Jordan. All children were born before his accession to the throne.

4. John *(1166-1216)*
At least 8 children from at least 5 mistresses.
It is believed that all the children were born during his first marriage to Isabella of Gloucester (1189-1199) and before his second marriage to Isabella of Angouleme. Almost all of them are believed to have been born before his accession to the throne.

5. James II *(1633-1701)*
At least 6 children from 2 mistresses.
Two children were born during his first marriage to Anne Hyde. Three children were born during his second marriage to Mary of Modena. One child was born between the two marriages. All of them were born before his accession to the throne.

6. Henry II *(1133-1189)*
At least 4 children from 3 mistresses.
Three of the four children were born during his marriage to Eleanor of Aquitaine. Three of them were born during his time as monarch. One child was born before his marriage and before his accession to the throne.

7=. Edward III *(1312-1377)*
3 children from 1 mistress.
At least two of the three children are thought to have been born during his marriage, before the death of his wife Philippa of Hainault. All children were born during his time as monarch.

7=. Edward IV *(1442-1483)*
At least 3 children from at least 2 mistresses.
All children are thought to have been born during his marriage to Elizabeth Woodville. All children were born during his time as monarch.

7=. George I *(1660-1727)*
3 children from 1 mistress.

Two of the three children were born before his divorce from his wife Sophia Dorothea of Celle, one of them was born afterwards. All of them were born in Hanover before his accession to the British throne.

10. Richard III *(1452-1485)*
2 children from 2 mistresses.
Both children were born before his marriage to Anne Neville, and before his accession to the throne.

11=. Stephen *(c.1092/97-1154)*
At least 1 illegitimate child.
Born before his marriage to Matilda of Boulogne, and before his accession to the throne.

11=. Richard I *(1157-1199)*
1 illegitimate child.
Born before his marriage to Berengaria of Navarre, and before his accession to the throne.

11=. Henry VII *(1457-1509)*
1 illegitimate child.
Born before his marriage to Elizabeth of York, and before his accession to the throne.

11=. Henry VIII *(1491-1547)*
1 illegitimate child.
Born during his marriage to Catherine of Aragon, and during his time as monarch.

11=. George II *(1683-1760)*
1 illegitimate child.
Born during his marriage to Caroline of Ansbach, and during his time as monarch. Note however that although George was widely

believed to be the father of this child he never acknowledged him publicly.

?. George IV *(1762-1830)*

It is widely believed that George IV fathered several children before his marriage to Caroline of Brunswick and before his accession to the throne. No firm evidence exists however to confirm paternity, and George himself, unlike his brother William IV, refused to publicly acknowledge any illegitimate children throughout his life.

Royal Mistresses

Royal mistresses have played a part in the history of the English/British monarchy for almost a thousand years, from the days of the early Norman kings up to our own times. Listed below, in chronological order, is a selection of the most notable mistresses of English/British monarchs.

Rosamund Clifford *(c.1140s/1150s-c.1176)*
Mistress to Henry II
Known for her good-nature, 'Fair Rosamund' was installed at Woodstock Palace by Henry II as his main mistress. Legends later grew that he built a labyrinth around the palace to protect her from his wife Eleanor of Aquitaine, who nevertheless found her and poisoned her. In reality however, the affair ended and Rosamund withdrew to private life in a nunnery.

Alice Perrers *(1348-1400)*
Mistress to Edward III
A lady in waiting to Edward's wife Queen Philippa, Alice was 15-years-old when she began an affair with Edward. He publicly acknowledged her as her official mistress after Philippa died and made lavish gifts to her, making her a very wealthy woman. After Edward died she was tried in Parliament by her enemies for corruption and was banished from the realm. She was a patron of Chaucer and is said to have been the model for the Wife of Bath in *The Canterbury Tales*.

Elizabeth Shore *(c.1445-c.1527)*
Mistress to Edward IV
Described by Thomas More as the merriest of Edward IV's several mistresses, Elizabeth (also called Jane) was a London merchant's daughter who was admired for her beauty, wit and good influence upon Edward. She had other lovers, and after Edward died Richard III forced her to make penance for her promiscuousness by walking through the streets of London dressed in penitential clothes.

Elizabeth Blount *(c.1500-1540s)*
Mistress to Henry VIII
'Bessie' Blount played an important part as a mistress to Henry VIII while he was married to Catherine of Aragon. By giving birth to Henry's illegitimate son, Henry Fitzroy, Elizabeth proved that Henry's failure to provide male heirs lay not with him but with his wife Catherine. A popular saying on the subject at that time was "Bless 'ee, Bessie Blount!"

Mary Boleyn *(c.1500s-1543)*
Mistress to Henry VIII
Anne Boleyn's elder sister was allegedly the mistress of the King of France before she came back to England and attracted Henry VIII's attentions. The affair was conducted while she was married to William Carey and some historians have argued that their children were in fact fathered by Henry. After her husband died and her affair with Henry ended she controversially married for love beneath her rank and was banished from court.

Barbara Villiers, Duchess of Cleveland *(1640-1709)*
Mistress to Charles II
Extravagant, foul-tempered and promiscuous, Barbara was the most notorious of Charles II's mistresses and the mother of five of his

illegitimate children, all of whom were ennobled. She was called the curse of the nation because of her greed, her meddling into politics, and her influence on Charles. Others however described her as great fun and very generous. Her other lovers were numerous and included John Churchill, Duke of Marlborough, as well as an actor and an acrobat. Her descendants by Charles II include Diana, Princess of Wales, and Sarah, Duchess of York.

Nell Gwyn *(1650-1687)*
Mistress to Charles II
Nell was one of the most famous figures of Restoration England because of her rags to riches story. After starting as an orange seller she became a prostitute, then a comedy actress and eventually she seduced the king. Samuel Pepys said she was a talented comedian on the stage and that she attracted Charles as much for her wit as for her beauty. Her barbs and tricks to other royal mistresses were legendary, but she was loyal and kind to her friends. On her deathbed, Charles famously asked those around him: "Let not poor Nelly starve."

Louise de Kerouaille, Duchess of Portsmouth *(1649-1734)*
Mistress to Charles II
'Fubbs', as Charles called her because of her plumpness, was a Frenchwoman sent to England by King Louis XIV to be Charles' mistress and also act as a spy. She grew very wealthy from Charles' presents but became hated by the people because of her Catholic faith. A very clever woman, she survived intrigues and changes of government to die at the age of 85 back in her native France. Her descendants through the son she conceived with Charles include Diana, Princess of Wales, and Camilla, Duchess of Cornwall.

Hortense Mancini *(1646-1699)*
Mistress to Charles II
Hortense was a niece of Cardinal Mazarin of France and one of five famous sisters celebrated for their beauty. After leaving her abusive husband at the age of 22 she became one of the most adventurous courtesans of her age, famed for her lesbian affairs. Deciding to try her luck in England as Charles' mistress, she arrived at court dressed as a man and quickly gained his affections. She lost his favour after having an affair with one of Charles' own daughters (see *Illegitimate Royal Children*), but he later forgave her.

Arabella Churchill *(1648-1730)*
Mistress to James II when Duke of York
Arabella was a kinswoman of Barbara Villiers and the sister of John Churchill, Duke of Marlborough. She became James' mistress shortly after becoming a Lady in Waiting to his first wife, Anne Hyde, with her own family encouraging the affair hoping for advancement. She was said to be all skin and bone, and to lack charm or ambition, however she possessed enough intelligence to retain James' affections for ten years.

Catherine Sedley, Countess of Dorchester *(1657-1717)*
Mistress to James II when Duke of York and when King
The daughter of a famous hellrake and a mother who went insane, Catherine was picked as a royal mistress by James after she became Lady in Waiting to his second wife, Mary of Modena. Like Arabella Churchill, she was notoriously plain but was famous for her wit. 'What he saw in any of us', she said of James years later, 'I cannot tell. We were all plain, and if any of us had wit he would not have understood it.' Charles II once joked that his brother's mistresses were imposed on him by his confessors as a penance.

Ehrengard Melusine von der Schulenburg, Duchess of Kendal *(1667-1743)*

Mistress to George I

Melusine's affair with George started in Hanover and continued in England after he ascended the British throne. She was nicknamed the Maypole by the London mob on account of her thin tall figure. Since George had divorced his wife Sophia Dorothea in Hanover before he became king, Melusine acted as his principal companion at court and at social functions in Britain. Robert Walpole said of her that she was 'as much a Queen of England as anyone was.'

Henrietta Howard, Countess of Suffolk *(1689-1767)*

Mistress to George II when Prince of Wales and when King

Henrietta became George's mistress when he was still Prince of Wales and was later made Woman of the Bedchamber to George's wife, Queen Caroline. She was noted more for her intelligence than her beauty, and it is said that George's punctual daily visits to her apartments were spent mostly talking and playing cards, prompting rumours that he kept a mistress more as a mark of status than for pleasure. After the affair ended she formed an intellectual circle in London that included Horace Walpole and Alexander Pope.

Mary Robinson *(1758-1800)*

Mistress to George IV when Prince of Wales

George IV's first public mistress when Prince of Wales was this successful London stage actress. George fell in love with her when he saw her playing Perdita in Shakespeare's *The Winter's Tale*, and offered her £20,000 to give up the theatre and be his mistress. She accepted but he soon tired of her, and he later dismissed her without ever paying the sum in full. Intelligent and learned, she later became a writer producing feminist tracts, novels and poetry.

Maria Fitzherbert *(1756-1837)*
Mistress to George IV when Prince of Wales
Mrs Fitzherbert was the great love of George's life. A patient and kind woman, she was one of the few people who could handle George's volatile personality. She was however twice widowed and a Catholic, and therefore completely unsuited to marry a future king. Nevertheless, the two were wed illegally and in secret in 1785 after George threatened to kill himself unless she agreed to be his wife. The marriage was soon annulled, and he later repudiated her to marry his cousin Caroline of Brunswick in order to have his debts paid. However he continued to have an on-and-off relationship with Maria for the rest of his life, and when he died he asked to be buried with her miniature around his neck.

Frances Villiers, Countess of Jersey *(1753-1821)*
Mistress to George IV when Prince of Wales
George was famously attracted to older women and Frances was 40 years old—nine years older than George—and a mother of 10 children when she became his mistress. A scintillating society woman, it was nevertheless said that she could not be happy without a rival to trouble and torment. To prove the point she first convinced George to marry his cousin Caroline of Brunswick and then set out to make her life at court very difficult. She remained George's principal mistress for about 10 years before he replaced her with another woman.

Elizabeth Conyngham, Marchioness Conyngham *(1769-1861)*
Mistress to George IV when King
Described as voluptuous and shrewd, Elizabeth decided to become George's mistress to improve her family's station, and succeeded on establishing herself as his last official mistress. He became besotted with her and most famously he was seen winking at her during his coronation ceremony. She was once called 'nothing but a hand to accept pearls and diamonds', and after George died she left the royal

palace with the Stuart Sapphire in her pocket (see *The Crown Jewels*), which she only handed back to the Crown after much wrangling.

Dorothy Jordan *(1761-1816)*
Mistress to William IV when Duke of Clarence
Originally born in Ireland as Dorothea Bland, Dorothy moved to England where she became one of the most famous stage actresses of her day. She eventually attracted the attention of William, then Duke of Clarence, who took her as a mistress and lived with her as a common-law wife for 20 years. She bore him 10 illegitimate children whilst also continuing to act occasionally. After their affair ended she was given a yearly allowance on condition that she never act again, but she forfeited it when she decided to go back to the stage. She eventually died in poverty in France where she had moved to escape creditors.

Lillie Langtry *(1853-1929)*
Mistress to Edward VII when Prince of Wales
Lillie was one of the best known celebrities of late Victorian England, famous for her beauty which was captured on portraits by the best artists of the day. She began a three-year affair with Edward when he was Prince of Wales after he became infatuated with her, and the two often met in a house in Bournemouth, on the southern English coast, away from prying eyes. She had a genius for self-promotion and after her affair ended she used her fame to become first an actress, then a stage producer, and later a racehorse owner.

Daisy Greville, Countess of Warwick *(1861-1938)*
Mistress to Edward VII when Prince of Wales
Daisy followed in the footsteps of her ancestress Barbara Villiers by seeking a place as a royal mistress when Edward was Prince of Wales. Her indiscretions and tendency to boast however forced Edward to discard her, and crucially she was also disliked by

Edward's wife Alexandra who thought her manipulative and insincere. After Edward died she tried to blackmail the Royal Family by threatening to publish personal letters she had received from him, but was eventually prevented from doing so.

Alice Keppel *(1868-1947)*
Mistress to Edward VII
Edward's last illicit love was described as the perfect mistress. A woman with perfect social graces and the ability to make everyone feel at ease, she was 29 when she started her affair with the 56 year-old king. Called 'La Favorita' in royal circles, she acted as friend, adviser and lover to Edward, all with the tacit approval of Queen Alexandra. As Edward lay dying, she was allowed to see him one last time to say her farewells and had to be dragged away in hysterics.

Wallis Simpson *(1896-1986)*
Mistress to Edward VIII
In the words of one of her biographers, Hugo Vickers, "the precise nature of Mrs Simpson's appeal to Edward could only be understood by him; probably he hardly understood it himself." Twice divorced and with other lovers, Wallis started as just one of Edward's mistresses before he became besotted with her and determined to make her his wife. There is evidence that Wallis preferred to remain a royal mistress instead, but Edward insisted in giving up the throne to marry her. They were wed six months after his abdication.

Royal Illegitimate Children

Illegitimate children of kings played an important part in the history of the monarchy until the 19th century, at which time bastards ceased to be acknowledged publicly. Listed below is a selection of the most notable illegitimate royal offspring since the Norman Conquest of 1066.

Robert Fitzroy, Earl of Gloucester *(c.1090-1147)*
Illegitimate son of Henry I, before his accession, by an unidentified mistress
Robert was most probably the first of Henry's many illegitimate children, and later became the most powerful noble in the realm during King Stephen's reign. A capable commander and respected earl, he played a key role in the Anarchy as the main ally and military commander of Empress Matilda, his half-sister.

Juliane de Fontevraud *(c.1090-after 1136)*
Illegitimate daughter of Henry I, before his accession, by a woman named Ansfrida
Juliane became famous in her time for going to war against her father after Henry allowed her young daughters to be taken hostage and be blinded by one of her enemies. As a revenge, Juliane tried to kill Henry with a crossbow as he was entering a castle once. They eventually reconciled, and she later entered a convent.

Matilda Fitzroy, Countess of Perche *(c.1090-1120)*
Illegitimate daughter of Henry I before his accession by a woman named Edith
After marrying Count Rotrou III of Perche (between Normandy and Maine in France) Matilda drowned in 1120 in the White Ship

disaster off the coast of Normandy. The story was told that Henry's legitimate heir to throne, William Adelin, her half-brother, lost his life in an attempt to save her.

Sybilla de Normandy, Queen of Scotland *(c.1092-c.1122)*
Illegitimate daughter of Henry I, before his accession, by Sybilla Corbet
Although illegitimate, Sybilla was married to King Alexander I of Scotland after Henry's accession and became the first daughter of an English king to become a Scottish Queen, starting a tradition that lasted 400 years. Her marriage was childless and she died young, but she and her husband founded Scone Abbey in Perthshire, the original site of the Scottish coronation stone.

Matilda Fitzroy, Duchess of Brittany *(before 1100-after 1128)*
Illegitimate daughter of Henry I before his accession by an unknown woman
Matilda married Conan III, Duke of Brittany and, differently from some her illegitimate siblings, she and her husband allied themselves with King Stephen during the Anarchy. Her great-granddaughter, Constance of Brittany, married one of the sons of King Henry II.

Reginald de Dunstanville, Earl of Cornwall *(c.1110-1175)*
Illegitimate son of Henry I by Sybilla Corbet
Also called Rainaldus or Rainaud, he took Matilda's side during the Anarchy and was made Earl of Cornwall by his half-brother Robert Earl of Gloucester. He later became a trusted advisor to Matilda's son, King Henry II, his own half-nephew, as well as one of the most powerful men in the kingdom thanks to the revenues from his Cornwall estates.

Gervaise of Blois, Abbot of Westminster *(c.1115/20-1160)*
Illegitimate son of Stephen before his accession by woman named Dameta

Made Abbot of Westminster by his father, Gervaise is said to have mismanaged the abbey's lands and to have given property away to his mother. He was dismissed from his post by his father's successor, King Henry II. His tomb can still be seen in Westminster Abbey today.

Geoffrey, Archbishop of York *(c.1152-1212)*
Illegitimate son of Henry II before his accession by a woman named Ykenai

Said to have been his father's favourite of all his children, Geoffrey helped Henry put down rebellions launched by his legitimate sons, prompting Henry to famously declare "My other sons are the real bastards, this is the only one who's proved himself legitimate!" He was made Bishop of Lincoln and Chancellor of England by his father, then Archbishop of York by his half-brother Richard I, but he quarrelled over church taxation with his other half-brother King John, and he died in exile in France.

William Longspee, Earl of Salisbury *(c.1167-1226)*
Illegitimate son of Henry II by Ida de Tosny

Called 'the flower of earls' by medieval chroniclers, William was known for his military prowess, loyalty and chivalry. He had good relationships with his royal half-brothers: Richard I married him to a wealthy heiress and created him Earl of Salisbury, and later he became a close ally of King John. He was one of the regents who governed England during the minority of his half-nephew Henry III.

Morgan, Provost of Beverley *(c.1180-c.1217)*
Illegitimate son of Henry II by Nesta of Iorweth ab Owain, wife of Sir Ralph Bloet
Morgan was born of an adulterous liaison, but his adoptive father, Sir Ralph Bloet, decided to raise him as if he was his own son. King John, Morgan's half-brother, made him Provost of Beverley and later nominated him to be Bishop of Durham, but Pope Innocent III refused to consecrate him on the grounds that he was known to be illegitimate. As a compromise, the pope offered Morgan to allow being consecrated if he would swear that he was the son of Nesta and Ralph Bloet. Morgan however refused to disavow Henry as his real father and was refused consecration, dying shortly after.

Joan, Lady of Wales *(c.1191-1237)*
Illegitimate daughter of John before his accession by a woman named Clementina
Although born illegitimate, Joan was eventually declared legitimate by the pope on the grounds that her parents had not been married to other people at the time of her birth. She was married to Llywelyn the Great, Prince of Wales, and enjoyed a happy marriage despite one brief affair Joan had with an English knight. Llywelyn was heartbroken when she died before him.

Oliver Fitzroy *(c.1191-c.1218/19)*
Illegitimate son of John, before his accession, by a woman named Hawise
Oliver fought at his father's side during the First Barons War, and after John's death he took part in the Fifth Crusade during which died at the siege of Damietta in Egypt. His body was brought back to England and he is buried in Westminster Abbey.

Arthur Plantagenet, Viscount Lisle *(c.1461/64-1542)*
Illegitimate son of Edward IV by Elizabeth Lucy
Arthur grew up at the court of his father Edward IV and later also became part of Henry VII's court. He was much loved by his half-nephew King Henry VIII who arranged an advantageous marriage for him and made him Constable of Calais in 1533. His luck turned however in 1540 when members of his household in Calais were accused of treason and Arthur was imprisoned in the Tower of London. After two years' imprisonment Henry VIII released him and cleared him of any wrongdoing, but Arthur was so excited at the news that he had a heart attack and died soon after.

John of Gloucester *(c.1468/70-c.1499)*
Illegitimate son of Richard III, before his accession, by an unknown woman
John was the only bastard officially acknowledged by Richard III, who knighted him in 1483 and made him Captain of Calais the year afterwards. He lost his position after his father died in 1485 and was initially tolerated by Henry VII who even granted him a pension. He was later imprisoned however when Henry faced challenges from pretenders, and was probably executed in the Tower of London around 1499.

Richard of Eastwell *(c.1469-1550)*
Illegitimate son of Richard III, before his accession, by an unknown woman
An old Kent tradition says that in 1546 an old man working as a bricklayer in Eastwell was discovered to be an illegitimate son of Richard III. He said he had been given into the care of a Kentish family when an infant, and found out that he was Richard III's son when he was taken to see his father on the eve of the Battle of Bosworth in 1485. He began to conceal his identity after Richard's death in fear for his life, until he was finally discovered in old age in Eastwell. There are no historical records backing this claim, except

the burial records in Eastwell itself which give the man's name as Richard Plantagenet.

Henry Fitzroy, Duke of Richmond and Somerset *(1519-1536)*
Illegitimate son of Henry VIII by Elizabeth Blount
Henry was the only surviving male child born to Henry VIII during his marriage to Catherine of Aragon. He was beloved of his father who bestowed title after title on him including a double dukedom, Lord High Admiral, and Lord President of the Council of the North, all before he turned 8 years old. He resembled his father in intelligence and athletic skills, and the relationship between the two was one of great affection. There was speculation at the time of Henry VIII's divorce from Anne Boleyn that he might legitimise him and make him his heir, but he died suddenly at the age of 17 of an illness.

James Scott, Duke of Monmouth and Buccleuch *(1649-1685)*
Illegitimate son of Charles II, before his restoration to the throne, by Lucy Walter
Charles's firstborn son, born whilst he was in exile, resembled his father in looks and gentlemanly qualities but lacked Charles' virtues of patience and common sense. As a Protestant he became the focus of discontented Whigs who wanted him to inherit the throne instead of Charles' Catholic brother James. He actively pursued his claim to the crown in the Exclusion Crisis of 1678-80, greatly displeasing Charles who exiled him abroad as a punishment. After James II's accession he came back to England to try depose his uncle in the failed Monmouth Rebellion of 1685 for which he was sentenced to death. The current line of the Dukes of Buccleuch is descended from him.

Charles FitzCharles, Earl of Plymouth *(1657-1680)*
Illegitimate son of Charles II, before his restoration to the throne, by Catherine Pegge
Born abroad while his father was in exile, Charles was raised in Europe. He arrived in England as a teenager in 1672 and was immediately acknowledged by Charles who granted him a pension. Newfound wealth and status however warped his character and he began to live a life of laziness and debauchery. He tried to redeem himself by joining military service and in 1679 commanded an English military expedition to Tangier, Morocco. He distinguished himself in leadership and bravery but he died of dysentery during the fighting there, aged only 23.

Anne Fitzroy, Countess of Sussex *(1661-1722)*
Illegitimate daughter of Charles II by Barbara Villiers
Anne was the most colourful of Charles' illegitimate children, allegedly conceived the night after Charles came back to England to reclaim his throne. Beautiful but also wilful and extravagant, she was rumoured to have had a lesbian relationship with Hortense Mancini, one of Charles' mistresses. She had a stormy relationship both with her husband, Thomas Lennard, Earl of Sussex, and her mother Barbara Villiers who tried to calm her spirits by sending her to a convent in France from which she escaped. She finally abandoned her husband in 1688 when she left the country at the Glorious Revolution to live with her exiled uncle James II in France.

Henry Fitzroy, Duke of Grafton *(1663-1690)*
Illegitimate son of Charles II by Barbara Villiers
Said to be the most beautiful of Charles' children, Henry was also considered the most able and the most popular because of his gallantry and common touch. He served both in the navy and in the army, and fought against his half-brother the Duke Monmouth during the Monmouth rebellion of 1685. He later supported William III's invasion of England against his uncle James II and died in

Ireland at the Siege of Cork fighting on behalf of William. He was an ancestor of Diana, Princess of Wales, and the current line of the Dukes of Grafton is descended from him.

Charlotte Fitzroy, Countess of Lichfield *(1664-1718)*
Illegitimate daughter of Charles II by Barbara Villiers
Charlotte was the favourite of Charles' children and inherited many of his character traits, like kindness and amiability. He looked visibly moved when he personally gave her away at her wedding to Edward Lee, Earl of Lichfield in 1677. She was the most prolific of his children, giving birth to at least 18 children over a 28-year period, ten of whom made it to adulthood. She was also a favourite of her uncle James II, and she supported his cause after he lost the throne in 1688.

George Fitzroy, Duke of Northumberland *(1665-1716)*
Illegitimate son of Charles II by Barbara Villiers
After training in the army abroad under Louis XIV, and possibly working as a spy in Venice, George rose to be colonel of the Life Guards regiment in England and held several offices under both James II and William III. He married rashly and secretly in 1686 to a widow of a regimental captain who was the daughter of a London poulterer. He later tried to divorce her, and when she refused he kidnapped her and sent her hostage to a convent in Flanders. They were forced to reconcile when the marriage was held to be binding by his uncle James II, though they had no children.

Charles Beauclerk, Duke of St Albans *(1670-1726)*
Illegitimate son of Charles II by Nell Gwyn
Nell Gwyn's eldest son became a valiant soldier who served under William III during his continental campaigns between 1693-1697. He was however often in financial difficulties as his mother had not been as greedy as other royal mistresses in seeking grants and

benefices for him. A committed Whig and believer in constitutional monarchy, six of his sons became members of the House of Commons. Over 2,000 people are descended from him today, including the present line of the Dukes of St Albans, a title Charles created especially for him.

Charles Lennox, Duke of Richmond and Lennox *(1672-1723)*
Illegitimate son of Charles II by Louise de Kerouaille
The fourth of Charles II's sons to bear his own name, this Charles was created a double duke by his father: of Richmond (in England) and of Lennox (in Scotland). Although intelligent and good-natured, he was also described as an inveterate turncoat who was both a Tory and a Whig, and a Catholic and an Anglican, as the situation demanded. He was a patron of the new game of cricket and did much to support the sport in its infancy. He is an ancestor of Diana, Princess of Wales and of Camilla, Duchess of Cornwall. The current line of the Dukes of Richmond and Lennox is descended from him.

Lady Mary Tudor, Countess of Derwentwater *(1673-1726)*
Illegitimate daughter of Charles II by Moll Davis
The youngest of Charles' officially recognised illegitimate children, Mary married Edward Radcliffe, Earl of Derwentwater, before becoming a widow and marrying twice more afterwards. Two her sons from her first marriage were later executed for taking part in different Jacobite rebellions against the House of Hanover: James Radcliffe in 1715 and Charles Radcliffe in 1745.

James Fitzjames, Duke of Berwick *(1670-1734)*
Illegitimate son of James II, before his accession, by Arabella Churchill
James II's most famous illegitimate son was raised abroad in France when his father was Duke of York, and became a celebrated military commander. He joined the army in England after his father became

King and was created Duke of Berwick. He was at his father's side during the crisis of the Glorious Revolution and later commanded James' troops at the Battle of the Boyne in Ireland in 1690. Afterwards he went back to France where he rose through military ranks to become Marshal of France, and fought for Louis XIV against William III in Flanders. A military man to the end, he died in his 60s on a battlefield in Germany when a cannonball sliced his head off his shoulder.

Petronilla Melusina von der Schulenburg, Countess of Walsingham, Countess of Chesterfield *(1693-1778)*
Illegitimate daughter of George I, when Elector of Hanover, by Melusine von der Schulenburg
Petronilla was one of three illegitimate daughters born to George I but never publicly acknowledged by him. Spirited and opinionated, she was one of the few people who stood up to her father when he disagreed with her. She married Philip Stanhope, 4th Earl of Chesterfield, a Whig politician who became famous as a writer of letters and essays. Besides the title carried by her husband, she was also created Countess of Walsingham in her own right by her father.

George Fitzclarence, Earl of Munster *(1794-1842)*
Illegitimate son of William IV, before his accession, by Dorothy Jordan
The eldest of William IV's 10 illegitimate children, George trained militarily and distinguished himself in the Napoleonic Wars in Spain under the Duke of Wellington. He also possessed intellectual talents and was a fellow of the Royal Society and Royal Geographical Society. He was however plagued with chronic depression, caused by unhappiness at his own illegitimate status. William made him Earl of Munster after George pleaded for a title and also made him Privy Councillor, but that did not cure George's innate unhappiness with his illegitimacy, as he imagined that if he had not been a

bastard he could have succeeded to the throne as a king's eldest son. Five years after his father died he shot himself at the age of 48.

Elizabeth Fitzclarence *(1801-1856)*
Illegitimate daughter of William IV, before his accession, by Dorothy Jordan

Elizabeth's claim to fame are her descendants. After marrying William Hay, Earl of Erroll, in 1820, she had four children. One of them, Agnes, married James Duff, Earl of Fife, and became the mother of Alexander Duff, who in 1889 married back into the Royal Family by marrying Princess Louise, daughter of the future Edward VII. Agnes' other descendants include historian John Julius Norwich and Prime Minister David Cameron, all of whom can claim royal descent from William IV.

Adolphus Fitzclarence *(1802-1856)*
Illegitimate son of William IV, before his accession, by Dorothy Jordan

Apprenticed into the Royal Navy at a young age, Adolphus, rose to the position of captain and commanded several ships. After his accession William IV made him captain of the Royal Yacht, the *Royal George*, a position which was later renewed by Queen Victoria at her accession. He reportedly burst into tears when Victoria confirmed his appointment, saying that as mere bastards he and his siblings 'did not dare to hope for anything.'

Kings Who Married With No Record of Mistresses or Illegitimate Children

Listed below are the English/British kings since the Norman Conquest of 1066 who were married and for whom there is no evidence of either mistresses or illegitimate children, either before or during their marriages.

William I *(c.1027/28-1087)*
Married to Matilda of Flanders. Nine children.

Henry III *(1207-1272)*
Married to Eleanor of Provence. Five children.

Edward I *(1239-1307)*
Married to Eleanor of Castile. Twelve children.
Married to Margaret of France. Three children.

Henry VI *(1421-1471)*
Married to Margaret of Anjou. One child.

Charles I *(1600-1649)*
Married to Henrietta Maria of France. Nine children.

George III *(1738-1820)*
Married to Charlotte of Mecklenburg-Strelitz. Fifteen children.

George V *(1865-1936)*
Married to Mary of Teck. Six children

George VI *(1895-1952)*
Married to Elizabeth Bowes-Lyon. Two children.

English/British Princesses Who Became Foreign Queens

Throughout the history of the monarchy daughters, and sometimes granddaughters, of monarchs were often married to other European rulers as part of diplomatic alliances between countries. Listed in this chapter is a selection of English/British princesses who were married to foreign kings and became Queens Consort of their new countries. They are listed chronologically from the start of their tenures as Queens. Note that the list includes only princesses who were married to kings or emperors. Those who married rulers of lower rank, like Dukes or Grand Dukes, are not included. English princesses who married Scottish kings before the unification of the two countries are also included, however the first English Queen of Scotland, Sybilla of Normandy, is not included on this list as she was not a princess but an illegitimate daughter of King Henry I. See her entry in *Royal Illegitimate Children*.

Matilda, Holy Roman Empress *(1102 - 1167)*
Daughter of Henry I
Married Holy Roman Emperor Henry V. Reigned 1114 to 1125
Matilda was betrothed to Henry V, who was in his 20s, when she was only 8-years-old and was married 4 years later. The marriage was childless. After he died she married Geoffrey Plantagenet and became her father's heir to the throne in England. When her claim to the English throne was denied at Henry I's death she fought her cousin Stephen for the crown (see Stephen in *Monarchs Facts Sheet*). She insisted on being addressed by the title of Empress for the rest of her life even after her first husband died.

Joan, Queen of Sicily *(1165 – 1199)*
Daughter of Henry II
Married William II, King of Sicily. Reigned 1177-1189
Joan was married at the age of 12 to William who was 10 years her senior. The marriage was childless, and after she became widowed her brother King Richard I tried to marry her to the brother of the Muslim leader Saladin. When that plan failed, she re-married to Count Raymond VI of Toulouse but the marriage was unhappy, and she ended her life taking refuge in a nunnery.

Eleanor, Queen of Castile *(1162 – 1214)*
Daughter of Henry II
Married Alfonso VIII, King of Castile. Reigned 1177 to 1214
A capable and cultured woman, Eleanor married the future King Alfonso VIII of Castile in 1174. She became well-respected in her new kingdom and wielded real power during her husband's reign. Their marriage was happy, producing 10 children, and after 40 years together she died of grief 4 weeks after her husband's death.

Joan, Queen of Scotland *(1210 – 1238)*
Daughter of King John
Married Alexander II, King of Scotland. Reigned 1211 to 1238
Married when she was only 10 and Alexander was 23 years old, Joan's tenure as queen was unhappy. Initially because of her young age, and later because of her inability to bear children, her relationship with her husband was distant and she did not play an important part in Scottish life. She chose to spend much of her time back in England where she died of an illness near London in the arms of her brother King Henry III.

Isabella, Holy Roman Empress *(1214 – 1241)*
Daughter of King John
Married Holy Roman Emperor Frederick II. Reigned 1235 to 1241
Isabella became the third wife of Frederick II, one of the Middle Ages' most enlightened and remarkable monarchs, after his first two wives died. Frederick lived mostly in Italy and Isabella travelled widely across the Italian peninsula accompanying him on affairs of state in a marriage that was described as happy. She also died before him, in childbirth, and was his final wife.

Margaret, Queen of Scotland *(1240 – 1275)*
Daughter of Henry III
Married Alexander III, King of Scotland. Reigned 1251-1275
Betrothed when both were about 3-years-old to arrange a peace between England and Scotland, Margaret and Alexander were eventually married when they were 10-11 years of age. Margaret was initially unhappy about her life in Scotland but things improved when her husband achieved his majority. Chroniclers spoke of her beauty, chastity and humility, and she was greatly missed after she predeceased her husband.

Joan, Queen of Scotland *(1321 – 1362)*
Daughter of Edward II
Married to David II, King of Scotland. Reigned 1329-1362
Joan was married at the age of 6 to the 4-year-old David, heir to the Scottish throne, as part of another diplomatic alliance between England and Scotland. They became King and Queen only a year later and remained married for 33 years. They grew apart however after David was captured by the English in 1346 and spent 11 years imprisoned in England. During that time he fell in love with a Welsh mistress and after his release he and Joan grew estranged, though they remained married. Her 33-year tenure made her the longest-serving Queen Consort in Scottish history before the unification of Great Britain in 1707.

Philippa, Queen of Portugal *(1360 – 1415)*
Daughter of John of Gaunt, granddaughter of Edward III
Married John I, King of Portugal. Reigned 1387-1415
Intelligent and well educated, Philippa married at the late age of 27 but went on to produce 9 children who established the new Portuguese royal house of Avis. Her children included Prince Henry the Navigator, the father of Portuguese maritime exploration. The marriage also established the Anglo-Portuguese alliance, the oldest foreign alliance in the world still in force today.

Philippa, Queen of Denmark, Norway and Sweden *(1394 – 1430)*
Daughter of Henry IV
Married Eric of Pomerania, King of Denmark, Norway and Sweden. Reigned 1406-1430
On her marriage to Eric of Pomerania Philippa became the first woman to be Queen Consort of all three Scandinavian kingdoms combined after they were joined in the Kalmar Union in the 1390s. Intelligent and learned, she became more popular than her husband, the rash and stubborn King Eric, and often she acted as regent in his place, including in 1428 when she led the defence of Copenhagen during a foreign naval attack.

Margaret, Queen of Scotland *(1489 – 1541)*
Daughter of Henry VII
Married James IV, King of Scotland. Reigned 1503-1513
The elder sister of Henry VIII, Margaret was the last English princess to become Queen of Scotland. Like her brother she had a taste for marriage and after James IV died, killed in battle by Henry's army, she re-married to a Scottish nobleman, divorced him, and then remarried again. All throughout she also played a major part in Scottish politics. Strong and determined, her great goal was to bring Scotland and England closer together, and her dream was fulfilled 60 years after her death when her great-grandson King James VI of Scotland ascended the English throne.

Mary, Queen of France *(1496 – 1533)*
Daughter of Henry VII
Married Louis XII, King of France. Reigned 1514-1515
The younger sister of Henry VIII, Mary was married for diplomatic reasons at age 18 to the 52-year-old Louis as his third wife. Louis had no sons despite his previous two marriages, and it is said that he exerted himself so much in the bedroom trying to conceive during the short marriage that he was dead three months after the wedding. Mary later remarried for love to Charles Brandon, Duke of Suffolk, and through this union she became the grandmother of Lady Jane Grey.

Elizabeth, Queen of Bohemia *(1596 – 1662)*
Daughter of James I
Married Frederick, King of Bohemia. Reigned 1619-1620
James I's only daughter, Elizabeth married in 1613 Frederick V, Elector Palatine of Germany, and in 1619 they were both offered the crown of Bohemia. They took residence in Prague as monarchs but lost their crowns shortly after when Frederick was defeated in battle by the Hapsburg emperor Ferdinand II. Because of their brief reign they were later referred to as the Winter King and Queen, and they subsequently also lost their original Palatine lands in Germany. Elizabeth spent the rest of her life in exile in the Netherlands, a widow for the last 30 years of her life. Her grandson George I later inherited the British throne.

Louise, Queen of Denmark and Norway *(1724 – 1751)*
Daughter of George II
Married Frederick V, King of Denmark and Norway. Reigned 1746-1751
Although married as part of a diplomatic alliance between Britain and Denmark, Louise and her husband grew to enjoy each other's company, despite Frederick's infidelities. Louise became a very popular Queen Consort, praised particularly for her efforts to speak

Danish and for enlivening life at the royal court after the stern reign of the previous monarch. She was greatly mourned after she died in childbirth, barely five years after becoming Queen.

Caroline Matilda, Queen of Denmark and Norway *(1751 – 1775)*
Daughter of Frederick Prince of Wales, granddaughter of George II
Married Christian VII, King of Denmark and Norway. Reigned 1766-1772
Christian VII, as the son of Queen Louise of Denmark and Norway (see above), was Caroline's first cousin once removed. Soon after the wedding it became clear that Christian was mentally ill and their relationship became troubled. As he sank into madness Caroline began an affair with his doctor, Johann Struensee, which enabled Struensee to usurp power and rule Denmark as unofficial regent for over a year. They were eventually both arrested, Struensee was executed, and Caroline was handed over to her brother King George III after her marriage was annulled. She ended her short life in exile in Hanover, dying of illness at the age of 23.

Charlotte, Queen of Wurttemberg *(1766 – 1828)*
Daughter of George III
Married to Frederick I, King of Wurttemberg. Reigned 1805-1816
When Charlotte married Frederick in 1797 he was only Duke of Wurttemberg, in south Germany. Her wedding was the object of great satire in the London press on account of the groom's enormous weight, however they had a happy marriage. In 1805 Frederick allied himself with Napoleon in exchange for the right of being raised from Duke to King of Wurttemberg. This provoked the anger of Napoleon's greatest foe and Charlotte's father, King George III, who refused to address her daughter as Queen. After Napoleon's defeat however their titles were recognized by all European nations, and by the British royal family.

Victoria, Empress of Germany *(1840 – 1901)*
Daughter of Queen Victoria
Married to Emperor Frederick III of Germany. Reigned March to June 1888
Victoria married Crown Prince Frederick of Prussia in 1858, and after the German Empire was proclaimed in 1871 they became Crown Prince and Princess of Germany. Their plans to establish a liberal democracy in Germany when Emperor and Empress were thwarted when Frederick developed throat cancer, and they reigned for only three months in 1888. Although a great patron of the arts and supporter of many charitable causes, she was referred to disparagingly as 'Die Englanderin', because of her foreign English origin. Because of her liberal views she had a difficult relationship with her son, Emperor Wilhelm II, who adopted militaristic, conservative policies instead.

Maud, Queen of Norway *(1869 – 1938)*
Daughter of Edward VII
Married to Haakon VII, King of Norway. Reigned 1905 to 1938
In 1896 Maud married Prince Carl of Denmark, her first cousin on her mother's side, who was later elected the first King of modern Norway in 1905. Maud embraced her new role by learning Norwegian and practicing national pastimes like skiing. She broke social conventions by supporting causes like the welfare of unwed mothers, and she organised charity drives during World War I. She never lost her attachment for Britain however, returning to the country every year to stay in a house she kept at Sandringham where she eventually died.

Victoria Eugenie, Queen of Spain *(1887 – 1969)*

Daughter of Princess Beatrice, granddaughter of Queen Victoria

Married Alfonso XIII, King of Spain. Reigned 1906 to 1931

Victoria Eugenie's queenship was full of tribulations, beginning with her wedding in 1906 when her bridal carriage procession was hit by an anarchist's bomb which left 15 dead. More strain came later when it was discovered that she had passed haemophilia to her first son and heir to the throne. Her relationship with Alfonso deteriorated so she dedicated herself into charity work instead and was instrumental in reorganising the Spanish Red Cross. Her troubled queenship ended in 1931 when the monarchy was abolished and she was forced to go into exile with her family. She worked tirelessly on behalf of the exiled monarchy however and her grandson was eventually restored to the Spanish throne 6 years after her death.

Marie, Queen of Romania *(1875 – 1938)*

Daughter of Prince Alfred, granddaughter of Queen Victoria

Married Ferdinand I, King of Romania. Reigned 1914 to 1927

Marie married Ferdinand in 1893 when he was Crown Prince of Romania. A very intelligent woman, she later proved to be a remarkable Queen, often assuming leadership roles in place of her weak husband. She played a key part in her country's conduct during the First World War and at the end she represented Romania at the victors' table, ensuring that the country's territory was doubled. Her political skills and popularity made her an early feminist icon, especially in America where she travelled to great acclaim in 1926.

Queen Victoria's Forty Grandchildren

Queen Victoria had nine children, and through them she became a grandmother forty times over a period of 32 years. Her grandchildren became part of the royal families of Germany, Spain, Russia, Sweden, Norway, Greece, Romania, as well as minor German principalities and British noble families. Listed below is basic information about each of her grandchildren, preceded by the identities of their parents, Queen Victoria's own children.

QUEEN VICTORIA (1819-1901), married in 1840 **PRINCE ALBERT OF SAXE-COBURG-GOTHA** (1819-1861): **9 children,** as described below.

Queen Victoria's Children

Victoria, Princess Royal (1840-1901), married in 1858 Frederick, Crown Prince of Prussia, later Emperor Frederick III of Germany (1831-1888): **8 children**

Albert, Prince of Wales later King Edward VII (1841-1910), married in 1863 Princess Alexandra of Denmark (1844-1925): **6 children**

Princess Alice (1843-1878), married in 1862 Prince Louis of Hesse, later Grand Duke of Hesse-Darmstadt and the Rhine (1837-1892): **7 children**

Prince Alfred, Duke of Edinburgh (1844-1900), married in 1874 Grand Duchess Maria Alexandrovna of Russia (1853-1920): **5 children**

Princess Helena (1846-1923), married in 1866 Prince Christian of Schleswig-Holstein (1831-1917): **5 children**

Princess Louise (1848-1939), married in 1871 John Campbell, Marquis of Lorne, later Duke of Argyll (1845-1914): **no children**

Prince Arthur, Duke of Connaught (1850-1942), married in 1879 Princess Louise Margaret of Prussia (1860-1917): **3 children**

Prince Leopold, Duke of Albany (1853-1884), married in 1882 Princess Helena of Waldeck-Pyrmont (1861-1922): **2 children**

Princess Beatrice (1857-1944), married in 1885 Prince Henry of Battenberg (1858-1896): **4 children**

The Forty Grandchildren:

The grandchildren are listed in order of birth. The title used in the identification is that given to the child at birth or soon thereafter. Other titles gained later in life are noted in the information that follows when relevant. Where known, the nickname used for the grandchild within the Royal Family has been included. Most names have been anglicised. Note that the list does not include two stillborn children: one born to Princess Helena in 1877 and one to Prince Alfred's wife in 1879.

1. Prince Wilhelm of Prussia *(27 Jan 1859-3 Jun 1941)*
Born to Victoria, Princess Royal
Became Emperor Wilhelm II of Germany in 1888, and later led his country against Britain in the First World War. He was forced to abdicate his throne in 1918 when the German Empire was abolished and lived the rest of his life in exile in the Netherlands.
Nickname: Willy

2. Princess Charlotte of Prussia *(24 Jul 1860-1 Oct 1919)*
Born to Victoria, Princess Royal
Known for her difficult personality, she married the Hereditary Prince of Saxe-Meiningen in 1878. She served as Duchess of Saxe-Meiningen, in Thuringia, from 1914 until the Duchy was abolished by the German Republic in 1918.
Nickname: Ditta

3. Prince Henry of Prussia *(14 Aug 1862-20 Apr 1929)*
Born to Victoria, Princess Royal
A career naval officer in the German Navy, he rose to the rank of Grand Admiral and commanded the German Baltic Fleet during the First World War. He was happily married to his cousin Princess Irene of Hesse (see 10. below).
Nickname: Harry

4. Princess Victoria of Hesse *(5 Apr 1863-24 Sep 1950)*
Born to Princess Alice
Reputed as the most intelligent of Queen Victoria's granddaughters, in 1884 she married Prince Louise of Battenberg, an officer in the British Royal Navy who rose to the rank of First Sea Lord in 1912. In 1917, during the First World War, they changed their family name from Battenberg to Mountbatten. She became the mother of Louis Mountbatten, Earl of Burma, and the grandmother of Prince Philip. Her daughter Louise became Queen of Sweden in 1950.

5. Prince Albert Victor of Wales *(8 Jan 1864-14 Jan 1892)*
Born to Albert, Prince of Wales
Second in line to the British throne during Queen Victoria's reign, he died of influenza at the age of 28 before his father became king. His fiancée, Mary of Teck, subsequently married his brother George (see 8. below).
Nickname: Eddy

6. Prince Sigismund of Prussia *(15 Sep 1864-18 Jun 1866)*
Born to Victoria, Princess Royal
He died of meningitis when only 21 months old. He was the first of Queen Victoria's grandchildren to die.

7. Princess Elizabeth of Hesse *(1 Nov 1864-18 Jul 1918)*
Born to Princess Alice
She married Grand Duke Sergei Alexandrovich of Russia in 1884. A popular figure in Russia because for her charitable works, following her husband's assassination in 1905 she became a Russian Orthodox nun. She was murdered by the Bolsheviks in 1918 during the Russian Revolution, and in 1992 she was proclaimed a saint in the Russian Orthodox Church.
Nickname: Ella

8. Prince George of Wales *(3 Jun 1865-20 Jan 1936)*
Born to Albert, Prince of Wales
Initially marked for a career in the navy, he became heir to the British throne at the age of 27 after the death of his brother Victor Albert (see 5. above). He became King George V in 1910.
Nickname: Georgie

9. Princess Victoria of Prussia *(12 Apr 1866-13 Nov 1929)*
Born to Victoria, Princess Royal
She married Prince Adolf of Schaumburg-Lippe, from the Principality of Lippe in modern Westphalia, in 1890. After his death in 1927 she controversially married a second time to Alexander Zoubkoff, a Russian playboy 35 years her junior who squandered much of her wealth.
Nickname: Moretta

10. Princess Irene of Hesse *(11 Jul 1866-11 Nov 1953)*
Born to Princess Alice
She married her first cousin Prince Henry of Prussia (see 3. above) in 1888, the two becoming known in the family as 'The Very Amiables'

because of their pleasant natures and happy marriage. She inherited the haemophilia gene from her mother and two of her sons died of the disease.

11. Princess Louise of Wales *(20 Feb 1867-4 Jan 1931)*
Born to Albert, Prince of Wales
She married Alexander Duff, Earl of Fife, in 1889 who was later created Duke of Fife by Queen Victoria. In 1905 she was created the fifth Princess Royal by her father King Edward VII. Her husband died from medical problems contracted when the entire family was shipwrecked off the coast of Morocco in 1911.

12. Prince Christian Victor of Schleswig-Holstein *(14 Aug 1867-29 Oct 1900)*
Born to Princess Helena
Said to be Queen Victoria's favourite grandson, he entered the British Army as a career officer and served mostly in Africa. He fought in the Third Ashanti War in Ghana in 1895-96, and in the Sudan campaign of 1898. He died in South Africa of malaria whilst serving in the Second Boer War, to the great grief of his family.
Nickname: Christle

13. Prince Waldemar of Prussia *(10 Feb 1868-27 Mar 1879)*
Born to Victoria, Princess Royal
He died of diphtheria aged 11, four months after the death of his cousin Princess Marie of Hesse of the same disease (see 25. below).
Nickname: Waldy

14. Princess Victoria of Wales *(6 Jul 1868-3 Dec 1935)*
Born to Albert, Prince of Wales
Despite having several suitors she never married, and served instead as her mother's companion and assistant until her mother's death in 1925. She was very close to her brother George (see 8. above) who died only 7 weeks after her.
Nickname: Toria

15. Prince Ernest Louis of Hesse *(25 Nov 1868-9 Oct 1937)*
Born to Princess Alice
He succeeded his father as Grand Duke of Hesse in 1892 and reigned until the Grand Duchy was abolished by the German Republic in 1918. His first unhappy marriage to his cousin Victoria Melita (see 29. below) was dissolved in 1901. He later remarried to Princess Eleonore of Solms-Hohensolms-Lich, who died tragically a month after him in a plane crash along with one of their sons and a grandson.
Nickname: Ernie

16. Prince Albert of Schleswig-Holstein *(28 Feb 1869-13 Mar 1931)*
Born to Princess Helena
Despite receiving a British military education like his brother Christian (see 12. above), he chose to enrol in the German Army instead where he rose to the rank of Lieutenant Colonel. During the First World War he asked to be excused from fighting against the British and served instead on domestic military duties in Berlin. He never married but fathered an illegitimate daughter who was later acknowledged as his offspring by his two sisters.

17. Princess Maud of Wales *(26 Nov 1869-20 Nov 1938)*
Born to Albert, Prince of Wales
She married her Danish cousin Prince Carl of Denmark in 1896, who in 1905 was elected the first modern King of Norway, taking the name of Haakon VII. Maud served as a popular and conscientious Queen Consort of Norway until her death.
Nickname: Harry, because of her tomboy behaviour as a child.

18. Princess Helena Victoria of Schleswig-Holstein (3 May 1870-13 Mar 1948)
Born to Princess Helena
She never married, serving instead as her mother's companion until her mother's death in 1923. Afterwards she became involved in many charitable organisations including the YMCA, the YWCA and

a nursing home founded by her mother at Windsor. She was also, together with her sister Marie Louise (see 24. below), an enthusiastic supporter of the arts, especially music.
Nickname: Thora

19. Princess Sophie of Prussia *(14 Jun 1870-13 Jan 1932)*
Born to Victoria, Princess Royal
She married Crown Prince Constantine of Greece in 1889, and later served as Queen Consort of Greece from 1913 to 1917, and from 1920 to 1922. Each of her three sons in turn became King of Greece.
Nickname: Sossy

20. Prince Frederick of Hesse *(7 Oct 1870-29 May 1873)*
Born to Princess Alice
A sufferer of haemophilia inherited from his mother, he died at the age of 2 when he fell 20 feet down a window and suffered a fatal bleed.
Nickname: Frittie.

21. Prince Alexander John of Wales *(6 Apr 1871-7 Apr 1871)*
Born to Albert, Prince of Wales
He died when he was only a day old after being born prematurely. His death greatly affected his mother.

22. Princess Margaret of Prussia *(22 Apr 1872-22 Jan 1954)*
Born to Victoria, Princess Royal
She married Prince Frederick Charles, Landgrave of Hesse in Germany, in 1893 who was briefly nominated as King of Finland in 1918 before turning down the honour. The mother of six children, including two sets of twins, two of her sons died in action during the First World War; a third son and two daughters-in-law died during the Second World War. She survived many other tribulations to die of old age at 81.
Nickname: Mossy

23. Princess Alix of Hesse *(6 Jun 1872-17 Jul 1918)*
Born to Princess Alice
She married Tsar Nicholas II of Russia in 1894 and reigned as Empress Consort of Russia until the Russian revolution in 1917. She was murdered in 1918 by the Bolsheviks along with her husband and children. She was a carrier of haemophilia, inherited from her mother, which she transmitted to her son Alexei.
Nickname: Sunny

24. Princess Marie Louise of Schleswig-Holstein *(12 Aug 1872-8 Dec 1956)*
Born to Princess Helena
She married Prince Aribert of Anhalt, in Germany, in 1891 but the marriage was childless and unhappy, and it was dissolved in 1900. She never remarried and settled instead in England where she devoted herself to charities and the arts, living together in later years with her sister Helena Victoria (see 18. above).
Nickname: Louie.

25. Princess Marie of Hesse *(24 May 1874-16 Nov 1878)*
Born to Princess Alice
She died at the age of 4 of a diphtheria infection that struck most of her family. Her mother died of the same infection a month afterwards.
Nickname: May

26. Prince Alfred of Edinburgh *(15 Oct 1874-6 Feb 1899)*
Born to Prince Alfred
He died at the age of 24 in mysterious circumstances after he supposedly shot himself. It is claimed that he suffered from syphilis, had a history of depression, and had contracted a secret marriage against his parents' wishes. None of this is proven however and his personal life prior to his death remains the subject of much speculation.
Nickname: Young Affie

27. Princess Marie of Edinburgh *(29 Oct 1875-18 Jul 1938)*
Born to Prince Alfred
One of the most eligible granddaughters of Queen Victoria, after turning down a marriage proposal from her cousin Prince George (see 8. above), she married Crown Prince Ferdinand of Romania in 1893. She later served as a very popular Queen of Romania from 1914 to 1927.
Nickname: Missy

28. Prince Harald of Schleswig-Holstein *(12 May 1876-20 May 1876)*
Born to Princess Helena
He died as an infant shortly after his birth.

29. Princess Victoria Melita of Edinburgh *(25 Nov 1876-2 Mar 1936)*
Born to Prince Alfred
Under pressure from her grandmother Queen Victoria she married her cousin Prince Ernest Louis of Hesse (see 15. above) in 1894. The marriage however was deeply unhappy and they divorced in 1901, after Queen Victoria's death. She later married her teenage sweetheart, Grand Duke Kiril Vladimirovich of Russia, to whom she was happily married for many years.
Nickname: Ducky

30. Princess Alexandra of Edinburgh *(1 Sep 1878-16 Apr 1942)*
Born to Prince Alfred
She married Prince Ernest of Hohenlohe-Langenburg in 1893, who briefly served as Regent of the Duchy of Saxe-Goburg-Gotha in Germany for her cousin Charles Edward before he came of age in 1900 (see 35. below). After the German Empire was abolished in 1918 she and her husband became disillusioned with their new bourgeois lives and became members of the Nazi party.
Nickname: Sandra

31. Princess Margaret of Connaught *(15 Jan 1882-1 May 1920)*
Born to Prince Arthur
She married Prince Gustav Adolf of Sweden in 1905, and in 1907 became Crown Princess of Sweden. The marriage was happy and produced five children but she died of infection at the age of 38 before her husband succeeded to the Swedish throne as King Gustav VI Adolf. Her descendants today include the monarchs of both Sweden and Denmark.
Nickname: Daisy

32. Prince Arthur of Connaught *(13 Jan 1883-21 Sep 1938)*
Born to Prince Arthur
A career officer in the British Army, he rose to rank of colonel and served in the Boer War and the First World War. He later served as Governor-General of South Africa in 1920-1924. He married his first cousin once removed Princess Alexandra, Duchess of Fife, daughter of Princess Louise (see 11. above).
Nickname: Young Arthur

33. Princess Alice of Albany *(25 Feb 1883-3 Jan 1981)*
Born to Prince Leopold
She married Prince Alexander of Teck, brother of the future Queen Mary, in 1904. He later served as Governor-General of both South Africa (1924-1931) and Canada (1940-1946), where Alice served as Viceregal Consort. She was the longest-lived of Queen Victoria's grandchildren and the last one to die, at the age of 97 in 1981.

34. Princess Beatrice of Edinburgh *(20 Apr 1884-13 Jul 1966)*
Born to Prince Alfred
She married Infante Alfonso, Duke of Galliera, a cousin of King Alfonso XIII of Spain, in 1909. The marriage was controversial as Beatrice initially refused to convert to Catholicism, and the union was later troubled by scandals because of her husband's affairs. Nevertheless, they remained married until her death.
Nickname: Baby Bee

35. Prince Charles Edward, Duke of Albany *(19 Jul 1884-6 Mar 1954)*
Born to Prince Leopold
Born four months after his father died, he inherited his father's title of Duke of Albany at birth. At the age of 16 he also became Duke of Saxe-Coburg-Gotha in Germany and was the last Duke to rule there before the Duchy was abolished by the German Republic in 1918. He controversially chose to fight for Germany during the First World War and was therefore stripped of all his British titles in 1919 by his cousin King George V (see 8. above). He later courted more controversy by joining the Nazi party and becoming a SA officer. Following denazification at the end of World War II he died as a private citizen, stripped of most of his wealth.
Nickname: Charlie

36. Princess Patricia of Connaught *(17 Mar 1886-12 Jan 1974)*
Born to Prince Arthur
She married Captain Alexander Ramsay in 1919, a Royal Navy officer who was awarded the Distinguished Service Order in the First World War. On her marriage she voluntarily relinquished her royal title of Princess and became known instead as Lady Patricia Ramsay, although she continued to be involved in royal events until her death.
Nickname: Patsy

37. Prince Alexander of Battenberg *(23 Nov 1886-23 Feb 1960)*
Born to Princess Beatrice
A very capable man, he joined first the Royal Navy, where he served until 1908, then the British Army where he rose to the rank of Captain during the First World War. He later also served as a Royal Air Force officer during the Second World War. Between the two wars he became the first member of the Royal Family to work for a living. At his death in 1960 he was the last surviving grandson of Queen Victoria.
Nickname: Drino

38. Princess Victoria Eugenie of Battenberg *(24 Oct 1887-15 Apr 1969)*
Born to Princess Beatrice
She married King Alfonso XIII of Spain in 1906 and reigned as Queen Consort until 1931 when the Spanish monarchy was abolished and they both went into exile. The marriage was fraught with tension as Alfonso blamed her for transmitting haemophilia to two of their children.
Nickname: Ena

39. Prince Leopold of Battenberg *(21 May 1889-23 Apr 1922)*
Born to Princess Beatrice
Named after his uncle Leopold who had died of haemophilia five years before his birth, he inherited the same disease from his mother. He managed to serve in the First World War I in a non-combat role, but he later died of haemophiliac complications from a hip operation at age 32. He never married.

40. Prince Maurice of Battenberg *(3 Oct 1891-27 Oct 1914)*
Born to Princess Beatrice
He joined the British Army and later enrolled in the same regiment of his cousin Prince Christian Victor (see 12. above), who had died whilst serving in the Boer War. Tragically, he too died in military service when he was killed in action at the First Battle of Ypres in 1914, in the first months of World War I.

Haemophilia in the Royal Family

Haemophilia appeared in the family of Queen Victoria in the 19th century. Through the royal intermarriages of Victoria's descendants it spread to other European royal families, and because of its rarity among the general population it began to be called 'the royal disease'. Following below is some basic information about haemophilia and the people it affected in the British Royal Family.

What is Haemophilia?

Haemophilia is an inherited genetic disorder preventing the blood to clot properly when blood vessels are broken, so that persons affected experience longer and potentially fatal bleeds. It was first mentioned in ancient times and began to be diagnosed medically in the 19th century. No cure exists for it but the condition can be controlled today with infusions of missing clotting factors via blood or plasma transfusions, given either as prophylaxis or after injuries. Before these infusions began to be used in the 1960s haemophilia sufferers usually died as a result of uncontrolled internal bleeding after falls and traumas.

There are two types of haemophilia: Haemophilia A, the most common, which affects 80% of all sufferers; and Haemophilia B, a rarer form which affects only 20% of haemophilia sufferers. In two-thirds of all haemophilia cases the condition is inherited, however in one-third of haemophilia sufferers the condition is the result of spontaneous genetic mutation at conception by non-carrier parents.

Haemophilia is found in both males and females, however due to the position of the faulty gene causing the disease in the human chromosome only males show symptoms of haemophilia. Females generally are carriers only, and it is extremely rare to find females showing symptoms of haemophilia. Because of genetic transmission mechanisms, female carriers can transmit the faulty gene to children of either gender, though the transmission is not automatic: some children will inherit the faulty gene whilst others will not, with no established pattern of transmission. Male carriers, on the other hand, exhibit automatic transmission patterns: all female children of male carriers inherit the faulty gene, but no male children of male carriers ever inherit the disease.

Origin in the Royal Family

Haemophilia in the British Royal family first appeared in Queen Victoria's children. It is thought that the genetic mutation causing haemophilia generated spontaneously either at Victoria's conception in 1818 or at the conception of her mother, Victoire of Saxe-Coburg-Saalfeld, in 1785. Some research suggests that children born to older parents have a higher chance of developing spontaneous mutations for haemophilia, in which case it is more likely that the faulty gene arose at Queen Victoria's conception as her mother was 32 at the time, and her father was 51. Research in 2009 on the remains of Tsarevich Alexei of Russia—a great-grandson of Queen Victoria—showed that Royal Family members carried the genetic mutation for Haemophilia B, the rarer form of haemophilia which affects only 0.002% of the human population.

Royal Family Members Who Were Carriers or Sufferers of Haemophilia

(✠ indicates death from haemophilia)

Queen Victoria *(1819-1901)*
Carrier. She transmitted haemophilia to three of her nine children: Princess Alice, Prince Leopold, and Princess Beatrice, as noted below.

THE LINE OF PRINCESS ALICE:

Princess Alice, Grand Duchess of Hesse-Darmstadt and the Rhine *(1843-1878)*
Carrier. Third child of Queen Victoria. Married Grand Duke Louis of Hesse-Darmstadt and the Rhine, and transmitted haemophilia to three of her seven children.

✠ **Prince Friedrich of Hesse** *(1870-1873)*
Sufferer. Fifth child of Princess Alice. He died of internal bleeding at the age of 2 years and seven months after falling 20 feet off a window. He was the first member of the Royal Family to die of the disease.

Princess Irene of Hesse *(1866- 1953)*
Carrier. Third child of Princess Alice. Married her cousin Prince Henry of Prussia and transmitted haemophilia to two of her three children.

✠ **Prince Waldemar of Prussia** *(1889-1945)*
Sufferer. First child of Princess Irene. Despite his condition he managed to live a normal life until his 50s and married, though no children were born for fear they would be sufferers also. He died of

a haemophilia attack at age 56 at the end of the Second World War, when blood could not be found for a needed transfusion.

✠ **Prince Heinrich of Prussia** *(1900-1904)*
Sufferer. Third child of Princess Irene, brother of Prince Waldemar. He died of a brain haemorrhage at age 4 after falling off a table.

Princess Alix of Hesse, later Empress Alexandra of Russia *(1872-1918)*
Carrier. Sixth child of Princess Alice. Married Tsar Nicholas II of Russia and transmitted haemophilia to at least one of her children (see below). It is unclear if any of her four daughters were carriers of haemophilia as they were all murdered during the Russian Revolution before marrying and having children. However some DNA research done on their remains in 2009 seems to indicate that one of them was a carrier.

Tsarevich Alexei of Russia *(1904-1918)*
Sufferer. Fifth child of Empress Alexandra of Russia. A known sufferer of haemophilia since he was a baby, he was supposedly healed of some haemophiliac episodes by his mother's mystic confessor Grigori Rasputin. He survived the disease until the age of 13 when he was murdered by the Bolsheviks during the Russian Revolution.

There are no known descendants of Princess Alice alive today who are either carriers or sufferers of haemophilia. The last known carrier, Princess Irene of Hesse, died in 1953.

THE LINE OF PRINCE LEOPOLD:

✠ **Prince Leopold, Duke of Albany** *(1853-1884)*
Sufferer and carrier. Seventh child of Queen Victoria. Leopold was the first member of the Royal Family to be diagnosed with haemophilia in 1853-54. Despite the limitations imposed by his condition he determined to live a full life: he attended university, travelled through Europe and North America, and fathered children. He died of a brain haemorrhage at the age of 31 after a minor fall off a staircase. He transmitted haemophilia to one of his two children (see below).

Princess Alice of Albany, later Countess of Athlone *(1883-1981)*
Carrier. First child of Prince Leopold. She married Prince Alexander of Teck and transmitted haemophilia to at least one of her three children. It is unclear if her third child, Prince Maurice, was a sufferer of haemophilia as he died aged 5 months of ill-health unrelated to the condition.

✠ **Prince Rupert of Teck, later Viscount Trematon** *(1907-1928)*
Sufferer. Second child of Princess Alice. Like his grandfather, Rupert refused to allow haemophilia to limit his life. He attended university, was a keen hunter who shot wild game in Africa, and even served as a train engine fireman during the General Strike of 1926. He died of a brain haemorrhage at age 20 after suffering a minor skull fracture in a car accident near Lyon, France. He never married.

There are no known descendants of Prince Leopold alive today who are either carriers or sufferers of haemophilia. The last known carrier, Princess Alice of Albany, died in 1981.

THE LINE OF PRINCESS BEATRICE:

Princess Beatrice *(1857-1944)*
Carrier. Ninth child of Queen Victoria. She married Prince Henry of Battenberg and transmitted haemophilia to at least two of her four children. It is unclear if her fourth child, Prince Maurice, who died in combat during World War I at the age of 23, was a sufferer of haemophilia.

✠ Prince Leopold of Battenberg, later Lord Leopold Mountbatten *(1889-1922)*
Sufferer. Third child of Princess Beatrice. In a tragic twist of fate, Leopold was named after his haemophiliac uncle who had died five years before his birth, and he also inherited the same disease. He tried to live a normal life and managed to serve in World War I in a non-combat role, but died at the age of 33 from haemophilia complications following a leg operation. He never married.

Princess Victoria Eugenie of Battenberg, later Queen of Spain *(1887-1969)*
Carrier. Second child of Princess Beatrice. She married King Alfonso XIII of Spain and transmitted haemophilia to two of her six children (see below).

✠ Alfonso, Prince of Asturias *(1907-1938)*
Sufferer. First son of Queen Victoria Eugenie and heir to the Spanish throne before the monarchy was abolished in 1931. Alfonso renounced his succession rights in 1933 to marry a Cuban commoner, whom he divorced in 1937. He remarried in 1937 to another Cuban commoner whom he also divorced in 1938. He died of internal bleeding in September 1938 after he drove a car into a telephone booth in Miami, Florida. He had no children from either of his wives.

✠ **Infante Gonzalo of Spain** *(1914-1934)*
Sufferer. Sixth child of Queen Victoria Eugenie. He died at age 20 of internal bleeding following a minor car accident in Austria, in a vehicle driven by his elder sister Beatriz. He never married.

There are no known descendants of Princess Beatrice alive today who are either carriers or sufferers of haemophilia. The last known carrier, Queen Victoria Eugenie of Spain, died in 1969. There is a very small chance however that the disease might still be present in some female descendants of Princess Beatrice who are descended exclusively through a female line.

Current Blood Relations of the British Royal Family to Other European Royal Families

The English, Scottish and British royal families have been intermarrying with other European royal houses for over 1,000 years, resulting in multiple distant relationships. The current relationships between the British and European royal houses however stem from more recent intermarrying that took place between the 19th and early 20th century. Listed below are the details of how the British Royal Family is currently most closely related to all the other European royal families. The families are listed roughly in the order of their sovereigns' closeness in blood to Queen Elizabeth II or Prince Charles.

The Royal Family of Norway

The two families are most closely related through King Edward VII (1841-1910), whose daughter Princess Maud married the future King Haakon VII of Norway in 1896. Queen Elizabeth II and King Harald V of Norway are second cousins.

The Royal Family of Denmark

The two families are most closely related through two equal lines. The first line stems from King Christian IX of Denmark (1818-1906), whose daughter Princess Alexandra of Denmark married the future King Edward VII in 1863. The second line stems from Queen Victoria (1819-1901), whose granddaughter Princess Margaret of Connaught married into the Swedish Royal Family in 1905. Princess Margaret's daughter, Princess Ingrid of Sweden, married the future King Frederick IX on Denmark in 1935. Queen Elizabeth II and

Queen Margrethe II of Denmark are third cousins through both lines.

The Royal Family of Sweden

The two families are most closely related through two equal lines, both descended from Queen Victoria (1819-1901). The first line stems from Prince Arthur, seventh son of Queen Victoria, whose daughter Princess Margaret of Connaught married the future King Gustav VI Adolf of Sweden in 1905. The second line stems from Prince Leopold, eighth son of Queen Victoria, whose granddaughter Princess Sibylla of Saxe-Coburg-Gotha married Crown Prince Gustav Adolf of Sweden in 1932. Queen Elizabeth II and King Carl XVI Gustaf of Sweden are third cousins through both lines.

The Royal Family of Spain

The two families are most closely related through King George I of Greece (1845-1913), the paternal grandfather of Prince Philip and a great-grandfather of Princess Sophia of Greece who married the future King Juan Carlos of Spain in 1962. Prince Charles and King Felipe VI of Spain are second cousins once removed through this line. Additionally, the two families are related through Queen Victoria (1819-1901), whose granddaughter Princess Victoria Eugenie married King Alfonso XIII of Spain in 1906. Queen Elizabeth II and King Felipe VI of Spain are third cousins once removed through this line.

The Grand Ducal Family of Luxembourg

The two families are most closely related through King Christian IX of Denmark (1818-1906), maternal grandfather of King George V, and a great-great-grandfather of Princess Josephine-Charlotte of Belgium who married the future Grand Duke Jean of Luxembourg in 1953. Queen Elizabeth II and Grand Duke Henri of Luxembourg are third cousins once removed.

The Royal Family of Belgium

The two families are most closely related through King Christian IX of Denmark (1818-1906), maternal grandfather of King George V, and a great-grandfather of Princess Astrid of Sweden who married the future King Leopold III of Belgium in 1926. Queen Elizabeth II and King Philippe of Belgium are third cousins once removed through this line. Additionally, the two families are distantly related through Duke Francis of Saxe-Coburg-Saalfeld (1750-1806), maternal grandfather of Queen Victoria and father of Leopold I, the first King of Belgium. Queen Elizabeth II and King Philippe of Belgium are fifth cousins through this second line.

The Royal Family of the Netherlands

The two families are related through multiple distant lines, the closest of which is through Tsar Paul I of Russia (1754-1801), a great-great-great-grandfather of Prince Philip and a grandfather of King William III of the Netherlands (1817-1890). Prince Charles and King Willem-Alexander of the Netherlands are fifth cousins through this line. Additionally, the two families are related through a common German ancestor, Duke Frederick II Eugene of Wurttemberg (1732-1797), a great-great-grandfather of both Queen Mary of Teck and of Queen Wilhelmina of the Netherlands. Queen Elizabeth II and King Willem-Alexander are fifth cousins once removed through this line.

The Princely Family of Monaco

The two families are most-closely related through Charles Louis, Hereditary Prince of Baden (1755-1801), an ancestor of both Prince Philip and Prince Louis II of Monaco who reigned 1922-1949. Prince Charles and Prince Albert II of Monaco are fifth cousins once removed through this line. Queen Elizabeth II and Prince Albert II of Monaco are also distantly related through John William Friso, Prince of Orange (1687-1711) (see below).

The Princely Family of Liechtenstein

The two families are distantly related through John William Friso, Prince of Orange, (1687-1711) who has been proven to be an ancestor of all the European royal houses existing today. Queen Elizabeth II and Prince Hans-Adam II of Liechtenstein are seventh cousins once removed through this line. Additionally, the two families are also related through Louis Rudolph, Duke of Brunswick-Wolfenbuttel (1671-1735), an ancestor of both Prince Albert, husband of Queen Victoria, and Prince Franz Joseph II of Liechtenstein who reigned 1938-1989. Queen Elizabeth II and Prince Hans-Adam II of Liechtenstein are eighth cousins through this line.

Queen Elizabeth II's Descent from William the Conqueror and from Alfred the Great

Queen Elizabeth II, and the rest of the present Royal Family, are direct descendants of both King William the Conqueror (c.1027/28-1087) and King Alfred the Great (c.848/49-899). Because of royal intermarrying through the centuries, Elizabeth II is actually descended from both kings through multiple lines, both British and foreign, counting different numbers of generations. The line of descent chosen below follows the official **Historical Line of Succession** to the English/British throne, particularly between Edward III and Queen Elizabeth York when the throne was contested by different lines during the Wars of the Roses.

According to the official Historical Line of Succession, there have been 32 generations between William the Conqueror and Elizabeth II, and 39 generations between Alfred the Great and Elizabeth II. If alternative lines of descent are followed during the Wars of the Roses, the numbers of generations can be reduced to 30 and 37 respectively.

The Historical Line of Succession

Queen Elizabeth II (1926-)
daughter of
King George VI (1895-1952)
son of
King George V (1865-1936)
son of

King Edward VII (1841-1910)
son of
Queen Victoria (1819-1901)
daughter of
Prince Edward, Duke of Kent and Strathearn (1767-1820)
son of
King George III (1738-1820)
son of
Frederick, Prince of Wales (1707-1751)
son of
King George II (1683-1760)
son of
King George I (1660-1727)
son of
Sophia, Electress Consort of Hanover (1630-1714)
daughter of
Elizabeth Stuart, Queen of Bohemia (1596-1662)
daughter of
King James I of England and VI of Scotland (1566-1625)
son of
Mary, Queen of Scots (1542-1587)
daughter of
King James V of Scotland (1512-1542)
son of
Margaret Tudor, Queen of Scotland (1489-1541)
daughter of
Queen Elizabeth of York (1466-1503)
daughter of
King Edward IV (1442-1483)
son of
Richard, 3rd Duke of York (1411-1460)
son of
Anne de Mortimer, Countess of Cambridge (1390-1411)
daughter of
Roger Mortimer, 4th Earl of March (1374-1398)
son of

Philippa of Clarence, 5th Countess of Ulster (1355-1382)
daughter of
Lionel of Antwerp, 1st Duke of Clarence (1338-1368)
son of
King Edward III (1312-1377)
son of
King Edward II (1284-1327)
son of
King Edward I (1239-1307)
son of
King Henry III (1207-1272)
son of
King John (1166-1216)
son of
King Henry II (1133-1189)
son of
Empress Matilda (1102-1167)
daughter of
King Henry I and Matilda of Scotland
(continues separately below)

Descent from William the Conqueror:

King Henry I (c.1068/69-1135)
son of
William the Conqueror (c.1027/28-1087).

Descent from Alfred the Great:

Matilda of Scotland (c.1080-1118)
daughter of
Margaret of Wessex, Queen of Scotland (c.1045/46-1093)
daughter of

Edward Aetheling (1016-1057)
son of
King Edmund Ironside (c.988/993-1016)
son of
King Aethelred the Unready (c.966/68-1016)
son of
King Edgar the Peaceful (c.943/44-975)
son of
King Edmund the Elder (c.920/21-946)
son of
King Edward the Elder (c.870s-924)
son of
King Alfred the Great (c.848/49-899).

The Current Line of Succession

The current Line of Succession is governed by the Succession to the Crown Act 2013, which replaced the previous Act of Settlement of 1701. Under the previous Act, the following succession rules used to be in force:

- Male preference primogeniture: brothers had precedence over sisters among siblings, and the descendants of brothers came before the descendants of sisters on a line-of-descent by line-of-descent basis. Older siblings had precedence over younger siblings (all males first, then all females), and older siblings' lines had precedence over younger siblings' lines.

- People who married Roman Catholics, who converted to Roman Catholicism, and who were raised Roman Catholics, were all excluded from the succession.

The new Succession to the Crown Act of 2013 had its origins in the Perth Agreement of 28 October 2011, when the heads of government of all Commonwealth Realms, sharing the British monarch as head of state, agreed to change the existing succession rules during a meeting in Perth, Australia. The subsequent Act was passed by the British Parliament on 25 April 2013 but only came into force on 26 March 2015, after similar legislation was approved in all other Commonwealth Realms. The new Act instituted these changes:

- Absolute primogeniture replaces male preference primogeniture: older siblings have precedence over younger siblings regardless of gender. Older siblings' descent lines have precedence over younger siblings' descent lines regardless of gender. The changes however only affect those born after 28 October 2011 (the date of the Perth Agreement). For those born before that date their place in the line of succession remains the same as it was under the Act of Settlement of 1701 (i.e. male-preference primogeniture applies).

- The restriction on marrying Roman Catholics has been removed and those who previously married Roman Catholics have been reinstated in the Line of Succession. However people who have converted to Roman Catholicism or have been raised Roman Catholics remain excluded from the succession.

- The first six people in the Line of Succession must seek the monarch's consent before marrying. Failure to obtain the monarch's consent results in their exclusion from the succession. This provision replaces a different Act, the previous Royal Marriages Act of 1772 which required all descendants of King George II, regardless of place in the line of succession, to obtain the current monarch's consent before marrying in order for the marriage to be legal in the United Kingdom.

The first 50 individuals in the Line of Succession as of 1 July 2019:

✠ Previously excluded from the Line of Succession for having married Roman Catholics, later reinstated according to the new succession rules.

♦ People whose place in the Line of Succession has been affected by absolute primogeniture.

Prince Charles' family

1. Prince Charles, Prince of Wales (b. 1948), eldest son of Queen Elizabeth II.

2. Prince William, Duke of Cambridge (b. 1982), elder son of Charles, Prince of Wales.

3. Prince George of Cambridge (b. 2013), first son of Prince William, Duke of Cambridge.
4. Princess Charlotte of Cambridge (b. 2015), daughter of Prince William, Duke of Cambridge.
5. Prince Louis of Cambridge (b. 2018), second son of Prince William, Duke of Cambridge.
6. Prince Harry of Wales, Duke of Sussex (b. 1984), younger son of Charles, Prince of Wales.
7. Archie Mountbatten-Windsor (b. 2019), son of Prince Harry, Duke of Sussex.

Prince Andrew's family
8. Prince Andrew, Duke of York (b. 1960), second son of Queen Elizabeth II.
9. Princess Beatrice of York (b. 1988), elder daughter of Prince Andrew, Duke of York.
10. Princess Eugenie of York (b. 1990), younger daughter of Prince Andrew, Duke of York.

Prince Edward's family
11. Prince Edward, Earl of Wessex (b. 1964), third and youngest son of Queen Elizabeth II.
12. James, Viscount Severn (b. 2007), son of Prince Edward, Earl of Wessex.
13. Lady Louise Windsor (b. 2003), daughter of Prince Edward, Earl of Wessex.

Princess Anne's family
14. Princess Anne, Princess Royal (b. 1950), daughter of Queen Elizabeth II.
15. Peter Phillips (b. 1977), son of Anne, Princess Royal.
16. Savannah Phillips (b. 2010), elder daughter of Peter Phillips.
17. Isla Phillips (b. 2012), younger daughter of Peter Phillips.
18. Zara Tindall (b. 1981), daughter of Anne, Princess Royal.
19. Mia Tindall (b. 2014) elder daughter of Zara Tindall.
20. Lena Tindall (b. 2018) younger daughter of Zara Tindall.

Descendants of Princess Margaret, the Queen's late sister, daughter of King George VI

21. David Armstrong-Jones, Earl of Snowdon (b. 1961), son of Princess Margaret.

22. Charles Armstrong-Jones, Viscount Linley (b. 1999), son of David Armstrong-Jones, Earl of Snowdon.

23. Margarita Armstrong-Jones (b. 2002) daughter of David Armstrong-Jones, Earl of Snowdon.

24. Lady Sarah Chatto (b. 1964) daughter of Princess Margaret.

25. Samuel Chatto (b. 1996) elder son of Lady Sarah Chatto.

26. Arthur Chatto (b. 1999) younger son of Lady Sarah Chatto.

The family of the Duke of Gloucester, grandson of King George V

27. Prince Richard, Duke of Gloucester (b. 1944), grandson of King George V.

28. Alexander, Earl of Ulster (b. 1974), son of Prince Richard, Duke of Gloucester.

29. Xan Windsor, Lord Culloden (b. 2007), son of Alexander, Earl of Ulster.

30. Lady Cosima Windsor (b. 2010), daughter of Alexander, Earl of Ulster.

31. Lady Davina Lewis (b. 1977), elder daughter of Prince Richard, Duke of Gloucester.

32. Senna Lewis (b. 2010), daughter of Lady Davina Lewis.

33. Tane Lewis (b. 2012), son of Lady Davina Lewis. ♦

34. Lady Rose Gilman (b. 1980), younger daughter of Prince Richard, Duke of Gloucester.

35. Lyla Gilman (b. 2010), daughter of Lady Rose Gilman.

36. Rufus Gilman (b. 2012), son of Lady Rose Gilman. ♦

The family of the Duke of Kent, grandson of King George V

37. Prince Edward, Duke of Kent (b. 1935), grandson of King George V.

38. George, Earl of St Andrews, (b. 1962), elder son of Prince Edward, Duke of Kent. ✠

(--) Edward, Lord Downpatrick (b. 1988), son of George, Earl of St Andrews. EXCLUDED AS A ROMAN CATHOLIC
(--) Lady Marina Windsor (b. 1992), elder daughter of George, Earl of St Andrew. EXCLUDED AS A ROMAN CATHOLIC
39. Lady Amelia Windsor (b. 1995), younger daughter of George, Earl of S Andrews.
(--) Lord Nicholas Windsor (b. 1970), younger son of Prince Edward, Duke of Kent. EXCLUDED AS ROMAN CATHOLIC
(--) Albert Windsor (b. 2007), eldest son of Lord Nicholas Windsor. EXCLUDED AS ROMAN CATHOLIC
(--) Leopold Windsor (b. 2009), second son of Lord Nicholas Windsor. EXCLUDED AS ROMAN CATHOLIC
(--) Louis Windsor (b. 2014), third son of Lord Nicholas Windsor. EXCLUDED AS ROMAN CATHOLIC
40. Lady Helen Taylor (b. 1964), daughter of Prince Edward, Duke of Kent.
41. Columbus Taylor (b. 1994), elder son of Lady Helen Taylor.
42. Cassius Taylor (b. 1996), younger son of Lady Helen Taylor.
43. Eloise Taylor (b. 2003), elder daughter of Lady Helen Taylor.
44. Estella Taylor (b. 2004), younger daughter of Lady Helen Taylor.

The family of Prince Michael of Kent, grandson of King George V
45. Prince Michael of Kent (b. 1942), grandson of King George V ✠
46. Lord Frederick Windsor (b. 1979), son of Prince Michael of Kent
47. Maud Windsor (b. 2013), elder daughter of Lord Frederick Windsor
48. Isabella Windsor (b. 2016), younger daughter of Lord Frederick Windsor
49. Lady Gabriella Windsor (b. 1981), daughter of Prince Michael of Kent

The family of Princess Alexandra of Kent, granddaughter of King George V
50. Princess Alexandra, Lady Ogilvy (b. 1936), granddaughter of King George V

The Current Royal Family

There is no formal definition in the United Kingdom of what constitutes membership of the Royal Family, however two general distinctions usually apply:

- ***Official Members*** of the Royal Family, related to the Monarch either by blood or by marriage, bear HRH (His/Her Royal Highness) titles, and carry official engagements on behalf of the Monarch (except minors).

- ***Unofficial Members*** of the Royal Family are closely related to the Monarch either by blood or by marriage, but bear no HRH titles and usually carry no official engagements on behalf of the monarch, leading instead private lives.

As of May 2019, the current Royal Family of the United Kingdom includes the following members:

THE MONARCH

HM Elizabeth II, The Queen
(b.1926)

OFFICIAL MEMBERS

(bearing HRH titles and carrying official engagements on behalf of the Queen, except minors)

HRH Prince Philip, the Duke of Edinburgh
the Queen's husband (b.1921)

HRH Prince Charles, the Prince of Wales
the Queen's firstborn son and heir to the throne (b.1948)

HRH Camilla, the Duchess of Cornwall
the Prince of Wales' wife (b.1947)

HRH Prince William, the Duke of Cambridge
the Prince of Wales' firstborn son (b.1982)

HRH Catherine, the Duchess of Cambridge
the Duke of Cambridge's wife (b.1982)

HRH Prince George of Cambridge
the Duke of Cambridge's first son (b.2013)

HRH Princess Charlotte of Cambridge
the Duke of Cambridge's daughter (b.2015)

HRH Prince Louis of Cambridge
the Duke of Cambridge's second son (b.2018)

HRH Prince Harry, the Duke of Sussex
the Prince of Wales' second son (b.1984)

HRH Meghan, the Duchess of Sussex
the Duke of Sussex's wife (b.1981)

Archie Mountbatten-Windsor
the Duke of Sussex's son (b.2019)

HRH Princess Anne, the Princess Royal
the Queen's daughter (b.1950)

HRH Prince Andrew, the Duke of York
the Queen's second son (b.1960)

HRH Princess Beatrice of York
the Duke of York's firstborn daughter (b.1988)

HRH Princess Eugenie of York
the Duke of York's second daughter (b.1990)

HRH Prince Edward, the Earl of Wessex
the Queen's third son (b.1964)

HRH Sophie the Countess of Wessex
the Earl of Wessex's wife (b.1965)

Lady Louise Windsor
the Earl of Wessex's daughter (b.2003)

James, Viscount Severn
the Earl's Wessex's son (b.2007)

HRH Prince Richard, the Duke Gloucester
the Queen's first cousin, grandson of King George V (b.1944)

HRH Birgitte, the Duchess of Gloucester
the Duke of Gloucester's wife (b.1946)

HRH Prince Edward, the Duke of Kent
the Queen's first cousin, grandson of King George V (b.1935)

HRH Katharine, the Duchess of Kent
the Duke of Kent's wife (b.1933)

HRH Princess Alexandra of Kent
The Queen's first cousin, granddaughter of King George V (b.1936)

HRH Prince Michael of Kent
the Queen's first cousin, grandson of King George V (b.1942)

HRH Marie Christine, Princess Michael of Kent
Prince Michael of Kent's wife (b.1945)

UNOFFICIAL MEMBERS
(often present at major public royal occasions, but not carrying official engagements on behalf of the Queen, and leading mostly private lives)

Vice Admiral Sir Timothy Laurence (b.1955), Princess Anne's second and current husband

The family of **Mr Peter Phillips** (b.1977), son of Princess Anne by her former husband Captain Mark Phillips

The family of **Mrs Zara Tindall** (b.1981), daughter of Princess Anne by her former husband Captain Mark Phillips

Jack Brooksbank (b.1986), Princess Eugenie's husband.

The family of **David Armstrong-Jones, Earl of Snowdon** (b.1961), the Queen's nephew, son of the late Princess Margaret

The family of **Lady Sarah Chatto** (b.1964), the Queen's niece, daughter of the late Princess Margaret

The children and grandchildren of **HRH Prince Richard, the Duke of Gloucester**

The children and grandchildren of **HRH Prince Edward, the Duke of Kent**

The children and grandchildren of **HRH Princess Alexandra of Kent**

The children and grandchildren of **HRH Prince Michael of Kent**

ADDITIONAL UNOFFICIAL MEMBERS

(not attending public royal occasions but sometimes present at private family events)

Sarah, Duchess of York (b.1959), former wife of Prince Andrew, the Duke of York, and mother of HRH Princess Beatrice and HRH Princess Eugenie

Captain Mark Phillips (b.1948), former husband of Princess Anne and father of Peter Phillips and Zara Tindall

CEREMONY AND CONSTITUTION

Royal Family Titles

Royal titles in the United Kingdom are both regulated by law and governed by tradition. In the case of the monarch, official titles are bestowed by Parliament according to tradition, and by other bodies national and local (see examples below). Royal titles for other members of the Royal Family are either bestowed by the monarch in the form of Letters Patent, or automatically granted in specific situations according to law or tradition. Following below is a list and brief explanations of these titles.

The Monarch's Titles

The monarch's principal title as used in the United Kingdom is as follows (adjusted for the gender of the monarch):

- **His/Her** Majesty, (*name*), by the Grace of God **King/Queen** of the United Kingdom of Great Britain and Northern Ireland, and of **His/Her** other Realms and Territories, Head of the Commonwealth, Defender of the Faith.

A modified form of this title is used in each of the other Commonwealth Realms of which the British monarch is Head of State, often excluding *Defender of the Faith*. The title *Head of the Commonwealth* was first used by George VI in 1949. The title *Defender of the Faith* was first used by Henry VIII in 1521.

Other Titles held automatically by the monarch include the following:

Supreme Governor of the Church of England
Title held since 1563 (see *The Monarchy and the Church*).

Duke of Normandy

Title held since 1066 when William the Conqueror acceded to the English throne. Although English monarchs lost possession of Normandy in 1204, the British monarch is still known informally as Duke of Normandy in the Channel Islands as the territory represents the last remnant of that dukedom still under the British crown. The title is used in the masculine form (in French, 'Duc') regardless of the gender of the monarch.

Duke of Lancaster

Title held since 1399 when Henry IV acceded to the throne, as he had been previously Duke of Lancaster. The title and dukedom were merged into the crown in 1413 at the accession of his son Henry V and have been held by every monarch since. It is used today for the Duchy of Lancaster, and is used in the masculine form regardless of the gender of the monarch.

Lord of Mann

Title held since 1765 after the Isle of Man came under the possession of the British Crown in George III's reign. The title is still used in the Isle of Man and is used in the masculine form regardless of the gender of the monarch.

In addition to the titles above, Queen Elizabeth II also holds the titles of **Duchess of Edinburgh, Countess of Marioneth, and Baroness Greenwich**, in virtue of the titles held by her husband Prince Philip.

HM and HRH

Kings, Queens Regnant and Queen Consorts (including Queen Dowagers and Queen Mothers) carry the titles of **His/Her Majesty,** shortened to **HM**. All other persons who are official members of the Royal Family carry, at the pleasure of the monarch, the title of **His/Her Royal Highness**, shortened to **HRH**.

Prince and Princess

Formal titles of Prince and Princess for members of the Royal Family only became customary in Great Britain after the accession of the German Hanoverian dynasty in 1714. The titles are currently regulated by Letters Patent issued by King George V in 1917. According to those Letters Patent, the titles of Prince and Princess of the United Kingdom—styled Prince/Princess (*Name*)—can only be borne by children of a monarch, by the grandchildren of a monarch in the male line, and by the eldest son of the eldest son of the Prince of Wales. Shortly before the birth of Prince William's first child in 2013, Queen Elizabeth II issued an additional Letter Patent establishing that all the children of the eldest son of the Prince of Wales can bear the title of Prince or Princess, regardless of number or gender. The title of Prince or Princess is however not compulsory: for example the children of Prince Edward, Earl of Wessex, though entitled, are not, in accordance to their parents' wishes, called Prince and Princess.

When a Prince marries, the legal status of Princess is, according to English law, transferred to his wife, but she does not become Princess in her own right—i.e. 'Princess (*Name*)'—as that particular style is meant to be borne only by those of blood royal as mentioned above. The spouse of a Prince of the United Kingdom must style herself after the husband's own title and be known, for example, as 'Princess Michael of Kent' (wife of Prince Michael of Kent), as opposed to Princess Marie Christine of Kent (i.e using her own name). Alternatively, spouses of a Prince can be known by any other title the Prince holds, for example as 'Catherine, Duchess of Cambridge' (wife of Prince William, Duke of Cambridge). No spouse of a Prince of the United Kingdom can style herself as 'Princess (*Name*)', unless she already bore that title before marriage, as for example was the case for Princess Marina, wife of Prince George, Duke of Kent, who was a Princess of Greece from birth. The monarch can however alter these rules and grant in certain cases the use of the title and style of 'Princess (*Name*)' to certain spouses in special circumstances. One such case happened in 1974 when Alice, Dowager Duchess of Gloucester, widow of Prince Henry, Duke of Gloucester, became known, by the Queen's permission, as 'Princess Alice, Duchess of Gloucester'.

Prince of Wales

The title of Prince of Wales was created by Edward I in 1301. The title is given to the heir apparent to the Crown—that is, the person who cannot be displaced in the line of succession by any future births. The title is not automatic and must be bestowed by the monarch, which means that some time may elapse between an heir apparent's birth and the time he becomes Prince of Wales. For example, the current heir to the throne, Prince Charles, only became Prince of Wales at the age of 9 in 1958. If the Prince of Wales dies before the monarch, the title merges back into the Crown and can be bestowed again to the next heir apparent. Similarly, the title merges back into the Crown when a Prince of Wales becomes King, to be bestowed later on the subsequent heir apparent. Traditionally, female heirs apparent have never been officially created Princesses of Wales in their own right, though this may happen in the future following the adoption of equal primogeniture through the Succession to the Crown Act of 2013. The title of **Earl of Chester** has been automatically granted together with the title of Prince of Wales since 1343.

The title of **Duke of Cornwall** is often borne together with the title of Prince of Wales but it is a separate title in the Peerage of England. The title was created in 1337 by Edward III for his eldest son, Edward the Black Prince. Differently from the title of Prince of Wales, the title of Duke of Cornwall is automatically inherited by the monarch's eldest living son, either on his father's accession or at birth. Only the eldest son of a monarch however, and no one else, can bear the title. That means for example that if the Prince of Wales or heir apparent to the throne is the grandson, brother, or nephew of the monarch, he cannot be Duke of Cornwall also, and the title is withheld. Female heirs apparent have so far also been excluded from bearing the title though this may change following the adoption of equal primogeniture through the Succession to the Crown Act of 2013. The title comes with its own estate of the Duchy of Cornwall, whose revenues usually fund the Prince of Wales' expenses and activities.

In Scotland, the Prince of Wales is known by the title of **Duke of Rothesay**, as well as **Earl of Carrick, Baron of Renfrew, Lord of the Isles** and **Prince and Great Stewart of Scotland**. These are the titles traditionally borne by the heir to the throne of Scotland, and were joined to the title of Prince of Wales after the crowns of England and Scotland were united in 1603. Like the title of Duke of Cornwall in England, these Scottish titles are automatically borne by the eldest living son of the monarch, and cannot be borne by anyone else.

Royal Duke

Royal Dukedoms are titles in the English and British Peerage that are generally reserved for male members of the Royal Family. They are given to the sons and male-line grandsons of a monarch, usually on reaching adulthood or upon marriage, and occasionally also to Prince Consorts. They are not automatic and must be bestowed by the monarch by Letters Patent like any other Peerage title. Titles can be inherited by subsequent male heirs, but they cease to be Royal Dukedoms once they are borne by persons who are no longer official members of the Royal Family (i.e. non-HRH). Once a title becomes extinct in the male line, it merges back into the Crown and can be recreated at a later time. Royal Dukedoms normally include the following titles:

** Currently in use as of June 2019*

*Duke of York (usually reserved for the second son of the monarch)
+Duke of Albany
*Duke of Cambridge
Duke of Clarence
+Duke of Cumberland
*Duke of Edinburgh
*Duke of Gloucester
*Duke of Kent
*Duke of Sussex

+ The titles of Duke of Albany and Duke of Cumberland have been suspended since 1917 when their German owners, descendants of children of King George III and Queen Victoria, were stripped of their titles for supporting German forces during the First World War. As of 2018 the titles remain suspended.

Princess Royal

The title of Princess Royal is a French royal title that was introduced to England by Queen Henrietta Maria, daughter of King Henri IV of France, after her marriage to King Charles I in 1625. The title is reserved for the firstborn daughter of the monarch and is borne exclusively until death. It is not automatic, and must expressly be bestowed by the monarch when the title is available since it can only be held by one person at a time. Consequently not all firstborn daughters of monarchs have carried the title of Princess Royal, and the ones who did hold it received it at different times in their lives.

As of May 2018, there have been seven women who have born the title of Princess Royal:

Mary *(1632-1660)*
Firstborn daughter of: Charles I
Tenure: 1642-1660
Other Titles: Princess of Orange

Anne *(1709-1759)*
Firstborn daughter of: George II
Tenure: 1727-1759
Other Titles: Princess of Orange

Charlotte *(1766-1828)*
Firstborn daughter of: George III
Tenure: 1789-1828
Other Titles: Queen of Wurttemberg

Victoria *(1840-1901)*
Firstborn daughter of: Victoria
Tenure: 1841-1901
Other Titles: Empress of Germany

Louise *(1867-1931)*
Firstborn daughter of: Edward VII
Tenure: 1905-1931
Other Titles: Duchess of Fife

Mary *(1897-1965)*
Firstborn daughter of: George V
Tenure: 1932-1965
Other Titles: Countess of Harewood

Anne *(1950-)*
Firstborn daughter of: Elizabeth II
Tenure: 1987-
Other Titles: *None*

British Honours and Decorations

Honours in the United Kingdom are divided between Orders of Chivalry, Decorations and Medals, Life Peerages, and Knights Bachelor titles. The monarch is considered the Fountain of Honours, and all honours and decorations must expressly be bestowed by him or her. Most honours today are awarded by the monarch under the advice of the government of the day, however a few honours remain in the monarch's personal gift (see below).

Most British honours are awarded yearly in two separate lists: on 1 January—the New Year's Honours List—and on the second/third Saturday in June—the Queen's Birthday Honours List. Special Honours lists are also issued on the resignation of a government and for unique royal occasions like coronations and jubilees. Currently, each of the two yearly Honours Lists contains between 1,000-1,350 individuals, the vast majority of whom receive introductory honours in the Order of the British Empire (see below). All honours are for life, and can only be revoked, or 'degraded', under special circumstances.

Listed on the next pages are the current Orders of Chivalry as well as the most significant decorations and medals.

ORDERS OF CHIVALRY

Given by the Monarch as a Personal Gift

(Listed in order precedence)

The Order of the Garter

Foundation: 1348 by King Edward III.

Purpose: The first and oldest order of chivalry, associated with England, it is awarded for distinguished achievements in someone's field, or for meritorious service to the monarch or the nation.

Membership: Restricted to 24 members who are citizens of the United Kingdom and other Commonwealth Realms. Members of the Royal Family are usually admitted as Royal Companions, whilst foreign monarchs are normally admitted as Stranger Companions. From the 18th to the 20th century appointments to the order were made on the advice of government. Appointments reverted into the monarch's personal gift in 1946.

Chapel: St George's Chapel, Windsor Castle.

The Order of the Thistle

Foundation: 1687 by King James VII of Scotland and II of England.

Purpose: The second-oldest order of chivalry, associated with Scotland, it is awarded for distinguished achievements in someone's field, or for meritorious service to the monarch or the nation.

Membership: Restricted to 16 members who are citizens of the United Kingdom and other Commonwealth Realms and who normally must have strong connections to Scotland. Members of the Royal Family are normally admitted as honorary members. From the 18th to the 20th century appointments to the order were made on the advice of government. Appointments reverted into the monarch's personal gift in 1946.

Chapel: St Giles' Cathedral, Edinburgh.

The Royal Victorian Order

Foundation: 1896 by Queen Victoria.

Purpose: Awarded for distinguished personal service to the monarch or to the institution of the monarchy.

Membership: Membership numbers are unlimited and open to citizens of any Commonwealth realm of which the British monarch is also head of state. Citizens from other countries may be admitted to the order as honorary members. Members of the Royal Family are often awarded this honour and there are currently 10 family members in the order. Total membership is currently between 40-45 members.

Chapel: The Savoy Chapel, London, and St George's Chapel, Windsor Castle.

The Order of Merit

Foundation: 1902 by King Edward VII.

Purpose: Awarded for distinguished achievement in the arts, sciences, culture, politics, the military, and fields of public service. Appointment to the Order is often considered the most prestigious honour in the United Kingdom after the Victoria Cross.

Membership: Restricted to 24 members who are citizens of any Commonwealth Realm. Citizens from other countries may be admitted as honorary members in unlimited numbers though admission is rare.

Chapel: The Chapel Royal, St James's Palace, London.

Given by the Monarch on the Government's Advice

(Listed in order precedence)

The Order of the Bath

Foundation: 1725 by King George I.

Purpose: Awarded to military officers and senior civil servants who achieved distinguished service in their careers. The order is

considered the highest honour that can be bestowed by the British government on civilians for public service.
Membership: Restricted to roughly 2400 members who are citizens of the United Kingdom and other Commonwealth Realms, though actual membership is lower at any one time. Ranks are divided between Knights or Dames Grand Cross, Knights or Dame Commanders, and Companions. Honorary membership is often conferred on foreign heads of state with good relations with the United Kingdom.
Chapel: Henry VII's Chapel, Westminster Abbey, London.

The Order of St Michael and St George

Foundation: 1818 by George, Prince Regent (later King George IV).
Purpose: Awarded to non-military government personnel who have performed important services in a foreign country, and to other people who performed important services in foreign and commonwealth affairs. The order is generally awarded to people working in foreign diplomacy, and to Governors-Generals of Commonwealth Realms.
Membership: Restricted to roughly 2250 members who are citizens of the United Kingdom and other Commonwealth Realms, though actual membership is lower at any one time. Ranks are divided between Knights or Dames Grand Cross, Knights or Dame Commanders, and Companions. Honorary membership is often conferred on selected foreign heads of state, and on foreign individuals with distinguished diplomatic achievements.
Chapel: St Paul's Cathedral, London.

Order of the British Empire

Foundation: 1917 by King George V.
Purpose: Awarded for public service, for services to charities and public welfare, and for achievement in all fields of human endeavour.

Membership: The order is the largest of all British orders. It is divided in five classes. The first three classes—Knights or Dames Grand Cross, Knights or Dame Commanders, and Commanders—are restricted to roughly 10,100 members combined. Membership numbers to the lower two classes, Officers and Members, is unlimited but no more than 2322 people may be appointed in any one year. The award is open to citizens of the United Kingdom, and of other Commonwealth realms that wish to nominate their citizens for the honour. Citizens from other countries may be admitted as honorary members.
Chapel: St Paul's Cathedral, London.

The Order of the Companions of Honour

Foundation: 1917 by King George V.
Purpose: Awarded for services to the arts, sciences, culture, politics, the military, and fields of public service. It is generally regarded as the junior class of the Order of Merit, the only difference being that members are appointed on the advice of the government.
Membership: Restricted to 65 members who are citizens of the United Kingdom and other Commonwealth Realms. Citizens from other countries may be admitted as honorary members.

DECORATIONS AND MEDALS

Awarded by the Monarch of the Government's Advice

(Listed in order of precedence. The awards below include the most senior award classes only.)

Victoria Cross

Category: Military
Foundation: 1856 by Queen Victoria.
Purpose: Awarded in exceptional circumstances for most conspicuous bravery, daring acts of valour, or extreme self-sacrifice

before the enemy in military combat. The Victoria Cross is the highest military decoration and highest honour in the United Kingdom, outranking all other honours including orders of chivalry.

George Cross

Category: Civilian/Military

Foundation: 1940 by King George VI.

Purpose: The George Cross is awarded to civilians for great acts of heroism in circumstances of extreme danger, either in wartime or peacetime. It is also awarded to military personnel for non-combat acts of heroism.

Distinguished Service Order

Category: Military

Foundation: 1886 by Queen Victoria.

Purpose: Awarded to military personnel for outstanding acts of leadership during active operations, and for distinguished leadership service.

Conspicuous Gallantry Cross

Category: Military

Foundation: 1993 by Queen Elizabeth II.

Purpose: Awarded to military personnel for acts of conspicuous gallantry during active operations against the enemy. It is considered a second level bravery award in the Armed Forces after the Victoria Cross.

Royal Red Cross

Category: Nursing

Foundation: 1883 by Queen Victoria.

Purpose: Awarded to military nursing personnel, or civilian nurses working for the military, for exceptional acts of bravery while performing nursing duties, or for exceptional devotion and competency over a long period of time. A second level award with the same name was created by King George V in 1917.

Distinguish Service Cross

Category: Military
Foundation: 1914 by King George V.
Purpose: Awarded to any member of the British Armed Forces for exemplary gallantry shown during active operations against the enemy at sea.

Military Cross

Category: Military
Foundation: 1914 by King George V.
Purpose: Awarded to any member of the British Armed Forces for exemplary gallantry shown during active operations against the enemy on land.

Distinguish Flying Cross

Category: Military
Foundation: 1918 by King George V.
Purpose: Awarded to any member of the British Armed Forces for exemplary gallantry shown during active operations against the enemy in the air.

The Sovereign's Guard

The monarchy has a special relationship with regiments in the British Army who have the honour and duty of guarding the Sovereign and other members of the Royal Family. These relationships began in the Middle Ages when select troops of knights provided protection to the monarch.
The present relationships between the British monarch and the regiments below began in the Tudor era and became formalised during the reign of Charles II at the Restoration. These regiments constitute the Sovereign's Guard, an elite group of soldiers who are charged with guarding the monarch and providing a ceremonial escort at major occasions.

The Sovereign's Guard is roughly divided between a **Ceremonial Guard** and a **Military Guard,** as described below. Some information about the Changing of the Guard follows at the end of this chapter.

THE CEREMONIAL GUARD

The monarch's Ceremonial Guard comprises the oldest military corps in Britain. Members are not full time soldiers but instead retired members of the Armed Forces or civilians, most of whom are called to perform ceremonial duties only on specific occasions. Although still charged with a formal degree of protection to the monarch, the guard's role is overwhelmingly ceremonial today. The four corps making up the ceremonial guard are listed below in order of foundation date.

The Yeomen of the Guard

History: The oldest military corps in Britain, it was founded by Henry VII at the Battle of Bosworth in 1485, and has been in attendance upon the sovereign ever since. Its original role was to act as personal bodyguard to the monarch at all times, including accompanying him into battle. Its last appearance on the battlefield was at the Battle of Dettingen in 1743 under George II.
Duties: Fully ceremonial today. The Yeomen of the Guard take part in the State Opening of Parliament, the Royal Maundy Service, the Garter Service, coronations, lyings-in-state, funerals, investitures, and garden parties.
Composition: Retired members from the British Armed Forces with a distinguished career of at least 22 years. Members are called for service only on specific occasions, and must retire by the age of 70.
Uniform: Tudor-era uniform in scarlet and gold, flat hat, collar ruff and ribbon-laced shoes. On some state occasions they carry medieval halberds.

The Yeomen Warders

History: Closely related to the Yeoman of the Guard, this corps was spun from them in Henry VIII's reign with the specific task of guarding the Tower of London, which they have done ever since. They were confirmed as a separate corps in Edward VI's reign. Their popular nickname of Beefeaters is thought to originate from the fact that the original Yeomen of the Guard were allowed to eat as much beef as they wanted from the King's table. The term then became associated specifically with the Yeomen Warders guarding the Tower of London.
Duties: The Yeomen remain the guardians of the Tower of London. Their main official role is to safeguard the Tower, its residents, and its visitors. In addition, they act as guides and storytellers to visitors to the Tower, and also take part in the Ceremony of the Keys at the

end of each day. Ceremonial roles outside the Tower include providing a guard of honour to the monarch during the coronation ceremony in Westminster Abbey.

Composition: Retired members from the British and Commonwealth Armed Forces with a distinguished career of at least 22 years, and who must be between 40-50 years of age on joining. There are currently 35-40 Yeomen Warders, plus a Chief Yeomen Warder, who must all live within the precincts of the Tower of London.

Uniform: A Tudor-era uniform of dark blue and red with a flat hat is used for everyday use at the Tower of London. The ceremonial uniform used for state occasions is almost exactly the same as the Yeomen of the Guard's, except that it lacks a shoulder belt worn across the chest.

The Gentlemen at Arms

History: Formed by Henry VIII in 1509, its original role was to provide a mounted escort to the monarch on the battlefield and on progress. They have however been acting solely as a ceremonial foot guard since 1660. Although the corps was founded after the Yeomen of the Guard, the Gentlemen have always been classed as the most senior bodyguard to the monarch because originally gentlemen outranked yeomen.

Duties: Fully ceremonial today. Gentlemen at Arms retain the privilege of providing the nearest guard to the sovereign at major ceremonial occasions like the State Opening of Parliament, State Visits, religious services for the orders of chivalry, and coronations.

Composition: Retired members of the British Army and Royal Marines who must be less than 55 years of age on joining and must retire by the age of 70. There are currently between 25 and 35 Gentlemen at Arms. The most senior officer, the Captain of the Corps, is a political appointment held by the Government Chief Whip in the House of Lords.

Uniform: Uniform of a heavy dragoon guard from the 1840s, including red coat with gold epaulettes, dark trousers, and helmets with white swan feathers. All gentlemen carry cavalry swords and ceremonial battle axes.

The Royal Company of Archers

History: Formed as a private archery club in 1676, the Company remains one of the oldest sporting clubs in the world. It was given the privilege of serving as the monarch's bodyguard in Scotland by George IV in 1822.
Duties: The Company serves as the monarch's ceremonial bodyguard when visiting Scotland, serving most notably during the Order of the Thistle service and at Garden Parties in Edinburgh. As a non-military body, its attendance at royal events must be requested specifically by the monarch. On a daily basis, the Company continues to function as a private archery club.
Composition: Members must be Scottish or have strong Scottish connections, and are elected to the club by current members.
Uniform: Dark green tunic with black facings, dark green trousers with black and crimson stripes, and a Balmoral bonnet adorned with an eagle feather and badge.

THE MILITARY GUARD

Unlike the ceremonial guard, the sovereign's Military Guard provides actual protection duties, mainly through guarding the royal palaces. It is also however involved in ceremonial duties, and with greater frequency and in greater numbers. The guard is composed of full-time soldiers who perform royal duties as part of their military rotation, alternating them with operational service, military exercises, and active combat abroad. The Guard is made of seven different regiments which include the most senior and prestigious regiments in the British Army, and are collectively known as the ***Household Division***. The Division's motto, *Septem Juncta In Uno* (Seven Joined In One) highlights the special relationship that holds them together in service to the monarch. The King's Troop, a regiment in the British Army with a special individual relationship to the monarch, is not part of the Household Division, but because it performs some of the same duties and enjoys the same privileges as the Household Division, it is designated as part of the ***Household Troops***.

The diagram below explains the relationship between the individual regiments of the Household Troops:

THE HOUSEHOLD TROOPS

- **I.** The Household Division *(Seven Joined in One)*
    - **1.** The Household Cavalry
        - **a.** The Life Guards
        - **b.** The Blues and Royals
    - **2.** The Household Guards
        - **a.** The Grenadier Guards
        - **b.** The Coldstream Guards
        - **c.** The Scots Guards
        - **d.** The Irish Guards
        - **e.** The Welsh Guards
- **II.** The King's Troop, Royal Horse Artillery

The Household Cavalry

The Household Cavarly is made up of two different regiments, the **Life Guards** and the **Blues and Royals**, and both have served as bodyguard to the monarch since the 1660s. Both regiments are split in two different units with different purposes. The ***Household Cavalry Regiment*** is an active unit in the British Army serving as a formation reconnaissance regiment as part of the Royal Armoured Corps. The ***Household Cavalry Mounted Regiment*** (described here) is a full time ceremonial unit providing the Queen's Life Guard in London, and serving on royal and state occasions. Members of the Life Guards and Blues and Royals are part of both units, and soldiers serve in both units separately at different points in their careers.

History

The Corps is made up of the two most senior regiments in the British Army, both tracing their origins to the English Civil War and Restoration of the monarchy in the mid 17th century:

The Life Guards. Officially the most senior regiment in the British Army, it had its origins in troops raised by Charles II while in exile abroad in the 1650s. At the Restoration of the monarchy in 1660 they were made the monarch's official military guard at Whitehall Palace. They have distinguished themselves in active service during the Monmouth Rebellion, the War of the Austrian Succession, Waterloo, World War I and World War II.

The Blues and Royals. The present regiment was amalgamated in 1969 from two previous cavalry regiments with illustrious histories:

- The ***Royal Horse Guards*** were originally founded in 1650 for Oliver Cromwell as part of the New Model Army. Parliamentarian officers were replaced by Royalists at the Restoration when the regiment was re-founded, and the regiment later went on to fight at the Battle of the Boyne, the Seven Years' War and the Battle of Waterloo.

- The ***Royal Dragoons*** were originally raised by Charles II in the 1660s to defend the city of Tangiers, Morocco, which the English had acquired as part of the dowry of Charles's wife Catherine of Braganza. They later fought in the War of the Spanish Succession, Waterloo, World War I and World War II.

Duties

When mounted, the regiments perform escort duties to the monarch at the State Opening of Parliament, Trooping the Colour, state visits and royal weddings. Dismounted duties include lining the monarch's walking route during the Garter Service at Windsor Castle, and lining staircases at the State Opening of Parliament. A dismounted division is also present at the Cenotaph ceremony on Remembrance Day. On a daily basis, the Household Cavalry provides the Queen's Life Guard, both mounted and dismounted, at Horse Guards—the ceremonial entrance to the Royal Palaces—which it has done since 1758 (see *Changing of the Guard* below).

Uniform

The ceremonial uniforms of both regiments are similar and include a tunic, a cuirass (chest armour plate), black jackboots, sword, and a metal helmet with a plume. The uniforms vary between the two regiments in the following differences:

The Life Guards

Tunic colour:	Red
Helmet plume colour:	White
Chin strap:	Worn below the lower lip

The Blues and Royals

Tunic colour:	Blue
Helmet plume colour:	Red
Chin strap:	Worn under the chin

The Foot Guards

The Foot Guards have served as a personal military guard to the monarch since the Restoration of the monarchy in 1660, however their role in guarding the Royal Palaces only became prominent in the 18th century after the royal court was moved to St James's Palace. Soldiers in the Foot Guards are involved in duties through a rotational system, alternating between military exercises and guarding the royal palaces. They are made up of five regiments: the **Grenadier Guards,** the **Coldstream Guards,** the **Scots Guards,** the **Irish Guards**, and the **Welsh Guards**. The monarch is always the Colonel in Chief of all five regiments. The history of the individual regiments is described below in order of regimental seniority.

History

The Grenadier Guards

The most senior infantry regiment in the British Army, the Grenadiers had their origins in troops raised abroad in the 1650s for the exiled Charles II and later combined in one regiment after the Restoration of the monarchy in 1660. The name Grenadier was adopted in 1815 after the regiment defeated Napoleon's French Imperial Grenadiers at the Battle of Waterloo. As an additional honour from that battle the Guards were allowed to adopt the French Grenadiers' bearskin hats, a privilege which was extended to all regiments of the Foot Guards in 1831. Besides Waterloo, the regiment distinguished itself in the War of the Spanish Succession, the Crimean and Boer Wars, and in major battles in World War I and World War II. Traditionally, the Grenadier Guards act as pallbearers to the monarch at his or her funeral.

The Coldstream Guards

The Coldstream regiment traditionally claims older origins than the Grenadiers in the British Army. It was formed by General George

Monck in Coldstream, Scotland, in 1650 as part of Cromwell's New Model Army. They first fought victoriously at the Battle of Dunbar against the Royalist Army in 1650, and were later among the troops Monck took to London in 1660 to force the Restoration of the monarchy. They were officially disbanded as a Republican regiment in 1660 and re-formed as a royal regiment in 1661, which is why they rank second to the Grenadier Guards in seniority. Their motto, 'Nulli Secundus' or 'second to none', points to their older history. The regiment fought valiantly during the capture of Gibraltar in 1704, the Napoleonic Wars, on the Western Front during World War I, and during the First Gulf War. Although it is named after a Scottish town, the regiment describes itself as 'fiercely English' and traditionally focuses recruitment in the northeast of England (where the first soldiers originated) and from the southwest (where George Monck was born).

The Scots Guards

The Scots Guards are the regiment with the oldest origins among the Foot Guards as they were originally raised by Charles I in the 1640s as royalist troops during the English Civil War. They later fought for his son Charles II at the battles of Dunbar and Worcester, but after his defeat at Worcester and flight into exile in 1650 the regiment was disbanded. It was expressly reformed by Charles II after the Restoration of the monarchy in 1661, after the Grenadiers and Coldstream, and so became the third officially formed regiment of Foot Guards. Known for their toughness and courage in battle, the Scots have participated in all major foreign engagements including Dettingen, the American War of Independence, Waterloo, the Crimean War (where they were among the first recipients of the Victoria Cross), and they received battle honours from most fighting theatres in World War I and World War II.

The Irish Guards

The Irish Guards were formed in 1900 by Queen Victoria to honour the Irish regiments who had fought courageously in the Boer War in South Africa. Since then the regiment has distinguished itself at the

Battle of the Somme during World War I, in World War II, and in the Balkans. Among its traditions is the presentation of fresh shamrock to the troops by a member of the Royal Family on St Patrick's Day, a tradition started by Queen Alexandra in 1901 and currently being continued by the Duchess of Cambridge. Queen Elizabeth the Queen Mother, who presented shamrocks to the Guards for over 50 years, had a special attachment to the Irish Guards: at her death the regiment had the special honour of bearing her coffin at her funeral.

The Welsh Guards

The Welsh Guards were created in 1915 by George V to complete the representation of the four British home nations in the Foot Guards. Since then they have served at the evacuation of Dunkirk, in the Falklands, and in Bosnia, Iraq and Afghanistan. The regiment has a special connection to the Prince and Princess of Wales, and provided the official escort at the funeral of Diana, Princess of Wales in 1997. They also provided the Royal Guard of Honour at Buckingham Palace for the wedding of Prince William, Duke of Cambridge in 2011.

Duties

The Foot Guards are the monarch's primary military protection in London and in Windsor, where they guard the royal palaces day and night. Their most famous ceremonial duties are the Changing of the Guard at the royal palaces, and the Trooping the Colour parade on the monarch's official birthday which is attended by all five regiments. Other duties include lining the streets at the State Opening of Parliament, providing a guard of honour at ceremonial events like state visits, and taking part in royal weddings and royal funerals. Ceremonial duties are usually shared between all regiments. Each regiment has its own band which may perform during royal ceremonies as well as other public events.

Uniform

The ceremonial uniform of the Foot Guards includes the famous bearskin hat, a scarlet tunic and dark blue trousers. The five individual Regiments all wear the same uniform but may be recognised by the following individual marks:

Grenadier Guards

Grouping of buttons on tunic:	Single
Collar badge:	Grenade
Plume on bearskin hat:	White, left side

Coldstream Guards

Grouping of buttons on tunic:	Twos
Collar badge:	Garter Star
Plume on bearskin hat:	Red, right side

Scots Guards

Grouping of buttons on tunic:	Threes
Collar badge:	Thistle
Plume on bearskin hat:	No plume

Irish Guards

Grouping of buttons on tunic:	Fours
Collar badge:	Shamrock
Plume on bearskin hat:	Blue, right side

Welsh Guards

Grouping of buttons on tunic:	Fives
Collar badge:	Leek
Plume on bearskin hat:	Green and white, left side

The King's Troop, Royal Horse Artillery

The King's Troop enjoys a special relationship with the monarchy. Although officially not part of the Household Division they are still in personal service to the monarch and are therefore called part of the Household Troops. Differently from the other corps described above however, they do not have a history of guarding the sovereign and only begun their special association in the 1940s.

History

Originally formed in 1793 as part of the Royal Regiment of Artillery, the Royal Horse Artillery was a horse mounted unit which was deployed in many conflicts including the Napoleonic Wars, the Crimean War, the Boer War and World War I. After the unit was mechanized in the 1930s a horse-mounted battery was retained to take part in ceremonial occasions, and was renamed The King's Troop by George VI himself during a visit to their barracks in 1947. After George VI's death, Queen Elizabeth II decreed that the royal masculine name be retained in honour of her father, regardless of the gender of the monarch on the throne.

Duties

The main ceremonial role of the King's Troop is firing Gun Salutes in the Royal Parks for official occasions including royal birthdays and anniversaries, state visits, Trooping the Colour, the State Opening of Parliament, and Remembrance Day. On those occasions mounted soldiers drive teams of horses pulling World War I-era field guns which are used to fire salutes. Other roles include taking part in the parades for Trooping the Colour, coronations and royal weddings. During royal ceremonial funerals (as opposed to State funerals) the King's Troop has the honour of pulling the gun carriage carrying the royal coffin as it happened at the funerals of Diana, Princess of Wales in 1997, and Queen Elizabeth the Queen Mother in 2002. The Troop also mounts the Queen's Life Guard at Horse Guard one month per year.

Composition

There are approximately 140 members in the King's Troop, and uniquely among the Household Troops they include both men and women. All the soldiers making up the unit are superb equestrians and serve in active duty, including combat areas.

Uniform

The uniforms worn on ceremonial occasions, including gun salutes, are in the Hussar style, dating back to the Napoleonic era when the original artillery regiment was first formed. The uniform includes a blue tunic with gilded frogging embroidery at the front, blue trousers with red stripes, a Hussar busby hat with plume, and a ceremonial sword.

THE QUEEN'S GUARD AND THE CHANGING OF THE GUARD

The duty and privilege of guarding the Royal Palaces is called the Queen's Guard (called the King's Guard when the monarch is male) or guard mounting. Since 1660 the Guard has been composed of regiments from the Household Division: the five regiments from the Foot Guards are charged with guarding royal palaces in London and Windsor, while the two regiments from the Household Cavalry are charged with guarding Horse Guard in London which is the ceremonial entrance on Whitehall to the royal palaces. There is a Queen's Guard in Edinburgh that is provided by the Royal Regiment of Scotland, or by whichever other regiment is resident in the city barracks at the time. Guard mounting at most locations is also occasionally provided by other regiments from the UK and the Commonwealth.

Individual battalions from regiments are rotated for duties during which they must provide an actual guard to the Royal Palaces. Sentries usually stay on duty for two hours at a time and must keep alert at all times. They may not eat, sleep, smoke, stand easy, sit or lie down during guard duties. Individual battalions normally take collective shifts guarding a royal residence, with each soldier taking a sentry shift. When all soldiers in a battalion have completed their shifts the group hands over sentry duties to another battalion of soldiers come to relieve them, i.e. there is a change in the guards posted at the residence.

The ceremony proper of the Changing of the Guard has its roots in German infantry drills imported into Britain by the Hanoverian kings in the 18th century and first refined during the reign of George II. The ceremony at Buckingham Palace is the biggest and most elaborate and dates back to the beginning of Queen Victoria's reign. A list of guard mounting and Changings of the Guard in the United Kingdom follows:

Guard Mounting and Changing of the Guard Locations in the United Kingdom:

Buckingham Palace, London

Four Foot Guards are posted when the monarch in is residence, two are posted at any other time. The Changing of the Guard ceremony used to take place at 11.30am every day between April and July, and on alternate days the rest of the year, however a new schedule began to be trialled in 2017 with new times being confirmed two months in advance.

St James Palace/Clarence House, London

Two Foot Guards used to be posted at the Pall Mall entrance of St James Palace, and two more at the Mall entrance of Clarence House, however this was discontinued in 2014-2016 due to security concerns. Currently two sentries are posted behind gates in Friary Court at St James Palace, while two sentries are posted behind gates in Stable Yard at Clarence House. The Changing of the Guard ceremony at St James Palace takes place together with the ceremony at Buckingham Palace. There is a small ceremony for changing the guard at Clarence House.

Horse Guards, Whitehall, London

A horse mounted guard provided by the Household Cavalry is posted at the entrance of Horse Guards, the official ceremonial entrance to the Royal Palaces, and is called the Queen's Life Guard. Mounted sentries and dismounted sentries are posted between 10am and 8pm. The Changing of the Guard ceremony is normally held every morning on the adjacent Horse Guards Parade.

The Tower of London

Two Foot Guards are posted at the Tower because it is still an official royal residence and the location of the Crown Jewels. One sentry is posted at the entry of the Jewel House, another before the Queen's House on Tower Green. There is no Changing of the Guard ceremony proper, however a simple opening and posting of the guards routine is performed every day before the Tower is open to visitors.

Windsor Castle, Berkshire

Foot Guards are mounted inside the Castle precincts. A ceremonial Changing of the Guard inside the Castle used to take place Monday to Saturday from April to July, and on alternate days the rest of the year, however a new schedule began to be trialled in 2017 with new times being confirmed two months in advance. The ceremony starts with the soldiers marching from their barracks through Windsor town centre to the Castle.

Edinburgh, Scotland

Sentries are posted before the Palace of Holyroodhouse and Edinburgh Castle when the monarch is in residence during Holyrood week, and when other members of the Royal Family are on official visits to Scotland. Changing of the Guard times vary.

Royal Gun Salutes

The practice of using gun salutes to honour royalty and other important dignitaries originated in the 18th century, and is said to have first begun in the British Royal Navy. The standard 21-gun salute began to be adopted internationally in the 19th century. Today, gun salutes in the United Kingdom are fired on major state occasions like the State Opening of Parliament and official state visits, and on major yearly royal anniversaries. They can also be fired to celebrate royal weddings, jubilee celebrations, and the birth of heirs to the throne. As of June 2019, scheduled Royal Gun Salutes are fired on the following dates in the United Kingdom:

6 February: The Queen's Accession Anniversary

21 April: The Queen's Birthday (actual)

2 June: The Queen's Coronation Anniversary

10 June: The Duke of Edinburgh's Birthday

Mid-June (Saturday): Trooping the Colour, The Queen's Birthday (official)

14 November: The Prince of Wales's Birthday

Note: *Gun salutes never take place on Sundays, so if any of the fixed dates above falls on a Sunday the gun salutes occur on the following day.*

In London, gun salutes are fired twice on the royal occasions listed above, once in one of the Royal Parks (either Green Park or Hyde Park) and once from the gun wharf of the Tower of London. In Hyde

Park and Green Park an extra 20 rounds are added to the basic 21-gun salute because they are Royal Parks, bringing the total Royal Gun Salute to 42 rounds. At the Tower of London, 20 rounds are added because the Tower is a royal fortress, and a further 21 rounds are added to honour the City of London, bringing the total Royal Gun salute there to 62 rounds. Gun salutes take place first in the Royal Parks at 12 noon (11am on the Queen's Official Birthday), and then at 1.00pm at the Tower of London. The salutes in the Royal Parks are usually fired by The King's Troop, Royal Horse Artillery; the ones at the Tower of London by the Honourable Artillery Company.

Gun Salutes can also be fired at any authorized military saluting stations in the UK including Windsor, Edinburgh, Cardiff, York, Plymouth, Dover, Hillsborough Castle in Northern Ireland, and many other places. A decision to fire a Royal Gun Salute across the UK is usually taken by the local government authority or military station.

Some Royal Ceremonies and Events Throughout the Year

Royal ceremonies and events have become part of the social and cultural life of the United Kingdom. Listed on the following pages are the most significant ceremonies and events in the yearly calendar, divided in two categories. Ceremonies and events **Attended by the Royal Family** require the presence of the monarch or a senior member of the Royal Family in order to take place. Ceremonies and events **Not Usually Attended by the Royal Family** commemorate specific royal events or maintain royal traditions, but do not require the presence of the monarch or a member of the Royal Family to take place (though Royal Family members may attend from time to time).

Attended by the Royal Family

Royal Maundy Service

Thursday before Easter

Rooted in an ancient Christian ceremony, the Royal Maundy religious service is held on the Thursday before Easter, the day commemorating the Last Supper and Jesus' washing of the disciples' feet. From medieval times until the late 17th century kings and queens regnant imitated Jesus' actions by washing the feet of a chosen group of poor people in public. Starting in the 18th century however monarchs began instead to give money to people in charitable need during religious ceremonies. Today the act has become purely ceremonial. The monarch hands out a small bag of commemorative coins to a group of recipients that has been chosen by the diocese where the ceremony takes place, based on their service to the community. Queen Elizabeth II has established the practice during her reign of holding the ceremony at a different church or cathedral in the UK every year, and she has herself performed the ceremony at every Anglican cathedral in England. The Maundy coins handed out are struck specifically for the occasion, and recipients receive them based on the age of the monarch: i.e., during the Maundy service held on the year Elizabeth II was 80 years old, she handed out a bag containing 80 pence worth of commemorative coins to 80 men and 80 women.

State Opening of Parliament

May/June

In the most visible display of the monarchy's constitutional functions, every year the monarch opens the new session of Parliament by travelling in state from Buckingham Palace to the Palace of Westminster and giving a speech in the House of Lords before the assembled Houses of Lords and Commons. The origins of the event go back to medieval times and rituals associated with it have been refined and added over the centuries, most recently by Edward VII between 1901 and 1910, and by Elizabeth II during her reign. The event was traditionally held in November/December until 2012 when it was moved to May/June.

Trooping the colour/The Monarch's Birthday Parade

Second/Third Sunday in June

The biggest royal celebration in the calendar year is the Trooping the Colour ceremony, a military parade that has been held to celebrate the monarch's birthday since 1748. Originally held on the actual birthday of the sovereign, since the reign of Edward VII—who was born in November—the ceremony has been held in June to take advantage of good weather. The monarch travels from Buckingham Palace between crowds assembled in The Mall to Horse Guards Parade where the main military exercise is held, and where he/she reviews the troops and receives royal salutes. Afterwards the monarch usually holds another review in front of Buckingham Palace, then joins the rest of the Royal Family on the Buckingham Palace balcony to greet the crowds and watch a Royal Air Force fly-past.

Garter Day

Third week of June

On the Monday of Ascot week (see below), the monarch holds a luncheon at Windsor Castle for the knights of the Order of the Garter, the oldest order of chivalry in the world founded at Windsor in 1348 (see *British Honours and Decorations*). Afterwards the knights and the monarch—everyone dressed in ceremonial robes and plumed hats—walk in procession among crowds gathered in the Windsor Castle courtyard to St George's Chapel, where they take part in the annual Order of the Garter service. Although dating back to medieval times, the present ceremonies were only revived by George VI in 1948 after they had fallen into disuse in the 18th century. Similar religious services for other chivalric orders attended by the monarch are held for the Order of the Thistle in Edinburgh; for the order of the Bath in Westminster Abbey, London; and for the Order of the British Empire at St Paul's Cathedral, London.

Royal Ascot

Third week of June

Ever since Queen Anne founded Ascot racecourse in 1711 the Royal Family has been involved in its most famous event, the five-day Royal Ascot meeting during the third week of June. On each of the five days the Royal Family opens the races by parading on the race track in horse-drawn carriages, a tradition started by George IV in the 1820s. They also present awards to some of the race winners. The Royal Family spend their time at Ascot in the Royal Enclosure, where a strict dress code is enforced, and admission is by sponsorship from existing members only.

Garden Parties

May-July

Garden parties were instituted by Queen Victoria in the 1860s and since then they have evolved into an informal event where people who have contributed to their community or the nation can meet the monarch and other members of the Royal Family. Guests lists are usually submitted to the palace by charities and other organisations, both national and local, ensuring that guests come from a wide spectrum. At least three garden parties are held in the gardens of Buckingham Palace each year, and one in the gardens of Holyroodhouse in Edinburgh, with an estimated combined total of 30,000 people attending the events. Held in the afternoon, the monarch and other members of the Royal Family arrive at 4pm and meet guests until 6pm, the national anthem playing as they arrive and when they leave. Special Garden Parties are also held to celebrate special anniversaries or charity causes.

Remembrance Day

Second Sunday in November

The Royal Family leads national commemorations on Remembrance Day, on the second Sunday in November, when all soldiers fallen since World War I are remembered. The main ceremony is held at the Cenotaph in London where the Royal Family is joined by politicians, the military, religious representatives and hundreds of veterans. The ceremony starts with a two minute silence after which the monarch lays a wreath at the foot of the Cenotaph, followed by other senior Royals doing likewise. The Royal Family also attends other related events in the same week including the Festival of Remembrance at the Royal Albert Hall.

The Diplomatic Reception

November/December

The biggest reception held at Buckingham Palace every year, this event is the highlight of the diplomatic calendar in Britain and is attended by over 1,500 people representing over 130 countries. During the event the monarch and other senior members of the Royal Family are formally presented to ambassadors and dignitaries in order of diplomatic precedence whilst moving through the state room of Buckingham Palace. Members of the Royal Family are expected to dress in their most formal evening wear, with the women wearing regalia, but because of the sensitive nature of diplomatic protocol no pictures or film are ever taken of the actual event.

Royal Variety Performance

November/December

George V instituted the first Royal Command Performance in 1912, held as a fundraiser for the Variety Artists Benevolent Fund, and the yearly charity event still continues to be held today. The performance usually takes place at the beginning of the Christmas season, either in London or selected theatres across the country, and is always attended either by the monarch or a senior royal. The choice of acts performing before the Royal Family is meant to reflect the wide spectrum of entertainment popular at the time, and past acts have included the Beatles, Luciano Pavarotti, Michael Jackson and Lady Gaga. The show is aired on British television as well as many other Commonwealth Countries and claims an audience of over 150 million viewers every year.

Not Usually Attended by the Royal Family

Commemoration of the Execution of Charles I

Last Sunday in January

Royalist members of the English Civil War Society, dressed in period costumes, commemorate the execution of Charles I on 30 January 1649 by marching from St James' Palace to Whitehall and holding an open-air service and review in Horse Guards Parade. A wreath is usually laid by the statue of Charles I in Trafalgar Square, or by the Banqueting House near the place where Charles was beheaded. The anniversary of Charles' death was observed in the Church of England on 30 January until 1859 as the Feast of St Charles the Martyr.

Ceremony of the Lilies and the Roses

21 May

Every year since 1923 students from Eton College in Windsor and King's College in Cambridge—both founded by Henry VI—gather on the anniversary of Henry's death at the Wakefield Tower in the Tower of London where he was murdered while praying in 1471. During a small ceremony at sundown the students lay separate flowers on the spot where Henry is said to have died: lilies are laid by Eton students and roses by King's College students. The ceremony is private and not opened to the public.

Oak Apple Day

29 May

A public holiday from 1660 until 1859, Oak Apple Day celebrated the restoration of the monarchy on 29 May 1660 with the accession of Charles II, after the monarchy had been previously abolished by the Republican Commonwealth in 1649. It took its name from an episode in the life of Charles II when he was defeated at the Battle of Worcester in 1651 and evaded capture by hiding in the trunk of an oak tree. The date was also significant as 29 May was Charles' own birthday. Oak Apple Day is still celebrated today at the Royal Hospital Chelsea, London, founded by Charles II in 1681, where it is called Founder's Day. A statue of Charles II in the courtyard of the hospital is garlanded with oak leaves for the occasion, and a member of the Royal Family sometimes visits on the day to meet former soldiers living on hospital grounds.

Swan Upping

July

By tradition, swans in English waters are owned by the monarch, though he or she can grant licenses for ownership to others. On the river Thames swans ownership is divided between the monarch and two City of London Livery companies: the Vintners Company and the Dyers Company. Every year in the third week of July a boating party of Swan Uppers, dressed in ceremonial clothes, travels up the Thames to mark the City liveries' swans from the Queen's Swans. In the past this was done by marking the swans' beaks, but this is done now by placing ID rings on the birds' legs. The original purpose of Swan Upping was to claim ownership of the swans for the purpose of eating them. Today the ceremony is used mainly to check the health of the swans' population in the Thames, though ownership is still marked. Monarchs or other members of the Royal Family do not usually attend Swan Upping however Elizabeth II attended the event in 2012, the first time in centuries that a monarch had done so.

The Cutting of the Christmas Glastonbury Thorn

December

Each year at the beginning of December a budding sprig from the Holy Thorn of Glastonbury, Somerset—a hawthorn that legend says was planted by Joseph of Arimathea—is cut in a small ceremony and sent to the monarch to adorn the royal table at Christmas time. The tradition started in the reign of James I when a sprig was sent to his wife, Anne of Denmark. The Glastonbury Holy Hawthorn variety is unusual in that after its usual blossoming in May it flowers a second time in December.

The National Anthem: *God Save the Queen*

The British National Anthem, *God Save the Queen* is the oldest complete national anthem in use in the world today. It is alternately known as *God Save the King/God Save the Queen* depending on the gender of the monarch on the throne at the time.

History

The origin of the music of *God Save the Queen* is shrouded in mystery. Some attribute it to a Dr John Bull (c.1563-1628) who might have written it in Antwerp in the early 17th century. Others say the music was written by French-Italian composer Jean-Baptiste Lully (1632-1687) for King Louis XIV of France in 1686. Others still say that, as with many other traditional tunes, it originated as a tavern drinking song.

The adoption of the song as the National Anthem arose during a time of national crisis, the Jacobite Rebellion of 1745. During the rebellion Charles Edward Stuart, the exiled Stuart pretende known as Bonnie Prince Charlie, invaded Britain in the hope of capturing the throne, and in September 1745 he defeated the army of King George II at Prestopans, Scotland. Following this battle patriotic fervour swept across England, and it was in this atmosphere that a tune called *God Save the King* began to be played in London theatres to rally the crowds. Traditionally, the first airing is set to have occurred on 28 September 1745, one week after the Battle of Prestopans, at the Theatre Royal in Drury Lane, sung to an arrangement by Thomas Arne, the writer of *Rule Britannia*. Its success spread to other theatres and out into the streets, and soon the song was being spontaneously sung whenever the King arrived to a public engagement, starting therefore a practice that survives to this day. The writer of the lyrics is unknown, and it is speculated that the words might have been written by players and writers working at Drury Lane and Covent Garden theatres in September 1745. When the first published version of the lyrics appeared in *The Gentleman's Magazine* in October 1745 it was credited 'as sung at both playhouses' in London.

As with many aspects of British tradition, there has never been a public proclamation or law making *God Save the Queen* the country's National Anthem. Its adoption came through the spontaneous embrace of the London and then British crowds in 1745 and in the years afterwards. It is a song that was first chosen by the people, and that only later became part of royal protocol and national tradition. The Jacobite Rebellion that served as the catalyst for the emergence of *God Save the King* was eventually defeated in April 1746 at the Battle of Culloden.

Verses

Because the adoption of *God Save the King* as the National Anthem happened through spontaneous popular use, there is no authorized version of its lyrics. However the following three verses, originally published in 1745, have become standard over the centuries. Only the first and third verse are generally sung. The references to the gender of the monarch change as required.

Verse 1

God save our gracious **King/Queen**!
Long live our noble **King/Queen**!
God save the **King/Queen**!
Send **him/her** victorious,
Happy and glorious,

Long to reign over us,
God save the **King/Queen**.

Verse 2 (usually not sung)

O Lord our God arise,
Scatter **his/her** enemies,
And make them fall:
Confound their politics,
Frustrate their knavish tricks,
On Thee our hopes we fix:
God save us all.

Verse 3

Thy choicest gifts in store
On **him/her** be pleased to pour,
Long may **he/she** reign.
May **he/she** defend our laws,
And ever give us cause,
To sing with heart and voice,
God save the **King/Queen**.

Alternative or additional verses have occasionally been introduced into the Anthem, for example in 1746, 1800, 1836 and 1919, but they never gained permanent usage.

Use

The National Anthem is played at the beginning or end of major public occasions including sporting competitions, military parades, political gatherings, and of course most royal events. On many of these occasions only the first verse is sung. On special occasions, like major royal ceremonies, both the first and third verses are sung. The National Anthem is normally also played when members of the Royal Family undertake official public engagements. Monarchs and their consorts are saluted with the entire Anthem, while other members of the Royal Family are saluted with only the first six bars (the first three lines of a verse). The first six bars are also played as the Vice Regal Salute for Governor-Generals in some Commonwealth Realms.

There is no proscribed way to stand or behave when the National Anthem is played, however a general practice has arisen for people to stand motionless with arms laid flat against the body, palm facing inward, and face staring forward. The monarch is expected to stand silently whilst the Anthem is played, and refrain from singing the song since the words are about himself/herself. Other members of the Royal Family are expected to sing it.

Other Uses

Over the last 200 years the success of *God Save the King/Queen* has prompted other countries to adopt its music, and create national anthems and patriotic songs of their own. National songs that have used its music include:

Past uses:

Heil dir im Siegerkranz, the national anthem of Prussia from 1795 to 1871, and afterwards of Imperial Germany from 1871 to 1918.

Molitva Russkikh, the first national anthem of Russia used between 1816 and 1833.

Bevare Gud vår Kung, the national anthem of Sweden used between 1805 and 1893.

Rufst Du, Mein Vaterland, the national anthem of Switzerland used between the 1850s and 1961.

Eldgamla Ísafold, Iceland's unofficial national anthem during the 19th century.

E Ola Ke Alii Ke Akua the national anthem of independent Hawaii between 1860 and 1866.

Current uses:

Kongesangen, the Royal Anthem of Norway, adopted in 1906 and still sung at royal occasions.

Oben Am Jungen Rhein, the current national anthem of Liechtenstein, adopted in 1920.

My Country, 'Tis of Thee, an American patriotic song with lyrics written in 1831.

God Save the Queen also remains the Royal Anthem played for Governor Generals in Commonwealth realms.

The Royal Residences

The monarchy of the United Kingdom possesses today more royal residences than any other European monarchy. These royal residences are used by the monarch and members of the Royal Family both as homes and to carry out functions associated with the monarchy. A list of these properties follows in the next pages, divided in the following categories:

- **Current State Residences:** state-owned palaces and houses that are currently used by the monarch and other members of the Royal Family.

- **Current Private Residences:** properties that are owned privately by the monarch and other members of the Royal Family, and are currently being used.

- **Historic Residences:** palaces, castles and houses that were royal residences in the past and remain Crown properties today, but that are no longer inhabited by the Royal Family.

- **Lost Residences:** palaces, castles and houses that were royal residences in the past, but that have disappeared today, either completely or with very few structures surviving.

CURRENT STATE RESIDENCES

State residences are palaces and houses that are owned by the state via the Crown. They are used as official residences for members of the Royal Family as well as for state functions and official ceremonial. They also often house offices of the Royal Household. They include the following residences.

Buckingham Palace, London

The Principal Residence of the Monarch in London, and Headquarters of the Monarchy.

History: An original smaller palace, known as Buckingham House, stood on the site in the 18th century. It was bought by George III for his growing family in 1761 and given as a residence to his wife Queen Charlotte. The present palace was built by George IV in the 1820s-1830s and was first used as a residence by Queen Victoria in 1837. The iconic balcony was installed by Victoria in the 1850s, and the present façade added in 1913 by George V. The palace was slightly damaged during World War II, and the Chapel that was destroyed during bombing was later turned into the Queen's Gallery, showcasing artworks from the Royal Collection to the public. Buckingham Palace has served as the focus of national celebrations for the last 100 years, including the end of the First and Second World Wars. The state rooms were first opened to the public in 1993.
Uses: The Palace is world-known as the official residence of the British monarch, and is the London residence of other members of the Royal Family. It is the venue for state visits, investitures, functions, audiences and garden parties. It continues to serve as the focus of national celebrations including royal weddings and jubilees.
Visiting: The State rooms are open between July and September. The Queen's Gallery and Royal Mews annexes are open all year round.

St James's Palace, London

The Official Senior Palace of the Monarchy

History: Built by Henry VIII in the 1530s on the site of a previous leper hospital from which it takes its name, St James's Palace was originally conceived as a leisure palace where Tudors and Stuarts could relax informally away from Whitehall (see *Lost Palaces* below). It was the birthplace of several Stuart monarchs in the 17th century, and the official court palace of the monarchy between the 1690s and 1830s. Its Chapel Royal has been the site of many weddings and christening over the last 300 years, including the weddings of George IV, Queen Victoria and George V.
Uses: As the oldest London royal residence still in use, St James's Palace is considered the official site of the royal court: foreign ambassadors are still accredited to the Court of St James's. The palace serves as administrative centre of the British monarchy and contains offices of the Royal Household. It is the venue of occasional state functions, and religious ceremonies are held in the Chapel Royal. The accession proclamations of new sovereigns to the public are made from the Proclamation Gallery overlooking Friary Court.
Visiting: The palace is not open to the public. The Chapel Royal is open to the public for religious services at certain times during the year.

Clarence House, London

Official Residence of the Prince of Wales

History: Built in the 1820s as a wing of St James' Palace, Clarence House was first used as a residence by William, Duke of Clarence, later King William IV, from whom the House takes its name. After his death in 1837 it was in turn a residence for Queen Victoria's mother, two of Victoria's sons (Prince Alfred and Prince Arthur), and Princess Elizabeth in 1950-1952 before her accession as Queen Elizabeth II. Thereafter, it famously became the residence for 50 years of Queen Elizabeth the Queen Mother, who received well-wishers by the entrance gates every year on 4 August for her birthday.

Uses: Currently the official London residence of the Prince of Wales and Duchess of Cornwall, it also houses offices of the Prince of Wales' household. It is often used by the Prince for receptions and social functions.

Visiting: The House is open during August for guided tours.

Kensington Palace, London

Official residence of the Duke and Duchess of Cambridge, and Prince Harry.

History: The palace was first bought and expanded by William III & Mary II in the 1690s and became the main London residence of monarchs from then until the 1760s. It was the childhood home of Queen Victoria and subsequently the residence of many royal family members until the 20th century. More recently, it was the official residence of Princess Margaret until 2002, of Prince Charles and Diana in the 1980s-1990s, and the principal mourning site for the death of Diana, Princess of Wales, in 1997.

Uses: The Palace is divided in two areas. The historic state apartments are open to the public as a visitor attraction. The private apartments serve as the official London residence of the Duke and Duchess of Cambridge, Prince Harry, and other royals. The palace also holds offices of different royal households, and is the site of receptions and functions.

Visiting: The historic state apartments are managed by Historic Royal Palaces and are open to visitors all year round. The private royal residences and offices are not open to the public.

Windsor Castle, Berkshire

The Oldest Continuously Occupied Royal Residence

History: The largest occupied castle in the world, Windsor Castle was originally built by William the Conqueror in the 1060s and later greatly expanded by Edward III in the 14th century. Edward founded the Order of the Garter there, and Edward IV, Henry VII and Henry VIII built St George's Chapel between the 1470s and 1540s. After the English Civil War the royal apartments were rebuilt by Charles II, and later George IV rebuilt and embellished the entire castle in the early 19th century. The castle was the site of George III's final 10-year confinement for madness, and the place where Prince Albert died in 1861. During the late 19th century it was the birthplace of many descendants of Queen Victoria and a gathering place for Europe's royal families. George V renamed the current royal dynasty after the castle in 1917. Part of the complex was destroyed by a large fire in 1992 and subsequently rebuilt. The castle and surrounding grounds have hosted the burial places of the Royal Family since 1810.

Uses: Currently the main weekend retreat of Queen Elizabeth II when she is in London, Windsor Castle is also used as her principal residence for a month around Easter and during Ascot Week in June. It is the site of the yearly ceremonies for the Order of the Garter, and an occasional venue for state visits, investitures and receptions. The Round Tower holds the Royal Archives, and the private royal apartments house the Royal Library. St George's Chapel is used for royal weddings and funerals, and the Frogmore Burial Grounds in Windsor Home Park are currently being used for royal family burials. The parkland surrounding the Castle contains other smaller royal residences including **Frogmore House** and **Royal Lodge**. **Fort Belvedere** and **Cumberland Lodge**, former royal residences still owned by the Crown, are currently being leased to tenants for other uses.

Visiting: The Castle's precincts and State rooms are open to visitors throughout the year. St George's Chapel is open on most days to visitors, and on Sundays for services. Frogmore House and the

Frogmore Burial Grounds are open to visitors on a few selected days during the year. The private royal apartments in the Castle and other private lodgings in the park are not open to the public.

Palace of Holyroodhouse, Edinburgh, Scotland
Official Residence of the Monarch in Scotland

History: Originally the site of an Abbey, the buildings began to be used by Scottish monarchs in the 14th century. It later became the main residence of the Stuart monarchs, including James IV and Mary Queen of Scots. Rebuilt by Charles II after the Restoration, it fell into disuse after the union of Scotland and England into one kingdom in 1707. It was briefly used as a base by Bonnie Prince Charlie during the Jacobite Rebellion of 1745. The Palace was completely renovated by George IV in the 1820s, and it became again a centre of Scottish royal court life during Queen Victoria's reign. George V instituted a program of official yearly ceremonies when the monarch would be in residence at the Palace which still continues today.
Uses: Investitures, receptions and garden parties are held once a year during Holyrood Week (June/July) when the monarch is in residence. Official ceremonies are also held by the Prince of Wales, as Duke of Rothesay, one week per year. Various other engagements and events are held throughout the year. The private royal apartments in the Palace are also used by the Royal Family when visiting Scotland.
Visiting: The state apartments, grounds, and the Queen's Gallery annex are open to visitors throughout the year. The Royal Family private apartments are not open to the public.

Hillsborough Castle, County Down, Northern Ireland

Official Residence of the Monarch in Northern Ireland

History: Originally built as a country house in the 18th century, the property was bought by the government in 1922 as a viceregal residence after the formation of Northern Ireland. It has been used by the Royal Family since the 1920s for ceremonial functions while in Northern Ireland, and also occasionally for holidays. It was the venue of several stages of the Northern Ireland peace process in the last 30 years.

Uses: The Castle is a working residence used by the Secretary of State for Northern Ireland, the official representative of the monarch in the country. It is used by the Royal Family when they visit Northern Ireland and serves as a venue for official functions and receptions.

Visiting: Guided tours are given on selected days from April to September, and by private arrangement at other times of the year. The gardens are open all year round.

CURRENT PRIVATE RESIDENCES

Private residences are palaces and houses that are owned directly by members of the Royal Family, and that are not subject to state control like the residences that are owned by the Crown. They were originally bought privately by individuals, they are passed down from person to person as inheritance, and are managed directly by the Royal Family. They include the following residences.

Sandringham House, Norfolk

History: Bought and expanded by Albert Edward, Prince of Wales (later Edward VII) in 1860s, it has been the birthplace of several Royal Family members and the place of death of kings George V and George VI. During the 20th century it became the Christmas retreat of the monarch and was the site of the first radio and TV Christmas messages.
Uses: The House is still used today by the Royal Family for Christmas celebrations and winter hunting, and serves as the official base of the monarch between December and February. The Sandringham Estate is privately owned by the Royal Family and used for farming, forestry and livestock breeding throughout the year.
Visiting: The house, gardens and a small museum are usually opened to visitors from April to November.

Balmoral Castle, Aberdeenshire, Scotland

History: Bought by Queen Victoria and Prince Albert in 1852 and rebuilt in 1856, Balmoral became a favourite retreat of Queen Victoria during her widowhood. It has continued to remain the summer residence of every monarch since the late 19th century.

Uses: It is used as a summer retreat by various members of the Royal Family who stay in various residences on the Balmoral estate. Occasionally the Castle is used to receive official foreign visits when the monarch is in residence. The Balmoral Estate, privately owned by the Royal Family, covers 50,000 acres and is used throughout the year for farming, hunting, fishing and hospitality. It includes forests and nature trails open to the public.
Visiting: The grounds and gardens, the Castle Ballroom and an exhibition area are open to visitors from April to July. All other rooms in the castle are not open to the public. Other parts of the estate are open all year round.

Other private residences used by individual members of the Royal Family include **Highgrove House**, country residence of the Prince of Wales, and **Gatcombe Park**, country residence of Princess Anne, both of them in Gloucestershire. **Bagshot Park**, a residence in Surrey owned by the Crown since the 18th century, is currently the private home of Prince Edward, Earl of Wessex, and his family.

HISTORIC RESIDENCES

Historic residences are palaces and houses that were official residences of the Royal Family in the past but are no longer inhabited today. Some of them, like the Tower of London and the Palace of Westminster, are still considered royal palaces and are used for functions associated with the monarchy. Others survive simply as visitor attractions. Except for the Royal Pavilion in Brighton, all the residences listed below are still owned by the Crown.

The Palace of Westminster, London

History: The oldest royal palace in England, originally built by Edward the Confessor in the 11th century, Westminster was the principal royal residence of English monarchs throughout the medieval period. It was the meeting place of the first parliaments in the 14th century, and after Henry VIII moved the royal court to Whitehall the palace became the permanent home of Parliament and the law courts. Guy Fawkes and his accomplices tried to blow up the building in the failed Gunpowder Plot of 1605, and Charles I tried by arrest MPs in it by forcing himself into the House of Commons in 1642, precipitating the English Civil War (no monarch has entered the House of Commons since). The original palace was destroyed by fire in 1834 with only a few buildings surviving including Westminster Hall, built in 1097 and one of the oldest medieval buildings in Europe. The new palace was later rebuilt in Gothic style and designed to accommodate the great ceremonies of state.
Current Use: Although used by the Houses of Parliament, the Palace retains its status as a royal residence. The monarch attends the yearly State Opening of Parliament at the palace when he or she delivers a speech from the Sovereign Throne in the House of Lords, which is the only throne in the realm in practical use.
Visiting: The palace is open to visitors for guided tours most of the year. Members of the public can attend debates in both Houses.

The Tower of London

History: The British monarchy's most famous fortress was originally built by William the Conqueror in the 1060s and expanded throughout the medieval period. Fortress, treasury, residence, armoury and mint, possession of the Tower was key to a monarch's power until the 17th century. It became a much feared prison during the Wars of the Roses, was the site of the Princes in the Tower's disappearance in 1483, and it saw the execution of Anne Boleyn, Catherine Howard and Lady Jane Grey during the Tudor period. It has been home to the Crown Jewels since the 14th century, and was the location of the Royal Mint until 1810. It was also the site of the earliest zoo in London. A visitor's attraction since the 17th century, the Tower also remained a prison and military barracks until the mid 20th century.
Current Use: Visitor attraction managed by Historic Royal Palaces. The Tower however still retains royal functions overseen by the Constable of the Tower, including the safekeeping of the Crown Jewels. It is home to the Beefeaters guards who both guard the Tower, act as stewards to visitors, and who live on site.
Visiting: Open all year round.

Edinburgh Castle, Scotland

History: Scotland's most historic building, Edinburgh's fortress was the centre of Scottish royal life and principal royal residence of Scottish Kings from the 12th to the 15th century. The object of much fighting by foreign invaders and Scottish factions, it was also the birthplace of King James VI/I. His son Charles I was the last monarch to stay at the Castle in 1633. After the Restoration in 1660 the Castle became home to a full time military garrison until 1923.
Current Use: Visitor attraction managed by Historic Scotland. The Castle retains a military garrison and is the location of the Scottish

National War Memorial, the Crown Jewels of Scotland, and the Stone of Scone.
Visiting: Open all year round.

Hampton Court Palace, Surrey

History: Thomas Wolsey built the original Tudor Palace south of London in the 1510s before Henry VIII appropriated in 1528 and enlarged it to accommodate the royal court. Henry's third wife, Jane Seymour, died at Hampton Court after giving birth to Edward VI there, and Henry also wed his sixth wife, Catherine Parr, at the palace. It was then used by Mary I, Elizabeth I, and greatly expanded by William III and Mary II. It was later embellished by George II who was the last monarch to live there. Queen Victoria opened the Palace to visitors in 1838.
Current Use: Visitor attraction managed by Historic Royal Palaces, who have their headquarters there. The Palace is furnished with royal treasures and items loaned from the Royal Collection. It also houses the Royal School of Needlework.
Visiting: Open all year round.

The Banqueting House, London

History: The only surviving part of the Palace of Whitehall (see *Lost Palaces* below), the Banqueting Hall was built by Inigo Jones for James I in 1619-1622, and was the first neoclassical building ever built in Britain. In the 1630s Charles I commissioned Rubens to paint a large series of canvases on its ceiling showing the divine right of kings, but ironically it was right in front of this building that Charles was later beheaded in 1649. Charles II and James II used the building for ceremonies of state, and William III and Mary II accepted their crowns from Parliament there in 1689 during the

Glorious Revolution. After the Palace of Whitehall burned down in 1694, the building was used as a Chapel Royal until 1893.
Current Use: Visitor attraction managed by Historic Royal Palaces. Also used for various receptions and events.
Visiting: Open all year round.

Kew Palace, London

History: Originally built in the 1630s as a private residence, this Dutch-style house was first used to house some of the children of George II in the 1720s. It then became one of the residences of Frederick Prince of Wales together with a nearby property called the White House. His son George III used both residences as a country retreat and to educate his children. He later was interned in both houses during his episodes of madness in the 1780s and 1800s. Kew Palace continued to be used by the royal family throughout George III's reign, and his wife Queen Charlotte died there in 1818. The house was subsequently abandoned and opened to the public by Queen Victoria in the 1890s, after which it was gradually restored. The nearby White House was demolished by 1802.
Current Use: Visitor attraction managed by Historic Royal Palaces. The house is furnished with original family items loaned from the Royal Collection.
Visiting: Open usually April to September.

White Lodge, Richmond Park, London

History: Built as a hunting lodge for George II in 1730, the house was later expanded and used as a residence by two of his daughters, Princess Amelia and Princess Mary. It was used briefly by Queen Victoria and Prince Albert to educate their son Albert, Prince of Wales, in the 1850s and later it was granted in the 1870s to Victoria's cousin, Princess Mary Adelaide, the mother of the future Queen

Mary of Teck. Mary grew up in the house and later stayed at White Lodge to give birth to her firstborn son, the future Edward VIII, in 1894. Mary's second son, the future George VI, and his wife Elizabeth Bowes-Lyon spent the first two years of their marriage in the 1920s living at White Lodge, after which the house began to be leased out privately.

Current Use: The building was leased for permanent use to the Royal Ballet School in 1955.

Visiting: Tours of the house and visits to a small museum on site can be arranged by contacting the Royal Ballet School.

Royal Pavilion, Brighton, West Sussex

History: This fanciful palace was built by George, Prince Regent as a seaside retreat in the 1810s, to indulge in his private pleasures. The Pavilion was built in extravagant Indian-Saracenic style on the outside and contains lavish Chinese interiors. It was one of George's principal residences during his later reign as King George IV, and the site of famous entertainments. After his death it was used by William IV as a family retreat, but was disliked by Queen Victoria who sold it to the town of Brighton after removing most of its furniture to Buckingham Palace and Windsor Castle.

Current Use: Visitor attraction managed by Brighton & Hove City Council. The council has restored much of the interior to its original appearance under George IV, and many original items on loan from the Royal Collection have been returned to the Pavilion.

Visiting: Open all year round.

Marlborough House, London

History: The house was first built by Sarah Churchill, Duchess of Marlborough, the great favorite of Queen Anne, and was completed in 1711. It was the London residence of the Dukes of Marlborough

until it came to the Crown in 1817. It was the home of Queen Adelaide after she became Queen Dowager in 1837, and then the home between 1863 and 1901 of Albert, Prince of Wales (the future Edward VII) who made it a famous centre of London society. Most of his children, including the future George V, were born there. It then became the London residence of Queen Alexandra and Queen Mary after they became Queen Dowagers. After Queen Mary died in 1953, Elizabeth II loaned it to the Commonwealth Secretariat but it remains a Crown property today.
Current Use: The building continues to be used by the Commonwealth as its Headquarters and Secretariat.
Visiting: Not open to visitors except for a weekend in September. Special group tours can be arranged upon request at other times in the year.

Osborne House, Isle of Wight

History: Queen Victoria and Prince Albert first bought this house in 1845 so that their family could enjoy a degree of normal life outside of London. The original house was completely rebuilt to Prince Albert's designs in the Italianate style. The estate had its own private beach, as well as a specially designed cottage on the grounds where royal children learned how to farm and cook. After Albert's death, Victoria spent much of her time at Osborne and died there in 1901. Her son Edward VII bequeathed most the house to the nation in 1902 after which it was turned for a brief period into a naval college. Queen Victoria's private apartments however were kept separate and sealed until they were finally opened to the public in 1954.
Current Use: Visitor attraction managed by English Heritage. The house is furnished with original family items loaned from the Royal Collection.
Visiting: Open all year round.

LOST RESIDENCES

Many more royal residences besides the ones listed above have existed in England in the past, including some of the most famous and lavish palaces ever used by the monarchy. Most of them have disappeared completely over the last 500 years, whilst for a few only some structures survive. Listed below is a selection of these lost residences including their fates.

Havering Palace, Essex

History: Havering, near London, was a royal possession since Anglo-Saxon times. William the Conqueror and its successors expanded the site into a small country palace and it became a favourite retreat of medieval English kings. Beginning with Queen Eleanor of Provence in the 13th century the palace was granted for the special use of Queens Consorts, with Queen Joan of Navarre dying there in 1437. James I and Charles I were the last monarchs to stay at Havering in the 17th century.
Fate: Havering Palace fell into disrepair during the English Civil War and was later sold off. Over the following centuries it became a ruin and was demolished in the early 19th century.

Woodstock and Beaumont Palaces, Oxfordshire

History: Henry I built both palaces near Oxford in the 1120s-1130s, Beaumont as a residence and Woodstock as a hunting lodge. Henry II expanded Woodstock into a palace and made use of both places, and his sons, kings Richard I and John, were both born at Beaumont. Woodstock Palace continued to be used as a royal residence by most medieval kings until the late 14th century, and was the birthplace of Edward the Black Prince in 1330. Elizabeth I was kept in house

arrests at Woodstock in 1554-55 during the reign of her half-sister Mary I.
Fate: Beaumont Palace was sold by Edward I in 1275 and later turned into a monastery which was dissolved during the Reformation in the 1530s. Woodstock Palace fell into neglect under the early Stuart kings and was much damaged by Parliament's forces during the English Civil War. The derelict Woodstock site was eventually given by Queen Anne in 1704 to John Churchill, Duke of Marlborough, as a reward for his military victory at the Battle of Blenheim. The last remnants of Woodstock Palace were razed in 1720 and Blenheim Palace was built on the site. The palace continues to be the residence of the Dukes of Marlborough and was the birthplace of Winston Churchill in 1874.

King's Langley Palace, Hertfordshire

History: The original manor of Langley, north of London, was first bought and rebuilt by Eleanor of Castile, wife of King Edward I, in the 1270s. It later became a favourite country residence of both Edward II and Edward III, whose son Edmund of Langley, the first Duke of York, was born there. Edward III also used the palace as a safe place to retire during the Black Plague in 1348-49. The palace was later used by Richard II and by subsequent Queens Consort until the late 15th century.
Fate: The palace became neglected under the Tudor monarchs and had fallen into decay by the reign of Elizabeth I. Only some ruins had survived by the 19th century, and even those have disappeared today.

Eltham Palace, Kent

History: This medieval palace near London was first acquired by Edward I and later became one of Edward III's favourite country

estates. It was frequently used by 15th century kings to host their Christmas celebrations there. Edward IV built a new great hall for the palace in the 1470s. The young Henry VIII grew up at Eltham and was famously instructed by the humanist Erasmus there.
Fate: The Palace was slowly abandoned after Henry VIII died and was stripped of much of its materials following the English Civil War. Its buildings were then converted in farming tenements and the Great Hall was used as a barn. Most buildings were finally pulled down in the 19th century, however the Great Hall has survived and can still be seen today.

Richmond Palace, Surrey

History: The site, on the Thames near London, was originally occupied by Sheen Palace, a medieval royal manor first occupied by Edward III who died there in 1377. Sheen was a favourite residence of Richard II and his wife Anne of Bohemia, and after Anne died in 1394 a distraught Richard had much of the residence razed to the ground. Henry V and Henry VI later rebuilt the palace but their buildings were mostly destroyed by a fire in 1497. Henry VII rebuilt Sheen and renamed it Richmond, and the new palace became one of his favourite residences. It was also a favourite palace of Queen Elizabeth I who died there in 1603. The early Stuart kings used it for hunting and to house royal children, especially Princes of Wales.
Fate: The Palace was sold by Parliament at the end of the Civil War and was dismantled for materials. A few buildings survived which were later used occasionally as royal lodgings during the reign of Charles II, however those also disappeared in the 18th century. Only the gatehouse from the Tudor palace remains today.

Greenwich Palace, London

History: Humphrey, Duke of Gloucester, brother of King Henry V, built an original manor at Greenwich, near London, in the 1430s and enclosed a park around it. This manor was later expanded by queens Margaret of Anjou and Elizabeth Woodville, and then completely rebuilt by Henry VII in 1499 to become one of the grandest palaces in Europe. It was the birthplace of Henry VIII and the site of many important events in his reign: his marriage to Catherine of Aragon; the birth of his daughters Mary I and Elizabeth I; the arrest of Anne Boleyn; and his marriage to Anne of Cleves. The palace continued to be used by Edward VI, who died there, and by Elizabeth I. James I commissioned Inigo Jones to build the Queen's House next to the Palace in the 1610s but otherwise the main residence was little used by the early Stuarts.
Fate: The Palace had fallen into disrepair by the English Civil War when it was further neglected and used as a war prison. Charles II tried to rebuild the palace after the Restoration with little progress, and it was eventually demolished by William and Mary in the 1690s to make way for the buildings of Royal Naval Hospital. James I's Queen's House has survived.

Whitehall Palace, London

History: The original palace, the property of the medieval Archbishops of York in London, was seized by Henry VIII in 1530 from Cardinal Wolsey, and used to replace Westminster Palace which had been damaged by a fire in 1512. Henry greatly expanded the new Whitehall palace to make it the centre of both court and government, with many buildings and blocks added over 20 years. Henry married both Anne Boleyn and Jane Seymour there and later died in the palace. All later monarchs continued expanding the palace so that by the later 17th century Whitehall covered 23 acres and had become the largest royal complex in Europe. James I added

the Banqueting House to the Palace in the 1620s, Charles I was executed on its grounds in 1649, and Charles II died there in 1685.
Fate: Most the palace complex was destroyed by a fire in 1698 and the remaining parts were incorporated into later buildings. The only notable structures left today are the Banqueting House and a set of wine cellars below the Ministry of Defence. The name Whitehall survives today in the road which now passes through the area, and has become a synonym for the British government.

Royal Palace of Hatfield, Hertfordshire

History: The palace, north of London, was originally built by Henry VII's Chancellor, Cardinal Morton, in 1485. It was seized by Henry VIII during the Reformation and turned into a residence for his children, Mary, Elizabeth and Edward, who all lived there together at one point in the 1540s. Elizabeth I was staying at Hatfield when she learned of her accession as Queen in 1558 and held her first council there.
Fate: James I exchanged the palace in the early 1600s for Theobald's House, a nearby mansion in Hertfordshire owned by his chief minister Robert Cecil, Earl of Salisbury, who was given Hatfield in return. Robert Cecil tore down most of the medieval royal building to build a new Jacobean palace, the present Hatfield House. The only part of the Tudor palace surviving today is the banqueting hall which can be seen in the grounds of Hatfield House.

Oatlands Palace, Surrey

History: This palace, south of London, was built by Henry VIII on land seized from a former monastery in the 1530s, and was used as a residence for his last three Queens. Catherine Howard was married to Henry at Oatlands in 1540. Oatlands thereafter became a favourite

country retreat of Elizabeth I, James I and Charles I, who all enjoyed hunting in its large deer park.
Fate: The palace was sold by Parliament during the English Civil War and later demolished for parts in 1651. A separate building in the palace park survived and was later used as a country house by Frederick Duke of York, a son of George III. This house has now been turned into a hotel.

Nonsuch Palace, Surrey

History: This fabled palace south of London was built by Henry VIII between 1538-1541 to rival King Francis I's grand castles in France. Built in a mixture of Tudor and Renaissance styles, its outside walls were decorated with lavish carvings and reliefs, earning it the name of 'none such' equal in England. It was first sold by Mary I in 1556 but reacquired by Elizabeth I in 1592 who made it one of her last favourite residences. It then continued to be used by the early Stuart kings who hunted in its park.
Fate: The Palace fell into disrepair during the English Civil War, and afterwards Charles II gave it to one of his mistresses, Barbara Villiers, Duchess of Cleveland. She had it dismantled and sold for materials in 1682-83 to pay her gambling debts. Some of its fabled carvings were preserved and are now housed in a local country house.

Old Somerset House, London

History: Originally built by the Earl of Somerset, Lord Protector to Edward VI and confiscated by the Crown in 1552 after his fall, this house was used by Princess Elizabeth during Mary I's reign and as council chambers after she became Queen Elizabeth I. Thereafter it was expanded and became the official residence of Stuart Queens Consort including Anne of Denmark, Henrietta Maria of France and

Catherine of Braganza. The palace became associated with the Catholic religion practiced by the last two queens and lost royal favour after the Glorious Revolution of 1688-89.
Fate: The palace fell into increasing neglect and disrepair throughout the 18th century, and it was finally demolished in the 1770s. George III agreed that the site should be redeveloped as public offices, and the present Somerset House was built to house them.

Carlton House, London

History: Bought by Frederick Prince of Wales in 1732, this mansion in St James's was later granted to George Prince of Wales in 1783 (the future George IV) who over the next 40 years enlarged it and made it one of the most lavish palaces in Europe, celebrated for its architecture and works of art. Carlton House became the de-facto main royal palace during George's tenure as Prince Regent in 1811-1820, and architect John Nash built Regent Street as a grand ceremonial approach to the house from Regent's Park.
Fate: After George ascended the throne as king in 1820 he decided the house was too small for a monarch, and decided instead to build Buckingham Palace down the Mall into the main royal residence. To save money during its building stage he decided to raze Carlton House to the ground in 1827, and its interiors and artworks were divided between Buckingham Palace and Windsor Castle. Waterloo Place, Carlton House Terrace and the Duke of York's steps now stand in its place.

Walter Bagehot on Monarchy

Walter Bagehot (1826-1877) was a Victorian writer, economist and political theorist who in 1867 published *The English Constitution*, a treatise on British government and its workings. His analysis on the monarchy set out in that book remains highly influential today and some of his ideas have become principles in the theory of constitutional monarchy. A selection of passages on the monarchy in *The English Constitution* follows below.

Note: Where Bagehot mentions 'the Queen', he refers specifically to Queen Victoria as the sovereign on the throne at the time.

On the Advantages of Monarchy

'The best reason why Monarchy is a strong government is that it is an intelligible government. The mass of mankind understand it.'

'So long as the human heart is strong and the human reason weak, royalty will be strong because it appeals to diffused feeling, and republics weak because they appeal to the understanding.'

(On an elected head of state) 'If the highest post in conspicuous life were thrown open to public competition, low ambition and envy would be fearfully increased. Clever base people would strive for it, and stupid base people would envy it. Political parties mix in everything and meddle in everything; they neither would nor could permit the most honoured and conspicuous of all stations to be filled except at their pleasure.'

On the Royal Family

'A family on the throne brings down the pride of sovereignty to the level of petty life.'

'A royal family sweetens politics by the seasonable addition of nice and pretty events. It introduces irrelevant facts into the business of government, but they are facts which speak to men's bosoms.'

'A princely marriage is the brilliant edition of a universal fact, and, as such, it rivets mankind.'

On the Constitutional Role of the Monarch

'To state the matter shortly, the sovereign has, under a constitutional monarchy such as ours, three rights—the right to be consulted, the right to encourage, the right to warn. And a king of great sense and sagacity would want no others. He would find that his having no others would enable him to use these with singular effect.'

'The characteristic advantage of a constitutional king is the permanence of his place. This gives him the opportunity of acquiring a consecutive knowledge of complex transactions, but it gives only an opportunity. The king must use it. There is no royal road to political affairs: their detail is vast, disagreeable, complicated, and miscellaneous. A king, to be the equal of his ministers in discussion, must work as they work; he must be a man of business as they are men of business.'

On the Prince of Wales

'All the world and all the glory of it, whatever is most attractive, whatever is most seductive, has always been offered to the Prince of

Wales of the day, and always will be. It is not rational to expect the best virtues where temptation is applied in the most trying form at the frailest time of human life.'

Bagehot's Advices and Warnings

'The nation is divided into parties, but the crown is of no party. Its apparent separation from business is that which removes it both from enmities and from desecration, which preserves its mystery, which enables it to combine the affection of conflicting parties—to be a visible symbol of unity. We must not bring the Queen into the combat of politics, or she will cease to be reverenced by all combatants; she will become one combatant among many.'

'Above all things our royalty is to be reverenced, and if you begin to poke about it you cannot reverence it. When there is a select committee on the Queen, the charm of royalty will be gone. Its mystery is its life. We must not let in daylight upon magic.'

'The benefits of a good monarch are almost invaluable, but the evils of a bad monarch are almost irreparable.'

The Monarchy and Government

The monarch is the formal head of all government branches of the United Kingdom. As the Queen in Parliament (or King in Parliament), the monarch is part of the legislature together with the House of Commons and the House of Lords. As the Crown, he or she is the formal head of the executive. As the Fount of Justice, he or she is the head of the Judiciary (see *The Monarchy and the Law*). In practice however, the actual functions invested in these roles have long been delegated to the Prime Minister, the Cabinet, and the rest of the Parliament and Judiciary. The actual constitutional functions performed by the monarch today are either ceremonial or advisory, and in all of them he or she is meant to remain neutral between parties. These constitutional functions are described in the following pages.

THE MONARCH'S FORMAL FUNCTIONS

As Walter Bagehot famously stated in the 19th century 'the Queen reigns but she does not rule.' The monarch's 'reigning' role includes performing important formal constitutional functions including the ones below.

Appointing the Prime Minister

The monarch is the formal head of the executive government but fully delegates the day-to-day power to her Chief Minister, her 'Prime' Minister, or PM. The Prime Minister can in principle be any person, however by convention he or she must be someone who can command the confidence of the majority of the House of Commons, therefore it is usually the leader of the party that won the most seats in a general election; or, in the event of a hung parliament, the leader of a coalition of parties with a Commons majority. In the event of a Prime Minister's resignation, the monarch takes the advice of the party that commands the majority of the Commons on who the next Prime Minister should be. In all cases, someone becomes Prime Minister only after the monarch has formally asked him or her to form a government, and is then appointed to the role by the monarch. This is usually done in person in a small informal ceremony at Buckingham Palace or one of the other royal residences soon after an election or change of government.

Opening Parliament

As the most ancient part of the three branches of the legislature—Monarch, Lords and Commons—it is the monarch's right to formally open the yearly session of Parliament during the State Opening of Parliament. As the formal head of the executive, the monarch reads the government's programme of action for the coming year during the ceremony, however the speech has been written by actual head of the executive, the Prime Minister.

Dissolving Parliament

Until 2010 the monarch always dissolved Parliament on the advice of the Prime Minister for periodic general elections that had to be held at least once every five years. This practice was modified by the Fixed-Term Parliaments Act of 2011 whereby Parliaments are now dissolved routinely every five years and the date of an election fixed in advance. The monarch however still retains the formal function of dissolving Parliament and is asked to exercise it when the five-year term expires. Additionally, the monarch continues to hold the power to dissolve Parliament on the advice of the Prime Minister, if for example the government loses a vote of confidence in the House of Commons, or the House as a whole recommends that an early general election should be held as it happened in 2017. On dissolving a parliament, the monarch immediately issues writs to summon a new parliament via a general election.

Royal Assent

For an Act of Parliament to come into force, it must receive Royal Assent from the monarch. According to the current convention, the monarch gives or withholds Royal Assent only on the advice of the Cabinet. In practice however, since Parliament is meant to reflect the will of the nation, the monarch never withholds Royal Assent to laws that have been passed in good faith by a majority of the House of Commons and the House of Lords, even if the Cabinet does not support them. It is important to note however that the monarch still retains in theory the power to veto laws that could seriously harm the nation, with or without the advice of the Cabinet, should there be a need.

Royal Assent today is given in writing, and a bill becomes law once the Assent is communicated to both Houses of Parliament. The last monarch to refuse Royal Assent was Queen Anne on 11 March 1708. On the advice of her council, Anne refused to assent to a bill forming a separate militia for Scotland after the Act of Union of 1707, for fear that it would provoke disloyalty and harm the new Union.

The Privy Council

The Privy Council is the oldest legislative body in the country, its roots laying in the group of counsellors that used to advise the monarch in medieval times. Its functions were taken over by the Cabinet in the 18th century, however the Council continues to exist today as an official body used to gain royal consent for government decisions that do not require a Parliament Act. It is made up mostly of government members and usually meets once a month in

Buckingham Palace where the monarch gives official approval to measures that have already been agreed by ministers. The Privy Council's main business includes government and civil service appointments, decisions regarding the Armed Forces, and laws affecting Crown Dependencies and Overseas Territories. It also approves and reviews Royal Charters for a wide variety of institutions like universities, professional bodies, towns and cities, the Bank of England, and the BBC. Since Queen Victoria's reign meetings of the Privy Council have been held standing up to keep meetings short, with the monarch giving consent to individual measures by simply saying 'Approved'.

THE MONARCH'S CONSULTATIVE FUNCTIONS

As formulated by Walter Bagehot in the 19th century, the monarch today retains three rights: the right to be consulted, the right to encourage, and the right to warn. These consultative functions are performed in several ways including the following:

Government Red Boxes

The monarch receives government documents on a daily basis, including Cabinet papers, parliamentary summaries, diplomatic and foreign dispatches, and other state items. They are famously delivered in red boxes, and access to them is limited to the monarch and the royal Private Secretary. Some of the documents require the Monarch's formal signature, but many of them are simply sent to keep the Monarch informed on what the government and Parliament are doing in domestic and foreign affairs, and so fulfil the Monarch's right to be consulted.

Ministerial Audiences

When in London, the monarch has as a weekly audience, or meeting, with the Prime Minister, and occasional meetings are also arranged when the monarch is staying outside of London. During these audiences the Prime Minister informs the monarch about any government business, the issues of the day, and any other subject they might want to discuss. It is during these meetings that the Monarch exercises the right to warn and encourage by offering his or her views. To protect the monarch's right to warn and encourage without interference no one is present during these meetings except the monarch and the Prime Minister, no notes are taken, and no information is divulged on what has been discussed. Similar meetings are also held from time to time between the monarch and other Cabinet members, as well as with the heads of the Armed Forces. In all cases, the monarch's views and wishes are not enforceable.

SCOTLAND, WALES AND NORTHERN IRELAND

Ever since the Scottish Parliament and Welsh Assembly were established in 1999, the monarch has exercised functions for those devolved governments similar to those exercised at the national level:

- The monarch appoints the Scottish First Minister and Welsh First Minister, following elections; and holds regular audiences with each First Minister.

- The monarch grants Royal Assent to legislation passed by the Scottish Parliament and Welsh Assembly, and is sent regular documents from both assemblies in red government boxes.

- The monarch is invited to open new sessions of the assemblies after each new election. Queen Elizabeth II has opened most new sessions of the Scottish Parliament and the Welsh Assembly since 1999.

The monarch holds similar constitutional functions in Northern Ireland, like granting Royal Assent to legislation, but does not have active involvement in the workings of the Northern Ireland Assembly. The monarch does not open new sessions of the Assembly nor hold regular audiences with the Northern Irish First Minister, though occasional informal audiences may be held.

THE ROYAL FAMILY AND VOTING

Although there is no law prohibiting them from doing so, neither the monarch nor other members of the Royal Family vote in general or local elections. In general elections the monarch must remain politically neutral as he or she will be appointing as Prime Minister the leader of whichever party gets the most votes. In other elections or referendums the monarch must remain neutral to provide a focus of unity and stability across party lines. The heir to the throne must abide by the same rules binding the monarch, while other members of the Royal Family abstain from voting to protect the monarchy's political neutrality.

Most Prime Ministers for a Monarch

The office of the Prime Minister (previously, and officially, called First Lord of the Treasury) was created between 1721-1742 by Robert Walpole, who served Kings George I and George II. Since then, there have been 55 persons serving as Prime Ministers to 10 monarchs. Listed below are the three monarchs who have had the most Prime Ministers as of July 2019.

1=. George III

Reign: 1760-1820

14 Prime Ministers

W= Whig T=Tory

Thomas Pelham-Holles, Duke of Newcastle	1757-1762	W
John Stuart, Earl of Bute	1762-1763	T
George Grenville	1763-1765	W
Charles Watson-Wentworth, Marquess of Rockingham	1765-1766 1782	W
William Pitt the Elder, Earl of Chatham	1766-1768	W
Augustus FitzRoy, Duke of Grafton	1768-1770	W

Frederick, Lord North	1770-1782	T
William Petty-FitzMaurice, Earl of Sherbourne	1782-1783	W
William Cavendish-Bentinck, Duke of Portland	1783 1807-1809	W
William Pitt the Younger	1783-1801 1804-1806	T
Henry Addington	1801-1804	T
William Wyndham Grenville, Lord Grenville	1806-1807	W
Spencer Perceval	1809-1812	T
Robert Banks Jenkinson, Earl of Liverpool	1812-1827	T

1=. Elizabeth II

Reign: 1952- present

14 Prime Ministers

C= Conservative La=Labour

Sir Winston Churchill	1951-1955	C
Sir Anthony Eden	1955-1957	C
Harold Mcmillan	1957-1963	C

Sir Alec Douglas-Home	1963-1964	C
Harold Wilson	1964-1970 1974-1976	La
Edward Heath	1970-1974	C
James Callaghan	1976-1979	La
Margaret Thatcher	1979-1990	C
John Major	1990-1997	C
Tony Blair	1997-2007	La
Gordon Brown	2007-2010	La
David Cameron	2010-2016	C
Theresa May	2016-2019	C
Boris Johnson	2019-	C

3. Victoria

Reign: 1837-1901

10 Prime Ministers

W= Whig C= Conservative Li=Liberal P=Peelite

William Lamb, Viscount Melbourne	1835-1841	W
Sir Robert Peel	1841-1846	C

Lord John, Earl Russell	1846-1852	W
	1865-1866	Li
Edward Smith-Stanley, Earl of Derby	1852	C
	1858-1859	
	1866-1868	
George Hamilton-Gordon, Earl of Aberdeen	1852-1855	P
Henry John Temple, Viscount Palmerston	1855-1858	W
	1859-1865	Li
Benjamin Disraeli	1868	C
	1874-1880	
William Ewart Gladstone	1868-1874	Li
	1880-1885	
	1886	
	1892-1894	
Robert Gascoyne-Cecil, Marquess of Salisbury	1885-1886	C
	1886-1892	
	1895-1902	
Archibald Primrose, Earl of Roseberry	1894-1895	Li

Note: Despite the lower number of individuals, Queen Victoria had the greatest turnaround of Prime Ministers for any monarch: 20 changes throughout her reign.

The Oath of Allegiance

The Oath of Allegiance is used to swear loyalty to the monarch. It is required from people wishing to become British citizens as well as from individuals in the United Kingdom who wish to take up certain public or civic positions. Its most basic form was standardized in 1868 and currently is as follows:

I *(name)* swear by Almighty God that I will be faithful and bear true allegiance to Her Majesty Queen Elizabeth II, her Heirs and Successors, according to law.

The name and gender of the monarch in the oath is changed at the beginning of each reign. People of non-Christian faiths can replace the words 'I swear by Almighty God' with an acceptable alternative. Those objecting to swearing a religious oath can choose to take a solemn affirmation of allegiance instead which has slightly different words:

I *(name)* do solemnly, sincerely, and truly declare and affirm that on becoming a British citizen, I will be faithful and bear true allegiance to Her Majesty Queen Elizabeth II, her Heirs and Successors, according to law.

The Oath of Allegiance is currently required to be sworn by the following categories of people:
(Note: this is not a complete list)

New British Citizens
Taken during citizenship ceremonies.

Members of the House of Commons

Taken after a general election or by-election. Until the oath is taken MPs may not receive a salary, take their seat, speak in debates or vote.

Members of the House of Lords

Taken on introduction to the House, and then at each new Parliament. Until the oath is taken Lords may not sit, receive a salary or vote in the House of Lords.

Note: there is no separate Oath of Allegiance taken by the Prime Minister and members of the Cabinet on taking up their offices as they normally already take the Oath as members of the House of Commons, or members of the House of Lords. Any member of the Cabinet who is not a member of either house however must swear the oath.

All Members of Parliament on the 'Demise of the Crown'

When a monarch dies (or otherwise abandons the throne), all members of Parliament are required to swear a new oath to the new monarch.

Members of the Scottish Parliament and of the Welsh Assembly

Taken after each election. Members of the Northern Ireland Assembly are not required to take an oath of allegiance.

Judges and Magistrates in England and Wales

A second judicial oath is also taken after the Oath of Allegiance. Members of the Judiciary in Scotland and Northern Ireland do not take the Oath of Allegiance.

All Members of the British Armed Forces, including the British Army, Royal Air Force, Royal Marines, and Royal Navy.

Until recently members of the Royal Navy were not required to take the Oath of Allegiance as the service was formed and still remains under the royal prerogative, therefore allegiance was implied. This changed recently and Royal Navy personnel are now asked to swear the Oath of Allegiance like the other branches of the Armed Forces.

Clergy licensed, appointed or admitted into the Church of England

Includes archbishops, bishops, priests, deacons, and any other office in the Church of England. The oath is required as the British monarch is the Supreme Governor of the Church of England.

Different Oaths of Allegiance to the Monarch

Members of the Privy Council swear a much longer oath, over 240 words long, which refers several times to "The Queen's Majesty" (or "The King's Majesty") instead of the monarch's actual name.

Police Officers in England and Wales swear a longer oath which currently starts with the words "I (*name*) solemnly and sincerely declare and affirm that I will well and truly serve the Queen in the office of ...." Police Officers' oaths in Scotland and Northern Ireland do not have references to the monarch.

The Monarchy and the Law

Beginning in Anglo-Saxon times, English kings took an active role in the development of English law and in establishing a uniform justice system in England. One of the first major legal codes of Anglo-Saxon England was compiled by Alfred the Great in the late 9th century, and his grandson Aethelstan later introduced penal reforms. Henry I established a central legal system and appointed the first itinerant judges; Henry II oversaw a reorganisation of secular and church law, and authorised the first jury systems; and Edward I introduced a major codification of all English laws during his reign.

In addition, medieval kings often judged cases while travelling throughout the kingdom and appointed judges to act on their behalf, establishing the principle that the monarch is the source of law and the guarantor of justice. This personal involvement ended following the Glorious Revolution in 1688-89 and today an independent judiciary administers justice on the monarch's authority, with the monarch having no personal involvement in the judicial process. The historical importance of the sovereign in the administration of justice however is reflected in the symbolic roles the monarch still plays in British law. These key symbolic roles are summarised below.

- The monarch is the Fount of Justice. Law and order are established and maintained in his or her name. Justice is administered in his or her name.

- The monarch swears in the coronation oath to 'cause law and justice, in mercy, to be executed in all judgements'.

- The monarch, on the advice of the government or legal panels, appoints all judges throughout the United Kingdom. Judges are called Her Majesty's Judges (or His Majesty when the monarch is male).

- In England and Wales, law courts are called the Queen's Courts (or King's Courts when the monarch is male). Senior Criminal Courts are called Crown Courts.

- Senior barristers and solicitors in the United Kingdom who have achieved distinction in their profession are called Queen's Counsel (or King's Counsel when the monarch is male). They are appointed to their office by the monarch upon the advice of a legal panel.

- In England and Wales criminal prosecutions are brought in the name of the monarch by the Crown Prosecution Service. Criminal cases brought by the state are usually titled 'R (for Regina or Rex, i.e. Queen or King) versus (*defendant*)'.

- The prison system in England and Wales is called Her Majesty's Prisons (or His Majesty when the monarch is male) and criminals are detained on the monarch's authority.

- The monarch, on the advice of Ministers, may exercises the prerogative of mercy in the form of free or conditional royal pardons.

Note: Different terms for law courts, the prosecution service and prisons are used in Scotland and Northern Ireland.

Sovereign Immunity

Because justice is carried out on the authority of the monarch as the Fount of Justice, the monarch cannot be sued as a person in his or her own courts, and cannot take part in any trial that is held on his or her authority, either as a defendant or a witness. This is done to preserve the dignity and authority of the monarch as the guarantor of justice. The 'Crown' however can be sued in its capacity as the state, government or public agencies.

The monarch is immune from arrest in all cases, and no arrest of any person can be made in the monarch's presence or within the verges of a royal palace. Judicial proceedings cannot be undertaken in a royal residence.

Other members of the Royal Family can be sued as persons, are not immune from arrest, and can take part in criminal or civil proceedings, including the Prince of Wales.

It is important to note that although the monarch cannot be sued for any breach of law, monarchs over the last 200 years have been careful to ensure that all their activities and those of their household are carried out in accordance with current laws.

The Monarchy and the Church

Ever since the Protestant Reformation of the English Church in the 16th century, the monarch has been the Supreme Governor of the Church of England. The title was first used in modified form by Kings Henry VIII and Edward VI who called themselves Supreme Head of the Church England. It was changed to Supreme Governor of the Church of England under Elizabeth I in 1563 after the Thirty Nine Articles of Religion were passed.

The Articles, still in force today, proclaim that the monarch is the ultimate authority in the Church, not because of any specific religious claim but simply because the monarch is said to have ultimate authority over all institutions within the kingdom, including the Church, as it was believed to have been for kings in ancient Israel as described in the Old Testament. The title is therefore jurisdictional rather than sacramental, meaning that the monarch has ultimate authority over the government of the Church in all its areas but does not claim spiritual authority nor takes part in practical governance.

Day-to-day spiritual leadership in the Church of England is exercised by the church's highest prelate, the Archbishop of Canterbury, whilst ultimate government of the Church is vested in a General Synod which meets every five years. The monarch however still holds formal and symbolic roles in the life of the Church, including the ones below.

- At his or her coronation the monarch must swear an oath to maintain the true profession of the Gospel and the Protestant religion in the UK; to preserve the settlement of the Church of England regarding its doctrine, worship and government; and to preserve the lawful rights and privileges of the clergy.

- The monarch bears the title of 'Defender of the Faith' among his or her official titles (see below).

- The monarch officially opens the General Synod of the Church of England every five years, and gives a speech at the opening ceremony.

- Measures passed by the General Synod must receive Royal Assent from the monarch in order to become legal. Measures that affect the nation as a whole are first sent to Parliament (who can either accept them or reject them but not amend them), and then are submitted for Royal Assent. Legislation on canon law only (governing the church's domestic affairs) goes directly to the monarch for Royal Assent.

- The monarch appoints all Church of England archbishops, bishops and deans of cathedrals on the advice of the Prime Minister and Church Commissions. Once appointed, these clergy must take an oath of allegiance to the monarch and may not resign without royal approval.

- Upon their licensing, all parish priests in the Church of England must swear an oath of allegiance to the monarch.

- Church of England religious services usually include prayers for the health and preservation of the monarch.

In order to fulfil the role of Supreme Governor of the church, the monarch and heirs to the throne must be in communion with the Church of England and be confirmed members in that faith.

The Title of 'Defender of the Faith'

'Defender of the Faith' used to be one of several titles that were bestowed by popes on virtuous Christian monarchs from the Middle

Ages onwards. The English title of Defender of the Faith was originally bestowed by Pope Leo X on King Henry VIII in 1521 as a reward for a treatise Henry wrote against Martin Luther, the *Assertio Septem Sacramentorum*, or 'Defence of the Seven Sacraments'. In its original meaning, the title proclaimed Henry a Defender of the Catholic Faith against Protestant heresies.

In one of the great ironies of history, Henry later used Martin Luther's same Protestant heresies to break relations with the Catholic Church and form the Church of England. As a consequence, the title of Defender of the Faith was revoked by Rome in 1538 when Pope Paul III excommunicated Henry VIII. The title however was re-conferred anew on Henry by the English Parliament in 1543-44, this time to signify his defence of the new Church of England's Protestant faith. The title was temporarily abolished by his Catholic daughter Mary I when she became Queen in 1553, but was re-adopted by her Protestant successor Elizabeth I in 1558. It has since been part of the official titles of all English, and later British, monarchs, signifying that the monarch is the defender of the Protestant faith professed by the Church of England and the Church of Scotland (see below).

Elizabeth II is the 21st monarch to bear this title since Henry VIII. Since 1714, the title has been stamped on all British coins in the shortened form FD or FID DEF, from the Latin *Fidei Defensor*. To note, the title of Defender of the Faith is applicable only to the monarchy of the United Kingdom and Northern Ireland, where the monarch is the Supreme Governor of the established Church of England and official protector of the Church of Scotland. In other Commonwealth realms where there are no state-sponsored churches the title is omitted.

The Monarchy and the Church of Scotland

The monarch has a separate, special relationship with the established Church of Scotland which, unlike the Church of England, is free from state control. The Church of Scotland is also Presbyterian in nature and does not possess an ecclesiastical hierarchy so the monarch is not its Supreme Governor. Supreme authority is vested in the Church's General Assembly. The monarch is a simple ordinary member of the Church of Scotland (insofar as he/she is also in communion with the Church of England), but also act as protector of its independence, and is required to swear an oath on accession to preserve its freedom.

As protector of the Church of Scotland, the monarch is represented by a Lord High Commissioner at yearly general meetings of the Church's General Assembly. The Lord High Commissioner's job is to open and close the General Assembly meetings, and to inform the monarch of the business undertaken. He or she has no voting power and cannot contribute to debates. Lord High Commissioners are appointed by the monarch every year and occasionally have included members of the Royal Family including the Prince of Wales, Princess Anne, Prince Andrew, and Prince Edward. Queen Elizabeth II is the only monarch in the last 300 years to have attended meetings of the General Assembly in person during her reign, in 1969 and 2002.

The Monarchy and the Armed Forces

The link between the monarchy and the Armed Forces is an ancient one, dating back to the time when kings led armies into battle. The last British king to personally lead troops into battle was George II in 1743 at the Battle of Dettingen, and today the monarch does neither lead troops nor is involved in military affairs. He or she however is still the official Head of all the British Armed Forces, and even though de-facto executive authority rests with the Prime Minister, the Cabinet and Parliament, the monarch and rest of the Royal Family retain important ceremonial and formal roles in military affairs, including the following:

- On enlistment, members of the British Armed Forces are required to take an oath of allegiance to the monarch as Head of the Armed Forces.

- The monarch is the only person who can declare war. This prerogative today is exercise by the Prime Minister and the government on behalf of the monarch.

- The monarch meets regularly with the Chief of the Defence Staff, the Service Chiefs, and the Defence Secretary, and also keeps regularly in touch with the work of the Services through a dedicated Defence Services Secretary who is normally a serving officer.

- The monarch and members of the Royal Family take part in the annual Cenotaph ceremony in November to commemorate the dead from all the wars. They also attend the festival of Remembrance in the same month held at the Royal Albert Hall.

- The monarch and other members of the Royal Family hold various appointments and honorary ranks in the Armed Forces (see next section), meant to foster a special link between the crown and the services.

- The monarch and senior members of the Royal Family personally bestow awards and decorations to members of the Armed Forces, usually in ceremonies at royal palaces.

- The monarch and members of the Royal Family undertake regular visits to units, ships and bases of all the British Armed Forces, both at home and overseas, to show support. They often visit troops deployed abroad in active operations, and welcome troops home.

In addition to the above, future monarchs and other members of the Royal Family are encouraged to serve in the Armed Forces for a period of time at some point in their lives to better understand its work and culture. Monarchs who experienced active service in the Armed Forces in the last 300 years have included George I, George II, William IV, Edward VII, George V, Edward VIII and George VI. Queen Elizabeth II served in the Women's Auxiliary Territorial Service based in London as a honorary Subaltern during the Second World War. Recent Royal Family members who have served in the British Armed Forces include the Prince of Wales, Prince Andrew, Prince William, and Prince Harry.

Some Notable Historical Acts of Royal Support for the Armed Forces

The link between the monarchy and the Armed Forces has been strengthened over the centuries by specific acts of royal support for active servicemen or wounded soldiers. Listed below are some notable instances of this support over the last 350 years.

1681: The Royal Hospital, Chelsea, London

Charles II founded the Royal Hospital in Chelsea in 1681 to provide for soldiers who were broken by age or war. The first soldiers were admitted in 1692 and the Hospital continues to serve as a retirement home for ex-servicemen and ex-servicewomen today, with a statue of its founder Charles II standing in its main courtyard. 'Chelsea Pensioners' must be over 65 and have served as regular soldiers in the British or Commonwealth Armed Forces.

1692: The Royal Naval Hospital, Greenwich, London

Queen Mary II founded the Royal Naval Hospital in 1692 as a naval counterpart to the Royal Hospital in Chelsea to provide for wounded sailors. She ordered that the Hospital be housed initially in the former royal palace of Greenwich, with new dedicated buildings erected afterwards. The Hospital served as a retirement home for sailors until 1869, after which the buildings housed the Royal Naval College until 1998. The Royal Naval Hospital survives today as a charity institution providing support for Royal Navy and Royal Marines ex-personnel.

1856: The Establishment of the Victoria Cross

Queen Victoria instituted the Victoria Cross in 1856 to recognize highest acts of bravery in the face of enemy action, to be awarded to any member of the Armed Forces regardless of rank. The design of the medal was chosen by Victoria and Prince Albert themselves. Victoria also personally awarded the first medals to 62 veterans of the Crimean War in a ceremony in 1857. The Victoria Cross remains today the highest military decoration in Britain, as well as the highest honour that can be bestowed in the kingdom.

1914: Princess Mary's Christmas Boxes

Princess Mary, daughter of King George V, was involved in a public fund established in 1914 to supply Christmas gifts to British troops during the first year of World War I. The gifts were tin boxes containing chocolates, sweets, tobacco and a personal greeting from King George V and Queen Mary, and bore the name 'Princess Mary's Christmas Gift Box'. It was delivered to over 350,000 soldiers and sailors in time for Christmas 1914. As everyone thought the war would finish in 1915 the fund was unfortunately not extended for the following years.

1918-1920: Honouring First World War Soldiers

At the end of the First World War George V sent a personal message to more than 150,000 British prisoners of war coming back home from Germany. He was also involved with the repatriation of the Unknown Warrior to Britain and with his burial in Westminster Abbey. George personally walked behind the Unknown Warrior's hearse in London during the memorial procession from Whitehall to Westminster Abbey, and on the same day he also opened the Cenotaph monument in Whitehall which commemorated all the dead from the First World War.

1939-1945: Field Visits to Troops during the Second World War

Although it is well known that King George VI and Queen Elizabeth visited bombed areas in Britain during the Second World War, the king's visits to British troops abroad are less known today. George VI first visited the British Expeditionary Force in France in December 1939. He then visited North Africa and Malta in June 1943 when he travelled over 6,000 miles in two weeks to visit military camps and battlefields. He also visited the Normandy beaches 10 days after D-Day in June 1944, he was in Southern Italy in July-August 1944, and he visited liberated Belgium in October 1944.

Royal Honorary Positions in the Armed Forces

Most members of the Royal Family hold honorary positions in the British Armed Forces, usually within individual regiments and units. These positions allow the monarchy to retain a personal link with the military, while at the same time individual units gain a royal patron who becomes involved in the life of the unit by sending messages of support, visiting troops, and awarding honours and regimental colours. In the British Army these royal honorary positions usually take the form of Colonel-in-Chief or Royal Colonel. In the Royal Navy the position is usually that of Commodore-in-Chief, while in the Royal Air Force it is normally Honorary Air Commodore. Listed on the following pages is a selection of current honorary appointments.

A Selection of current Royal Honorary Positions (as of June 2017)

**This is not a complete list*

Note: Prince Philip's Royal Honorary Positions pre-date his official retirement in August 2017.

The Queen

Army

Colonel-in-Chief of the Life Guards
Colonel-in-Chief of the Blues and Royals
Colonel-in-Chief of the Grenadier Guards
Colonel-in-Chief of the Coldstream Guards
Colonel-in-Chief of the Scots Guards

Colonel-in-Chief of the Irish Guards
Colonel-in-Chief of the Welsh Guards
Colonel-in-Chief of the Royal Regiment of Scotland
Colonel-in-Chief of the Duke of Lancaster's Regiment
Colonel-in-Chief of the Royal Mercian and Lancastrian Yeomanry
Colonel-in-Chief of the Royal Welsh
Colonel-in-Chief of the Royal Scots Dragoon Guards
Colonel-in-Chief of the Corps of Royal Engineers
Colonel-in-Chief of the Royal Tank Regiment
Colonel-in-Chief of the Malawi Rifles
Colonel-in-Chief of the Corps of Royal Military Police
Colonel-in-Chief of the Adjutant General's Corps
Colonel-in-Chief of the Queen's Royal Lancers
Captain-General of the Royal Regiment of Artillery
Captain-General of the Honourable Artillery Company
Captain-General of Combined Cadet Force
Honorary Colonel of the Queen's Own Warwickshire and Worcestershire Yeomanry

Royal Air Force
Air Commodore-in-Chief of the Royal Air Force Regiment
Air Commodore-in-Chief of the Royal Auxiliary Force
Air Commodore-in-Chief of the Royal Observer Corps
Royal Honorary Air Commodore of Royal Air Force Marham
Royal Honorary Air Commodore of the 603 (City of Edinburgh) Squadron

The Duke of Edinburgh

Army
Field Marshal of the British Army
Colonel-in-Chief of The Queen's Royal Hussars
Colonel-in-Chief of the Rifles

Colonel-in-Chief, Army Cadet Force
Colonel-in-Chief of the Corps of Royal Electrical and Mechanical Engineers
Colonel-in-Chief of the Intelligence Corps
Royal Colonel of the Highlanders, 4th Battalion, The Royal Regiment of Scotland
Honorary Colonel of the Leicestershire and Derbyshire Yeomanry
Colonel of the Grenadier Guards

Royal Navy
Lord High Admiral of the United Kingdom
Captain-General of the Corps of Royal Marines

Royal Air Force
Marshal of the Royal Air Force
Air Commodore of the University Air Squadron

The Prince of Wales

Army
Colonel-in-Chief of the Parachute Regiment
Colonel-in-Chief of the Royal Dragoon Guards
Colonel-in-Chief of the Army Air Corps
Colonel-in-Chief of the Royal Gurkha Rifles
Colonel-in-Chief of the Queen's Dragoon Guards
Colonel in Chief of the Mercian Regiment
Royal Colonel of the Black Watch, 3rd Battalion, The Royal Regiment of Scotland
Royal Colonel of the 51st Highland, 7th Battalion, The Royal Regiment of Scotland
Royal Honorary Colonel of the Queen's Own Yeomanry
Colonel of the Welsh Guards

Royal Navy
Commodore-in-Chief of Plymouth, Royal Naval Command

Royal Air Force
Honorary Air Commodore, Royal Air Force Valley

The Duchess of Cornwall

Army
Royal Colonel of the 4th Battalion, The Rifles

Royal Navy
Commodore-in-Chief of the Naval Medical Services
Commodore-in-Chief, Naval Chaplaincy Service

Royal Air Force
Honorary Air Commodore, RAF Halton
Honorary Air Commodore, RAF Leeming

The Duke of Cambridge

Army
Colonel of the Irish Guards

Royal Navy
Commodore-in-Chief of HMNB Clyde
Commodore-in-Chief of the Royal Navy Submarine Service
Commodore-in-Chief of Scotland

Royal Air Force
Honorary Air Commandant, RAF Coningsby

The Duchess of Cambridge

Royal Air Force
Honorary Air Commandant of the Air Training Corps

Prince Harry

Royal Navy
Commodore-in-Chief of Small Ships and Diving

Royal Air Force
Honorary Air Commandant, RAF Honington

The Princess Royal

Army
Colonel-in-Chief of the King's Royal Hussars
Colonel-in-Chief of Worcestershire and Sherwood Foresters Regiment (29/45 Foot)
Colonel-in-Chief of the Royal Corps of Signals
Colonel-in-Chief the Royal Army Veterinary Corps
Royal Colonel of the Royal Scots Borderers, 1st Battalion, Royal Regiment of Scotland
Royal Colonel of the 52nd Lowland Regiment, 6th Battalion, Royal Regiment of Scotland
Colonel of the Blues and Royals
Commandant-in-Chief of the First Aid Nursing Yeomanry (Princess Royal's Volunteer Corps)

Royal Navy
Admiral and Chief Commandant for Women in the Royal Navy
Commodore-in-Chief of HMNB Portsmouth

Royal Air Force
Honorary Air Commodore, RAF Lyneham
Honorary Air Commodore of the University of LondonAir Squadron

The Duke of York

Army
Colonel-in-Chief of the $9^{th}/12^{th}$ Royal Lancers (Prince of Wales's)
Colonel-in-Chief of the Small Arms School Corps
Colonel-in-Chief of the Yorkshire Regiment ($14^{th}/15^{th}$ 19th and 33rd / 76th Foot)
Royal Colonel of the Royal Highland Fusiliers, 2nd Battalion, Royal Regiment of Scotland

Royal Navy
Commodore-in-Chief of the Fleet Air Arm
Admiral of the Sea Cadet Corps

Royal Air Force
Honorary Air Commodore, Royal Air Force Lossiemouth

The Earl of Wessex

Army
Royal Colonel of the 2nd Battalion, The Rifles
Royal Honorary Colonel of the Royal Wessex Yeomanry
Royal Honorary Colonel of the London Regiment

Royal Navy
Commodore-in-Chief of the Royal Fleet Auxiliary

Royal Air Force
Honorary Air Commodore, Royal Air Force Waddington

The Countess of Wessex

Army
Colonel-in-Chief of Queen Alexandra's Royal Army Nursing Corps
Colonel-in-Chief of the Corps of Army Music
Royal Colonel of the 5th Battalion of the Rifles

Royal Air Force
Honorary Air Commodore, Royal Air Force Wittering

The Duke of Kent

Army
Colonel of the Scots Guards
Colonel-in-Chief of the Royal Regiment of Fusiliers
Deputy Colonel-in-Chief of the Royal Scots Dragoon Guards

Royal Air Force
Honorary Air Commodore, RAF Leuchars

The Duchess of Kent

Army
Colonel-in-Chief of The Prince of Wales's Own Regiment of Yorkshire
Deputy Colonel-in-Chief of Adjutant Generals Corps
Deputy Colonel-in-Chief of Royal Dragoon Guards

The Duke of Gloucester

Army
Colonel-in-Chief of the Royal Anglian Regiment
Colonel-in-Chief of the Royal Army Medical Corps
Royal Colonel of the 6th (V) Battalion, The Rifles
Royal Honorary Colonel of the Royal Monmouthshire Royal Engineers (Militia)

Royal Air Force
Honorary Air Commodore, of RAF Odiham
Honorary Air Commodore of 501 (County of Gloucester) Squadron, Royal Auxiliary Air Force
Honorary Air Marshal, Royal Air Force

The Duchess of Gloucester

Army
Colonel-in-Chief of the Royal Army Dental Corps
Deputy Colonel-in-Chief of the Adjutant Generals Corps
Royal Colonel of the 7th (V) Battalion, The Rifles

Princess Alexandra of Kent

Army
Deputy Colonel-in-Chief of The Queen's Royal Lancers
Royal Colonel of the 3rd Battalion, The Rifles
Royal Honorary Colonel of The Royal Yeomanry

Royal Air Force
Patron and Air Chief Commandant of Princess Mary's Royal Air Force Nursing Service
Honorary Air Commodore, RAF Cottesmore

Prince Michael of Kent

Army
Royal Honorary Colonel of the Honourable Artillery Company

Royal Navy
Honorary Vice Admiral of the Royal Naval Reserve
Commodore-in-Chief of the Maritime Reserves

Royal Air Force
Honorary Air Marshal, RAF Benson

ARTS AND TREASURES

The Royal Collection

The Royal Collection is the art collection of the British monarchy. It comprises all the art objects, treasures and decorative items that have been gathered by British monarchs over the last 500 years. One of the largest and most important art collections in the world, it contains over one million items and is unique for still remaining in the possession of its founding royal family, instead of being dispersed or re-settled in state museums like other European royal collections from the past.

Composition

The Collection contains objects collected mainly from the 1660s onwards. Earlier works that were collected and commissioned by medieval and Tudor monarchs were mostly lost during the Republican Commonwealth in the 1650s after the monarchy was abolished. Medieval and Tudor works that are part of the Royal Collection today were largely re-acquired after 1660 or bought anew by later monarchs. Among the great royal patrons to add to the Collection in the last 350 were Charles II, George III, George IV, Queen Victoria and Prince Albert, and Queen Mary, consort of King George V. Queen Mary was also instrumental in cataloguing the Collection in detail and re-discovering previously lost items.

Because it was formed primarily through the interests of individual monarchs and Royal Family members, the Royal Collection is not thematic in scope like a museum, but rather reflects the individual tastes of the people who assembled it. The Collection comprises:

- **Visual Art**: Over 5,000 paintings (with particular strength in Italian, Dutch and British paintings), 10,000 watercolours, and over 3,000 miniatures.

- **Drawings and Prints:** 20,000 Old Masters drawings and over 500,000 prints, including works by Michelangelo, Leonardo, Holbein and Durer.

- **Sculpture**: 1,400 items including pieces in marble, bronze and terracotta. Over half of the collection—900 pieces—are British, the rest includes works from antiquity, European sculptors and modern works.

- **Ceramics**: A large collection of European ceramics including the best collection of French 18th century porcelain in the world, Dutch Delft ware, and an encyclopaedic collection of British ceramics.

- **Silver and gold plate**: Thousands of items collected and commissioned from the 1660s to the early 20th century, including church and coronation plate, dinner services, representational table pieces and decorative items.

- **Furniture**: One of the largest collections of antique furniture in the world, of which many pieces are still in their original settings. It includes the most important collection of Louis XVI French furniture in the world.

- **Tapestries and textiles**: Over 100 Flemish, French and British tapestries, including priceless Tudor masterpieces. The textile holdings also comprise bed furnishings, historic costumes, coronation dress, and a dedicated lace collection.

- **Arms and Armour**: Tudor and Stuart armour including personal royal pieces, firearms and swords from the 17th century onwards, and the largest collection of Oriental arms and armour in Western Europe.

- **Oriental Art**: A large collection of items from India, China and Japan which includes porcelain, jades, ivories, furniture and gold items.

- **Photographs**: Over 450,000 items including a priceless collection of early 19th century photographs.

Additionally, the Collection includes books, illuminated manuscripts, maps, clocks, insignia, coins, glass, jewellery and objects d'art.

Where to see the Royal Collection

What makes the Royal Collection unique is that many of its works can still be seen in the original royal palaces for which they were commissioned. The Collection is spread between all the royal residences across the United Kingdom. Those include the occupied residences—Buckingham Palace, Clarence House, St James's Palace, Kensington Palace, Windsor Castle, Sandringham House, Balmoral Castle, Holyrood Palace and Hillsborough Castle—as well as many unoccupied historic residences including the Tower of London, Hampton Court Palace, Kew Palace, Osborne House and the Brighton Pavilion. All these residences, except for St James's Palace, are open to the public daily or at some point during the year. Many objects are routinely moved between royal residences, although items that are particularly associated with a certain residence are usually left in place permanently.

Works can also be seen on exhibitions held at the Queen's Gallery at Buckingham Palace, the Queen's Gallery at Holyrood Palace, and the Drawings Gallery at Windsor Castle. Outside the royal residences and galleries, over 3,000 objects from the Collection have been permanently loaned to museums around Britain including the British Museum, the National Gallery and the Victoria & Albert

Museum in London; the Royal Armouries in Leeds; the National Museum of Wales; and the National Galleries of Scotland. People interested in exploring the Royal Collection do not necessarily need to visit sites in person as the Royal Collection website features photographs and descriptions of over 250,000 of its best items online.

Ownership & Management

The Collection is the property of the monarch, but it is not owned by him or her as a private individual. Rather, it is held in trust for the nation, to be handed down intact to the next monarch. Although monarchs and other members of the Royal Family can add to the Royal Collection, items from it cannot be sold or disposed away as they are considered national heritage. Not all works of art or decorative items that are bought by monarchs automatically enter the Royal Collection—some of them can remain the private property of the individual for their own lifetime—however most privately bought property enters the Collection eventually, and currently everything that was acquired before 1936 is officially considered part of the Collection.

The Collection is officially constituted as a department of the Royal Household, however it does not receive public funds or subsidies. It is administered through the Royal Collection Trust, a registered charity which has been chaired by Prince Charles since 1993. The Trust is responsible for the conservation, restoration and cleaning of Collection items; for displaying the Collection to the public; and for acquiring new works. Their work is funded by public admission fees to the royal palaces—like Windsor Castle and Buckingham Palace—entrance fees to the Royal Collection galleries; and sales from the Royal Collection shops in London, Windsor, Edinburgh and online.

Artists Represented in the Royal Collection

Listed below is a selection of famous artists represented in the Royal Collection, either through paintings, sculptures or decorative arts. Because the Royal Collection reflects the tastes of the monarchs who assembled it, it is not complete in artistic scope and has both strengths and weaknesses. This is shown for example in the strong collection of 17th century Dutch paintings assembled by George IV, and in the vast Italian Renaissance art acquired by Charles I, Queen Victoria and Prince Albert. Conversely, the Collection contains little Spanish art or 19th century French impressionist works.

Italian

14th Century: Duccio, Bernardo Daddi.

15th Century: Gentile da Fabriano, Fra Angelico, Pietro Perugino, Andrea Mantegna, Giovanni Bellini.

16th Century: Leonardo da Vinci, Michelangelo, Raphael, Bronzino, Andrea del Sarto, Correggio, Pontormo, Lorenzo Lotto, Jacopo Bassano, Parmigianino, Dosso Dossi, Titian, Tintoretto, Veronese.

17th Century: Caravaggio, Domenichino, Guido Reni, Artemisia Gentileschi, Luca Giordano, Guercino, Gian Lorenzo Bernini, Francesco Borromini.

18th Century: Canaletto.

19th Century: Antonio Canova.

Flemish

15th Century: Hugo van der Goes, Hans Memling.

16th Century: Quentin Matsys, Joos van Cleve, Peter Brueghel the Elder.

17th Century: Jan Brueghel the Elder, Marcus Gheeraerts the Younger, Peter Paul Rubens, Anthony van Dyck, David Teniers the Younger.

Dutch

17th Century: Daniel Mijtens, Frans Hals, Rembrandt van Rjin, Johannes Vermeer, Jan Steen, Pieter de Hooch, Albert Cuyp, William van der Velde the Younger, Meydert Hobbema.

German

16th Century: Albrecht Durer, Hans Holbein the Younger, Lucas Cranach the Elder, Lucas Cranach the Younger.
18th Century: Johann Zoffany.
19th Century: Franx Xavier Winterhalter.

French

16th Century: Francois Clouet.
17th Century: Simon Vouet, Georges de la Tour, Claude Lorrain, Nicolas Poussin.
18th Century: Louis-Francois Roubiliac, Jean-Etienne Liotard
19th Century: Claude Monet.

British

16th - 17th Century: Nicholas Hilliard, Isaac Oliver, Peter Lely, Godfrey Kneller, Grinling Gibbons.
18th Century: William Kent, William Hogarth, Thomas Chippendale, Joshua Reynolds, Thomas Gainsborough, George Stubbs, William Beechey, Benjamin West.
19th Century: Thomas Lawrence, Edwin Landseer, William Powell Frith, John Singer Sargent.
20th Century: Walter Sickert, Augustus John, L.S. Lowry, Graham Sutherland, John Piper.

Royal Patrons of the Arts

One of the functions of monarchy has always been to patronise art in all its forms and to gather great collections for magnificent display at the royal court. Following below is a list of the people who are generally considered to have been England's and Britain's greatest royal patrons of the arts, including a special mention to the greatest of them all, King George IV.

Richard II
(1367-1400)
Although he was a failure politically, Richard II presided over a great flowering of the arts during his reign. He rebuilt Westminster Hall and filled it with new sculptures, commissioned illuminated manuscripts, and left us the earliest contemporary paintings we have of an English King. He was also patron to writers Geoffrey Chaucer and John Gower, and his court was one of the most fashion-conscious in Europe.

John, Duke of Bedford
(1389-1435)
John was a younger brother of King Henry V and regent of the English possessions in France in 1422-1434, during the Hundred Years War. He commissioned many lavish illuminated manuscripts while in France, including the magnificent Bedford Hours, now in the British Library. He also assembled a great collection of gold plate and fine household items, one of which, the enamelled Royal Gold Cup, is considered a medieval treasure of the British Museum.

Henry VIII

(1491-1547)

Henry competed with other monarchs, especially King Francois I of France, in creating the most splendid Renaissance court in Europe. To that end he brought artists to England to be in his service including painter Hans Holbein, miniaturist Lucas Horenbout and sculptor Pietro Torrigiano. He also commissioned hundreds of expensive tapestries from Flanders to adorn his palaces. He expanded the royal residences by appropriating Hampton Court and Whitehall from Cardinal Wolsey, and he built St James Palace and Nonsuch Palace, all of which he embellished with the latest decorations.

Elizabeth I

(1533-1603)

Despite being notoriously close-fisted when it came to doling out money, Elizabeth I encouraged the development of selected arts during her reign. She employed miniaturists Nicholas Hilliard and Isaac Oliver, under whom the art of miniature painting reached new heights, and promoted the production of hundreds of images celebrating her eternal youth as Virgin Queen. She also inspired writers like Edmund Spenser who wrote *The Faerie Queen* in her honour, and supported the development of theatre in London by famously supporting William Shakespeare.

Anne of Denmark

(1574-1619)

James I's Queen Consort was a patron of artists, writers and musicians. She employed the poet Ben Jonson to produce masques at court, and the architect Inigo Jones to build the Queen's House in Greenwich in the new Italian classical style. She also built up a significant art collection, favouring Dutch and Italian artists, once saying to a minister that she took more pleasure in her pictures than in affairs of state.

Charles I

(1600-1649)

Charles, the son of Anne of Denmark, inherited his mother's artistic interests and became one of the greatest art collectors in the history of the monarchy. A skilled connoisseur, he bought works from all over Europe—particularly favouring Titian—and brought to England the Raphael Cartoons to be woven into tapestries at the Mortlake factories. In 1627 he purchased the great Gonzaga art collection from Italy containing masterpieces by Michelangelo, Caravaggio and Mantegna which, together with his other purchases, created the greatest art collection in Western Europe (see *Lost Royal Treasures* for the fate of Charles I's collection). At his own court, he hired Anthony Van Dyck as court painter, and commissioned works by Rubens as well as sculptures by Bernini and Hubert le Sueur.

Charles II

(1630-1685)

Charles was famously more interested in science than in the arts—he founded the Royal Society and the Royal Observatory—however his artistic contributions are still noteworthy. Besides recovering much of his father's art collection, which had been dispersed by the Republican Commonwealth, he collected Old Masters paintings and drawings including a large collection of Leonardo Da Vinci's notebooks. He commissioned Peter Lely to paint the ladies of his court, he encouraged and patronised Christopher Wren's work as an architect, and employed woodcarving virtuoso Grinling Gibbons to decorate his new Baroque apartments at Windsor Castle.

Caroline of Ansbach

(1683-1737)

As Queen Consort to King George II Caroline liked to surround herself with writers and artists. She made important acquisitions for the Royal Collection in the form of paintings, miniatures, drawings and cameos. She was also a patron of architect William Kent and sculptor Michael Rysbrach.

Frederick Prince of Wales

(1707-1751)

Frederick, the son of Queen Caroline and father of George III, was a lover of art who expanded the Royal Collection by acquiring Old Masters works by Van Dyck, Rubens, Hals and Poussin. He was also a patron of painters and architects, including William Kent who built new residences for him as well as a sumptuous state barge. A skilled musician himself, he supported opera companies and commissioned musical works.

George III

(1738-1820)

During his long reign George III did much to encourage British arts and craftsmanship. Besides commissioning works from Allan Ramsay, Benjamin West and Thomas Gainsborough, he also founded the Royal Academy of Arts and patronised makers of clocks and scientific instruments. He added many masterpieces to the Royal Collection by buying large Italian collections in bulk, and amassed a fabled library of thousands of books and maps which were later given to the British Museum by his son, George IV.

Britain's Greatest Royal Patron: George IV

(1762-1830)

George IV was arguably Britain's greatest patron of the arts. His obsession with art collecting was legendary. He bought indiscriminately in vast scale, from silver and gold plate to jewels, paintings and sculptures, print collections, armours and antique guns. After the French Revolution he ransacked the market for the former belongings of the French Royal Family, creating in the process the greatest collection of Sevres porcelain and Louis XVI

French furniture in the world. He was just as compulsive with paintings, of which he was a connoisseur, especially acquiring works by Flemish and Dutch masters like Rubens and Rembrandt. At Carlton House alone at one point in 1816, 136 paintings hung in the state rooms, 67 were in the private quarters, and 250 more were in storage. He supported contemporary British artists like George Stubbs, Thomas Lawrence and William Beechey; he convinced the British government to buy the 38 paintings that became the nucleus of the National Gallery; and was instrumental in securing the Elgin Marbles for the British Museum. He also had a taste for refined jewels, and for his coronation in 1821 he commissioned the magnificent Jewelled Sword, and the State Diadem that has been worn by Queens ever since. George's taste however was at its grandest in architecture. To him we owe one of the most fantastical-looking buildings in Britain, the Royal Pavilion in Brighton, while in London he created Regent Street and Regents Park, and rebuilt Buckingham Palace. At Windsor, George repaired the Castle to give it its present medieval appearance, and remodelled the interior to what it is today.

Queen Victoria and Prince Albert

(1819-1901, 1819-1861)

Victoria and Albert supported many types of British art together before Albert died in 1861. Their patronage included commissioning paintings and sculptures from Edwin Landseer, Franz Winterhalter and Francis Chantrey; supporting the new art of photography; and founding new museums in South Kensington, London, with the proceeds of the Great Exhibition of 1851. They also championed Medieval and early Renaissance art by adding paintings to the Royal Collection and encouraging public museums to do likewise.

Queen Mary

(1867-1953)

Art and family history were Queen Mary's great passions and she combined the two by exploring, re-organising and carefully cataloguing the entire Royal Collection. An indefatigable researcher, she re-acquired thousands of items that had once belonged to the Royal Family including silver, jewellery, bibelots and furniture. Mary also made the collection available for study to scholars and was a supporter of several art museums, to which she often loaned Royal Collection items for exhibitions.

Queen Elizabeth the Queen Mother

(1900-2002)

Both as Queen and Queen Mother, Elizabeth Bowes-Lyon patronised many contemporary British artists, buying and commissioning works from Augustus John, Graham Sutherland, John Piper and Paul Nash among others. She also collected French impressionist art and assembled a splendid collection of Chelsea porcelain.

Great Treasures Owned by the Monarchy

Among the over one million items it holds the Royal Collection counts important individual treasures and collections of world renown. The items below are considered to be the most important and are listed in rough chronological order from their creation date.

The Leonardo Notebooks

The Royal Collection owns over 200 manuscript pages from Leonardo Da Vinci's notebooks, written between 1478-1518 and acquired by King Charles II between 1660-1685. Although not the largest collection of Leonardo notebook pages in the world, the so-called 'Windsor Codex' contains some of Leonardo's finest art drawings and the largest collection of his anatomical studies. Carefully kept in preservation storage, some the drawings are often shown to the public during special exhibitions at the royal palaces.

The Raphael Cartoons

The great Renaissance master Raphael painted these large cartoon paintings in 1515-16 to serve as models for tapestries to be hung in the Vatican. Depicting stories of St Peter and St Paul from the New Testament, they are considered some of his greatest works and are the largest commission he ever undertook. Of the original 10 cartoons seven have survived and are part of the Royal Collection. They were purchased by Charles I in 1623 when he was Prince of Wales and have remained in Britain ever since. In 1699 William III installed them in a specially built gallery at Hampton Court Palace where however only copies exist today. Queen Victoria permanently lent the original cartoons in 1865 to the Victoria and Albert Museum in London where they still hang today in a specially designed gallery.

Portrait Miniatures

Counting over 3,000 pieces, the Royal Collection's holdings of miniatures is one of the largest in the world, and includes some of the earliest miniatures ever made in Europe at the start of the 16th century. The collection covers over 300 years of development in the art, from the court of Henry VIII to that of Queen Victoria, and is particularly strong on royal portraits. Visual likenesses of several Tudor royals and courtiers are known only from miniatures held in the Royal Collection. Works are regularly on show to the public at the royal palaces and in special exhibitions.

The Abraham Tapestries

Commissioned by Henry VIII to celebrate the birth of his son Edward in 1537, these tapestries are only a small surviving part of Henry VIII's immense tapestries collection which at his death counted over 2,000 large pieces. Officially called *The Story of Abraham Cycle,* this tapestries set was made in the 1540s and consists of ten large pieces showing different episodes from the life of the Hebrew patriarch. They were woven in Flanders in gold thread and cost Henry VIII over 2,000 pounds, the equivalent of two battleships in contemporary money. When the Royal Collection was auctioned off in the 1650s after the abolition of the monarchy the tapestries were valued to be the most expensive item in the collection and considered so important that Oliver Cromwell kept them from being sold. They can currently be seen at Hampton Court Palace in London.

Canaletto Paintings

The Canaletto holdings in the Royal Collection, consisting of 50 paintings and over 140 drawings, are considered to be the largest and finest group of works by the Venetian artist in existence. The bulk of the collection was bought by George III in 1762 from Joseph Smith, the British Consul in Venice who had been one of Canaletto's patrons. Most of the paintings record detailed views of 18th century Venice but also include views of London painted while Canaletto was living in England in 1746-1755. Most of the paintings can be seen in the occupied and historic royal palaces, and in special exhibitions.

Sevres Porcelains

The collection of Sevres porcelains owned by the British Monarchy is largely acknowledged to be the finest in the world. Numbering hundreds of pieces, the collection was mostly assembled by George IV from the time he was Prince of Wales in the 1780s until his death in 1830. Many of the pieces were made for the French Kings Louis XV and Louis XVI, and were bought by George after the French monarchy was abolished at the French Revolution in the 1790s. The collection includes complete, elaborate dinner services which are still used during state banquets. Other pieces include vases, urns and table decorations which normally adorn the state rooms of the royal palaces.

Faberge Works

There are over 500 Faberge pieces in the Royal Collection, representing the largest and most important private Faberge collection in the world, both in variety and quality. It includes four of the famous Russian Imperial eggs, but also small boxes, cigarette cases, crystal flowers, figurines, bibelots, and the largest set of miniature carved animals that Faberge ever created. The collection was started in the late 19th century by Albert, Prince of Wales, and his wife Alexandra of Denmark, and was greatly expanded after they became King and Queen in 1901. Later monarchs and other members of the Royal Family continued to add pieces throughout the 20th century, with the latest additions made by the present Prince of Wales. Many of the objects are regularly shown to the public during special exhibitions at the royal palaces.

Queen Mary's Doll House

The most unique treasure in the Royal Collection, Queen Mary's Doll House is claimed to be the largest and most beautiful doll house in the world. Built between 1921-1924, it was created to be a gift for Queen Mary from the British public, to thank the Royal Family for their support during the First World War. More than 1,500 artists and craftsmen made contributions to the project, with many famous firms, including McVities, HMV and Rolls Royce, fashioning special miniature items for the house. The house is built in 1:12 scale and measures 1.52 metres high by 2.59 metres wide. Everything is built in the highest quality and with the finest materials. It contains three floors, and a basement garage filled with replicas of contemporary royal cars. It has working electricity, working lifts, and hot and cold water running in the bathrooms. There are hand-painted portraits of Royal Family members throughout the house, and the cellar is stocked with tiny bottles filled with actual vintage wine. The most important room in the house is considered to be the Library which is stocked with 300 volumes of real tiny books, including some with original works by Arthur Conan Doyle, Thomas Hardy and Rudyard Kipling, as well as the smallest book ever printed from type, *The Mite*. Queen Mary's Doll House is on permanent show to the public at Windsor Castle.

Lost Royal Treasures

Over the last 800 years many valuable artistic items that belonged to the monarchy have been lost, either through disasters or human agency. Listed below are the most famous royal treasures that no longer exist, or are no longer in the Royal Collection. They are listed in chronological order of disappearance.

King John's Treasure

Lost: 1216

As reported by medieval chroniclers, King John lost much of his royal treasure in October 1216 while marching across the East of England, during his war against rebellious barons. The baggage train carrying his treasure was caught in the rising tides of The Wash mudflats, near King's Lynn in Norfolk, and disappeared into sand and water. Among the possessions lost were jewels and gold plate used by his brother Richard the Lionheart and father Henry II, and the regalia that his grandmother Matilda had worn as Empress of Germany which included her crown and golden wand. None of the lost items have ever been recovered from The Wash. Some historians claim that John never actually lost these treasures but arranged their disappearance in order to sell or melt the items as he tried to raise funds to fight his barons. Whatever the truth, the fact remains that Empress Matilda's regalia and other jewels that were accounted for during John's reign had vanished by the time he died.

The Three Brothers Jewel

Lost: 1640s

The Three Brothers jewel was a Tudor brooch consisting of three large rubies (or spinels) set as a triangle around a large diamond, with pearls in between. It was bought by King Edward VI in 1551 and later became one of the favourite jewels of Queen Elizabeth I. She can be seen wearing it on her bodice in the famous 'Ermine Portrait' at Hatfield House, Hertfordshire, as well as on her tomb effigy in Westminster Abbey. On Elizabeth's death the jewel passed to the Stuart monarchs and later disappeared during the English Civil War. It is thought to have been pawned or sold to raise funds for Charles I's cause.

The Mirror of Great Britain Jewel

Lost: 1640s

The Mirror of Great Britain was a large, magnificent jewel created by King James I in 1604 to celebrate the union of the crowns of England and Scotland on his accession. Made out of gold, in the shape of a hand-held mirror, it contained four diamonds and a ruby. One of the diamonds was the 'Great Harry' which had belonged to James's mother Mary Queen of Scots. Another was the famous Sancy Diamond, which James had bought from France. James can be seen wearing the finished jewel as a hat ornament in a portrait by John de Critz held in the National Gallery of Scotland. On the accession of his son Charles I the jewel was broken up and pawned to pay for royal debts, and its gems were later sold and dispersed during the English Civil War. The Sancy diamond eventually re-appeared in France and became part of French Crown Jewels, and can be seen today in the Louvre Museum in Paris.

The Old Crown Jewels

Lost: 1650s

After Charles I's execution and the abolition of the monarchy in 1649 Parliament ordered the original coronation regalia to be dismantled and destroyed. The gold was melted and the gems were put up for sale. Among the pieces that were lost were the original St Edward's Crown; the Tudor Imperial State Crown and sceptres; the Queens Consorts Crown; the child-size crown made for Edward VI's coronation; Llewellyn's Coronet, worn by the Welsh Princes of Wales; and the coronet said to have been worn by Henry V at the Battle of Agincourt. Except for the Tudor Imperial State Crown and sceptre there are no visual records of what these items looked like. Some of the individual gems that were sold were recovered later at the Restoration of the monarchy, and were re-set in the newly re-minted Crown Jewels in 1660-1661. The others gems were lost.

Charles I's Art Collection

Lost: 1650s

Charles I is said to have owned the greatest painting collection ever assembled by a British Monarch. His collection was strong on Italian artists with many works coming from the great Gonzaga Renaissance collection that he bought from Italy in the 1620s, but it also included gifts and purchases from Spain, the Netherlands and Germany. Artist Peter Paul Rubens remarked on a visit to Whitehall that "when it comes to fine pictures I have never seen such a large number in one place as in this royal palace." The collection was broken apart and sold by the Republican Commonwealth in the early 1650s after the monarchy was abolished. Some paintings were kept in England and were later returned to the Royal Collection. The vast majority however, including the most spectacular, were sold abroad and never returned. Many of them can be seen today in museums all over Europe, including Caravaggio's *Death of the Virgin* and Leonardo's *St John the Baptist,* in the Louvre, Paris; Raphael's *La Perla* and Albrecht Durer's *Self Portrait,* in the Prado, Madrid; and Titian's *Young Woman in a Fur Coat,* in the Kunsthistorisches Museum, Vienna.

The Holbein Whitehall Mural

Lost: 1698

Hans Holbein the Younger's most celebrated work was a mural he painted in the Privy Chamber of the Palace of Whitehall, London, in 1537. It celebrated the Tudor dynasty by showing lifesize, full-length portraits of King Henry VII, King Henry VIII, and their wives Elizabeth of York and Jane Seymour. The figure of Henry VIII in particular, in his famous astride pose, was said to have been so lifelike and imposing that many visitors felt intimidated in its presence. The mural was lost when the Palace of Whitehall was destroyed by fire of 1698, however a small, faithful copy made in 1667 survives in the Royal Collection.

Bernini's Bust of King Charles I

Lost: 1698

The great Baroque sculptor Gianlorenzo Bernini created a celebrated marble bust of Charles I in 1636. As he was unable to travel to England to see his subject in person, he used as a model the famous painting of *Charles I in Three Positions* by Anthony van Dyck which had been expressly painted to provide Bernini with a visual model whilst working in Italy. The finished bust was sent to England and became a favourite of both Charles I and his wife Henrietta Maria who praised it for its lifelikeness. It was sold with the rest of Charles I's art collection in the 1650s and was later recovered by his son, Charles II, but it was destroyed in the Whitehall Palace fire of 1698. A copy of it exists today in the Royal Collection, however opinions differ on whether it is a actual copy of the original.

Michelangelo's Statue of Cupid

Lost: 1698

This statue by Michelangelo, sculpted when he was only 20-years-old, caused a sensation in Italy when it was first unveiled in 1496. Depicting a sleeping cupid, it was so faithful to classical roman statues that many thought it was a newly discovered archaeological treasure, with people initially refusing to believe that a young contemporary artist had sculpted it. It came to Charles I in the 1620s when he bought the Gonzaga Collection from Italy, and was still part of the Royal Collection after the English Civil War. It is believed to have been destroyed in the Whitehall Palace fire of 1698.

The Painted Chamber, Palace of Westminster

Lost: 1834

Built by Henry III from 1226 onwards, the Painted Chamber was one of the great artistic treasures of the medieval Palace of Westminster. Its walls were decorated with colourful murals of biblical history scenes, including elaborate battles from the life of Judas Maccabeus, miracles by the prophet Elisha, and the fall of Jerusalem. There were also representations of vices and virtues, and a full length painting of the coronation of Edward the Confessor in 1042. Over the centuries these murals began to be neglected until they were finally whitewashed in the 18th century. Parts of them were rediscovered during restorations in 1800 and sparked great public interest, but even these survivals were lost when the Old Palace of Westminster was destroyed by fire in 1834. Watercolours copies done in 1819 however have survived.

The Armada Tapestries

Lost: 1834

This spectacular set of tapestries was commissioned by Lord Howard of Effingham, who was Lord Admiral during the Spanish Armada invasion of 1588, to celebrate England's victory over the Spanish. There were 10 large tapestries, each 4.4 metres high by 8.7 metres wide, depicting the movements of English and Spanish ships at different times during the invasion. They were woven in the Netherlands and cost £1,582, the equivalent of about £5-10 million today. King James I bought the tapestries in 1616 for the same amount of money, and in the 1660s they were hung in the House of Lords of the Old Palace of Westminster where over time they became a beloved national symbol of Parliament. They were lost in 1834 when the Old Palace of Westminster was destroyed by fire. Drawings of the tapestries survived however, and smaller painting reproductions of five of them were hung again in the Palace of Westminster in 2010.

The Crown Jewels

The Crown Jewels of the United Kingdom comprise the items used during the coronation ceremony and other official state functions, like the State Opening of Parliament. They are the visual symbols of monarchy and the essence of authority, transcending any single person who wears them. England has had Crown Jewels at least since the time of Edward the Confessor, but the original medieval jewels were destroyed by the Republican Commonwealth in 1649 after the abolition of the monarchy. The only item said to have survived the destruction is a 13th century golden spoon used in the anointing part of the coronation ceremony. A new set of Crown Jewels was created after the Restoration of the monarchy in 1660, to which other items have been added ever since.

The Crown Jewels do not belong to members of the Royal Family but to the British State, which in matters related to monarchy is often referred to as 'The Crown'. The coronation jewels re-created at the Restoration were paid for by the English government and have always belonged to the Crown. Other items, like the George IV State Diadem and Queen Victoria's Small Diamond Crown, started life as personal royal possession but were later bequeathed to the Crown by individual monarchs.

It is impossible to place a monetary value on the British Crown Jewels because on top of their material worth must be added their historical and constitutional worth which is incalculable, consequently the Jewels have never been insured. Since the 14th century they have been stored for safekeeping in the Tower of London where they are currently kept in a maximum security area which is open to visitors during the Tower's visiting hours. In accordance with a law dating back to medieval times, the Jewels can never leave British soil (legend says the injunction goes back to the time King John lost his jewels in the waters of the Wash in the 13th century, see *Lost Royal Treasures*).

The descriptions of the Crown Jewels in this chapter have been divided into appropriate categories: Coronation Regalia, Other State Jewels, and a distinct group called The Great Gems of State which describe important historic gems deserving a category of their own. The end of the chapter also includes sections on the Honours of Wales and Honours of Scotland, the separate crown jewels of those two British home nations. Note that only the most important items have been chosen for individual description here. Unless noted, all jewels are kept in the Tower of London.

The Coronation Regalia

The Crown Jewels proper include the items used to invest the monarchs and their consorts during the coronation ceremony in Westminster Abbey. They include crowns, sceptres, rings, orbs and swords, as well as items used for anointing and for symbolic use only. The most important items worn or handled by monarchs and their consorts during the ceremony are described below.

St Edward's Crown

The most venerable item in the Crown Jewels, St Edward's Crown is used for the actual act of crowning the monarch during the coronation ceremony. It is named after the original crown of St Edward the Confessor that was used to crown all English monarchs until 1625, after which it was destroyed by the Republican Commonwealth in 1649. The current crown was made after the Restoration of the monarchy to crown Charles II in 1661, and is said to contain some gold from the original St Edward's Crown. It contains over 400 precious and semi-precious stones and is made of solid gold, weighing 2.23 kilos. Because of its heavy weight it is only used briefly during the coronation ceremony, and some monarchs in the past have chosen to be crowned with the lighter Imperial State Crown instead, with St Edward's Crown being born in procession.

The Imperial State Crown

During the Middle Ages St Edward's Crown was considered so holy that it was never allowed to leave Westminster Abbey, so another crown had to be made to be worn at official occasions in other places. In the 15th century, this crown came to be known as the Imperial State Crown, not because England presided over an empire, but because English monarchs began to claim that they received their authority directly from God and were not subject to any earthly power like the Pope (i.e. they were like an Emperor, who was not subject to the Pope). Ever since the 17th century the Imperial State Crown has been worn yearly during the State Opening of Parliament, and also at the end of the coronation ceremony when the monarch leaves Westminster Abbey. As such, it is the most frequently used of the coronation jewels and has had to be replaced or remade several times since the Restoration because of wear and tear.

The present Imperial State Crown was made in 1937 for the coronation of George VI and is almost identical in design to the previous crown which had been made for Queen Victoria in 1838. It is made of gold, platinum and silver and contains 2,868 diamonds, 17 sapphires, 11 emeralds, 5 rubies and 273 pearls. Among them are some of the most famous jewels in English history including St Edward the Confessor's Sapphire, the Black Prince's Ruby, Queen Elizabeth's Pearls, the Stuart Sapphire and the Second Star of Africa Diamond (see *The Great Gems of State* below). The Imperial State Crown is considered the first symbol of the state, and as such an image of it is often included on official documents and on government buildings. During the State Opening of Parliament, it is taken to the Palace of Westminster in its own carriage and given its own procession into the building. Because of its symbolism and the historical gems it features this crown is often considered the most important of the Crown Jewels.

The Sovereign's Sceptres

Ever since the Middle Ages monarchs in England have been crowned with two sceptres. The largest sceptre, the **Sovereign's Sceptre with Cross**, symbolizes kingly power and justice, and is placed in the monarch's right hand during the coronation ceremony. The current sceptre was made in 1661 for the coronation of Charles II. It is 92cms long, made of gold, and contains diamonds, rubies, sapphires and emeralds. In 1910, in preparation for the coronation of George V, the top of the sceptre was set with the 530.2-carat First Star of Africa, the largest colourless cut diamond in the world, cut from the famous Cullinan diamond found in 1905 in South Africa (see *The Great Gems of State* below). The **Sovereign's Sceptre with Dove**, also known as the Rod of Equity and Mercy, symbolizes the monarch's spiritual authority and duties to the people, and is placed in the monarch's left hand at the coronation ceremony. It is also made of gold, with groupings of diamonds, emeralds, sapphires and rubies, but is longer at 110cms, and carries an enamelled dove with outstretched wings at the top of the staff. This sceptre remains virtually the same since it was first made for Charles II in 1661.

The Orb

The orb surmounted by a cross symbolizes Christ's dominion over the world and is therefore meant to remind the sovereign who holds it that all earthly power is subject to God. Orbs were first used in the coronations of medieval monarchs, but only began to be used regularly in English coronation ceremonies in the 17th century. The current orb was made for the coronation of Charles II in 1661 and despite being hollow weighs over 1 kilo. It is set with 365 diamonds plus rubies, emeralds, sapphires, pearls, and one large amethyst supporting a jewel-encrusted cross atop the orb. It has been used in every coronation since 1661.

The Sovereign's Ring

Like a wedding ring, the sovereign's ring symbolizes the union between the monarch and the people, and is placed on the fourth finger of the monarch's right hand at the coronation. Until the 19th century coronation rings were personal and a new one was made for every sovereign. This changed in 1902 when Edward VII used the coronation ring that had been made for William IV in 1831, and this ring has been used at coronations ever since. It is made of gold and has 14 diamonds, five rubies and one large sapphire, all arranged in the shape of a red cross over a blue field, resembling a Union Jack.

The Jewelled Swords of Offering

There are five swords used during the coronation ceremony. One of them, the Jewelled Sword of Offering, is presented to the monarch with the exhortation that it should be used to protect good and fight evil, and is then offered back by the monarch to God at the altar after presentation. The current sword was made for the coronation of George IV in 1821 and has been described as the most beautiful and most expensive sword ever made. The blade is made of Damascus steel and is engraved with blue and gold heraldic decorations. The scabbard is covered in gold and set with over 2,000 diamonds, emeralds, sapphires and rubies, all arranged to form the flower symbols of England, Scotland and Ireland. The hilt is set with hundreds more diamonds and sapphires forming oak leaves and acorns, and the handles are in the shape of diamond-encrusted lion heads with small rubies for eyes. After being used by George IV in 1821 the sword was not used again until 1902 for the coronation of Edward VII, but it has been used to crown every monarch since. It was a personal possession of the Royal Family until Edward VII made it one of the Crown Jewels in 1902.

The Queen Consort's Regalia

This particular regalia is used to crown female consorts of male monarchs in a separate crowning ritual at the end of the coronation ceremony. It features items similar to the ones used to invest the monarch, and includes a crown, sceptres, a ring, but not an orb or a sword.

Because of wear and tear, changes in fashion, and unavailability at particular times, there have been and remain several **Queen Consort's Crowns** in the Crown Jewels:

- The **State Crown of Mary of Modena**, the first Queen Consort's crown since the Restoration, was made for the coronation of James II's consort in 1685. It was used to crown only two consorts: Mary of Modena, and Caroline of Ansbach in 1727. It is made of gold, silver and pearls, and was originally set with hundreds of diamonds but these have now been replaced with quartz crystals. It is normally exhibited with the other Crown Jewels in the Tower of London.

- **Queen Adelaide's Crown** was made in 1831 for the coronation of William IV's consort Queen Adelaide of Saxe-Meinengen. A new crown was deemed necessary at the time since Mary of Modena's Crown was considered unfit for use after 100 years of neglect (Queen Charlotte, consort of King George III, was crowned in 1761 with one of her personal crowns that is no longer in the Crown Jewels or Royal Collection). Queen Adelaide's Crown was only worn at her coronation and has not been used since. Now stripped of its gems, the empty gold and silver frame survives in a separate room at the Tower of London.

- **Queen Alexandra's Crown** was made in 1902 for the coronation of Edward VII's consort Alexandra of Denmark. Once again a new crown was deemed necessary in 1902, this time to reflect the increased world status of the British monarchy since 1831. This crown was bigger than the previous ones and contained eight half-arches in the continental style, a design inspired by Queen Alexandra herself who contributed ideas to its creation. Made of gold and silver, it was originally set with over 3,000 diamonds including the famous Koh-i-Noor diamond upon the front cross. The crown is now set with paste stones and is shown in a separate room at the Tower of London.

- **Queen Mary's Crown** was made for the coronation of George V's consort Mary of Teck in 1911. Queen Mary commissioned this new crown intending it to be used by all future Queen Consorts. Its design was inspired by Queen Alexandra's Crown, with eight half-arches, but was taller and closer in style to British crowns. It is made of gold and silver and Mary had it set exclusively with diamonds, over 2,200 of them including originally the Koh-i-Noor (transferred from Queen Alexandra's Crown) and the newly cut Cullinan III and IV diamonds (see *The Personal Jewels of the Royal Family—Gems*). These three stones have now been removed and replaced with quartz crystals, however the crown is still set with the other original diamonds. It is exhibited with the other Crown Jewels at the Tower of London.

- **Queen Elizabeth the Queen Mother's Crown** was made for the coronation of George VI's consort Queen Elizabeth Bowes-Lyon in 1937. Necessity dictated that this crown be made because Queen Mary, in a break with tradition, decided to attend the coronation of her son George VI wearing her own Queen Consort's Crown, so another one had to be made for Queen Elizabeth. This crown is simpler in style, with only four arches, and is made of platinum instead of gold. It contains over 2,800 diamonds including the Koh-i-Noor at the front, transferred from the previous crown. It was the last Queen Consort crown to be used on a public occasion when it was placed on the coffin of Queen Elizabeth the Queen Mother at her funeral in 2002.

As with the Sovereign, two sceptres are used to crown Queen Consorts. The **Queen Consort's Sceptre with Cross**, placed in the Queen Consort's right hand, symbolizes earthly power. It is made of gold, measures 65cms and resembles in style the Sovereign's Sceptre with Cross. The **Queen Consort's Ivory Rod with Dove**, symbolizing mercy and delivered into the left hand, is much longer at 95cms and is made of ivory held together by gold fittings. Its gold monde at the top and gold pommel at the bottom are enamelled with the national flowers of England, Scotland and Ireland. Unlike the Sovereign's Sceptre with Dove, the wings of the dove at the top of this sceptre are folded. Both sceptres were made for the coronation of James II and Mary of Modena in 1685 and have been used to crown all Queen Consorts ever since.

The **Queen Consort's Coronation Ring** contains a large ruby surrounded by 14 diamonds and is placed on the fourth finger of the Queen Consort's right hand at her crowning. Like the Sovereign's Ring, it symbolizes union with the nation. The ring was first made for the coronation of Queen Adelaide of Saxe-Meiningen in 1831 and has been used to crown all Queen Consorts since.

Mary II's Double Regalia

For the joint coronation of William III and Mary II in 1689 two new pieces had to be created to crown Mary as monarch in her own right together with her husband. One of them was an additional Orb, similar to the Sovereign's Orb but 7cms smaller in circumference. The other was a second Sovereign's Sceptre with Dove, exactly as long as the existing one. A coronation ring was also made for Mary but it has not survived among the Crown Jewels. A separate crown was not made as she was crowned with the Queen Consort's Crown made for Mary of Modena in 1685. (It is unclear why a separate Sovereign's Sceptre with Cross was not made for Mary II). Mary II's Orb, and Sceptre with Dove have not been used since 1689.

Other State Jewels

Besides the coronation regalia, there are other state jewels that are owned by the Crown and that are used, or have been used, on official occasions. The three most important of these items are described below.

The George IV State Diadem

Although not kept with the Crown Jewels in the Tower of London, this State Diadem belongs to the Crown and has become closely identified with state functions like the State Opening of Parliament and state banquets. The Diadem was created in 1821 for the coronation of George IV, who wanted a jewel bearing flower symbols of Britain: the circlet features bouquets of flowers made of English roses, Scottish thistles and Irish shamrocks, alternating with Maltese crosses. It is 19cm wide, 7.5cm high, and is set with 1,333 diamonds and 169 pearls. George IV only wore it once around a velvet cap during his coronation's procession to Westminster Abbey, and following his death in 1830 it has been used by Queens only. Queen Victoria wore it on official portraits early in her reign, and later it was worn occasionally by Queens Consorts until 1952. The Diadem is today most closely associated with Queen Elizabeth II who has worn it at the State Opening of Parliament since 1952 and on many official portraits, including her official image on postage stamps and coins.

Queen Victoria's Small Diamond Crown

After Prince Albert's death in 1861 Victoria insisted on wearing widow's clothing for the rest of her life, and therefore refused to wear the Imperial State Crown at official occasions as she considered it too large and colourful for a widow to wear. To solve this problem a new smaller crown was created in 1870 set exclusively with colourless diamonds, which could be worn by widows. Victoria wore it often on official occasions and on portraits over the last 30 years of her life, and it became her most identifiable piece of jewellery. The tiny crown is only 10cms wide by 10cms high and weighs only 140grams, but is still set with over 1,100 diamonds. After Victoria's death it became an official state jewel. It was occasionally worn by Queen Alexandra and Queen Mary, but it has remained unused since 1937. It can be seen together with the Crown Jewels in the Tower of London.

The Imperial Crown of India

This large crown was created specifically for the Delhi Durbar of 1911 held to celebrate the accession of George V as Emperor of India. George planned to attend the ceremony in India in person wearing one of the crowns he had worn at his coronation in Westminster Abbey, but it was pointed out to him that British law forbids the Crown Jewels to be removed from British soil. A new crown therefore had to be made in London by the crown jewellers at a cost of £60,000, or approximately £4 million in today's money. The crown has a gold and silver frame, is set with 6,000 small diamonds, and contains large emeralds, sapphires and rubies that were donated by Indian princes. George V wore it at the Delhi Durbar on 12 December 1911, however the crown's weight made it difficult to bear it in the hot Indian sun. George wrote in his diary at the end of that day: "Rather tired after wearing the crown for 3 and a half hours, it hurt my head as it is pretty heavy." After the Durbar the crown was taken back to Britain and placed in the Tower of London, where it remains today. It has not been used since 1911. However—as Beefeaters in the Tower are often fond of saying—if a monarch should have a need to wear an official crown abroad, this is the only crown that can be removed from the country.

The Great Gems of State

The Crown Jewels used in the coronation service contain some of the most historic gems in the nation's history. These gems were either owned by famous figures, or were silent witnesses to important historical events, or are of enormous value because of their quality. They are considered individual treasures on their own and rank as one of the greatest collection of state gems in the world. The most important ones are described below.

St Edward the Confessor's Sapphire

The oldest gem in the Crown Jewels, this deep blue sapphire was owned by St Edward the Confessor, the last monarch of the Anglo-Saxon House of Wessex who died in 1066. The sapphire therefore is older than the Tower of London itself where it is kept, and is the historical link to Anglo-Saxon England in the Crown Jewels. Legend says it was originally set in a ring King Edward gave for alms to a beggar who then revealed himself to be St John the Evangelist. Medieval art often depicted this miracle by showing Edward with the sapphire ring in his hand. Edward arranged to be buried with the ring, but the sapphire was retrieved from his coffin in 1163 in the presence of Thomas Becket. It was then stored in the royal treasury in the Middle Ages, sold by the Commonwealth in 1649, and then re-bought at the Restoration in 1660. It was first set at the top of the Imperial State Crown in 1821, in the same position it holds today.

The Black Prince's Ruby

Set prominently at the front of the Imperial State Crown, this 170-carat deeply red stone is not actually a ruby but a spinel, though its weight and size still make it one of the biggest spinels in the world. It probably originated in Central Asia and was first recorded in Europe in the 14th century. In 1367 King Pedro I of Castile gifted it to Edward the Black Prince, the first English owner of the stone, as a reward for his winning support at the Battle of Najera in Spain. Tradition says the gem was later worn by Henry V at the Battle of Agincourt, where it was almost lost in the melee of battle. It was then noted among the jewels of Queen Elizabeth I, and like other Crown Jewels it was sold by the Commonwealth in 1649, but then re-acquired at the Restoration. It was first placed in the Imperial State Crown at the coronation of James II in 1685 and has been set at the front ever since.

Queen Elizabeth's Pearls

Tradition says that three large pearls hanging from the crossing in the Imperial State Crown once belonged to Queen Elizabeth I. They had first belonged to the 16th century French Queen Consort Catherine de Medici, who had received them as a wedding gift from her cousin Pope Clement VII. Catherine in turn gifted them to her daughter-in-law, Mary Queen of Scots, who eventually brought them to Scotland in 1561. After Mary lost the Scottish throne and fled to England in 1568 the pearls somehow came into the possession of her cousin, Queen Elizabeth I. At Elizabeth's death the pearls were inherited by her successor, James I—Mary's son—and he gave them to his daughter who was also called Elizabeth and who became Queen of Bohemia (therefore another Queen Elizabeth). She took the pearls abroad with her in 1613 before coming back to England in 1660, so the pearls escaped Republican destruction in 1649. There were originally a larger number of pearls but by the reign of Queen Victoria only three large pearls survived, and they were set hanging from the middle of the Imperial State Crown's crossing where the arches meet. A fourth pearl hanging there was supplied by the crown jewellers in 1838.

The Stuart Sapphire

The Stuart Sapphire, set in the Imperial State Crown, is an ancient 104-carat oval stone that was first recorded in the possession of the medieval kings of Scotland in 1214. In 1296 King Edward I took the stone to England during the Scottish Wars, but it was later returned to Scotland by his grandson, Edward III. It was then passed down the Stuart dynasty of Scottish kings from which it took its name before it was united with the English Crown Jewels. Like other jewels, it was sold by the Commonwealth in 1649 but was re-acquired at the Restoration. James II famously took the stone with him into exile at the Glorious Revolution in 1688 and afterwards it was owned by his heirs, the Stuart pretenders to the throne. It was finally reunited with the Crown Jewels in 1814 after the death of the last Stuart pretender. George IV famously gave the gem to his last great mistress, Lady Elizabeth Conyngham, who wore it at George's coronation, and after his death in 1830 the stone had to be discreetly recovered from her as she initially refused to give it back. Queen Victoria first set the sapphire at the front of the Imperial State Crown in 1838, but it was later transferred to the back of the crown in 1909 to make way for the Second Star of Africa.

The Koh-I-Noor

The origins of the Koh-I-Noor, meaning 'Mountain of Light', are shrouded in Indian myth. Its first historical mention is from the 14th century when it was set as an eye in the statue of a Hindu goddess in Southern India. From then until the 19th century the stone changed hands many times as a spoil of war between the rulers of India and Central Asia, until finally it came into the hands of the rulers of Punjab in the 1830s. When the British East India Company annexed the Punjab in 1849 they demanded the Koh-I-Noor as a tribute, and the gem was sent to Queen Victoria in England. Already famous because of its history and legends, the stone was exhibited at the Great Exhibition of 1851 where it was seen by over a million people. Disappointment with its lack of sparkle however led to its re-cutting in 1852, supervised by Prince Albert, when the stone was cut to 105.6 carats losing 40% of its volume. By this time a legend had grown that the Koh-I-Noor brought misfortune to its owners, and that the rulers of the Punjab had given it to the British in the hope that they would lose their grip on India. When that clearly did not happen, the legend was modified to say that the gem brought great misfortune to male owners but great fortune to female owners, since the stone had technically become the property of Queen Victoria. Consequently, a royal practice was started for the Koh-I-Noor to be passed down from woman to woman in the Royal Family. After Victoria's death, the stone was handed down as inheritance from Queen to Queen at each monarch's accession, and was in turn set into the Queen Consort Crowns of Queen Alexandra, Queen Mary and Queen Elizabeth the Queen Mother. At the death of Queen Elizabeth the Queen Mother in 2002 the Koh-I-Noor was inherited by her daughter Queen Elizabeth II, the current owner. At present however the gem remains set into the Crown of Queen Elizabeth the Queen Mother kept in the Tower of London.

The First and Second Stars of Africa

The First Star of Africa and the Second Star of Africa are the biggest gems cut from the Cullinan Diamond, the biggest diamond ever found in the world. When initially discovered in 1905 in the Premier Mine near Pretoria, South Africa, the rough diamond weighed 3,106 carats or over half a kilogram (1.6lb). Besides its size it was also notable for its purity and extraordinary blue-white colour. It was immediately named after Thomas Cullinan, the owner of the mine, who sold it to the new South African government of the Transvaal. The government in turn presented to King Edward VII in 1907 as a token of loyalty to the British Crown following the previous Boer Wars. The diamond was famously sent to London under a ruse: a decoy strongbox was placed on a steamboat headed to England where it was guarded night and day, while the real diamond was sent over by regular parcel post in an ordinary box. Edward VII promised to include the Cullinan in the British Crown Jewels for posterity and the diamond was subsequently cut into separate stones in Amsterdam in 1908, with the biggest two gems joining the Jewels in 1909. The biggest stone, renamed The First (or Great) Star of Africa was set at the top of the Sceptre with Cross. At 530.2 carats it remains the largest colourless cut diamond in the world. The second stone, weighing 317.4 carats and renamed The Second (or Lesser) Star of Africa, was set at the front of the Imperial State Crown, below the Black Prince's Ruby. Seven other stones, smaller in size, were also cut from the Cullinan in 1908 and later became personal possessions of the Royal Family (See *The Personal Jewels of the Royal Family—Gems*).

The Honours of Wales

Wales possesses its own Crown Jewels, called the Honours of Wales, which are used in the official investiture ceremony of the Prince of Wales. This ceremony has roots in medieval investitures however the current public ceremony only had its start in 1911 when it was first performed in Caernarvon Castle to invest Edward Prince of Wales, son of King George V (the future Edward VIII). Only one other investiture has been performed since then, for Prince Charles in 1969. The Honours include items used in these investiture ceremonies as well as coronets worn by Princes of Wales in the past. They include the following:

The **Coronet of the Prince of Wales** only contains one arch crossing the head, from ear to ear, as opposed to the four arches found on monarchs' crowns. A small orb topped by a cross rises in the middle of the arch. The Honours of Wales include three coronets that have been used by Princes of Wales in the past, all similar in design:

- The **Coronet of Frederick Prince of Wales** was made for the eldest son of George II in 1728. It was the first coronet made for a Prince of Wales since the Restoration and was cast in solid gold with no gems. It was used for all Princes of Wales until 1901, however it was seldom worn on the head, rather it was carried on a cushion in procession before the Prince on state occasions. It is now kept with the Crown Jewels in the Tower of London.

- The **Coronet of George Prince of Wales** was created for the son of Edward VII to wear at his father's coronation in 1902. Made of gilt silver, it was later worn by George's own son, Edward Prince of Wales, for his father's coronation as George V in 1911, and also for Edward's investiture in Caernarvon Castle that same year. For reasons unknown, and contrary to tradition that says the Crown Jewels must not leave the country, when Edward abdicated as King Edward VIII in 1936 he took the coronet with him into exile and kept it until his death in 1972. It was later returned and placed in the Tower of London with the other Crown Jewels where it remains today.

- The **Coronet of Charles Prince of Wales** was created in 1969 for his investiture at Caernarvon Castle. Its creation was necessary as the existing coronet was still in the possession of the Duke of Windsor and taken abroad after he abdicated the throne (see above). It is made of gold, platinum, diamonds and emeralds, and designed in modern style. Although it retains all the design elements of the previous coronets, it also includes symbols associated with Prince Charles including 13 diamonds on the top orb that are arranged as the constellation of Scorpio, the Prince's star sign. The coronet has in the past been on show at the National Museum of Wales in Cardiff but is currently back in the Royal Collection.

The other Honours of Wales consist in a ring, a gold rod and a sword, all made in 1911 for the investiture of Edward Prince of Wales:

- The **Ring** is made of gold and is in the shape of two dragons coming together holding a single amethyst in their mouths and claws.

- The **Rod** is also made of gold and is 85cms long (2 feet 8 inches), with the top part featuring the dragon of Wales and a single amethyst.

- The **Investiture Sword** has a steel blade etched with the motto of the Prince of Wales on one side, "Ich Dien", while the other side is etched with the words "Iorwerth Tywysog Cymru", Welsh for "Edward Prince of Wales". The hilt of the sword is in the shape of two dragons entwined bearing a coronet.

These three items are not often on public display and are currently stored in the Royal Collection in London. Plans have been proposed for these items, plus the Coronet of Charles Prince of Wales, to be exhibited permanently in a new heritage centre in Wales but no action has been taken yet as of May 2018.

The Honours of Scotland

Scotland possesses its own Crown jewels, called the Honours of Scotland, which are the oldest regalia in the United Kingdom dating back to the late 15th to early 16th centuries. Differently from the English Crown Jewels, they escaped destruction by the Republican Commonwealth in the 1650s thanks to the resourcefulness of several Scots who smuggled them out of Edinburgh and hid them in the north of the country. They were last used in a coronation ceremony in 1651 for the Scottish coronation of Charles II (before they were hid), and from 1660 to 1707 they were ceremonially used to open the Old Parliament of Scotland. After the Union of the English and Scottish Parliaments in 1707 the Jewels were locked away in Edinburgh Castle until they were re-discovered in 1818. Since then they have been on show in the Crown Room at Edinburgh Castle, except for a short period of time during the Second World War when they were again hidden for safety. Under the terms of the Act of Union of 1707 the Jewels cannot be taken out of Scotland. The Honours of Scotland proper comprise the following three items.

- The **Crown of Scotland** was cast for James V in 1540 using material from a previous crown of date unknown. It is made of solid gold and contains 43 precious stones and 68 Scottish freshwater pearls, with most of the gems coming from the previous crown. The crown was used in the coronation ceremonies of Mary Queen of Scots and James VI of Scotland, and to crown Charles I and Charles II at their separate Scottish coronations in 1633 and 1651. It is currently used in special ceremonies like the official opening of the Scottish Parliament in 1999 and the opening of the permanent Parliament building in 2004.

- The **Sceptre** is silver gilt and was a gift from Pope Alexander VI to King James IV of Scotland in 1494. It was remodelled by King James V in 1536 and in its present form features small figures of the Virgin and Child, St James and St Andrew in its top finial, all surrounded by golden dolphins and topped by a polished rock crystal.

- The **Sword of State** was a gift from Pope Julius II to King James IV of Scotland in 1507. A tall sword measuring 1.35ms, the blade is etched with figures of the apostles Peter and Paul, and the handle is silver gilt and decorated with oak leaves. The blade bears a scar from when it was once broken: tradition says it happened in 1652 when the Crown Jewels were smuggled out and hid to protect them from Cromwell's Republican troops.

Also shown in the Crown Room of Edinburgh Castle together with the items above is the **Stuart Coronation Ring**, which tradition says was worn by Kings Charles I, Charles II and James II at their coronations in the 17th century. James II took the ring with him into exile in 1688 and it was then passed down the Stuart pretenders to the throne until the last pretender bequeathed it on his death in 1807 to George Prince of Wales, the future George IV. William IV first loaned the ring to Edinburgh Castle to be displayed with the

Honours of Scotland in 1830 but it remains part of the Royal Collection and is not an official Honour of Scotland. The ring is made of gold and silver, and is topped with a flat ruby engraved with a cross. A circle of 26 diamonds, a later 18th century addition, surrounds the ruby.

The Personal Jewels of the Royal Family

The Personal Jewels of the Royal Family comprise items that are worn by female family members on official occasions, royal visits and public appearances. They are visual representations of monarchy but, unlike the Crown Jewels, they are not owned by the state but by members of the Royal Family, or by the monarchy as part of the Royal Collection. The jewels came into royal possession in a variety of ways: as gifts from the public on important royal occasions like weddings or jubilees; as official gifts during state visits; as gifts between Royal Family members; and occasionally as legacies from friends of the Royal Family.

All the jewels that came into royal possession before 1936 are considered now part of the Royal Collection, and are therefore heritage held in trust for the nation. Jewels that were bought privately or bestowed as private gifts to members of the Royal Family after 1936 are still considered private possessions and can be disposed of at will, especially if they come in the possession of individuals who are not official members of the Royal Family (like for example happened in 2002 when some of Princess Margaret's jewels were sold by her son after her death). Generally however, all jewels that are bought by or gifted to the monarch, the Prince of Wales, and other future heirs to the throne are considered to have entered the Royal Collection automatically.

The present Personal Jewels collection was started by Queen Victoria in the 1850s. Only a few items pre-date her reign as most of the jewels owned by previous queens were lost to the Kingdom of Hanover in 1858 after a lengthy legal battle over Queen Charlotte's will (the Kingdom of Hanover split from the British Crown in 1837

at the accession of Queen Victoria and was inherited by Queen Charlotte's fifth son, Ernest Augustus, who claimed that most of his mother's jewels belonged by right to the Hanoverian Crown, not the British one). Queen Mary greatly expanded the collection both before and after becoming Queen, between the 1890s and 1920s, and Queen Elizabeth II has added many items during her reign.
Differently from the Crown Jewels, the Personal Jewels can be taken outside the country and so are frequently worn during foreign state visits. They are not stored in the Tower of London but are kept instead within the occupied Royal Residences where they are not accessible for public viewing. Many however are regularly exhibited in themed exhibitions by the Royal Collection. It is impossible to ascertain the exact number of items in the Personal Jewels collection as there is no official catalogue, and their total worth has never been publicly appraised. Only the most significant and historic items are described in this chapter, divided between Tiaras, Necklaces, Parures, Brooches and Gems. All items are listed in chronological order of creation within each section.

TIARAS

The Oriental Circlet

Also called the Indian Ruby Tiara, this circlet was designed by Prince Albert in 1853 using Indian motifs like Mogul arches and lotus flowers. As originally created, it contained diamonds and opals on a gold frame, and Queen Victoria wore it in this way when Prince Albert was alive but stopped wearing it after his death. Afterwards it passed to Queen Alexandra who replaced the opals with the current rubies. This circlet was a favorite of Queen Elizabeth the Queen Mother who wore it frequently until the end of her life in 2002.

The Vladimir Tiara

This tiara was originally made in the 1880s for the Grand Duchess Vladimir (Maria Pavlovna) of Russia, aunt of Tsar Nicholas II, who was described as the grandest of all the Grand Duchesses of Russia. A magnificent tiara, it had to be smuggled out of the country in 1917 during the Russian Revolution and was later sold by the Grand Duchess' family in 1921. It was bought by Queen Mary who repaired it and later bequeathed it to her granddaughter Queen Elizabeth II. The tiara is made of 15 interlocking gold circles covered in diamonds, with large pendant pearls usually hanging from the circles. The circles can also be left empty, or can be filled with other gems like the Cambridge Emeralds (see below). Queen Elizabeth II has worn the tiara in each of these forms regularly during her reign.

Queen Alexandra's Kokoshnik Tiara

This tiara was a gift to Alexandra of Denmark from the 'Ladies of Society' in 1888 to celebrate her Silver Wedding anniversary to the Prince of Wales. Alexandra specifically requested that it be modeled on the kokoshnik, the traditional Russian folk headdress that was popular at the Russian Imperial court at the time, and that had been worn as a tiara by her sister, Russian empress Maria Feodorovna. It contains 488 diamonds spread across 61 platinum bars, set as a fringe on a gold frame. Alexandra wore it frequently both as Princess of Wales and as Queen, and later bequeathed it to Queen Mary. Queen Elizabeth II inherited it in 1953 and has worn it regularly throughout her reign.

The Girls of Great Britain and Ireland Tiara

Queen Mary received this tiara as a gift on her wedding day in 1893 when she became Duchess of York. It was a present from a committee of women from Britain and Ireland who raised money to purchase it from the crown jeweller, Garrard's. The tiara's frame is made of gold and silver and is filled entirely with diamonds, arranged in scrolls and flower leaves. Queen Mary gave the tiara to her granddaughter Princess Elizabeth as a wedding gift in 1947 and since then it has become one of Queen Elizabeth II's most recognizable tiaras, often used at state banquets and other official occasions. It is also worn by the Queen on her portrait used on banknotes and coins, both in Britain and some Commonwealth countries.

The Delhi Durbar Tiara

The largest tiara in the Royal Collection, this grand headdress with lyres and scrolls was first worn by Queen Mary at the Delhi Durbar ceremony in 1911. It is made of gold, platinum and diamonds, many of them recycled from a previously dismantled tiara. As worn at the Delhi Durbar it was decorated with a ring of 10 of the Cambridge Emeralds (see below), but Queen Mary removed the emeralds in the 1920s. She later gave the tiara to Queen Elizabeth Bowes-Lyon who rarely wore it in her lifetime, and at her death it passed to Queen Elizabeth II. It has lately been loaned to Camilla, Duchess of Cornwall who has worn it on state occasions.

The Cambridge Lover's Knot Tiara

Queen Mary commissioned this piece in 1914 to resemble a tiara that had been worn by her grandmother, Princess Augusta, Duchess of Cambridge. Made of gold, silver and diamonds, it contains 19 large pearls hanging from arches ties by lover's knot bows, from which the tiara takes the second part of its name. Queen Elizabeth II inherited the tiara at Queen Mary's death in 1953 and wore it regularly during the first years of her reign. In 1981 she loaned it to Diana, Princess of Wales who made it her most recognizable piece of jewelry, wearing it at state functions, receptions and on official portraits. The tiara was returned to the Queen after Diana's divorce from Prince Charles in 1997 and it was not seen again until 2015 when it began to be worn by the current Duchess of Cambridge.

Queen Mary's Fringe Tiara

Queen Mary had this tiara created in 1919 using diamonds from a previous similar tiara that had been used by both Queen Adelaide of Saxe Meiningen and by Queen Victoria (it is sometimes called the Hanoverian Tiara because of the origins of the diamonds contained in it). As refashioned by Queen Mary, the tiara contains 47 diamond bars divided by smaller diamond spikes on a gold and silver frame. It can be dismantled from its frame and also be worn as a fringe necklace. Queen Mary gave it to Queen Elizabeth Bowes-Lyon in 1936 who owned it until her death in 2002 but she wore it sporadically as Queen Mother. The tiara was famously worn as 'something borrowed' by Princess Elizabeth at her wedding in 1947 (when it famously broke and had to be repaired on the day), and also by Princess Anne at her wedding in 1974.

The Greville Tiara

Dame Margaret Greville (1863-1942), an heiress and famous society hostess, was a personal friend of both Queen Mary and Queen Elizabeth Bowes-Lyon. When she died childless in 1942 she left her personal jewelry collection containing over 60 pieces to Queen Elizabeth, including this tiara. Also called the Boucheron tiara, after the jewelry firm that created it, it is one of the largest tiaras in the Royal Collection, with diamonds mounted on a honeycomb-shaped frame. It was one of the Queen Mother's favourite tiaras and after her death it passed to Queen Elizabeth II. She has currently loaned it to Camilla, Duchess of Cornwall, who wears it frequently at official functions including the State Opening of Parliament. The other jewelry pieces bequeathed by Mrs Greville included earrings, brooches and necklaces, all of which have been worn frequently by women in the Royal Family.

The Burmese Tiara

Queen Elizabeth II commissioned this tiara in 1973 using two wedding presents she had received in 1947: 96 rubies from the Burmese people, and diamonds from a tiara given by the Nizam of Hyderabad (see below). The gift of the 96 diamonds was symbolic as in Burmese belief rubies have the power to protect the human body from 96 diseases. The tiara is made of a gold and silver frame supporting ruby-filled flowers, surrounded by diamonds. Queen Elizabeth II has worn this tiara often since 1974.

NECKLACES

Queen Anne's and Queen Caroline's Pearls

Possibly the oldest personal jewels in the Royal Family, these two individual, single-strand pearl necklaces are said to have been belonged separately to Queen Anne, the last Stuart monarch who died in 1702, and to Caroline of Ansbach, Queen Consort of King George II, who died in 1727. Queen Anne's necklace contains 46 pearls, Queen Caroline's has 50 pearls. Although individual heirlooms, they are usually worn together, with their combined weight adding to over two kilos. They were worn by Princess Elizabeth on her wedding day in 1947.

The Coronation Necklace

Created in 1858 for Queen Victoria, this necklace has been worn by five queens in succession. It takes its name from having been worn at the coronation ceremony of Queen Alexandra in 1902, Queen Mary in 1911, Queen Elizabeth Bowes-Lyon in 1937, and Queen Elizabeth II in 1953. It consists of a string of 25 large diamonds set in gold and silver, plus a single 22.48-carat pendant known as the Lahore Diamond. The necklace comes with a matching set of diamond earrings, called the Coronation Earrings.

Queen Alexandra's Dagmar Necklace

One of the most elaborate jewels in the Royal Collection, this necklace was a present from King Frederick VII of Denmark to her cousin Alexandra on her wedding to the Prince of Wales in 1863. It was designed in the Byzantine style with several gold strings, swags and scrolls, and includes 2,000 diamonds and 118 pearls. Its centerpiece is an enameled pendant in the form of a Dagmar Cross, a traditional Danish decoration based on a cross worn by Queen Dagmar of Denmark in the 13th century. In true Byzantine style, the cross contains silk from King Cnut's tomb as well as a fragment of the True Cross. The cross pendant is removable, and the pendant-less necklace was last worn by Queen Elizabeth II in the 1950s.

Queen Victoria's Golden Jubilee Necklace

This necklace was a gift to Queen Victoria from a committee of ladies for her Golden Jubilee in 1887. It is made of clusters of gold, pearls and diamonds on a gold string, and the centre cluster is topped by a small silhouette of a crown. Queen Victoria was said to have been very pleased with the gift, but it was not a favourite item of Queens Consorts afterwards. Queen Elizabeth II has worn it frequently during her reign, especially during state visits and at the State Opening of Parliament where it has made more appearances than any other necklace.

The South African Necklace

Princess Elizabeth received this necklace as a 21st birthday gift from the government of South Africa, while visiting the country with her parents in 1947. It originally contained 21 large diamonds but Elizabeth shortened it to 15 after she became Queen, turning the rest into a bracelet. Since then she has referred to the necklace on occasions as her 'best diamonds'.

The Nizam of Hyderabad Necklace

One of Princess Elizabeth's wedding gifts in 1947 was a tiara and necklace paid for by the Nizam of Hyderabad, one of India's last princes, reputed the richest man in the world at the time. Princess Elizabeth chose the gifts herself at the London branch of Cartier while the bill was sent to the Nizam. Elizabeth wore both necklace and tiara during her first years as Queen, however she later dismantled the tiara to create two brooches, and used the spare diamonds to create the Burmese tiara in 1974 (see above). The necklace remains intact however and has been worn regularly by the Queen, who also has loaned it to the Duchess of Cambridge. Oriental in design, it is made of platinum and includes over 50 diamonds.

The King Faisal and King Khalid Necklaces

Both these necklaces were gifts from the Kings of Saudi Arabia to Queen Elizabeth II, and both were designed by the American jeweler Harry Winston. The King Faisal Necklace was an official gift to the Queen during that King's state visit to Britain in 1967. It has over 300 diamonds set in platinum, with a combined diamond weight of over 80 carats. The King Khalid necklace, also made of platinum and diamonds, was an official gift to the Queen during her state visit to Saudi Arabia in 1979. Both necklaces have been worn regularly by Elizabeth II over the last 40 years, and have also been loaned to other members of the Royal Family.

PARURES

The Delhi Durbar Parure

Perhaps the most exotic-looking set of jewels in the Royal Collection, this parure was a gift from King George V to Queen Mary on her 44th birthday, and was expressly created to be worn at the Delhi Durbar of 1911. It was designed with Indian motifs and contains a large part of the Cambridge Emeralds (see below). Besides the large Delhi Durbar tiara (see above), the parure includes earrings, a bracelet, a stomacher, and a necklace. The earrings are set with oval emeralds surrounded by 11 diamonds. The bracelet is made of gold and platinum with three large emeralds. The stomacher, worn on the breast, is filled with hundreds of small diamonds and seven large emeralds, two of which can be detached to be worn as a brooch. Finally, the Delhi Durbar Necklace is a uniquely designed diamond necklace with seven large Cambridge Emeralds alternating with six large diamonds, and from which hang two separate pendants: a large drop-shaped emerald from one string, and the Cullinan VII diamond from another string (see below). The parure was often worn complete by Queen Mary throughout her life however the items have not been worn together since Queen Elizabeth II inherited the set in 1953. The Queen prefers to wear the parure reduced to necklace, earrings, brooch and bracelet, without the tiara and stomacher, and in this guise she has worn it often throughout her reign.

Queen Elizabeth II's Sapphire Set

This set started with a gift from King George VI to his daughter Princess Elizabeth on her wedding in 1947. It originally included a 19th century gold necklace and earrings with large sapphires and diamonds. After becoming Queen, Elizabeth added a large sapphire pendant to the necklace that can also be used as a brooch, and in 1963 she completed the parure by purchasing a sapphire and diamond tiara, and a bracelet. The parure has been worn often by the Queen at official functions.

The Brazilian Aquamarine Parure

The President of Brazil presented a necklace and earrings to Queen Elizabeth II on her coronation in 1953 that was set with the finest aquamarines sourced in Brazilian mines. After collecting more quality aquamarines in the following years, Brazil then presented the Queen with an additional bracelet and brooch in 1958. The Queen then completed the parure by commissioning an aquamarine tiara from the crown jewelers made with more Brazilian stones. She was worn the full set often on official occasions, and as individual pieces separately. Most the pieces have platinum frames and also contain diamonds.

BROOCHES

Prince Albert's Sapphire Brooch

Prince Albert gave this jewel, a gold brooch with a large sapphire surrounded by 12 diamonds, to Queen Victoria as a present on the day before their wedding in 1840. Victoria wore it frequently until Albert died in 1861, and it was later worn by all Queen Consorts. It has been worn frequently by Queen Elizabeth II, especially on important occasions including President Kennedy's reception at Buckingham Palace in 1961, and Prince William's christening in 1982.

The Bow Brooches

Bow brooches have been a favourite item of wear of every queen from Queen Victoria to Queen Elizabeth II. Four items in particular have been used more than any other:

- **Queen Victoria's Bow Brooches** is a set of three brooches commissioned by Victoria in 1858 that contain over 500 diamonds in total. They have been worn by all Queens in many guises ever since.

- **The Kensington Bow Brooch** was a wedding gift from the residents of Kensington, London, to Queen Mary in 1893 when she became Duchess of York. It is made of gold, silver and diamonds, and features a large pendant pearl.

- **The Dorset Bow Brooch** was another wedding gift to Queen Mary in 1893 from the county of Dorset. It is also made of gold, silver and diamonds.

- **The True Lover's Knot Brooch**, the largest of the bow brooches, was acquired by Queen Mary in 1932 and is studded with diamonds. It is usually worn by Queen Elizabeth II on important occasions like the wedding of Prince William in 2011, and at official state visits.

All the bow brooches came into the possession of Queen Elizabeth II at the death of Queen Mary in 1953. She has worn them often, particularly during the Remembrance Day ceremony at the Cenotaph in November, when any of the brooches can be used to secure a small bouquet of Remembrance poppies to her dress.

The Guards Badge

The Guards Badge is a regimental brooch that combines the badges of the five regiments of the Foot Guards: the Grenadier Guards, Coldstream Guards, Scots Guards, Irish Guards and Welsh Guards. The individual badges are delicately rendered in fine precious stones inside an oval which is surrounded by an inscription saying 'Quinque Juncta in Uno', i.e. Five Joined In One, the motto of the Foot Guards. The brooch was created for Queen Mary and has become associated with Trooping the Colour. Queen Elizabeth II has been wearing it at the annual ceremony every year for the last 20 years.

The Rhodesian Flame Lily Brooch

One of the most beautiful brooches in the collection, this jewel was a 21st birthday gift to Princess Elizabeth in 1947 from the children of

Southern Rhodesia when the country was still part of the British Empire. It is said that 42,000 Rhodesian schoolchildren gave a little bit of their pocket money to contribute to the purchase of the brooch. It is shaped like Rhodesia's national flower, the flame lily, and contains over 300 diamonds set in platinum. This was the first jewel Elizabeth II wore publicly as Queen when she arrived back in the United Kingdom from Kenya in February 1952.

The Williamson Diamond Brooch

Shaped like a jonquil flower, this brooch contains at its centre the Williamson Diamond, a 23.6-carat rare pink diamond said to be the finest of its kind in the world. It is named after Dr John T. Williamson, the Canadian owner of the mine in Tanganyka where the diamond was found, and who gave the jewel to Princess Elizabeth as a wedding present in 1947. The brooch has a platinum frame set with 203 diamonds making up the petals, stalk and leaves of a flower. The Williamson Diamond is set as the central gem in the middle of the petals. Queen Elizabeth II wore this brooch for her Silver Jubilee in 1977, Prince Charles' wedding in 1981, and Prince Edward's wedding in 1997.

The Commonwealth Brooches

A number of brooches in the Personal Jewels collection are associated with specific Commonwealth countries and are often worn to honour those nations. They include:

- **The Canadian Maple Leaf Brooch:** a diamond encrusted brooch in the shape of Canada's national symbol, it was a gift by King George VI to his wife Queen Elizabeth ahead of their royal tour of Canada in 1939. It is primarily used in Canada-related events and during royal tours of the country.

- **The New Zealand Fern Brooch:** a Christmas gift to Queen Elizabeth II from the women of Auckland, New Zealand during the royal tour of 1953, it represents one of the symbols of the country, the silver fern, in platinum and diamonds. It is often worn on official New Zealand royal portraits.

- **The Australian Wattle Brooch:** given to Queen Elizabeth II as a gift by the people of Australia during the royal tour of 1954, it is made in the shape of Australia's national flower, the golden wattle, and is set with yellow, white and blue diamonds.

- **The Jamaican Doctor Bird Brooch:** This brooch was given by the people of Jamaica to Queen Elizabeth II during her Golden Jubilee tour of the country in 2002. It represents Jamaica's national bird, a species of hummingbird only found on the island. It is made of platinum, silver, diamonds, rubies, sapphires, plus Jamaican granite and marble.

- **The Botswana Flower Brooch**: made of gold and diamonds in the shape of a spray of millet, Botswana's main crop, it was given to Elizabeth II from the President of Botswana in 2007.

The Centenary Rose Brooch

This very personal brooch was a gift from Queen Elizabeth II to her mother, Queen Elizabeth the Queen Mother, for her 100th birthday in 2000. It features a hand-painted Queen Elizabeth rose (named after the Queen Mother) on rock crystal, surrounded by 100 diamonds. After the Queen Mother died at the age of 101 Queen Elizabeth II began to wear the brooch herself.

GEMS

The Cambridge Emeralds

The origins of this set of large cabochon (i.e. smooth) emeralds are obscure but they probably originated in India where they would have been owned by royalty. After they appeared in Europe in the 19th century they were offered as a prize in a charity lottery held in Frankfurt in 1818, which was won by the Duke and Duchess of Cambridge, the son and daughter-in-law of King George III and grandparents of Queen Mary. They were passed down the Cambridge family line until they finally came to Queen Mary in 1910. It is unclear how many emeralds were or are contained in the set but estimates suggest between 30 and 40, of different shapes and of a bright shade of green. Queen Mary placed most of them in the original Delhi Durbar Parure (see above) but only 20 of them remain in that set today, with nine in the Delhi Durbar necklace alone. The ones that were on the Durbar tiara were later removed and are now occasionally worn in the Vladimir Tiara (see above). A few emeralds have also been set separately in other jewels.

The Timur Ruby

Once considered the largest ruby in the world this unfaceted stone is now known to be a spinel, weighing 352.5 carats. Indian tradition holds that the gem was once owned by Timur, also known as Tamerlane, the great 13th century ruler of Central Asia. It was later owned by his descendants, the Mughal Emperors of India, four of whom inscribed their names on the stone, including Akbar, Jahangir and Aurangzeb. The ruby then passed through the hands of Persian and Afghan rulers as a spoil of war during the 18th and 19th centuries. The last Indian owner was the Maharajah of the Punjab who relinquished the ruby to the British East India Company in 1849 along with the Koh-I-Noor diamond. The gem was taken to England, where it was first discovered that it was not a ruby but a spinel, and given to Queen Victoria in 1851. She placed it in a specially designed gold and diamond necklace which she sometimes wore before Prince Albert died in 1861. The necklace and the ruby have not been worn by anyone else since, but are sometimes shown as part of Royal Collection exhibitions.

The Cullinan Diamonds

The Cullinan Diamond, found in South Africa in 1905, remains at 3,106 carats the largest diamond ever found. After it was presented to King Edward VII in 1907 it was sent to the firm of Asscher's in Amsterdam to be cut in separate stones. (for more history see *The First and Second Star of Africa* in *The Crown Jewels*). The diamond was eventually cut by Asscher's into nine large stones and 96 smaller stones. In the process, the Cullinan lost 2,050 carats of its weight, or 62.25% of its original size. The nine principal stones were renamed Cullinan I to IX in order of size, from largest to smallest. Cullinan I and Cullinan II, weighing 530.2 and 317.40 carats, were renamed the First Star and the Second Star of Africa and were set into the British Crown Jewels by King George V. Cullinan VI was bought privately by King Edward VII as a present for his wife Queen Alexandra during the diamond cutting process in 1908. The remaining stones were left with the firm of Asscher's as payment for the cutting and polishing of Cullinan I and II, however the government of the Transvaal eventually bought the six remaining large diamonds once they were cut and polished, and presented them to Queen Mary in 1910 to celebrate the founding of the Union of South Africa that year. Today, they continue to be used as personal jewels by the Royal Family, especially Queen Elizabeth II. They include:

- **Cullinan III and IV**, respectively 94.40 and 63.60 carats, were at first placed by Queen Mary in her Queen Consort Crown at the 1911 coronation. Since then they have usually been worn together as a brooch, with the pear-shaped Cullinan III hanging as a pendant from the cushion-shaped Cullinan IV. Queen Elizabeth II usually wears this brooch on special occasions only, the last time at her Diamond Jubilee celebrations in 2012.

- **Cullinan V** is heart-shaped and weighs 18.8 carats. It is set in a platinum brooch which can also be fit into larger pieces, like the stomacher in the Delhi Durbar parure. The diamond was also set individually in Queen Mary's crown at the 1937 coronation of George VI. Queen Elizabeth II has often worn it in its main setting as a brooch.

- **Cullinan VI**, weighing 11.5 carats and purchased by Edward VII as a present for Queen Alexandra, was modified by Queen Mary in 1925 to serve as a pendant on other jewels. It is marquis-cut (oblong) and is currently hanging as a pendant from Cullinan VIII on a brooch.

- **Cullinan VII** weighs 8.8 carats and is also marquis-cut. It is permanently set as a pendant in the Delhi Durbar neckace together with nine of the Cambridge emeralds (see *Delhi Durbar Parure* and *Cambridge Emeralds* above).

- **Cullinan VIII**, weighing 6.8 carats, is emerald-cut and was placed in a platinum brooch similar in style to the brooch of Cullinan V. It is currently worn with Cullinan VI as a pendant.

- **Cullinan IX** is the smallest diamond at 4.4 carats and is pear-shape cut. It is set in a platinum ring that Queen Elizabeth II has often worn together with the other Cullinan stones.

The Royal Philatelic Collection

The Royal Philatelic Collection is the personal stamps collection of the British Monarchy. Housed in St James's Palace, London, it is said to be the world's most comprehensive and important collection of postage stamps from Great Britain and the British Commonwealth.

History

The first serious stamp collector in the Royal Family was Prince Alfred, second son of Queen Victoria, who was given his first collector's stamps in 1856, only 16 years after the first postage stamp was issued in Britain. He went to on to become a serious collector and became Honorary President of the Royal Philatelic Society. Alfred eventually sold his collection to his brother, the future Edward VII, and he in turn passed it to his own son, the future George V, who became the greatest stamp collector in the history of the Royal Family.

George V once remarked to his personal philatelic advisor: "I wish to have *the* best collection & not *one of* the best collections in England." His passion was well known, and upon his marriage in 1893 members of the Royal Philatelic Society made him a wedding gift of 1,500 postage stamps from around the Empire. He amassed a remarkable stamp collection, mostly through bulk purchases of current and old stamps (he was often given first offer by dealers of collections up for sale) but also through judicious purchases of rare issues. In 1904, when he was Prince of Wales, he famously bought at auction a rare, unused 1847 Two Pence Blue issue from the Mauritius Post Office, paying a record price of £1,450 for it. When an unwitting courtier later told him that some 'damned fool' had spent over £1,400 on one silly stamp, George famously replied "I was that damned fool!" By a curious coincidence, George became King on 6 May 1910, the 70th anniversary of the first postage stamp being used in Britain.

After George V's death his collection passed to Edward VIII, who briefly considered selling it, and then to George VI and to Elizabeth II, thereby establishing a pattern for the collection being passed down from monarch to monarch. Although neither George VI nor Elizabeth II inherited George V's personal passion for stamps, they both continued to add to the collection through purchases of new issues and rare stamps, helped by the Keeper of the Royal Philatelic Collection, a permanent post created by George V. The Collection continues to grow today.

The Collection

The collection consists almost entirely of British and Commonwealth material, and its strength is in the completeness of its British holdings, particularly the very first British postal issues of the 1840s. There are also stamps with errors, oddities, and rare British Empire and Commonwealth issues. Besides stamps, the collection also includes stamp designs, proofs and colour trials including rare watercolours sketches for the first proposed Penny Black stamp of 1840. Because the monarch must approve any new stamp issue in the United Kingdom, proofs and stamp design sheets have been continually added to the collection over the last century. There is very little material in the Collection from outside the British Commonwealth, the only exception being a stamp album said to have belonged to Tsarevich Alexis of Russia.

It is not known how many stamps are in the Collection as it has never been officially counted for total numbers. George V's own collection is stored in 328 'Red' albums, each containing about 60 pages. Additions made by George VI are stored in 'Blue' albums, and those made by Elizabeth II are in 'Green' albums. Not all stamps acquired since George V however have been mounted, and the Royal Philatelic Collection estimates that there is probably enough material to fill another 2,000 albums.

Value and Access

It is impossible to put a monetary value on the Royal Philatelic Collection: nothing comparable in size and completeness has ever been sold on the market before, and it also includes items like designs and proofs which have never been auctioned previously. Among the most expensive individual items in the Collection are the Penny and Twopence Mauritius Post Office stamps acquired by George V at auction in 1904 (see above). These two stamps were the first ones issued by a colony of the British Empire in 1847, only seven years after the first British issues, and less than 30 examples of them are in existence today. Based on recent past auctions, both items are now valued at between £1-1.5 million each.

Unlike items in the Royal Collection, the Royal Philatelic Collection does not belong to the nation but is privately owned by the monarch. Because of its importance and uniqueness however it is not considered a personal asset to trade in, but a family heirloom to hand down to future generations. Because much of the Collection is fragile, and much of it is still un-mounted, it is not unfortunately on general display to the public, and remains stored at St James's Palace in London. Many items however are regularly shown at exhibitions in Britain and around the world, a practice that was started by King George VI in the 1940s.

Notable Royal Music

Monarchs and princes have employed musicians for personal entertainment or to exalt the monarchy since the Middle Ages. Famous composers employed directly by the royal court since the time of Henry VIII have included Thomas Tallis, Orlando Gibbons, Henry Purcell, George Frideric Handel, Thomas Arne, Arthur Sullivan and Edward Elgar. Following below is a list of famous musical pieces that were either composed for, of popularised by, the British monarchy.

The Prince of Denmark's March

By Jeremiah Clarke, c.1700

This popular composition for trumpets was originally written by the organist of St Paul's Cathedral in honour of Prince George of Denmark, Queen Anne's husband, two years before she became Queen and he became Royal Consort. It was famously played at the wedding of Prince Charles and Diana Spencer in 1981, and remains a popular musical choice for weddings in the UK today.

The Water Music Suites

By George F. Handel, 1717

Handel, the favourite composer of the early Hanoverian monarchs, created some of the most memorable music associated with the British monarchy (see other pieces below). The *Water Music Suites* were composed expressly for King George I after he requested a concert to be played during a regatta party he was to take part in London on 17 July 1717. On that day, the composition was played by musicians on barges accompanying the King, and George I was so pleased with the music that he asked for the concert to be repeated three times. The *Suites* have since become one of Handel's most famous pieces of music.

Zadok the Priest

By George F. Handel, 1727

Handel's greatest musical contribution to the British monarchy was *Zadok the Priest,* one of the four Coronation Anthems he composed for the coronation of George II in 1727. With its compelling crescendo, its explosion of choir and trumpets in the middle, and glorious declarations of 'God Save the King' at the end, the anthem has become closely identified with the monarchy itself. It has been played during the anointing of the monarch at every coronation since 1727, and has become one of the most popular pieces of classical music in Britain today.

Rule, Britannia!

Music by Thomas Arne, lyrics by James Thomson, 1740

This most patriotic of British songs started life as part of a masque written by Thomas Arne for Frederick Prince of Wales, son and heir of George II. The masque, called *Alfred,* centred on the life of King Alfred the Great and was first performed at Cliveden, the Prince's country home, on 1 August 1740. In its original form *Rule, Britannia* was meant to be a song of protest from the Prince's party against the policies of his father, King George II, who was accused of not doing enough to expand Britain's sea power. It was however picked up by the London theatres a few years later to great popular acclaim, and eventually became a patriotic hit song by the 19th century, when Britain was actually ruling the seas.

Music for the Royal Fireworks

By George F. Handel, 1749

Towards the end of his life Handel produced yet another memorable piece of music for the monarchy. The *Music for the Royal Fireworks* suite was commissioned by George II to accompany a grand fireworks display on 27 April 1749, held to celebrate the end of the War of the Austrian Succession in which Britain had been victorious. By this time Handel's fame was such that 12,000 people attended the rehearsal alone the week before. The work remains popular with audiences today and is often played together with the *Water Music Suites* during concerts.

Wedding March

By Felix Mendelssohn, 1842

Written as incidental music for his version of William Shakespeare's *A Midsummer Night's Dream* in 1842, Mendelssohn's *Wedding March* became popular after it was used at the wedding ceremony of Queen Victoria's eldest daughter, Victoria the Princess Royal, in London in 1858. Mendelssohn was Victoria and Albert's favourite composer and the march was played three times throughout the day: it was performed by the band of the Grenadier Guards in the courtyard of Buckingham Palace before the wedding party left for the chapel; it was played at the end of the wedding ceremony in the Chapel Royal of St James's Palace; and was played back at Buckingham Palace in the afternoon during the official wedding dejeuner for the guests. It has been played at wedding ceremonies all over the world ever since, becoming Mendelssohn's most popular piece of music.

Land of Hope and Glory

Music by Edward Elgar, lyrics by AC Benson, 1901-1902

'I've got a tune that will knock 'em - knock 'em flat!' Edgar wrote to a friend after he first wrote the music to *Land of Hope and Glory* as part of his *Pomp and Circumstance Marches* in 1901, the year Edward VII became king. He was right: at the *March*'s London premiere in October 1901 people rose as the tune ended and asked for a double encore. A year later the song was included in Elgar's *Coronation Ode* composed for Edward VII's coronation, and AC Benson was commissioned to write appropriately grand words to accompany the music, legend says at the suggestion of Edward VII himself. Since then, *Land of Hope and Glory* has been played at the end of each coronation ceremony and has become an expression of British patriotism, as shown yearly during its performance at the Last Night of the Proms. The original wordless tune has also developed a parallel life in the United States and Canada where it is traditionally played during graduation ceremonies in colleges and high schools.

I Was Glad

By Hubert Parry, 1902

Parry—who also wrote the music to the patriotic English hymn *Jerusalem*—composed *I Was Glad* for the coronation of King Edward VII in 1902. The anthem takes its name from the first words of Psalm 122, traditionally sung at British coronations since 965, and Parry's version has been played at every coronation since 1902 while the monarch processes up Westminster Abbey at the beginning of the ceremony. It was also played at the royal weddings of Prince Charles in 1981 and Prince William in 2011, and remains a frequently played piece of church music throughout Britain and the Commonwealth today.

Crown Imperial

By William Walton, 1937

The BBC commissioned this triumphant march from famed composer William Walton in 1936. It was meant to be performed at Edward VIII's coronation in 1937 but after his abdication it ended up being performed instead at the crowning of his successor, George VI. At the time, Walton was criticized for composing a march that was unrepresentative of his contemporary work and that sounded more like one of Elgar's *Pomp and Circumstances* marches, however *Crown Imperial* has since become one of Walton's most famous pieces. It was played at Elizabeth II's coronation in 1953, and at the royal weddings of Prince Charles and Prince William.

Candle in the Wind 1997

Music by Elton John, lyrics by Bernie Taupin, 1973, 1997

The original *Candle in the Wind*, released in 1973, was originally written as a tribute to Marilyn Monroe. In 1997 Elton John and Bernie Taupin reworked the song with new lyrics to pay tribute to Diana, Princess of Wales after her sudden death in a Paris car crash. Elton John performed the song in Westminster Abbey during Diana's funeral and a single was publicly released a week later, reaching the No.1 spot on most charts across the world. By the end of 1997 *Candle in the Wind 1997* had become the biggest-selling single of all time in the UK—a title it still retains—and later went on to become one of the biggest-selling singles in the world of all time, with a total of over 33 million copies sold to date.

Notable Royal Artists

Over the centuries many members of the Royal Family received instructions in artistic disciplines, particularly painting and music. The following Royal Family members distinguished themselves in particular arts or produced some artistic work of renown.

Henry VIII *(1491-1547)*
Musician, Composer
A monarch of many talents, Henry VIII's greatest artistic gift was music. He played the lute, virginals, recorder and organ, sang with a fine voice, and composed both secular and sacred music. A manuscript kept in the British Library records 33 compositions to his name including the popular tunes *Pasttime With Good Company, Green Groweth the Holly*, and *Oh, My Heart!*.

Mary Queen of Scots *(1542-1587)*
Needlework artist
Mary learned the art of embroidery as a young child at the French court and kept practicing it all her life. Her most famous works were embroidered whilst she was imprisoned in England between 1569-1587 and include pictures of animals, flowers and emblems, some of them set in elaborate compositions. Some of her work can be admired today at the Victoria and Albert Museum in London, and at Oxburgh Hall in Norfolk.

Anne of Denmark *(1574-1619)*
Actress, Musician
James I's wife commissioned and starred in elaborate court plays called 'masques', which were famed for their magnificent sets and

lavish costumes. Between 1604 and 1611 she is known to have acted in six masques—four of them written by Ben Jonson—on one occasion famously performing when six months pregnant. Anne was also a skilled musician, playing the lute, virginals and the lyra viol.

Prince Rupert of the Rhine *(1619-1682)*
Draughtsman, Printmaker
Charles I's nephew was one of the first people in England to experiment with mezzotint, a printing technique to reproduce artwork that improves the quality of dark and light tones. Some scholars actually credit him with being one of the inventors of this technique. His most famous mezzotint work, *The Great Executioner,* was partly inspired by the execution of his uncle Charles I.

George III *(1738-1820)*
Draughtsman, Amateur Architect, Musician
George was particularly fond of architecture and from his youth produced many drawings of classical buildings, architectural vistas and landscapes. Forty-five such drawings survive in the Royal Collection today, as well as over 100 architectural plans made by the king for study or pleasure. George was also a competent musician playing the harpsichord and the flute, and was particularly fond of playing Handel music.

Princess Elizabeth *(1770-1840)*
Draughtsman, Painter, Decorator
All six of George III's daughters received training in drawing and painting but the most talented was Princess Elizabeth, George's third daughter. Elizabeth was a skilled draughtswoman who produced individual paintings, miniatures and prints, all of which are kept in the Royal Collection. She also painted fans and porcelain, and decorated some rooms at Frogmore House with images of flowers and Chinoiserie.

Queen Victoria *(1819-1901)*
Draughtsman, Painter
Victoria was taught how to draw as a child and later learned how to paint watercolours. She became a very competent artist and was particularly good at capturing people, especially children. She could paint from life as well as from memory though she preferred real subjects instead of works of imagination. Her sketchbooks, kept in the Royal Collection, contain hundreds of drawings, paintings and watercolours. They include portraits of her family and courtiers, landscapes from Scotland, seascapes from the Isle of Wight, and views from the places she visited.

Prince Albert *(1819-1861)*
Composer, Designer, Painter, Architect
Victoria's Prince Consort was probably the most multi-talented person to ever be part of the British Royal Family. Besides being able to draw and paint, he designed jewellery and furniture, drew architectural plans for both Osborne House and Balmoral, sang and played the piano. He also composed music. There are over 40 musical compositions to his name including songs, hymns, and a *Te Deum* that was played at Queen Victoria's Golden Jubilee Service in St Paul's Cathedral in 1887.

Princess Louise *(1848-1939)*
Sculptor, Painter
Victoria and Albert's fourth daughter inherited her parents' talents for drawing and produced striking portraits of Queen Victoria kept today in the Royal Collection. Her greatest talent however was sculpting which she learned at the National Art Training School in Kensington, London, and in the studio of sculptor Joseph Edgar Boehm. Her most famous work is the statue of her mother that still stands before Kensington Palace, London, which she sculpted in 1890-1893. Other works include beautiful busts of some of her siblings, and a soldiers' memorial in St Paul's Cathedral in London.

Queen Mary *(1867-1953)*
Painter, Needlework Artist
George V's Queen Consort could draw and paint in watercolours, but her real talent was in needlework and weaving. Her greatest work was a large carpet she wove between 1941 and 1950 when she was in her seventies. The carpet is made up of 12 panels filled with floral designs, each panel signed 'Mary R', and contains over 1 million stitches. Mary donated it to charity in 1950 to raise money for Britain after the Second World War, and today it can be seen at the National Gallery of Canada in Ottawa.

Prince Charles *(1948-)*
Painter
Prince Charles received initial training in painting during the 1970s and 1980s from several artists including Edward Seago. Over the years he has become a skilled watercolourist and his work is often shown in exhibitions under the name of Arthur G. Carrick (Arthur and George are two of his four Christian names, while Earl of Carrick is one of his official titles). His work focuses on landscapes, especially from royal estates in Scotland and Norfolk, and also views from his travels. Prints and lithographs of his works are regularly sold to raise money for charities, however the paintings themselves are never sold.

Sarah Armstrong-Jones *(1964-)*
Painter
Princess Margaret's daughter studied painting at the Camberwell School of Art, and later also at the Royal Academy School where she won two prizes in 1988 and 1990. Following her studies she became the first modern royal to take up art as a professional career and her artwork is currently being handled by the Redfern Gallery, a private art gallery for contemporary artists in London. She specializes in still lifes and landscapes, mostly abstract.

Royal Writers

Most monarchs and members of the Royal Family have left written records in the form of letters, journals and government papers. A select few however have distinguished themselves with their writing skills by becoming published authors. Listed below are royal family members who are known to have written books throughout the centuries. At the end of the list a special mention is made about Queen Victoria's voluminous writing output besides her two published books.

Alfred the Great
(849-899)
One of the first English kings who could read and write, Alfred initiated a program to educate the English people which included making classical books available in the common English tongue. He himself translated works by Gregory the Great, Boethius and St Augustine from Latin into English, wrote dedicated prologues for each work, and in many cases edited the books to make sure the works would have relevance to his subjects' lives.

Henry VIII
(1491-1547)
Before his break with Rome in the 1530s Henry had written a book, in Latin, against the Protestant heresies of Martin Luther called *Assertio Septem Sacramentorum* (A Defence of the Seven Sacraments). Published in 1521, it went through several editions and was even translated into German. Although it is thought the King had considerable help from theologians who prepared the bulk of the

book in advance, Henry added his own material and certainly edited the finished work.

Catherine Parr

(c.1512-1548)

Henry VIII's sixth wife was an erudite woman who published three religious works during her lifetime. Her first book, *Psalms and Prayers* (1544) was merely an anonymous English translation from Latin of a work by John Fisher, Bishop of Rochester. Her second work, *Prayers and Meditations,* was a collection of original prayers published in 1545 and is credited with being the first book published by an English Queen under her own name. Catherine's third book, *The Lamentation of a Sinner* (1547), was a highly praised Protestant theological work describing the search for salvation through faith alone.

James I

(1566-1625)

A well-trained scholar in politics, theology and language, James I produced the most intellectual works ever written by a British monarch. His most famous books explored royal political theory: *The True Law of Free Monarchies* (1598) carefully laid down the theory of the divine right of kings, while *Basilikon Doron* (1599) described the duties and responsibilities of a successful monarch. Other books included *Essays of a Prentise in the Divine Art of Poesie* (1585), a book on poetry; *A Counterblaste to Tobacco* (1604), a prescient treatise on the bad effects of smoking on one's health; and *Demonologie* (1597), a Socratic dialogue on witchcraft and demonic possession.

Queen Victoria

(1819-1901)

Besides putting more words to paper than any other British royal in history (see below), Victoria published two books during her lifetime, both about her experience of life in Scotland. *Leaves from the Journal of Our Lives in the Highlands,* adapted from her personal diaries, was published in 1868 to enormous success, and was followed 16 years later by *More Leaves from a Journal of a Life in the Highlands.* Victoria also wrote a memoir of John Brown which she planned to publish privately, however she was dissuaded from doing so by her private secretary and the manuscript was eventually destroyed.

John Campbell, Duke of Argyll

(1845-1914)

The Duke of Argyll—Princess Louise's husband and Queen Victoria's son-in-law—was a prolific author who wrote travelogues, biographies, novels and tracts between 1867 and 1910. His books included *A Trip to the Tropics and Home to America* (1867), *Canadian Pictures Drawn with Pen and Pencil* (1885), and a popular biography of Queen Victoria published after her death in 1901 entitled *V.R.I: Her Life and Empire.* He also published a biography of Lord Palmerston and a two-volume autobiography.

Queen Marie of Romania

(1875-1938)

Marie was a daughter of Prince Alfred, Duke of Edinburgh, a granddaughter to Queen Victoria, who married the heir to the throne of Romania and later became Queen of that country. During and after her time as Queen she wrote over 30 books and tracts including fairytales, patriotic works about Romania, and a highly acclaimed three-volume autobiography, *The Story of My Life* (1934).

Princess Marie Louise

(1872-1956)

Shortly before her death in 1956 Princess Marie Louise, a granddaughter of Queen Victoria, published a memoir entitled *My*

Memories of Six Reigns in which she recalled her 'rich experience' during the reigns of Victoria, Edward VII, George V, Edward VIII, George VI and Elizabeth II. Her candid recollections included an account of her unhappy marriage to a German prince, and Victoria's confession to Marie Louise that she never actually uttered the phrase "We are not amused."

Princess Alice of Albany

(1883-1981)

Like her cousin Marie Louise, Alice, Queen Victoria's last surviving granddaughter, also wrote a volume of memoirs, published in 1966 under the title *For My Grandchildren*. Her recollections ranged from her memories of Queen Victoria to the coronation of Elizabeth II. They included her experiences whilst serving as Viceregal Consort in South Africa and Canada, and frank impressions on many famous people of her time like WE Gladstone, Kaiser Wilhem II and Winston Churchill.

Princess Michael of Kent

(1945-)

Prince Michael of Kent's wife has authored half a dozen books since 1986. Four of them are non-fiction works on royal history, including a book on famous royal brides, *Crowned in a Far Country* (1986), and one on famous royal mistresses, *Cupid and the King* (1991). Two of her books have been novels based on the lives of two famous 15th century French women, Yolande of Aragon and Agnes Sorel.

Charles, Prince of Wales

(1948-)

The Prince of Wales' writing skills first came to the fore in 1980 when he published a children's book called *The Old Man of Lochganar*, a story set on the Royal estate of Balmoral in Scotland. Since then he has also published *A Vision of Britain: A Personal View of*

Architecture (1989), and *Watercolours* (1991). He also co-authored a number of books on the Highgrove Estate and about sustainable living, and has written a number of lectures on art, history and the environment.

Sarah, Duchess of York

(1959-)

Prince Andrew's former wife has been the author of numerous books since 1989. The majority have been children's stories, including a series of books on *Budgie the Little Helicopter,* and one on a nursery doll called Little Red. She also co-wrote two books on Queen Victoria, two memoirs, and a series of self-help books for Weight Watchers, one of which was inventively titled *Dining with The Duchess.*

Empress of Words: A Short Assessment of Queen Victoria's Writing Output

Queen Victoria's writing output throughout her life belies belief. If one were to add all the words contained in the Bible, the entire works of William Shakespeare, the *Lord of the Rings* and the entire *Harry Potter* book series, the total would be equivalent to less than half the words Victoria put to paper throughout her life. It has been estimated that, between her journals and letters, Victoria wrote down between 1,000 and 2,000 words every few days, adding up to over 10 million words by the time she died in 1901.

Her daily writing practice began in 1832, when at the age of 13 she was given a diary by her mother to record her impressions during a trip to Wales. From that moment forward she never stopped writing and continued keeping a diary for her entire life, the last entry dictated to her daughter Princess Beatrice on 13 January 1901, nine days before her death at the age of 81. Her collected diaries today run to 141 volumes, numbering over 43,000 pages, however this is still less than half the words Victoria originally wrote down in them. On her death she left instructions to her daughter Princess Beatrice to edit the diaries for anything controversial, a task that Beatrice carried out with ruthless efficiency and that, to the great consternation of scholars and other members of the Royal Family, included destroying most of the original diaries written in Victoria's hand.

Besides her diaries, Victoria was also one of the most prolific letter-writers of the 19th century, an era when letter-writing was already a daily routine for many. After her eldest daughter Vicky married into the German imperial family and left England in 1858 Victoria kept up correspondence with her for over 40 years, totalling over 3,700 letters. She similarly kept regular correspondence with all her children and grandchildren after they moved away from home, and also with other heads of state in Europe. When publishers began to search the Royal Archives for her letters in 1904 they were faced with 460 volumes of correspondence to choose from. To these must also be added all the letters that were kept by the original recipients and are now scattered between state archives and private collections, making an official tally of all the letters Queen Victoria wrote in her lifetime virtually impossible to accomplish.

Her journals however—or rather what was left of them after editing—have been carefully organised over the years and have recently been made available to everyone through an official British Monarchy website, *queenvictoriasjournals.org*. The website shows photos of every page of the journals, typed transcriptions for every page, as well as some recovered original excerpts from the diaries that escaped Princess Beatrice's destruction. The journals, as well as the letters, contain accounts and views from virtually everything that took place in her life, making Victoria the most documented monarch in British history, and perhaps world history as well.

William Shakespeare's Royal Plays

William Shakespeare composed 11 plays on the royal history of England (10 in the accepted canon, plus one—*Edward III*—recently attributed to him). Most of the plays deal with the Wars of the Roses, particularly the rise and fall of the House of Lancaster, and end with the accession of Henry VII who united the warring factions of Lancaster and York and brought peace to England. All but one of the plays (*Henry VIII*) were written during the reign of Queen Elizabeth I who was Henry VII's granddaughter, and the whole cycle was written as a cautionary tale against political factionalism which the Tudors had brought to an end.

Shakespeare used contemporary history chronicles to write his plays, particularly Edward Hall's *Chronicle* of 1548 and Holinshed's *Chronicle* of 1578, so the basic historical facts of his plays are correct. However he also took considerable historical liberties, both for dramatic effect and to satisfy Tudor propaganda. This is obvious for example in the creation of his most famous royal character, Richard III, who is based more on Tudor myth than actual facts.

A short description of each royal history play by William Shakespeare follows in the next pages. The 'Events Covered' sub-sections record only the royal events described in the play, not necessarily their historical accuracy.

The Plays

(in order of composition)

Henry VI, Part I

Written: 1589-90.
Period described: c.1422-1445.
Events covered: The minority of Henry VI; English fighting in France during the Hundred Years War; the rise and fall of Joan of Arc; the start of infighting between Lancastrians and Yorkists.
Memorable line: "Here I prophesy: this brawl today / Grown to this faction in the Temple Garden / Shall send between the red rose and the white / A thousand souls to death and deadly night." The Earl of Warwick to Richard Duke of York, Act 2, Scene 4.
Interesting fact: Following Tudor chronicles, Shakespeare set the beginning of the Wars of the Roses in London's Temple Gardens where Lancastrians and Yorkists first identify with red and white roses. This incident however has no basis in fact.

Henry VI, Part II

Written: 1590-91.
Period described: c.1445-1455.
Events covered: The beginning of the Wars of the Roses; the influence of Queen Margaret of Anjou over the weak Henry VI; the murders of Humphrey Duke of Gloucester and the Duke of Suffolk; the designs of Richard, Duke of York to seize the crown; Jack Cade's Rebellion; the First Battle of St Albans.
Memorable line: "The first thing we do, let's kill all the lawyers": Jack Cade's follower, Dick, Act IV, Scene 2.
Interesting fact: Eleanor of Gloucester's attempt to use witchcraft to predict the King's death is based on actual events.

Henry VI, Part III

Written: 1590-91.
Period described: c.1455-1471.
Events covered: The Wars of the Roses battles continue; the death of Richard Duke of York; the seizure of the throne by Edward IV and his marriage to Elizabeth Woodville (Lady Grey); the brief restoration to the throne of Henry VI and his subsequent murder in the Tower of London; the triumph of the House of York.
Memorable line: "Here burns my candle out, ay, here it dies / Which whiles it lasted gave King Henry light. / O Lancaster! I fear thy overthrow / More than my body's parting with my soul!" Lord Clifford's dying speech after the Battle of Towton, Act II, Scene 6.
Interesting fact: The play contains more battle scenes than any other of Shakespeare's plays, and sets the stage for the rise of Richard III in the next royal history play.

Richard III

Written: 1592-93.
Period described: 1470s-1485.
Events covered: Richard, Duke of Gloucester, plots his way to the throne by murdering rival claimants including his brother, George, Duke of Clarence; Richard's usurpation of the throne after the death of Edward IV; the murder of his nephews, the Princes in the Tower; the Battle of Bosworth, resulting in Richard III's death and the accession of Henry VII.
Memorable lines: "Now is the winter of our discontent / Made glorious summer by the sun of York" Richard, Duke of Gloucester, Act I, Scene 1. "A horse! A horse! My kingdom for a horse!" King Richard III, Act V, Scene 4.
Interesting fact: From about 1700 to the 1850s the play was performed in England and the United States in a bowdlerized

version which cut out half the play and added new text. The original Shakespearean text began to be restored in 1845.

King John

Written: 1595-96.
Period described: c.1200-1216.
Events covered: John's usurpation of the crown from his nephew Arthur of Brittany and Arthur's murder; the barons' rebellion against John; Richard I's illegitimate son, Philip the Bastard, takes revenge for his father's death; John clashes with King Philip II of France and with papal authority; France's invasion of England; King John's death.
Memorable lines: "This England never did, nor never shall / Lie at the proud foot of a conqueror." Philip the Bastard, Act V, Scene 7.
Interesting fact: Shakespeare completely left out Magna Carta from the play, but invented the character of Philip the Bastard, based on the shady historical figure of Philip of Cognac, to represent English civic duty and patriotism.

Edward III

Written: 1590-94.*_Only partly composed by Shakespeare._
Period described: c.1337-1356.
Events covered: Edward's claim to the French throne and the beginning of the Hundred Years War; the Black Prince's successes at the Battle of Crecy and Battle of Poitiers; the story of the Burghers of Calais; the English conquests in France.
Memorable lines: "Tell him, the Crown that he usurps, is mine / and where he sets his foot, he ought to kneel. / 'Tis not a petty Dukedom that I claim / but all the whole Dominions of the Realm." King Edward III, Act I, Scene 1.

Interesting fact: The play was not included in the first Shakespeare Folio of 1623 and has only recently been admitted into the Shakespeare canon. It had been banned during the reign of Scottish-born King James I because it contained many slurs and jokes against the Scots.

Richard II

Written: 1595.
Period described: 1398-1399.
Events covered: The play covers only the last two years of Richard II's reign focusing on the events leading to his deposition including: the banishment of Henry Bolingbroke; the death of John of Gaunt and the seizure of his property by Richard; Henry Bolingbroke's return from exile and his seizure of the crown; Richard II's deposition and his death in Pontefract Castle.
Memorable lines: "Not all the water in the rough rude sea / can wash the balm from an anointed king" King Richard II, Act III, Scene 2. "For God's sake, let us sit upon the ground / and tell sad stories of the death of kings." King Richard II, Act III, Scene 2.
Interesting fact: On the eve of his failed rebellion against Queen Elizabeth I in February 1601 the Earl of Essex and his supporters paid a handsome sum to Shakespeare's company to perform *Richard II* in London. Essex and his supporters hoped to rally popular support to their cause by staging a play about a royal deposition, however this appeal failed. Elizabeth I did not hold a grudge against the company for performing the play.

Henry IV, Part I

Written: 1596-97.
Period described: 1402-03.

Events covered: King Henry IV's struggle for legitimacy after the deposition of Richard II; Owen Glyndwor's rebellion in Wales; the misspent youth of the Prince of Wales (Prince Hal); the Percy rebellion; the Battle of Shrewsbury.
Memorable lines: ""I am the Prince of Wales, and think not, Percy / to share with me in glory anymore. / Two stars keep not their motion in one sphere." Prince Hal, Act V, Scene 4. "The better part of valour is discretion." Falstaff, Act V, Scene 4.
Interesting fact: Both Henry IV plays include one of Shakespeare's most popular characters, the larger-than-life drinking wit Sir John Falstaff, who spends most of his time carousing with young Prince Hal, the future Henry V. The character was so popular when first presented that Queen Elizabeth I requested that a new play be written specifically for him, which became *The Merry Wives of Windsor.*

Henry IV, Part II

Written: 1598.
Period described: 1403-13.
Events covered: The Archbishop of York and his allies plot against Henry IV; Prince John, Henry IV's second son, deceives the plotters, arrests them, and has them executed; Henry IV's illness and death; Prince Hal becomes King Henry V and reforms his ways.
Memorable lines: "Uneasy lies the head that wears a crown." King Henry IV, Act III, Scene 1.
Interesting fact: There is no conclusive evidence on whether King Henry IV's death scene, where his son Hal takes the crown from him while his father is still alive, is based on actual events. Henry's death in the Jerusalem Chamber however, fulfilling a prophecy that he would die 'in Jerusalem', is based on true accounts.

Henry V

Written: 1598-99.
Period described: 1413-20.
Events covered: Henry V's resumption of the Hundred Years War with France; the Southampton Plot; the siege of Harfleur; the Battle of Agincourt; the conquest of France; Henry's marriage to Catherine of Valois, daughter of the French King.
Memorable lines: "Once more unto the breach, dear friends, once more / Or close the wall up with our English dead!" King Henry V, Act III, Scene 1. "The game's afoot / Follow your spirit: and upon this charge / Cry — God for Harry! England and Saint George!" King Henry V, Act III, Scene 1. "We few, we happy few, we band of brothers. / For he to-day that sheds his blood with me / Shall be my brother." King Henry V, Act IV, Scene 3.
Interesting fact: Tradition holds that this was the first play performed in the newly constructed Globe Theatre in London in 1599.

Henry VIII

Written: 1612-13.**Only partly composed by Shakespeare.*
Period described: 1521-36.
Events covered: Henry's divorce from Catherine of Aragon; the fall of Cardinal Wolsey; Henry's marriage to Anne Boleyn and her coronation; the death of Catherine of Aragon; courtiers plot against Archbishop Cranmer; the birth of Princess Elizabeth, later Queen Elizabeth I.
Memorable lines: "Had I but serv'd my God with half the zeal / I serv'd my king, he would not in mine age / Have left me naked to mine enemies." Cardinal Wolsey, Act III, Scene 2.
Interesting fact: During a performance of *Henry VIII* at London's Globe Theatre in 1613 a cannon shot fired as part of the play sparked

a fire on the thatched roof which burned the whole theatre to the ground.

"This Scepter'd Isle..."

Shakespeare's *Richard II* contains one of the most famous passages in all of English literature, the 'Scepter'd Isle' speech delivered by John of Gaunt in Act II, Scene 1, praising England as a distinct glorious world. The speech has often been used to lionise England, however the original speech is delivered in the play not in the spirit of praise but of warning: John of Gaunt laments that what was once a glorious land has been reduced to shameful exploitation by Richard and his cronies. The sense of the speech can be fully understood when reproduced in full:

"This royal throne of kings, this scepter'd isle,
This earth of majesty, this seat of Mars,
This other Eden, demi-paradise,
This fortress built by Nature for herself
Against infection and the hand of war,
This happy breed of men, this little world,
This precious stone set in the silver sea,
Which serves it in the office of a wall,
Or as a moat defensive to a house,
Against the envy of less happier lands,
This blessed plot, this earth, this realm, this England,
This nurse, this teeming womb of royal kings,
Fear'd by their breed and famous by their birth,
Renowned for their deeds as far from home,
For Christian service and true chivalry,
As is the sepulchre in stubborn Jewry,
Of the world's ransom, blessed Mary's Son,
This land of such dear souls, this dear dear land,
Dear for her reputation through the world,

Is now leased out, I die pronouncing it,
Like to a tenement or pelting farm:
England, bound in with the triumphant sea
Whose rocky shore beats back the envious siege
Of watery Neptune, is now bound in with shame,
With inky blots and rotten parchment bonds:
That England, that was wont to conquer others,
Hath made a shameful conquest of itself.
Ah, would the scandal vanish with my life,
How happy then were my ensuing death!"

MISCELLANEA

Royal Towns and Settlements

Many places in the United Kingdom bear names associated with the monarchy. The majority of them are historic settlements that received the words 'King', 'Queen' or 'Regis' in their names centuries ago because they originally belonged to the monarchy. Others received royally-related names more recently as a way to honour a particular monarch, while a more select group comprises towns and boroughs that have been granted the privilege of bearing the title 'Royal' in their official names. All these types of royal settlements are described below.

Royal Towns, Boroughs and Counties

The privilege of bearing the title 'Royal' in their official names has been granted only to a few towns, boroughs and counties in the United Kingdom. The practice started in the late 19th-early 20 century, either to confirm an existing but unofficial royal status, or to honour particular royal events. These towns, boroughs and counties have the privilege of calling themselves 'Royal' in all official documents and public signage, regardless of whether the word Royal is part of the actual name (i.e. 'the Royal Borough of Kensington and Chelsea' or 'the Royal Town of Caernarfon'). The privilege must be expressly bestowed by the monarch, usually by Letters Patents. As of June 2019, only four boroughs, five towns and one county have been bestowed this Royal privilege. All but two have historical links with the monarchy.

Royal Boroughs

The Royal Borough of Kingston upon Thames, London

The oldest Royal borough in England, Kingston upon Thames has been considered royal ever since the 10th century when seven Anglo-Saxon kings were crowned in the ancient town. King George V confirmed the right of the borough to bear a Royal title in 1927.

The Royal Borough of Windsor and Maidenhead, Berkshire

The site of Windsor Castle, Windsor was first mentioned as belonging to the King in the reign of Henry I in the 1130s and has been considered royal ever since. When the new, larger borough of Windsor and Maidenhead was created in 1974 the Royal title was confirmed for the new authority.

The Royal Borough of Kensington and Chelsea, London

The Royal Borough of Kensington was granted the Royal honour in 1901 by King Edward VII in memory of his mother Queen Victoria who was born in Kensington Palace in 1819. When the borough of Kensington was amalgamated with the borough of Chelsea in 1965 the Royal title was transferred over.

The Royal Borough of Greenwich, London

Greenwich was the birthplace of Henry VIII, Mary I and Elizabeth I, and was the site of the ancient Royal Palace of Placentia. It was declared a Royal Borough in 2012 to commemorate the Diamond Jubilee of Queen Elizabeth II.

Royal Towns

The Royal Town of Sutton Coldfield, West Midlands

Now a suburb of Birmingham, the original town of Sutton Coldfield was granted a Royal title in perpetuity by Henry VIII in 1528 after a petition by Bishop John Vezey who was born in the town. The town was assumed to have lost its title after it was incorporated into

Birmingham in the 19th century, however after a successful petition in 2014 the government recognized that Sutton Coldfield could indeed use the title of Royal Town in perpetuity.

Royal Leamington Spa, Warwickshire

The town was known as Leamington Priors until the 19th century when it was developed into a fashionable spa town. It was renamed Royal Leamington Spa in 1838 by Queen Victoria who had visited the town in 1830 as a young princess, and who patronised the town again with a visit later in 1858.

Royal Tunbridge Wells, Kent

King Edward VII granted the Royal prefix to the spa town of Tunbridge Wells in 1909 in recognition of its long associations with the monarchy. Queen Henrietta Maria was the first royal to visit the town in 1629 to take the waters, and was later followed by Charles II and Queen Anne in the late 17th century. Queen Victoria and Prince Albert also visited in the 19th century.

The Royal Town of Caernarfon, Wales

Caernarfon's royal associations go back to the reign of Edward I in the 1280s when Caernarfon Castle was built as an official royal seat of government in Wales, and the future Edward II was born there in 1284. Queen Elizabeth II honoured these associations in 1963 by granting royal status to the borough of Caernarfon. When that borough was abolished in 1974 and Caernarfon became a town council the Royal title was transferred to the town's official name.

Royal Wootton Bassett, Wiltshire

This small town in Wiltshire captured the nation's imagination between 2007 and 2011 when most of its population turned out to honour the last journeys of fallen soldiers being repatriated from Iraq and Afghanistan, which by necessity had to travel through the town from Royal Air Force Base Lyneham nearby to reach the medical coroner in Oxford. Simple hearse rides soon turned into full funerary processions during which the entire town came to a standstill to pay silent respects to the dead soldiers, many of whom were young boys of 18-20 years of age. The processions ended in 2011 when RAF Base Lyneham closed and the repatriations were moved to RAF Base Brize Norton, however in recognition of the role Wootton Basset played in honouring hundreds of fallen soldiers the government petitioned Queen Elizabeth II to grant the Royal prefix to the town, which she granted in perpetuity at the end of 2011.

Royal Counties

The Royal County of Berkshire

Queen Elizabeth II granted the unique title of Royal County to Berkshire in 1958 in recognition of the county's strong links with the monarchy. Berkshire contains the town of Windsor, Windsor Castle, and the 5,000-acres royally-owned Windsor Great Park.

Historic Royal Settlements

Many settlements in Britain bear words in their names recalling their royal origins and associations, some of them going back 1,000 years or more. Towns and villages bearing 'King' or 'Queen' in their names often indicate that the land on which the town stands today was once owned by a monarch or his consort. Another way of marking royal possession was to append the Latin word 'Regis', meaning 'of the King' to the name of the settlement, with some settlements having borne both 'Regis' and 'King' in their names throughout their histories. Other settlements, like Queensferry, indicate origin rather than possession. Following below is a selection of some of the most notable historic royal settlements in Great Britain, listed in rough chronological order of when they received their royal names.

Kingston Upon Thames, Surrey

Widely considered the oldest town in England to bear the name Kingston, it was originally thought that the name derived from the ancient coronation stone (the 'King's Stone') used to crown Anglo-Saxon kings in the town between 899-979. New research however has shown that the settlement bore the name of Cyninges Tun, meaning 'settlement of the King' as far back as the year 838.

Kingsclere, Hampshire

The first mention of Kingsclere comes from King Alfred the Great's will in the late 9th century, when the village was part of a royal manor. The name was formalised in the 12th century.

Kingswinford, West Midlands

Originally the possession of Anglo-Saxon kings, the name means 'ford for the King's swine.' The manor was listed as a royal possession in the Domesday Book, and was also known as Swinford Regis during the Middle Ages.

Milton Regis, Kent

The ancient settlement of Milton in Kent was already described as belonging to the King in Anglo-Saxon times, and is known to have been part of King Edward the Confessor's possessions in the 11th century. It was first described as Middleton Terra Regis in the Domesday Book in 1086.

Rowley Regis, West Midlands

This Black Country historic parish was first recorded bearing the suffix Regis in a survey of 1140 during the reign of King Stephen, when the estate was noted to be royal hunting grounds.

Queen Camel, Somerset

This oddly named town achieved its name through two different sources: Camel is a modern contraction of the ancient Celtic word Cantmael, possibly meaning 'bare hill district'; the Queen prefix was added in the 13th century, possibly because the village's estate belonged to Queen Eleanor of Provence, wife of King Henry III.

King's Sutton, Northamptonshire
The village of Sudtone was first listed as belonging to the King as a royal manor in the Domesday Book of 1086. It was recorded as Sutton Regis in 1252, and finally renamed as Kings Sutton from 1294.

Lyme Regis, Dorset
The Regis suffix was first added to the town's name in 1284 after Edward I granted a Royal Charter to Lyme.

Kingston Upon Hull, Yorkshire
Originally called Wyke on Hull, King Edward I renamed the town Kingston upon Hull after he bought the estate which contained the town in 1293.

North Queensferry and South Queensferry, Scotland
Both places derive their name from the ferry service established by Queen Margaret of Scotland, wife of King Malcolm III, in the late 11th century to help pilgrims make their way to the holy church of St Andrews in Fife, beyond the Firth of Forth. The name Queensferry began to be used widely from the year 1300.

Kings Langley, Hertfordshire
The original village of Langley gained its royal prefix after a royal manor was built there in the 13th century which later became Kings Langley Palace. The palace all but disappeared by the 17th century.

Bere Regis, Dorset
An improbable local legend says that this village in Dorset, which had been royal property since Saxon times, acquired its name when King John visited the area and was so pleased with the quality of the local beer that he decreed that the place be called Beer Regis. In

reality, the name Bere is of Anglo-Saxon origin, and the first mention of a royal prefix occurs in 1303 when it was first called Kingsbere. The name Bere Regis was first recorded in the 16th century, and both royal names were used interchangeably until the 18th century when the present name was permanently adopted.

Houghton Regis, Bedfordshire
Houghton was first mentioned as a royal manor in the Domesday Book in 1086. The town was briefly called Kyngshouton in the 13th century, with the name Houghton Regis first recorded in 1353.

Prince Risborough, Buckinghamshire
Although a royal manor since the reign of King Harold Godwinson in 1066, Risborough only acquired its princely name between the 1340s and 1370s when it was owned by Edward the Black Prince, son of King Edward III. The manor was subsequently held by other Princes of Wales.

Beeston Regis, Norfolk
Originally named Beeston-next-to-the-sea, the village became Beeston Regis after Henry of Lancaster became King Henry IV in 1399, presumably because the land was part of a Lancastrian estate.

Kingsbury Regis, Somerset
This small hamlet, now part of Milborne Port, received its unique double royal name in two stages. The name Kingsbury was first recorded in the 13th century to note that the manor belonged to the King and to separate it from other estates. The Regis suffix was first recorded in 1431 when the estate passed to the Beaufort royal line.

King's Lynn, Norfolk
This town was originally called Bishop's Lynn in the Middle Ages when it was under the control of the Bishop of Norwich. After the dissolution of the monasteries in the 1530s the area came under the royal control of King Henry VIII and was renamed King's Lynn.

Grafton Regis, Northamptonshire
Grafton was originally the family seat of the Woodville family and was for a time called Grafton Woodville. It was the birthplace of Elizabeth Woodville and the site of her secret marriage to King Edward IV in 1464. After the Woodville manor came into the hands of King Henry VIII—Elizabeth's grandson—he renamed the town Grafton Regis.

Queen Charlton, Somerset
The Queen prefix was given to the village of Charlton after King Henry VIII gifted the town's estate to his sixth wife, Catherine Parr, in the 1540s.

Kingstanding, Birmingham
According to a local legend this settlement received its colourful name in 1642 at the beginning of the English Civil War when King Charles I addressed local people at the site while standing on a mound at the centre of the village (i.e. 'king standing'). The name however seem to predate the event and it is thought to originate with the practice of medieval kings standing on the same mound—a Neolithic barrow—while hunting deer in the area.

Other Royally Named Towns

The following towns are neither Royal Towns nor historic royal settlements but received instead their royal names more recently to honour particular individuals or events.

Princetown, Devon
Charles Tyrwhitt, secretary to George Prince of Wales (later George IV), founded this village in Dartmoor National Park in 1785 on land owned by the Duchy of Cornwall. It was therefore named after the Prince of Wales who owned the Duchy. Dartmoor Prison was later built on the same grant of land near the town.

Queensferry, Flintshire, Wales

This ferry town on the River Dee, on the Welsh border with England near Chester, was first renamed Kingsferry in the 1820s to celebrate the accession of King George IV. It was then renamed Queensferry in 1837 at the accession of Queen Victoria and the name has remained unchanged ever since.

Queen Adelaide, Cambridgeshire

Although the area had scattered farms since the Middle Ages, this hamlet north of Cambridge expanded and was officially charted in the 1840s around a new railway station. It took its name from a nearby pub called The Queen Adelaide, which in turn was named after Queen Adelaide of Saxe-Meiningen, consort of William IV, who was a popular Queen Dowager at the time.

Bognor Regis, West Sussex

After spending three months in Bognor recuperating from surgery in 1929 King George V agreed to the residents' request that the suffix Regis be added to the town's name, in recognition of the fact that during that time the entire Royal Family had been spending time in the seaside resort. The town however was not made a Royal Town, which is why its case is peculiar and is listed separately in this section.

London's Royal Parks

London possesses eight Royal Parks that are owned by the Crown and are open to the public. Five are located in central London while three are located in the outer suburbs, together adding up to roughly 5,000 acres of land available for public recreation during opening hours. Almost all of them began as royal hunting reserves and were gradually opened to the public over the centuries, often after major redesigns. The Crown Lands Act of 1851 opened all Royal Parks to the public, however they still remain under ownership of the Crown as part of the monarchy's hereditary possessions. In central London, Crown ownership of Green Park, St James's Park and Hyde Park/Kensington Gardens ensured that their land remained free from development and create large green spaces at the centre of the capital.

The parks are run by the Royal Parks agency, a government body managing the land on behalf of the Crown, and their funding comes directly from the government, not from the Royal Household or local councils. Each park has individual opening hours during which the public has free access to its land and facilities, and they are policed by a dedicated unit of the London Metropolitan Police. Listed on the following pages are individual descriptions for each park.

The Eight Royal Parks

Green Park

Location: Central London, between Piccadilly and Buckingham Palace.
Dimensions: 40 acres (16 hectares).
History: The smallest of the Royal Parks has its origins in land first bought for royal use by King Charles II in 1668. In the 18th century it was the site of popular fireworks entertainments including Handel's premiere of *Music for the Royal Fireworks* in 1749. The park was also a popular rendezvous for duels. It was open to the general public in 1826.
Features: The Canada Gate by the Buckingham Palace forecourt; the Canada Memorial to soldiers who died in the First and Second World Wars; the RAF Bomber Command Memorial; the park is one of two used for royal gun salutes.

St James's Park

Location: Central London, between Whitehall and Buckingham Palace.
Dimensions: 57 acres (23 hectares).
History: The oldest of the Royal Parks in central London takes its name from a leper hospital dedicated to Saint James that stood on the site in the 13th century. King Henry VIII first enclosed the area as royal hunting grounds in the 1530s after building the adjacent St James's Palace. King James I turned the grounds into a park in the early 1600s and kept a large collection of animals in it. Charles II had the park redesigned, introduced a water canal, and opened it to the public in the 1660s after which unfortunately it became a popular site for lewd encounters. The present park was the romantic creation

of John Nash for King George IV in the 1820s after which it became a fashionable place.

Features: St James's Park Lake, with a pelican colony on a small island; the Blue Bridge over the lake with romantic views of Buckingham Palace; the Tiffany Jet Fountain; the Household Guards Memorial; the National Police Memorial; the South African Royal Artillery Memorial.

Hyde Park

Location: Central London, between Mayfair and Kensington Gardens.

Dimensions: 350 acres (142 hectares).

History: Central London's largest open space was once a manor owned by the monks of Westminster Abbey. Henry VIII seized the land during the dissolution of the monasteries in the 1530s and turned it into a deer hunting reserve. Charles I first opened the park to the public in 1637, and during the English Civil War earthworks were built in it by Parlamentarians to defend Westminster from Royalist attacks. William III and Mary II built Kensington Palace at the western edge of the Park in the 1690s and created a route on the southern edge which came to be called Rotten Row (thought to be a corruption of the French 'Route De Roi'). The route became the first street in England to be lit at night, to allow the people to travel in safety from Westminster to Kensington. Queen Caroline of Ansbach, consort of King George II, formally divided Hyde Park in two by commissioning the Serpentine Lake and creating Kensington Gardens on the western side of the park in the 1730s. The present Hyde Park was largely redesigned in the 1820s under George IV, and in 1851 it was the site of the Great Exhibition, housed in the Crystal Palace on the south side of the park. From the mid-19th century to the 20th century Hyde Park was often the site of political demonstrations and protests.

Features: Apsley Gate; the Queen Elizabeth the Queen Mother Gates; the statue of Achilles commemorating the Duke of Wellington; the Diana Princess of Wales Memorial Fountain; the 7th July 2005 Terrorists Attacks Memorial; the Reformers Tree Memorial; Speakers' Corner, where everyone is entitled to speak out on public issues; public boating on the Serpentine Lake; the park is one of two used for royal gun salutes.

Kensington Gardens

Location: Central London, between Kensington and Hyde Park.
Dimensions: 242 acres (98 hectares)
History: William III and Mary II created the first gardens after they moved into Kensington Palace at the edge of Hyde Park. Queen Caroline of Ansbach then expanded the gardens in the 1730s by annexing 300 acres from Hyde Park and formally separating the two parks, making Kensington Gardens a private royal enclosure. Queen Caroline also added the Round Pond in front of Kensington Palace and the Broad Walk as the main path through the Gardens north to south. Very few changes were made in the following centuries so that the 18th century park remains in essence unchanged to this day. The royal grounds were initially opened to the public in the mid-18th century, but only on Saturdays and only to those who were respectfully dressed. General admission was granted to all in the 19th century. In 1997 Kensington Gardens was the main site of mourning for the death of Diana, Princess of Wales—who had lived in Kensington Palace—with thousands of flowers laid at the southwestern edge of the park in front of her former home.
Features: Kensington Palace; the Queen Victoria and King William III statues; the Albert Memorial; the Peter Pan Statue; the Italian Gardens; the Serpentine Art Gallery; the Round Pond and the Long Water.

Regent's Park

Location: On the northern edge of Central London, between Marylebone and Camden Town.
Dimensions: 490 acres (197 hectares).
History: Generally acknowledged as the most beautiful of the Royal Parks, Regent's Park also started life as a deer hunting reserve for Henry VIII in the 16th century. After the Civil War the deer reserve became neglected and from the 1660s until the 1810s the area, then on the edge of London, was leased out to small tenant farmers. The future George IV, when Prince Regent, created the present park in the 1810s by commissioning architect John Nash to design a new space in the fashionable Regency style. Nash was also commissioned to build a new ceremonial route from the park to Carlton House, the Prince Regent's palace in St James's, creating in the process Regent Street. When finished, the park was also named after the Prince Regent. Additional formal gardens were laid in the 1930s, but in essence the park today remains as Nash envisioned it. It was first opened to the public by William IV in the 1830s.
Features: Queen Mary's Gardens; the Boating Lake; the Open Air Theatre; sports grounds; the London Zoo occupies the northeastern corner of the park.

Greenwich Park

Location: Greenwich, South-East London.
Dimensions: 180 acres (73 hectares).
History: The oldest of the Royal Parks, Greenwich was first created by Humphrey, Duke of Gloucester, uncle of King Henry VI, from 1427 onwards. It later passed through the hands of Queen Margaret of Anjou, the Yorkist Kings, and finally Henry VII in the 1480s who built the Palace of Placentia on its grounds. Henry VIII, Mary I and Elizabeth I were all born in that palace and greatly favoured the park which was filled with deer for hunting. Legend says that Sir

Walter Raleigh laid down his cloak over a puddle for Queen Elizabeth I while walking in the park one day. King James I enclosed the park with a brick wall in the early 17th century, much of which still exists. Charles II commissioned a redesign of the park in the 1660s-1670s and also built the Royal Observatory on a hill in the eastern portion of the park. The park was first opened to pensioners from the Royal Naval Hospital nearby in the 18th century, and to the general public afterwards. The Prime Meridian line that marks Longitude 0 and established Greenwich Mean time passes through the park and takes its name from it.
Features: The National Maritime Museum; the Queen's House; the Royal Observatory; the Prime Meridian; Queen Elizabeth's oak; flower gardens; deer herds.

Bushy Park

Location: Between Kingston upon Thames and Hampton, South-West London.
Dimensions: 1,100 acres (445 hectares).
History: The land making up this large, semi-rural park in the London suburbs was first seized by Henry VIII from Cardinal Wolsey in 1529, together with the palace of Hampton Court nearby. Henry turned it into a deer hunting reserve, and although hunting is no longer practiced today both red deer and fallow deer still roam the park. King Charles I brought water to the Park in 1638-39 by building a 12-mile canal from the river Colne west of London in order to supply water to Hampton Court Palace, a massive engineering feat for the time. Christopher Wren later embellished the park by using the water canal to build the Diana Fountain, and he also created Chestnut Avenue as a ceremonial route to the north entrance to Hampton Court. The future William IV served as Ranger of Bushy Park for twenty years before he became king and lived at Bushy House on the northern side of the park. During the Second

World War the park housed temporary headquarters for General Eisenhower's Allied Expeditionary Forces.
Features: The Diana Fountain; Chestnut Avenue; Bushy House; the USAAF Memorial; water gardens; herds of red deer and fallow deer.

Richmond Park

Location: Between Richmond, Wimbledon and Kingston upon Thames, South-West London.
Dimensions: 2,500 acres (1,010 hectares).
History: The largest Royal Park in London had its origins in the royal manor of Sheen owned by the Plantagenet kings outside the capital. The Park was initially enclosed in 1637 by Charles I who introduced 2,000 deer to use as a hunting reserve. He also built eight miles of brick walls to enclose the park, most of which still stand, though he preserved the people's right of way through the park. When Princess Amelia, daughter of King George II, was made Ranger of Richmond Park in the 1750s she tried to stop public access into the park but was taken to court by the citizens of Richmond who won the case against her, and the park has been open to the public ever since. Vistas, ponds and other features were added to the park in the 18th century and it has remained relatively unchanged since then. Several royal residences have been built in the park since the 18th century. White Lodge was completed by George II in 1730 and was the home of Queen Mary's family, the Tecks, in the 19th century. Thatched House Lodge currently serves as the residence of Princess Alexandra.
Features: King's Henry's Mound with views of London and St Paul's Cathedral; White Lodge; Pembroke Lodge; Isabella Plantation; the Pen Ponds; herds of red deer and fallow deer.

Other Royal Parks

There are two more parks in London that are owned by the Crown but that are not part of the official Royal Parks:

Hampton Court Park, next to Bushy Park, is part of the Hampton Court Palace estate and is managed by Historic Royal Palaces. The park covers 700 acres and is open to the public separately from the Palace's visiting hours. Amenities include The Long Water, the Golden Jubilee Fountain and other ponds. The park has been opened to the public since 1894, and since 1990 has been the site of the yearly Hampton Court Flower Show, currently the biggest flower show in the world.

Buckingham Palace Gardens are the private grounds of Buckingham Palace. They cover 42 acres and are not opened to the public. Parts of them however can be walked through during the yearly Summer Opening of Buckingham Palace.

London's Royal Statues

The British capital is home to the largest collection of public royal statues in Britain. This includes official memorials, historic monuments and architectural features. Following below is a list of these statues divided in two categories: monarchs and other notable royals. It only includes statues in the open air serving as public monuments and visual memorials, therefore statues of monarchs inside buildings are not included. They are listed in chronological order of birth of their subjects. Equestrian statues are noted in parenthesis. Regarding exact location, note that postcodes are approximate as British postcodes only cover buildings serving as mailing addresses, not exact geographical locations, so the postcodes listed below are for the buildings closest to the site of the statues.

Statues of Monarchs

Alfred the Great
Location: Trinity Church Square, Borough, SE1 4HT.

Edward the Confessor
Location: Top of Westminster School War Memorial column, The Sanctuary, in front of Westminster Abbey, SW1P 3PA.

Richard I
(*Equestrian*) Location: Old Palace Yard, Palace of Westminster, SW1P 3JY.

Henry III
Location: Top of Westminster School War Memorial column, The Sanctuary, in front of Westminster Abbey, SW1P 3PA.

Henry VIII
Location: Henry VIII Gate entrance, St Bartholomew Hospital, Smithfield, EC1A 7BE.

Edward VI
Location: Outside main entrance of St Thomas' Hospital, Westminster Bridge Road, Lambeth, SE1 7EH.
Note: A second statue of Edward VI, formerly outside, now stands inside one of the hospital's main corridors.

Elizabeth I
Location: Façade of St Dunstan-in-the-West church, 186a Fleet Street, City, EC4A 2HR.

Location: Top of Westminster School War Memorial column, The Sanctuary, in front of Westminster Abbey, SW1P 3PA.

Location: Courtyard of Westminster School, by Westminster Abbey, Deans Yard, SW1P 3PF.
(Note: the courtyard is not always open to the public)

James I
Location: Temple Bar Gate, Paternoster Row, St Paul's, EC4M 7DX.

Charles I
(*Equestrian*) Location: Charing Cross traffic island, South end of Trafalgar Square, WC2N 5DU.

Location: Temple Bar Gate, Paternoster Row, St Paul's, EC4M 7DX.

Charles II
Location: Soho Square Gardens, Soho, W1D 3QE.

Location: Central Courtyard, Royal Hospital Chelsea, SW3 4SR.

Location: Temple Bar Gate, Paternoster Row, St Paul's, EC4M 7DX.

James II
Location: In front of National Gallery (west side), Trafalgar Square, WC2N 5DN.

William III
(*Equestrian*) Location: St James's Square Gardens, St James's, SW1Y 4LE.

Location: South front of Kensington Palace, Kensington, W8 4PX.

Anne
Location: Front of St Paul's Cathedral, City, EC4M 8AD.

Location: By 15 Queen Anne's Gate, Westminster, SW1H 9BU.

Location: Queen Square Gardens, Bloomsbury, WC1N 3AR.
(Note: a definite identification of this statue has never been made, with some claiming that it represents instead Queen Charlotte of Mecklenburg-Strelitz.)

Location: Market House, Market Place, Kingston upon Thames, South London, KT1 1JS.

George I
Location: Atop the spire of St George's Church, Bloomsbury, WC1A 2SA.

George II
Location: Golden Square, Soho, W1F 9DJ.

Location: Main Esplanade, Old Royal Naval College, Greenwich, SE10 9NN.

George III
Location: Courtyard of Somerset House, Strand, WC2R 0RN.

(Equestrian) Location: Corner of Pall Mall and Cockspur Street, Westminster, SW1Y 5DL.

George IV
(Equestrian) Location: Trafalgar Square, Westminster, WC2N 5DS

William IV
Location: North Entrance of National Maritime Museum, off King William's Walk, Greenwich, SE10 9NF.

Victoria
Location: Victoria Memorial, in front of Buckingham Palace, SW1A 1AA.

Location: East front of Kensington Palace, Kensington Gardens, W8 4PX.

Location: Temple Bar Memorial, Fleet Street/Strand, EC4Y 1BD.

Location: North entrance of Blackfriars Bridge, City, EC4V 4DY.

Location: Entrance of 14-15 Carlton House Terrace, St James's, SW1Y 5AH.

Location: Victoria Square, Victoria, SW1V 0RB.

Location: Front entrance of Victoria and Albert Museum, South Kensington SW7 2RL.

Location: Top of Westminster School War Memorial column, The Sanctuary, in front of Westminster Abbey, SW1P 3PA.

Location: Front of Croydon Central Library, Katherine Street, Croydon, South London, CR9 1ET.

Edward VII

(Equestrian) Location: Waterloo Place, St James's, SW1Y 5ER.

Location: Outside Tooting Broadway Underground Station, Tooting, SW17 0SU.

Location: Front entrance of Victoria and Albert Museum, left side, South Kensington SW7 2RL.

(As Prince of Wales) Location: Temple Bar Memorial, Fleet Street/Strand, EC4Y 1BD.

George V

Location: Gardens between Westminster Abbey and Abingdon Street, facing the Palace of Westminster, SW1P 3JX.

George VI

Location: Carlton Gardens steps, leading to The Mall, St James's, SW1Y 5AA.

Monarchs who reigned since the Norman Conquest of 1066 with no public statues in London:

William I, William II, Henry I, Stephen, Henry II, John, Edward I, Edward II, Edward III, Richard II, Henry IV, Henry V, Henry VI, Edward IV, Edward V, Richard III, Henry VII, Mary I, Mary II, Edward VIII, Elizabeth II.

Note: All statues of Queen Elizabeth II erected so far in the United Kingdom are outside the Greater London boundaries.

Other Notable Royal Statues

Queen Eleanor of Castile
1st Wife of Edward I
Location: Eleanor Cross monument, forecourt of Charing Cross Railway Station, Strand, WC2N 5HX.

Queen Anne Boleyn
2nd Wife of Henry VIII
Location: Church Hill, Carshalton, South London, SM5 3PD.

Queen Anne of Denmark
Wife of James I
Location: Temple Bar Gate, Paternoster Row, St Paul's, EC4M 7DX.

Prince Frederick, Duke of York
Son of George III
Location: Atop the Duke of York Column, Duke of York Steps, between Waterloo Place and The Mall, St James's, SW1Y 5AH.
Note: Commemorated as Commander-in-Chief of the British Army from 1795 to 1809, and 1811 to 1827.

Prince Edward, Duke of Kent
Son of George III, Father of Queen Victoria
Location: Park Crescent gardens, Marylebone, W1B 1LT

Prince Albert
Husband of Queen Victoria
Location: Albert Memorial, Kensington Gardens, W2 2UH.

Location: Rear courtyard of Royal Albert Hall, Kensington, SW7 2AP.

(Equestrian) Location: Holborn Circus, Holborn, EC1N 2HP.

Location: Front entrance of Victoria and Albert Museum, South Kensington SW7 2RL.

Prince George, Duke of Cambridge
Grandson of King George III, Cousin of Queen Victoria
(Equestrian) Location: Whitehall, in front of Old War Office building, Westminster, SW1A 2AX.
Note: Commemorated as Commander-In-Chief of the Forces from 1856 to 1895.

Queen Alexandra
Wife of Edward VII
Location: Rear courtyard of Royal London Hospital, near Stepney Way, Whitechapel, E1 1BB.

Queen Elizabeth Bowes Lyon
Wife of George VI
Location: Carlton Gardens steps, leading to The Mall, St James's, SW1Y 5AA.

Royal Coaches

Royal Family members make use of many forms of transport to travel to and from engagements, however the most popular form of transport are the royal ceremonial coaches. These are horse-drawn carriages employed at most state and formal occasions, some of which have been in use for over a century. Besides allowing the Royal Family to travel in traditional pomp and style, these ceremonial coaches also allow the public a better view of the Royal Family.

There are over 100 coaches and carriages available to the Royal Household. The most famous and most frequently used coaches are described below, in chronological order of their creation. They are all housed in the Royal Mews of Buckingham Palace, London, where they can be viewed by the public.

The Gold State Coach

The oldest, most important and most magnificent of the ceremonial coaches is the Gold State Coach, commissioned by King George III in 1762. Built to celebrate Britain's victories against France during the Seven Years' War (1754-1763), the coach was first used by George III in November 1762 for the State Opening of Parliament. A true work of art of monumental proportions, the Gold State Coach is 24 feet long, 8 feet wide and 13 feet high, and weighs over 4 tons. Its wood is sculpted and gilded, and includes many marine decorations that were meant to symbolize Britain's new dominance of the sea following the Seven Years' War. Three cherubic figures on the roof symbolizing the spirits of England, Scotland and Ireland are sculpted holding a crown, sceptre and sword of state.

The Coach requires 8 horses to pull it, all of which are always dressed in the 'No. 1 State Harness', an 18th century royal harness made of Morocco leather and gilt brass that is only used with the Gold State Coach. The weight of the Coach is such that it can only travel at walking speed, and 30-40 yards are needed to bring it to a complete stop when in full motion. Differently from all other ceremonial coaches, only the Monarch can ride in the Gold State Coach (accompanied by other members of the Royal Family if so desired). It has been used by monarchs at every coronation since 1821, and until the Second World War it was used occasionally to travel to the State Opening of Parliament. Queen Elizabeth II also used it during the processions for her Silver Jubilee in 1977 and Golden Jubilee in 2002.
Despite its glorious appearance the Gold State Coach is known to be a particularly rough ride. William IV compared it to a ship tossing in the rough seas, and George VI described his coronation procession as the worst ride of his life. The coach however was completely overhauled for the coronation of Elizabeth II in 1953.

The Irish State Coach

The first Irish State Coach was built in Dublin in 1803-04 and was bought by Queen Victoria during a visit to the city in 1852. It was one of Victoria's favourite coaches and was also used by Edward VII, however it burned down in 1911 while being refurbished in London with only part of the ironwork surviving. The present coach was re-built in 1911 and was completely restored in 1988-89 based on original designs. Its roof's gilded decorations, dating back from Queen Victoria's later reign, are unique: besides English roses, Scottish thistles and Irish shamrocks the decorations also include small palms, symbolizing Victoria's title of Empress of India. From 1946 to 2013 this was the coach routinely used to convey the monarch to and from the State Opening of Parliament, after which it was replaced by the newer and grander Diamond Jubilee State Coach.

The Scottish State Coach

One of the oldest coaches in the collection, this carriage was initially built in 1830 for Prince Adolphus, Duke of Cambridge, one of the sons of King George III, who used it at the coronation of his brother William IV in 1831. After many years of family use it was sold to William Keppel, Earl of Albermarle—an ancestor of Camilla, Duchess of Cornwall—who converted it to a simple landau. The Keppel family then returned it to the Royal Family in 1920 as a gift to Queen Mary, Prince Adolphus' granddaughter. Queen Elizabeth II had the coach rebuilt and modified in 1968-69 when it was decorated with Scottish emblems including the Scottish Royal Coat of Arms, the badge of the Order of the Thistle, and a copy of the Crown of Scotland upon the coach's roof. The new coach was first used by the Queen in Edinburgh in 1969 and has been used on many state and royal occasions since, including the Silver Jubilee of 1977 and Prince William's wedding in 2011. The coach has larger glass windows than other coaches and a glass roof, allowing more light into the interior and a better view of the riders for onlookers.

The Glass Coach

This carriage was built in 1881 and was bought by the monarchy in 1911 to use at George V's coronation that year. Since then it has become associated with royal weddings, particularly with driving royal brides to the church. Lady Elizabeth Bowes-Lyon first used it in this way in 1923 for her wedding to the Duke of York (later King George VI), and it was later used at the weddings of Princess Alexandra in 1963, Princess Anne in 1973, Diana, Princess of Wales in 1981, and Sarah, Duchess of York in 1986. Queen Elizabeth II however used the coach to only ride back from Westminster Abbey in 1947 after her marriage to Prince Philip, using instead the Irish State Coach for the inward ride. It is known to be a very comfortable coach with excellent suspensions, so it is often used at royal events to transport members of the Royal Family or dignitaries.

The Alexandra State Coach

Considered by experts to be one of the finest coaches ever built, the Alexandra State coach was bought in 1893 for Alexandra of Denmark, Princess of Wales, later Queen Alexandra, from whom it takes its name. She and her husband, King Edward VII, used the coach often in London both before and after they became King and Queen in 1901. After Edward VII's death in 1910 the coach was used by Alexandra as Queen Dowager until her death in 1925. Its decorations are said to include as many as 67 painted and sculpted crowns, and perhaps for that reason the coach has been used exclusively since 1962 to convey the Imperial State Crown to the Palace of Westminster for the annual State Opening of Parliament, together with the Cap of Maintenance and the Sword of State. On those occasions a special cushioned table with an overhead spotlight is used to show off the Crown during its procession to and from Westminster.

The 1902 State Landau

The most frequently used of the State Coaches, the 1902 State Landau (that is, a luxury open carriage) was built for King Edward VII's coronation in that year, though owing to the King's ill health during the coronation ceremonies he only used it for the first time in October during a visit to the City of London. It is lavishly decorated with gold leaf and crimson satin lining, and painted in a lighter shade of maroon than the other coaches. It has been the coach of choice during Queen Elizabeth II's reign to welcome foreign Heads of State to Britain during State Visits, and is frequently used as such in London, Windsor, and Edinburgh (weather permitting as it is an open coach). The Landau has also played a prominent part during famous royal occasions: it was used by the Queen during royal processions for her Silver Jubilee in 1977 and Diamond Jubilee in 2012, and was also used to carry royal newlyweds back to Buckingham Palace after the weddings of Prince Charles (1981), Prince Andrew (1986) and Prince William (2011).

The Australian State Coach

This coach was a gift from the people of Australia to Elizabeth II on the occasion of the Australian Bicentenary in 1988, and was first used at the British State Opening of Parliament in November that year. Its design is similar to the Irish State Coach but it is decorated with Australian heraldic symbols and Queen Elizabeth II's personal flag as Head of the Commonwealth. It was the first coach built by W.J. Frecklington and is one of the most modern of the coaches with electric windows and central heating. It is often used by the Queen to welcome Heads of State during official State Visits, and by other members of the Royal Family on important royal occasions.

The Diamond Jubilee State Coach

The Diamond Jubilee State Coach is one of the most spectacular ever created. The coach was designed and built by Australian W.J. Frecklington—who previously built the Australian State Coach—to celebrate the Diamond Jubilee of Queen Elizabeth II. Finished in 2010, it was originally named State Coach Britannia and only assumed its current name after coming into royal service in 2014. Since then it has replaced the Irish State Coach as the carriage used to convey the monarch to the State Opening of Parliament. The coach is both a remarkable feat of engineering and a luxurious work of art. It is 18ft long, 7ft 2in wide and 10ft 8in high; weighs over 3 tons; and was built with all modern conveniences, including electric

windows, hydraulic stabilisers and heating. Much of the exterior wood is gilded with 23.5 carat gold-leaf, its lamps are made of Edinburgh crystal, and the door handles are decorated with diamonds and sapphires.
The coach's most remarkable feature however are the dozens of historical items incorporated in its body. W.J. Frecklington wanted to create something special to mark the rare occasion of a sovereign marking a Diamond Jubilee, and to that end he gathered fragments, mostly made of wood, from historic buildings, churches, ships and artefacts representing over 2,000 years of British history. The majority are stored in the coach's cabin forming the inner wooden panelling and are carefully marked by small plaques. Among them are items from Westminster Abbey, Canterbury Cathedral, Blenheim Palace, Old London Bridge, 10 Downing Street, Edinburgh Castle, the Mayflower ship, Isaac Newton's Apple Tree, a Spitfire plane, a button from a soldier's uniform who served on the Western Front, and Robert Stephenson's Rocket locomotive. In addition, the sculpted crown on the roof of the coach is made out of wood from HMS Victory, Horatio Nelson's flagship at Trafalgar, and the finial cross contains a capsule holding gold, frankincense and myrrh, to honour the Christian associations of the monarchy. A compartment within the cabin also stores two microcards containing a copy of the Magna Carta and the Domesday Book.

Countries Officially Visited by Queen Elizabeth II, 1952-2018

Queen Elizabeth II is the most travelled monarch in British history. A list of the countries and territories where the Queen made official visits during her reign follows below. It includes official royal visits made to Commonwealth countries as well as state visits to non-Commonwealth countries. It does not include repeat visits, so each country is listed only once on the year Elizabeth II first visited. It also does not include visits Elizabeth undertook as Princess before her accession to the throne, nor her stay in Kenya in February 1952 at the time of her accession.

Country	**First Visited as Queen**
1950s	
Bermuda	1953
Jamaica	1953
Panama	1953
Fiji	1953
Tonga	1953
New Zealand	1953
Australia	1954
Cocos Islands	1954
Sri Lanka	1954
Yemen (Aden)	1954
Uganda	1954
Libya	1954

Malta	1954
Gibraltar	1954
Norway	1955
Nigeria	1956
Sweden	1956
Portugal	1957
France	1957
Denmark	1957
Canada	1957
USA	1957
The Netherlands	1958

1960s

India	1961
Pakistan	1961
Nepal	1961
Iran	1961
Italy	1961
Vatican City	1961
Ghana	1961
Liberia	1961
Sierra Leone	1961
Gambia	1961
Ethiopia	1965
Sudan	1965
West Germany	1965
Barbados	1966
Guyana	1966
Trinidad and Tobago	1966
Grenada	1966
Saint Vincent and the Grenadines	1966
Saint Lucia	1966
Dominica	1966
Monserrat	1966

Antigua and Barbuda	1966
St Kitts and Nevis	1966
Anguilla	1966
British Virgin Islands	1966
Turks and Caicos Islands	1966
Bahamas	1966
Belgium	1966
Brazil	1968
Chile	1968
Austria	1969

1970s

Turkey	1971
Thailand	1972
Singapore	1972
Malaysia	1972
Brunei	1972
Maldives	1972
Seychelles	1972
Mauritius	1972
Kenya	1972
Yugoslavia	1972
Cook Islands	1974
Norfolk Island	1974
New Hebrides	1974
Solomon Islands	1974
Papua New Guinea	1974
Indonesia	1974
Mexico	1975
Hong Kong	1975
Japan	1975
Finland	1976
Luxembourg	1976
Western Samoa	1977

Kuwait	1979
Bahrain	1979
Saudi Arabia	1979
Qatar	1979
United Arab Emirates	1979
Oman	1979
Tanzania	1979
Malawi	1979
Botswana	1979
Zambia	1979

1980s

Switzerland	1980
Tunisia	1980
Algeria	1980
Morocco	1980
Nauru	1982
Kiribati	1982
Tuvalu	1982
Cayman Islands	1983
Bangladesh	1983
Jordan	1984
Belize	1985
China	1986
Spain	1988

1990s

Iceland	1990
Namibia	1991
Zimbabwe	1991
*Germany	1992
Hungary	1993

Russia	1994
South Africa	1995
Poland	1996
Czech Republic	1996
South Korea	1999
Mozambique	1999

** Germany is here counted as a different country from West Germany which Elizabeth II had visited previously. On this visit the Queen visited cities in the territory of the former East Germany which she had never visited before.*

2000s

Lithuania	2006
Latvia	2006
Estonia	2006
Slovenia	2008
Slovakia	2008

2010s

Ireland	2011
TOTAL VISITED	**116**

The three countries most visited by Queen Elizabeth II between 1952-2018 are all Commonwealth realms of which she is Head of State:

1.	**Canada**	22 visits
2.	**Australia**	16 visits
3.	**New Zealand**	10 visits

Outside of Commonwealth countries, the three countries most visited by the Queen between 1952-2018 have been the following:

1. **West Germany/Germany** 7 visits
2. **France** 6 visits
3. **United States** 5 visits

Notable countries never officially visited by Elizabeth II as Queen include Argentina, Cuba, Israel, Egypt, Iraq and the Philippines. Elizabeth also never visited Greece as Queen, however she made a visit to the country in 1950 as Princess Elizabeth accompanied by her husband Prince Philip.

Notable Films on Royal History

The history of the British monarchy has provided subjects for many films over the last century. Listed on the following pages are the most notable films on royal history since the 1930s with a bite-size review of both the subject treated and the quality of the movie. Academy Awards (Oscars) won by a film are also noted where relevant. Note that only films where royal history is the main subject are listed. Adaptations of Shakespeare's plays and other major works of literature (for example *Ivanhoe* and *The Prince and the Pauper*) are not included.

The Private Life of Henry VIII (1933)
Director: Alexander Korda
Starring: Charles Laughton (Henry VIII), Merle Oberon (Anne Boleyn), Elsa Lanchester (Anne of Cleves), Binnie Barnes (Catherine Howard).
The first great royal talkie, part drama, part comedy, with a larger-than-life performance of Henry by Charles Laughton.
★*Academy Award for Best Actor (Charles Laughton)*

Nell Gwynn (1934)
Director: Herbert Wilcox
Starring: Anna Neagle (Nell Gwynn), Cedric Hardwicke (Charles II), Jeanne De Casalis (Duchess of Portsmouth).
Enjoyable, old-fashioned romp on the exploits of Nell Gwynn at the court of Charles II.

The Crusades (1935)
Director: Cecil B. DeMille
Starring: Richard Wilcoxon (Richard I), Loretta Young (Berengaria of Navarre), Ian Keith (Saladin).
A grand Cecil B. DeMille epic centred on a romanticized love-story between Richard I and Berengaria of Navarre taking place during the Third Crusade.

Tudor Rose (1936)
(Also released as 'Nine Days A Queen')
Director: Robert Stevenson
Starring: Nova Pilbeam (Lady Jane Grey), John Mills (Guilford Dudley), Cedric Hardwicke (Earl of Warwick).
Stagey historical adaptation of the tale of Lady Jane Grey which is liberal with facts, but is saved by the central character's compelling performance.

Mary of Scotland (1936)
Director: John Ford
Starring: Katherine Hepburn (Mary Queen of Scots), Friedrich March (Earl of Bothwell), Florence Eldridge (Elizabeth I).
Melodramatic retelling of the troubled life of Mary Queen Scots, with some glaring historical inaccuracies but of great cinematic value.

Fire Over England (1937)
Director: William K. Howard
Starring: Flora Robson (Elizabeth I), Laurence Olivier (Michael Ingolby), Vivien Leigh (Cynthia Burleigh), Leslie Banks (Earl of Leicester).
Timeless, patriotic (even if slightly fictional) account of England's triumph over the Spanish Armada, featuring the definite big screen portrayal of Queen Elizabeth I.

Victoria the Great (1937)
Director: Herbert Wilcox
Starring: Anna Neagle (Queen Victoria), Anton Walbrook (Prince Albert) H.B. Warner (Lord Melbourne), Mary Morris (Duchess of Kent).
Reverential and celebratory black-and-white biopic of Queen Victoria's life covering events from her accession to her Diamond Jubilee.

Sixty Glorious Years (1938)
Director: Herbert Wilcox
Starring: Anna Neagle (Queen Victoria), Anton Walbrook (Prince Albert) C. Aubrey Smith (Duke of Wellington), Felix Aylmer (Lord Palmerston), Joyce Bland (Florence Nightingale).
Colour sequel to *Victoria the Great* where the same cast covers further events from the Queen's life, this time up to her death.

Tower of London (1939)
Director: Rowland V. Lee
Starring: Basil Rathbone (Richard III), Vincent Price (George, Duke of Clarence), Boris Karloff (Mord the Executioner).
Largely imagined portrayal of Richard III's rise to the throne, where he methodically eliminates everyone on his path to power like a mob don.

The Private Lives of Elizabeth and Essex (1939)
Director: Michael Curtiz
Starring: Bette Davis (Elizabeth I), Errol Flynn (Earl of Essex), Vincent Price (Walter Raleigh).
Classic Hollywood re-interpretation of the doomed relationship between Elizabeth I and her late favourite the Earl of Essex, long on glamour and romance, slightly shorter on accuracy.

Mrs Fitzherbert (1947)
(Also released as 'A Court Secret')
Director: Montgomery Tully
Starring: Peter Graves (George, Prince of Wales), Joyce Howard (Mrs Fitzherbert).
Almost forgotten (and rather stiff) recital on the love affair between George Prince of Wales and the commoner Mrs Fitzherbert.

Bonnie Prince Charlie (1948)
Director: Anthony Kimmins
Starring: David Niven (Bonnie Prince Charlie), Margaret Leighton (Flora MacDonald), Elwyn Brook-Jones (Duke of Cumberland).
Worthy Technicolor caper chronicling Bonnie Prince Charlie's adventures in Britain during the 1745 Jacobite Rebellion.

Saraband for Dead Lovers (1948)
Director: Basil Dearden
Starring: Joan Greenwood (Sophia Dorothea of Celle), Peter Bull (Prince George), Stewart Granger (Count Konigsmark), Francoise Rosay (Electress Sophia of Hanover).
The doomed tale of George I's spurned wife, Sophia Dorothea, gets an airing in this largely faithful, compelling saga.

Young Bess (1953)
Director: George Sidney
Starring: Jean Simmons (Princess Elizabeth), Charles Laughton (Henry VIII), Deborah Kerr (Catherine Parr), Stewart Granger (Thomas Seymour).
Brilliant portrayal of a fiery, young Elizabeth I, replete with lavish costumes and Hollywood stars.

Beau Brummell (1954)
Director: Curtis Bernhardt
Starring: Stewart Granger (Beau Brummell), Peter Ustinov (George Prince of Wales), Robert Morley (George III), Elizabeth Taylor (Lady Patricia Belham).
Embellished costumed drama on the famous arbiter of fashion and his friendship with George, the Prince Regent, who is memorably played by Peter Ustinov.

The Virgin Queen (1955)
Director: Henry Koster
Starring: Bette Davis (Elizabeth I), Richard Todd (Sir Walter Raleigh), Joan Collins (Elizabeth Throckmorton).
Bette Davis once again plays Elizabeth I in a romantic, partly fictional story focusing on her relationship with Sir Walter Raleigh.

Becket (1964)
Director: Peter Grenville
Starring: Peter O'Toole (Henry II), Richard Burton (Thomas Becket), John Gielgud (King Louis VII of France).
Character-driven account of the struggle between King Henry II and Thomas Becket, with some historical flaws.
★*Academy Award for Best Adapted Screenplay*

A Man For All Seasons (1966)
Director: Fred Zinnemann
Starring: Paul Schofield (Thomas More), Robert Shaw (Henry VIII), Leo McKern (Thomas Cromwell).
Sophisticated adaptation of a successful play charting Thomas More's fall from power at the court of Henry VIII, largely accurate and brilliantly acted.
★*Academy Award for Best Picture, Best Director, Best Actor (Paul Scofield), Best Adapted Screenplay, Best Cinematography, Best Costume Design*

The Lion In Winter (1968)
Director: Anthony Harvey
Starring: Peter O'Toole (Henry II), Katherine Hepburn (Eleanor of Aquitaine), Anthony Hopkins (Prince Richard the Lionheart).
Brilliantly acted adaptation of a stage play depicting a weekend into the dysfunctional life of King Henry II's power-hungry family, compressed for facts but faithful in spirit.
★*Academy Award for Best Actress (Katherine Hepburn), Best Adapted Screenplay, Best Musical Score*

Alfred the Great (1969)
Director: Clive Donner
Starring: David Hemmings (King Alfred), Michael York (King Guthrum), Prunella Ransome (Queen Ealhswith).
Ponderous and almost forgotten British epic on the life of Saxon England's greatest king.

Anne of the Thousand Days (1969)
Director: Charles Jarrott
Starring: Genevieve Bujold (Anne Boleyn), Richard Burton (Henry VIII), Irene Papas (Catherine of Aragon), Anthony Quayle (Thomas Wolsey).
Traditional retelling of the rise and fall of Anne Boleyn, praised for Genevieve Bujold's portrayal of Anne.
★*Academy Award for Best Costume Design*

Cromwell (1970)
Director: Ken Hughes
Starring: Richard Harris (Oliver Cromwell), Alec Guinness (Charles I), Dorothy Tutin (Queen Henrietta Maria).
Flawed big-budget saga on the English Civil War centred on Oliver Cromwell, notable for Alec Guinness' portrayal of Charles I.
★*Academy Award for Best Costume Design*

Mary Queen of Scots (1971)
Director: Charles Jarrott
Starring: Vanessa Redgrave (Mary Queen of Scots), Glenda Jackson (Elizabeth I), Timothy Dalton (Lord Darnley), Patrick McGoohan (Earl of Moray).
Over-dramatic palaver depicting a saintly Mary Stuart fighting, and losing, against an evil world.

Henry VIII and His Six Wives (1972)
Director: Waris Hussein
Starring: Keith Michell (Henry VIII), Charlotte Rampling (Anne Boleyn), Donald Pleasance (Thomas Cromwell), Bernard Hepton (Thomas Cranmer).
Brilliant, if somewhat skimmy, historical chronicle of Henry VIII's marital life, adapted from a successful 1970 BBC mini-series.

Lady Jane (1986)
Director: Trevor Nunn
Starring: Helena Bonham Carter (Lady Jane Grey), Cary Elwes (Guilford Dudley), Jane Lapotaire (Mary I).
Idealistic, romantic account of the rise and fall of Lady Jane Grey and her husband Guilford Dudley, noteworthy for its Royal Shakespeare Company cast.

The Madness of King George (1994)
Director: Nicholas Hytner
Starring: Nigel Hawthorne (George III), Helen Mirren (Queen Charlotte), Rupert Everett (George, Prince of Wales).
Factually liberal, yet touching account of King George III's first madness bout of 1788-89.
★*Academy Award for Best Art Direction*

Braveheart (1995)
Director: Mel Gibson
Starring: Mel Gibson (William Wallace), Patrick McGoohan (Edward I), Sophie Marceau (Isabella of France).
Flawed Hollywood epic on the struggle between Scottish patriot William Wallace and King Edward I of England, completely riddled with historical inaccuracies.
★*Academy Award for Best Picture, Best Director, Best Cinematography, Best Sound Editing, Best Make-up*

The Bruce (1996)
Directors: Bob Carruthers and David McWhinnie
Starring: Sandy Welch (Robert the Bruce), Brian Blessed (Edward I), Oliver Reed (Robert Wishart).
Patriotic, if somewhat confused, account of Robert the Bruce's life and struggles as King of Scotland.

Mrs Brown (1997)
Director: John Madden
Starring: Judy Dench (Queen Victoria), Billy Connolly (John Brown), David Westhead (Prince of Wales).
Decorous yet insightful exploration of the relationship between Queen Victoria and her Highland servant John Brown.

Elizabeth (1998)
Director: Shekhar Kapur
Starring: Cate Blanchett (Elizabeth I), Joseph Fiennes (Earl of Leicester), Geoffrey Rush (Francis Walsingham), Richard Attenborough (Lord Burghley).
Historical travesty where Elizabeth I and other real-life characters inhabit in a shockingly fictionalised version of real events.
★*Academy Award for Best Make-up*

To Kill A King (2003)
Director: Mike Barker
Starring: Tim Roth (Oliver Cromwell), Rupert Everett (Charles I), Dougray Scott (Sir Thomas Fairfax).
Historically messy and cinematically rambling flop revolving around the Parliamentary victory in the Civil War and the execution of Charles I.

The Queen (2006)
Director: Stephen Frears
Starring: Helen Mirren (Elizabeth II), James Cromwell (Prince Philip), Michael Sheen (Tony Blair).
Somewhat over-critical interpretation of the events surrounding Diana, Princess of Wales' death, focusing mostly on Elizabeth II and Tony Blair.
★*Academy Award for Best Actress (Helen Mirren)*

Elizabeth: The Golden Age (2007)
Director: Shekhar Kapur
Starring: Cate Blanchett (Elizabeth I), Geoffrey Rush (Francis Walsingham), Samantha Morton (Mary Queen of Scots).
Slightly less inaccurate sequel to *Elizabeth* (1998), notable for lavish sets and pathos, but still very much historical shamwork.
★*Academy Award for Best Costume Design*

The Other Boleyn Girl (2008)
Director: Justin Chadwick
Starring: Natalie Portman (Anne Boleyn), Scarlett Johansson (Mary Boleyn), Eric Bana (Henry VIII).
Lush, highly fictionalised tale of the two Boleyn sister's lives and their relationships with Henry VIII, itself based on Philippa Gregory's historical guesswork.

The Young Victoria (2009)
Director: Jean-Marc Vallee
Starring: Emily Blunt (Queen Victoria), Rupert Friend (Prince Albert), Miranda Richardson (Duchess of Kent).
Elegant, worthy portrayal of Queen Victoria's adolescence, accession to the throne, and her falling in love with Prince Albert.
★*Academy Award for Best Costume Design*

The King's Speech (2010)
Director: Tom Hooper
Starring: Colin Firth (George VI), Helena Bonham-Carter (Queen Elizabeth), Guy Pearce (Edward VIII).
Oscar-winning, largely accurate account of how George VI overcame his stammering to perform his duties as King.
★*Academy Award for Best Picture, Best Director, Best Actor (Colin Firth), Best Original Screenplay*

W.E. (2011)
Director: Madonna
Starring: Andrea Riseborough (Wallis Simpson), James D'Arcy (Edward VIII).
Stylish, yet widely panned tale of a modern New York housewife's obsession with Edward VIII and Wallis Simpson's love story.

Ironclad (2011)
Director: Jonathan English
Starring: James Purefoy (Thomas Marshall), Paul Giamatti (King John).
Partly fictionalised account of King John's siege of Rochester Castle in 1215 during the First Barons War.

Diana (2013)
Director: Oliver Hirschbiegel
Starring: Naomi Watts (Princess Diana) Naveen Andrews (Dr Hasnat Khan).
Soppy flop describing the last two years of Diana's life and her relationship with London heart surgeon Hasnat Khan.

Mary Queen of Scots (2013)
Director: Thomas Imbach
Starring: Camille Rutheford (Mary Queen of Scots), Aneurin Barnard (Lord Darnley), Sean Biggerstaff (Earl of Bothwell).
Swiss-produced, sympathetic portrait of Mary Stuart, based on a popular 1935 Austrian biography. Half-spoken in French.

A Royal Night Out (2015)
Director: Julian Jarrold
Starring: Sarah Gadon (Princess Elizabeth), Bel Powley (Princess Margaret), Rupert Everett (George VI).
Frothy, highly fictionalised account of Princess Elizabeth and Princess Margaret's one night out in London during VE celebrations in 1945.

Victoria and Abdul (2017)
Director: Stephen Frears
Starring: Judy Dench (Queen Victoria), Ali Fazal (Abdul Karim), Eddie Izzard (Bertie, Prince of Wales).
The fascinating relationship between Queen Victoria and her last confidant, her Indian servant Abdul Karim, is explored in this beautifully photographed though slightly underwhelming biopic.

Some Notable Royal Pets

Every monarch since Henry VIII has owned pets, with dogs the clear favourites, and pet owning has been the norm among Royal Family members since at least the 16th century. Listed below are some of the most notable royal pets of the last 500 years, all of them dogs but with one notable exception. They are listed in rough chronological order.

Cut

Pet owner: King Henry VIII

Cut was a dog belonging to Henry VIII who seems to have had a knack for getting lost. Court financial records from the 1530s show that Henry VIII twice rewarded people for bringing the lost dog back to court. He once gave a man 10 shillings 'for bringing Cut the kinge's spanyell ayen', and later gave 4 shillings and 8 pence 'to a poure woman in rewarde for bringing ayenne of Cut, the kinge's dog.'

Mary Queen of Scots' Terrier

Pet owner: Mary Queen of Scots

This unnamed small Skye Terrier belonging to Mary Queen of Scots achieved immortality when it accompanied its mistress to her execution in February 1587 by sneaking its way unnoticed under her skirts. No one realised its presence until after Mary was beheaded and the dog began to howl from under the skirts of her lifeless body. It refused to depart the decapitated body, staining itself with the blood spilling on the floor, and had to be carried away by force. It is said that Mary's blood could not completely be washed away from its fur, and that the terrier died soon afterwards by refusing to eat.

Jewell

Pet owner: King James I

The story goes that once while King James I and his wife Queen Anne of Denmark were out hunting deer Anne mistook her aim and shot instead Jewell, one of James' favourite hound dogs. The King immediately lost his temper and 'stormed exceedingly awhile', but calmed himself once he learned his wife was the accidental culprit. To make sure Anne would not feel too aggrieved by her mistake, he sent her a diamond worth £2000, 'as a legacie from his dead dogge.'

Boy

Pet owner: Prince Rupert of the Rhine

The most famous royal pet of the 17th century, Boy was a white poodle belonging to Prince Rupert, a nephew of Charles I and famous Royalist Commander during the English Civil War. Boy accompanied its master everywhere on military campaigns, even onto the edge of battlefields. It always seemed to survive unharmed, so a myth grew among Roundheads that it was indestructible and had supernatural powers, including the ability to speak foreign languages and to put hexes on its enemies. A pamphlet was even published in 1643 criticizing the influence Boy had on Charles I's war council, and describing its attitude to religion as 'most popish.' Boy's invincibility was finally disproved when it died at the Battle of Marston Moor chasing its master into the fray after someone forgot to tie it to the baggage train. Its fame by then was such that its death was recorded in the Parliamentary Journal as the slain 'accursed cur' of which 'so much had been said across the country'.

Rogue

Pet owner: King Charles I

Rogue was one of Charles I's favourite spaniels who stayed by his side during the last year of his life, from his imprisonment at Carisbrooke Castle in 1648 to his execution in London in January 1649. On the last day of Charles' life Rogue accompanied him as he walked across St James's Park to his place of execution in Whitehall, and after Charles's death it was paraded in the capital as a royal trophy by Roundhead soldiers. Its later fate is unknown.

Eos

Pet owner: Prince Albert

Prince Albert's favourite dog, Eos was a female greyhound that Albert raised from a puppy in Germany and that became his faithful companion for 11 years. It accompanied its master to England and was painted several times by Edwin Landseer for the Royal Collection. In 1841 it was accidentally shot during a shooting party by Prince Ferdinand of Saxe-Coburg-Gotha, Queen Victoria's uncle, and its fame was such by then that bulletins about its recovery were followed anxiously by royal families across Europe. Eos eventually recovered and later died of natural causes in 1844 at Osborne House, where it is commemorated today with a life-size bronze sculpture in the gardens.

Dash

Pet owner: Queen Victoria

Queen Victoria's first great canine companion was a King Charles spaniel that had originally been given as a gift to her mother when Victoria was 14 years old. It soon became Victoria's inseparable friend following her wherever she went. 'Dear Dashy', as she called it, continued being Victoria's favourite pet after her accession as Queen, and she famously recorded in her diary how she came back to Buckingham Palace after her coronation ceremony to give Dash a bath. It died in 1840 and was buried in Windsor Home Park, where its gravestone records 'His attachment was without selfishness, his playfulness without malice, his fidelity without deceit.'

Noble IV

Pet owner: Queen Victoria

Queen Victoria owned several border collies during her life, three of which were named Noble, however it was the fourth collie to bear this name which became perhaps her favourite dog. Described as a sweet-natured creature, Noble IV had been given as a gift to Victoria in 1872 and had the special task of guarding Victoria's gloves. She described it as 'the most biddable dog I ever saw, and so affectionate and kind; if he thinks you are not pleased with him, he puts out his paws and begs in such an affectionate way.' When it died at the advanced age of 16 at Balmoral in 1887 Victoria was distraught. It was buried in the grounds of Balmoral where a lifesize bronze memorial still stands on its grave.

Turi

Pet owner: Queen Victoria

This Pomeranian dog was Queen Victoria's last favourite pet and can be seen with her in several photographs taken in the last years of her life. It has the claim of being the last pet Victoria ever cuddled as she lay on her deathbed at Osborne House in 1901, asking specifically that Turi be brought to her as one of her last wishes. After her death it was adopted by one of Victoria's daughters-in-law, Princess Helena, Duchess of Albany, the widow of Prince Leopold.

Alix

Pet owner: Queen Alexandra of Denmark

A gift from the Tsar of Russia to Queen Alexandra when she was Princess of Wales in 1895, Alix was a Borzoi dog that bore as its name Alexandra's nickname in the Royal Family. Borzois were bred exclusively for the Russian Imperial family and were unknown in Britain before the 1860s, so by the time this dog arrived in the country in the 1890s its breed had become one of the priciest in Europe. Alix was exhibited many times at dog shows during its lifetime, including Crufts, receiving over 100 awards. It was reported that people queued for hours at these exhibitions just to see Alexandra's celebrated Borzoi.

Caesar

Pet owner: King Edward VII

Caesar was a male Wire Fox Terrier and Edward VII's favourite dog. It became famous throughout the world in 1910 when it took the place of honour at its master's funeral procession, walking behind Edward's coffin before all the kings of Europe. While Edward was alive Caesar had its own personal valet to tend to its needs, and a collar around its neck proclaiming 'I am Caesar, I belong to the King'. Edward even had the jewellery firm of Faberge create a small precious stone figurine of the dog with a gold collar and ruby eyes which remains in the Royal Collection today. After Edward's death, Caesar went to live with his widow, Queen Alexandra, until it died from an operation in 1914. It is buried in the gardens of Marlborough House, London, but a life-size statue of him curls at the feet of Edward VII's effigy on his tomb in St George's Chapel, Windsor.

Charlotte

Pet owner: King George V

One of the most unique pets in royal history, Charlotte was a female, grey-pink parrot belonging to King George V, a gift from his sister Victoria. An infamously temperamental parrot, George was nevertheless devoted to it. On most mornings he would bring Charlotte, perched on his finger, to the breakfast table where it would forage among people's plates for something to eat. On the odd occasion when it made a mess on the table the King always tried to cover the item with some tableware before others could notice it. Charlotte would then follow its master into his study where guests were often surprised to see a parrot on a stand next to the King. It was with him for over 20 years until George's death in 1936, after which it accompanied George's funeral party back to London from Sandringham. Its later fate is unclear.

Slipper

Pet owners: Wallis Simpson and King Edward VIII

Slipper was a Cairn terrier Edward VIII gave as a gift to Wallis Simpson at the beginning of their romance in 1934, when he was still Prince of Wales. During the abdication crisis of December 1936 Wallis took the dog with her when she moved to France, in the expectation that she, Edward and Slipper would soon be reunited together. Slipper however died soon after its arrival in France when it was bitten by a viper. Wallis Simpson described in her memoirs how 'his loss on the eve of my reunion with David (Edward) seemed to me a frightful omen'. At the time she wrote to Edward: 'he was our dog—not yours or mine but ours—and he loved us both. Now the principal guest at our wedding is no more.' After giving the dog a funeral Wallis and Edward commemorated Slipper with a diamond medallion which hung in a place of honour in their Paris home.

Dookie

Pet owners: Princess Elizabeth and Princess Margaret

Dookie was the first Pembroke Corgi to be owned by the Royal Family, starting a love affair with the breed that persists to this day. It was bought by the Duke of York, the future George VI, for his daughters Princess Elizabeth and Princess Margaret in 1933. It was a male officially called Rozavel Golden Eagle but its name was soon changed to Dookie, a shortened version of Duke of York. Both princesses became very attached to the dog, which was described as a born sentimentalist, and it was soon joined by another corgi named Jane. Both dogs were photographed with the Duke of York's whole family for a special book published in 1936 entitled *Our Princesses and Their Dogs*, the sale of which boosted the popularity of the breed in Britain. Dookie died in the early 1940s.

Susan

Pet owner: Queen Elizabeth II

After the death of Dookie, Princess Elizabeth received another Pembroke corgi for her 18th birthday in 1944, another gift from her father King George VI. This time it was a female called Susan who became one of Elizabeth II's all-time favourite dogs, even going on honeymoon with her and Prince Philip in 1947. Susan was bred several times and became the ancestress of all the corgis owned by Elizabeth II since, counting 14 generations of descendants over the last 60 years. In her adult years she developed a propensity for biting—her victims included a policeman, a sentry and the royal clock winder—which she seems to have passed down to her descendants. Susan died in 1959 and was buried at Sandringham, with a headstone memorial designed by Elizabeth II herself.

Some Rules to Follow When Meeting the British Monarch

There is no obligatory code of behaviour when meeting the British monarch, the only thing that is expected is courtesy. The following rules however have long been part of royal protocol and can be used by people who wish to follow tradition:

- If sitting, rise from your seat when the monarch arrives. Stand when the monarch stands, and do not sit down unless invited to do so, or unless it is generally expected (i.e. a formal dinner or a play). Remember to also rise when the monarch leaves. The only persons who are exempt from these rules are Queens Consort and former monarchs (the late Queen Elizabeth the Queen Mother was exempt from rising from her seat in the presence of her daughter).

- Do not turn your back to the monarch when in close proximity at official functions. It is generally acceptable to do so however during mingling activities.

- Do not introduce yourself to the monarch. Officials, hosts or royal aides will do that for you when it is your turn.

- On meeting the monarch, men should bow and women should curtsy. Bows should be simple bows from the neck and shoulders only. Curtsies are performed by placing your right foot behind the left foot and bending the knees briefly while keeping the upper body straight. Bows and curtsies should also be performed when bidding goodbye to the monarch. Bows and curtsies are not required from citizens of countries of which the

Queen is not Head of State (i.e. Commonwealth republics and other foreign countries).

- Do not offer your hand for a handshake. If the monarch offers a hand for a handshake however do shake it, but without gripping or pumping.

- Refrain from touching the monarch, even if affectionately meant. The monarch will generally do not mind if this rule is broken, but other people are likely to take offense, especially in official situations.

- Generally, do not start speaking with the monarch until invited to do so. He or she will normally start a conversation with you.

- Address the monarch the first time as 'Your Majesty', and subsequently throughout the conversation with 'Ma'am'—which should rhyme with 'Pam'—if the monarch is a woman, or 'Sir' if a man. Use 'Your Majesty' again when addressing the monarch for the last time before he or she departs.

- During conversation, do not address the monarch by using 'you'. Instead address the monarch in the third person by using 'Your Majesty' (for example: "Has Your Majesty enjoyed the weather today?").

- Do not ask personal questions in conversation. If mentioning other members of the Royal Family refer to their titles, not to their personal names (for example, say 'the Prince of Wales', not 'Charles').

- At the dinner table, everyone should stop eating their courses after the monarch has finished eating and cleared the plate. Generally however, if the monarch has finished eating before others diners he or she will always leave a small amount of food on the plate to allow others to finish their courses.

It is important to note that breaking any of the rules above will not incur any royal displeasure so long as general courtesy is still employed. The Royal Household's guidelines on meeting the monarch are only that people should adopt rules of courtesy with which they are comfortable.

How to Write to Members Of The Royal Family

Members of the Royal Family can normally only be contacted by post. Following below are some rules and advice on how to write a letter plus current mailing addresses.

Some Rules and Advice

Debrett's 'Rules of Etiquette' advises that only close personal friends should write directly to members of the Royal Family, everyone else should write to the Private Secretary, Equerry or Lady-in-Waiting of the person they wish to contact. This practice however is rarely followed today, and the British Monarchy website encourages people to write directly to a Royal Family member (though correspondence will be dealt in any case by a Private Secretary, Equerry or Lady-in-Waiting first, and then if appropriate passed to the person the letter is addressed to). Letters and cards may be sent for birthdays, anniversaries, weddings, royal births, royal deaths; to inform a particular Royal Family member of local achievements, charity and royal patronage issues; and about matters related to the Crown. Letters showing support for a particular cause patronised by a member of the Royal Family are also welcome.

Letters should formally open with 'Your Majesty', or more simply 'Sir' or 'Madam' when writing to the monarch; and with 'Your Royal Highness' or 'Sir' / 'Madam' when writing to other members of the Royal Family. Letters should end with 'Yours Sincerely' or 'Yours Faithfully'. In the case of the monarch a more formal closing can be used as follows: 'I have the honour to be, Madam/Sir, Your Majesty's humble and obedient servant'. Envelopes should be addressed to 'His Royal Highness', 'Her Royal Highness' or 'Their Royal Highnesses', followed by the titles and addresses listed below. In the case of the Monarch or Queens Consort, envelopes should be addressed to 'His Majesty the King' and 'Her Majesty the Queen'.

Senders should be aware that neither The Queen nor any member of the Royal Family intervene in political issues or personal disputes, so letters of this nature will receive a standard response. Unsolicited packaged gifts should also not be sent as they will not be opened for security reasons, and unsolicited vouchers or gift certificates will also be returned. Hand-made drawings on paper or photographs however are acceptable. Senders should not expect a direct response from a member of the Royal Family. All responses, acknowledgements, and letters of thanks are normally composed and signed by Private Secretaries, Equerries or Ladies-in-Waiting, though a Royal Family member may sometimes append a personal signature.

Addresses:

Mailing addresses are current as of June 2018. Correct postage should always be affixed to the envelope.

The Queen, The Duke of Edinburgh, The Duke of York, Princess Beatrice of York, Princess Eugenie of York, The Princess Royal, Princess Alexandra of Kent:
Buckingham Palace
London SW1A 1AA

The Prince of Wales, The Duchess of Cornwall:
Clarence House
London SW1A 1BA

The Duke of Cambridge, The Duchess of Cambridge, Prince George, Princess Charlotte, Prince Louis, The Duke of Sussex, The Duchess of Sussex:
Kensington Palace
London W8 4PU
(correspondence can also be sent to Clarence House)

The Earl of Wessex, The Countess of Wessex:
Bagshot Park
Bagshot
Surrey GU19 5PL

The Duke of Gloucester, The Duchess of Gloucester, Prince Michael of Kent, Princess Michael of Kent:
Kensington Palace
London W8 4PU

The Duke of Kent:
St James's Palace
London SW1A 1BQ

The Duchess of Kent:
Wren House
Palace Green
London W8 4PY

SOURCES

The following sources were consulted in the writing of this book.

PRINTED SOURCES (BOOKS):

Works on the British Monarchy, its History and Collections:

Allison, Ronald, and Sarah Riddell, Eds. *The Royal Encyclopedia*. (London: Macmillan Press, 1991).

Beauclerk-Dewar, Peter and Roger Powell. *Royal Bastards. Illegitimate children of the British Royal Family*. (Stroud, Glos.: The History Press, 2008).

Clark, Pam; Julie Crocker; Allison Derrett; Laura Hobbs; and Jill Kelsey. *Treasures From the Royal Archives*. (London: Royal Collection, 2014).

Crofton, Ian. *The Kings and Queens of England*. (London: Quercus, 2006).

Cussans, Thomas. *'The Times' Kings and Queens of the British Isles*. (London: HarperCollins, 2004).

De Guitaut, Caroline. *Diamonds. A Jubilee Celebration*. (London: Royal Collection, 2012).

Dodson, Aidan. *The Royal Tombs of Great Britain*. (London: Gerald Duckworth, 2004).

Doran, Susan. *The Tudor Chronicles, 1485-1603*.(London: Quercus, 2011).

Erickson, Carolly. *Brief Lives of the English Monarchs*. (London: Constable, 2007).

Hallam, Elizabeth, Gen. Ed. *The Plantagenet Chronicles*. (London: Weidenfeld and Nicolson, 1986.)

Hardman, Robert. *Monarchy. The Royal Family at Work*. (London: Ebury Press, 2007).

Hill, Michael. *Right Royal Remarks. From William I to Elizabeth II*. (London: Robson Books, 2003.)

Hilliam, David. *Crown, Orb and Sceptre. The True Stories of English Coronations*. (Stroud, Glos.: The History Press, 2009).

Hilliam, David. *Kings, Queens, Bones and Bastards*. (Stroud, Glos.: The History Press, 2004).

Hilton, Lisa. *Queens Consort. England's Medieval Queens*. (London: Phoenix, 2009).

Humphrys, Julian. *The Private Life of Palaces*. (Hampton Court, Surrey: Historic Royal Palaces, 2007).

Keay, Anna. *The Crown Jewels. The Official Illustrated History*. (London: Thames & Hudson, 2012).

Loades, David. *Princes of Wales. Royal Heirs in Waiting*. (London: The National Archives, 2008).

Longford, Elizabeth, Ed. *The Oxford Book of Royal Anecdotes*. (Oxford: Oxford University Press, 1989).

Matson, John. *Dear Osborne*. (London: Hamish Hamilton, 2009).

Oakey, David. *The Queen's Year. A Souvenir Album*. (London: Royal Collection, 2010).

Parsons, Tom. *100 Treasures of Buckingham Palace*. (London: Royal Collection, 2008).

Phillips, Charles. *The Complete Illustrated Encyclopedia of Royal Britain*. (London: Hermes House, 2008).

Plumb, J.H., and Huw Wheldon. *Royal Heritage. The Story of Britain's Royal Builders and Collectors*. (London: BBC, 1977).

Powell, Roger. *Royal Sex. Mistresses and Lovers of the British Royal Family*. (Stroud, Glos.: Amberley, 2010).

Roberts, Hugh. *The Queen's Diamonds*. (London: Royal Collection, 2012).

Starkey, David. *Crown and Country. The Kings and Queens of England: A History*. (London: HarperPress, 2010).

Strong, Roy. *Coronation. A History of Kingship and the British Monarchy*. (London: HarperCollins, 2005).

Struthers, Jane. *Royal Palaces of Britain*. (London: New Holland Publishers, 2004)

Vickers, Hugo. *The Royal Line of Succession. Official Souvenir Guide*. (London: Royal Collection Trust/Scala, 2012).

Weir, Alison. *Britain's Royal Families. The Complete Genealogy.* (London: Vintage, 2008).

Williamson, David. *Brewer's British Royalty. A Phrase and Fable Dictionary*. (London: Cassell, 1996).

Wilson, Derek. *The Plantagenets. The Kings That Made Britain.* (London: Quercus, 2011).

Wright, Peter. *The Story of the Royal Maundy*. (London: Pitkin Guides, 1990).

Royal Biographies:

Ashley, Maurice. *Charles II. The Man and the Statesman*. (London: The History Book Club, 1971).

Battiscombe, Georgina. *Queen Alexandra*. (London: Sphere Books, 1972).

Bradbury, Jim. *Stephen and Matilda. The Civil War of 1139-53*. (Stroud, Glos: Sutton Publishing, 2005).

Bradford, Sarah. *George VI*. (London: Penguin, 2011).

Donaldson, Frances. *Edward VIII*. (Aylesbury, Bucks: Futura Publications, 1976).

The Duke of Windsor. *A King's Story. The Memoirs of HRH the Duke of Windsor*. (London: Cassell and Company, 1951).

Fraser, Antonia. *King Charles II*. (London: Weidenfeld and Nicolson, 1979).

Fraser, Antonia. *The Six Wives of Henry VIII*. (London: Phoenix, 2003).

Fraser, Flora. *Princesses. The Six Daughters of George III.* (London: John Murray, 2004).

Fulford, Roger. *Royal Dukes. The Father and Uncles of Queen Victoria.* (London: Fontana, 1973).

George III, His court and His Family. A New Edition in Two Volumes. (London: Henry Colburn and Co., 1821).

Greig, Geordie. *The Kingmaker: The Man Who Saved George VI.* (London: Hodder and Staughton, 2011).

Hammerton, John, Ed. *Our King and Queen. A pictorial Record of their Lives Complete in One Volume*. Silver Jubilee Edition. (London: The Amalgamated Press, 1935).

Hardman, Robert. *Our Queen*. (London: Hutchinson, 2011).

Hibbert, Christopher. *Charles I. A Life of Religion, War and Treason.* (Basingstoke, Hampshire: Palgrave Macmillan, 2007).

Hibbert, Christopher. *George III. A Personal History*. (London: Viking, 1998).

Hibbert, Christopher. *Queen Victoria. A Personal History*. (London: HarperCollins, 2001).

Hibbert, Christopher. *The Virgin Queen. The Personal History of Elizabeth I.* (London: Penguin, 1992).

Lacey, Robert. *Royal. Her Majesty Queen Elizabeth II*. (London: Little, Brown, 2002).

Longford, Elizabeth. *Victoria*. (London: Abacus, 2011).

Magnus, Philip. *King Edward The Seventh.* (London: John Murray, 1977).

Matusiak, John. *James I: Scotland's King of England.* (Stroud, Glos: The History Press, 2015).

Morris, Marc. *A Great And Terrible King. Edward I and the Forging of Britain*. (London: Hutchinson, 2008).

Mortimer, Ian. *The Fears of Henry IV. The Life of England's Self-Made King*. (London: Vintage Books, 2008).

Mortimer, Ian. *The Perfect King. The Life of Edward III, Father of the English Nation*. (London: Jonathan Cape, 2006).

Neale, J.E. *Queen Elizabeth I.* (Harmondsworth, Middlesex: Pelican, 1965).

Penn, Thomas. *Winter King: Henry VII and the Dawn of Tudor England.* (London: Penguin, 2012).

Plowden, Alison. *Caroline and Charlotte. Regency Scandals*. (Stroud, Glos.: Sutton Publishing, 2005).

Pope-Hennessy, James. *Queen Mary, 1867-1953*. (London: George Allen and Unwin Limited, 1959).

Rappaport, Helen. *Queen Victoria. A Biographical Companion*. (Oxford: ABC-CLIO, 2003).

Rex, Peter. *William the Conqueror. The Bastard of Normandy*. (Stroud, Glos: Amberley, 2011).

Rose, Kenneth. *George V*. (London: Orion, 2000).

Salway, Lance. *Queen Victoria's Grandchildren*. (London: Collins and Brown, 1991).

Shawcross, William. *Queen Elizabeth the Queen Mother. The Official Biography*. (London: Macmillan, 2009).

Skidmore, Chris. *Edward VI, the Lost King of England*. (London: Phoenix, 2008).

Somerset, Anne. *Queen Anne. The Politics of Passion. A Biography*. (London: HarperPress, 2012).

Van Der Kiste, John. *Queen Victoria's Children*. (Stroud, Glos.: Sutton Publishing, 2003).

Van Der Zee, Henri and Barbara. *William and Mary*. (London: Penguin, 1988).

Warner, Marina. *Queen Victoria's Sketchbook*. (London: Book Club Associates, 1979).

Warren, W.L. *King John*. (London: Yale University Press, 1961).

Weintraub, Stanley. *Albert. Uncrowned King*. (London: John Murray, 1997).

Weir, Alison. *Children of England. The Heirs of King Henry VIII*. (London: Pimlico, 1997).

Weir, Alison. *Eleanor of Aquitaine. By the Wrath of God, Queen of England*. (London: Pimlico, 2000).

Weir, Alison. *Elizabeth The Queen*. (London: Pimlico: 1999).

Weir, Alison. *Isabella. She-Wolf of France, Queen of England*. (London: Pimlico, 2006).

Weir, Alison. *Henry VIII. King and Court*. (London: Vintage, 2008).

Weir, Alison. *The Six Wives of Henry VIII*. (London: Pimlico, 1997).

General Works on British History:

Davies, Norman. *The Isles. A History*. (London: Macmillan, 2000).

Downing, Taylor, and Maggie Millman. *Civil War*. (London: Collins&Brown/Channel 4, 1991).

Lacey, Robert. *Great Tales From English History*. (London: Abacus, 2008).

Lee, Christopher. *This Sceptred Isle, 55bc-1901*. (London: Penguin/BBC, 1998).

Lewis-Stempel, John, Ed. *England, the Autobiography*. (London: Penguin, 2006).

Royle, Trevor. *Civil War. The Wars of the Three Kingdoms, 1638-1660*. (London: Abacus, 2005).

Royle, Trevor. *The Wars of the Roses. England's First Civil War*. (London: Abacus, 2010).

Schama, Simon. *A History of Britain*. 3 Volumes. (London: BBC Worldwide, 2003).

Vincent, Nicholas. *A Brief History of Britain 1066-1485*. (London: Robinson, 2011).

Weir, Alison. *Lancaster and York. The Wars of the Roses*. (London: Arrow Books, 1996).

Guidebooks:

Begent, Peter J. *The Romance of St George's Chapel, Windsor Castle*. 16th edition. (Windsor: Society of the Friends of St George's and the Descendants of the Knights of the Garter, 2001).

Dolman, Brett; Sebastian Edwards; Susanne Groom; and Marc Meltonville. *Explore Hampton Court Palace. Souvenir Guidebook.* (Hampton Court, Surrey: Historic Royal Palaces, 2008).

Edwards, Sebastian. *Discover Kew Palace. Official Guidebook.* (Hampton Court, Surrey: Historic Royal Palaces, 2006).

Haynes, John, and Clare Murphy. *Kensington Palace. The Official Guidebook.* (Hampton Court, Surrey: Historic Royal Palaces, 2007).

Keay, Anna. *The Crown Jewels. Official Guidebook.* (Hampton Court, Surrey: Historic Royal Palaces, 2002).

Marsden, Jonathan. *Clarence House. Official Souvenir Guide.* (London: Royal Collection, 2011).

Marsden, Jonathan. *Buckingham Palace. Official Souvenir Guide.* (London: Royal Collection, 2006).

Marsden, Jonathan, and Matthew Winterbottom. *Windsor Castle. Official Souvenir Guide.* (London: Royal Collection, 2009).

Robinson, John Martin. *Queen Mary's Doll's House. Official Souvenir Guide.* (London: Royal Collection, 2012).

Thurley, Simon; Edward Impey; and Peter Hammond. *The Tower of London. The Official Guidebook.* (Hampton Court, Surrey: Historic Royal Palaces, 2007).

Thurley, Simon; Susanne Groom; and Susan Jenkins. *The Banqueting House. Whitehall Palace.* (Hampton Court, Surrey: Historic Royal Palaces, 2000).

Turner, Michael. *Osborne. English Heritage Guidebook.* (London: English Heritage, 2012).

Vickers, Hugo. *The Royal Mews at Buckingham Palace. Official Guidebook.* (London: Royal Collection, 2009).

Other Works:

Alder, John. *Constitution and Administrative Law.* (London: Palgrave MacMillan, 2013).

Blackburn, Robert. "Crown and Crown Proceedings". *Halsbury's Laws of England. Volume 29 (2014).* (London: LNUK, 2014)

Carroll, Alex. *Constitution and Administrative Law.* (London: Pearson Longman, 2007).

Cohen, M.J., and John Major. *History in Quotations.* (London: Weidenfeld and Nicolson, 2008).

Crispino, Enrica. *Leonardo.*(Florence, Italy: Giunti, 2002).

Dunton-Downer, Leslie, and Alan Riding. *Essential Shakespeare Handbook.* (London: Dorling Kindersely, 2004).

Maltin, Leonard, Ed. *Leonard Maltin's Movie Guide 2009.* (London: Plume, 2008).

McDonogh, Katharine. *Reigning Cats and Dogs. A History of Pets at Court since the Renaissance.* (London: Fourth Estate, 1999).

Montague, Trevor. *A to Z of Britain and Ireland*. (London: Sphere, 2009).

Roden, Timothy J.; Craig Wright; and Bryan R. Simms. *Anthology for Music in Western Civilization. Volume I: Antiquity through the Baroque.* (Boston, MA, USA: Schirmer Cengage Learning, 2010).

Tydeman, William, Ed. *The Medieval European Stage, 500-1550.* (Cambridge: Cambridge University Press, 2001).

Mills, A.D. *A Dictionary of British Place Names*.(Oxford: Oxford University Press, 2011).

ONLINE SOURCES:

Official Royal Websites:

The British Monarchy official website: www.royal.gov.uk (old website) and www.royal.uk (new website).

The Prince Of Wales official website: www.princeofwales.gov.uk

The Royal Collection: www.royalcollection.org.uk

Balmoral, Scottish Home to the Royal Family, official website: www.balmoralcastle.com

The Sandringham Estate official website: www.sandringhamestate.co.uk

Edinburgh Castle Official Website: www.edinburghcastle.gov.uk

Historic Royal Palaces: www.hrp.org.uk

The Royal Parks, London: www.royalparks.org.uk

Queen Victoria's Journals, A Royal Archives website: www.queenvictoriasjournals.org

Reference, Information Sites and Web Resources:

BBC History: www.bbc.co.uk/history

BBC News: http://news.bbc.co.uk

British History Online: www.british-history.ac.uk

British Pathe': www.britishpathe.com

Luminarium, anthology of English literature. Luminarium Encyclopedia Project: www.luminarium.org

Oxford Dictionary of National Biography: www.oxforddnb.com

Oxford Reference: www.oxfordreference.com

Public Monuments and Sculpture Association: www.pmsa.org.uk
The Times Digital Archive, 1785-2006: http://gale.cengage.co.uk/times-digital-archive/times-digital-archive-17852006.aspx

The Victorian Web resource website: www.victorianweb.org

Wikipedia: www.wikipedia.org

Government Resources:

Gov.uk: www.gov.uk

Legislation.gov.uk: www.legislation.gov.uk

The Privy Council Office: http://privycouncil.independent.gov.uk/

The UK Parliament official website: www.parliament.uk

The UK Prime Minister official website: https://www.gov.uk/government/organisations/prime-ministers-office-10-downing-street

Church and Religious Websites:

The Abbey Church of St Mary and Melor, Amesbury: www.maryandmelor.com

Biblical Studies: https://biblicalstudies.org.uk/

The Church of England official website: www.churchofengland.org

The Church of Scotland official website: www.churchofscotland.org.uk

Douai Abbey official website: www.douaiabbey.org.uk

St George's Chapel, Windsor Castle official website: www.stgeorges-windsor.org

Westminster Abbey official website: www.westminster-abbey.org/

British Armed Forces and other Military-Related Websites:

The British Army official website: www.army.mod.uk

British Military Awards and Decorations: https://www.gov.uk/topic/defence-armed-forces/military-awards-commemorations

Changing of the Guard at Buckingham Palace, an unofficial information site: http://changing-guard.com

The Greenwich Hospital Royal Navy Charity official website: www.grenhosp.org.uk

The Household Division official website: www.householddivision.org.uk

Old Comrades Associations of the Household Cavarly: http://householdcavalry.co.uk/

The Queen's Body Guard of the Yeoman of the Guard, by Yeoman William Norton: www.yeomenoftheguard.com

The Royal Hospital Chelsea official website: www.chelsea-pensioners.co.uk

Trooping the Colour, an unofficial information site: www.trooping-the-colour.co.uk

Museums and Educational Institutions:

The American Film Institute: www.afi.com

British Film Institute Screen Online: www.screenonline.org.uk

The British Library official website: www.bl.uk

The British Postal Museum and Archive Blog: https://postalheritage.wordpress.com

Elmbridge Museum, Surrey: http://elmbridgemuseum.org.uk

The Guards Museum, London: www.theguardsmuseum.com

The Household Cavalry Museum, London: www.householdcavalrymuseum.co.uk

Kingston Upon Hull history centre: www.hullhistorycentre.org.uk

Lyme Regis Museum official website: www.lymeregismuseum.co.uk

Museo Nazionale Scienza e Technologia Leonardo da Vinci, Milan, Italy: www.museoscienza.org

Museum of the History of Science, Oxford: www.mhs.ox.ac.uk

The National Archives: www.nationalarchives.gov.uk

The National Army Museum, London: www.nam.ac.uk

The National Gallery of Canada, Ottawa: www.gallery.ca

Royal Museums Greenwich: www.rmg.co.uk

Tunbridge Wells Museum and Art Gallery official website: www.tunbridgewellsmuseum.org

The Victoria and Albert Museum, London, official website: www.vam.ac.uk

Local Authorities Resources:

Beeston Regis Parish Council website: http://beestonregispc.norfolkparishes.gov.uk

Bere Regis village website: www.bereregis.org

Bognor Regis information site: www.bognor-regis.co.uk

Epsom and Ewell History Explorer: www.epsomandewellhistoryexplorer.org.uk

Grafton Regis Village website: www.grafton-regis.co.uk

A History of Birmingham Places and Placenames A to Y by William Dargue: https://billdargue.jimdo.com/placenames-gazetteer-a-to-y/places-k/kingstanding/

Houghton Regis Town Council official website: www.houghtonregis.org.uk

Kingsclere Heritage Association blog: https://kingsclereheritageassociation.wordpress.com

King's Langley Local History and Museum Society: www.kingslangley.org.uk

King's Lynn online information site: www.kingslynnonline.com

King's Sutton, Northamptonshire information site: www.kingssutton.org

Kingswinford, West Midlands history website: www.kingswinford.com

Kinneff Old Kirk, Guardians of the Honours of Scotland, 1651-1660: www.kinneffoldchurch.co.uk/

The London Borough of Greenwich, official website: www.royalgreenwich.gov.uk

The London Borough of Richmond upon Thames, official website www.richmond.gov.uk

Rowley Regis Village website: http://rowleyvillage.webs.com

Genealogy and Heraldry:

Debrett's Online: www.debretts.com

Heraldica, a site about heraldry: www.heraldica.org

Medieval Lands. A Prosopography of Medieval European Noble and Royal Families: http://fmg.ac/Projects/MedLands/

The Peerage. A Genealogical Survey of the Peerage of Britain as well as the Royal families of Europe: www.thepeerage.com/

Blogs and Dedicated Sites:

British Royal Family History: www.britroyals.com

English Monarchs: www.englishmonarchs.co.uk

From Her Majesty's Jewel Vault: http://queensjewelvault.blogspot.co.uk/

Regency History: www.regencyhistory.net
Royal Magazin blog: http://royal-magazin.de/

The Royal Order of Sartorial Splendour: http://orderofsplendor.blogspot.co.uk

Unofficial Royalty, the site for royal news and discussion: www.unofficialroyalty.com

Other Sites:

All about Elgar: www.elgar.org

The Armada Paintings project: http://armada.parliament.uk/history.html

The Ceremony of the Lilies and Roses at the Tower of London, Spitafields Life website: http://spitalfieldslife.com/2011/05/24/the-ceremony-of-the-lilies-the-roses-at-the-tower-of-london/

Department of Canadian Heritage: www.canada.ca/en/canadian-heritage.html

Eltham Palace and Gardens, official English Heritage website: www.english-heritage.org.uk/visit/places/eltham-palace-and-gardens

Faberge, official website: www.faberge.com

GB Stamps, Great Britain Philately: www.gbstamps.com

The Jacobite Heritage: www.jacobite.ca

Linn's Stamp News: www.linns.com

Marlborough House, the Commonwealth official website: http://thecommonwealth.org/marlborough-house

Measuring Worth: www.measuringworth.com

The National Archives Currency Converter: www.nationalarchives.gov.uk/currency/

Newmarket Racing Site: www.newmarket-racing.org

The Queen's Swan Marker: www.royalswan.co.uk

The Redfern Gallery, London: www.redfern-gallery.com

The Royal Variety Charity: http://www.royalvarietycharity.org

Somerset House, official website: www.somersethouse.org.uk

The State Coach Britannia: http://royalcoach.downau.com via http://archive.is

Welsh Corgi News: www.welshcorgi-news.ch

AUDIOVISUAL SOURCES:

Documentaries:

David Starkey's Monarchy. First Series. (Channel 4: 2004).

David Starkey's Monarchy. Second Series. (Channel 4: 2006).

David Starkey's Monarchy. Third Series. (Channel 4: 2007).

David Starkey's Music and Monarchy. 4 Episodes. (BBC: 2013).

Days of Majesty. (ITV: 1993).

Richard III: The New Evidence. (Channel 4: 2014).

Royal Deaths and Diseases. "Episode 5: Tainted Blood". (Channel 4: 2003).

Royal Paintbox. Artists of the Royal Family. (ITV: 2013).

Films:
(used to compile the section 'Notable Films on Royal History')

A Man For All Seasons. (1966). Dir: Fred Zinnemann.

Alfred the Great. (1969). Dir: Clive Donner.

Anne of the Thousand Days. (1969). Dir: Charles Jarrott.

Beau Brummell. (1954). Dir: Curtis Bernhardt.

Becket. (1964). Dir: Peter Grenville.

Bonnie Prince Charlie. (1948). Dir: Anthony Kimmins.

Braveheart. (1995). Dir: Mel Gibson.

Cromwell. (1970). Dir: Ken Hughes.

Diana. (2013). Dir: Oliver Hirschbiegel.

Elizabeth. (1998). Dir: Shekhar Kapur.

Elizabeth: The Golden Age. (2007). Dir: Shekhar Kapur.

Fire Over England. (1937). Dir: William K. Howard.

Henry VIII and His Six Wives. (1972). Dir: Waris Hussein.

Lady Jane. (1986). Dir: Trevor Nunn.

Mary of Scotland. (1936). Dir: John Ford.

Mary Queen of Scots. (1971). Dir: Charles Jarrott.

Mrs Brown. (1997). Dir: John Madden.

Nell Gwynn. (1934). Dir: Herbert Wilcox.

Saraband for Dead Lovers. (1948). Dir: Basil Dearden.

The Bruce. (1996). Dir: Bob Carruthers and David McWhinnie.

The King's Speech. (2010). Director: Tom Hooper.

The Lion In Winter. (1968). Dir: Anthony Harvey.

The Madness of King George. (1994). Dir: Nicholas Hytner.

The Other Boleyn Girl. (2008). Dir: Justin Chadwick.

The Private Life of Henry VIII.(1933) Dir: Alexander Korda.

The Private Lives of Elizabeth and Essex. (1939). Dir: Michael Curtiz.

The Queen. (2006). Dir: Stephen Frears.

The Virgin Queen. (1955). Dir: Henry Koster.

The Young Victoria. (2009). Dir: Jean-Marc Vallee.

To Kill A King. (2003). Dir: Mike Barker.

Tower of London. (1939). Dir: Rowland V. Lee.

Young Bess. (1953). Dir: George Sidney.

The Imperial Crown graphic used throughout the book was created by The Vector Lab, and was downloaded free as advertised for commercial and personal use on 3 February 2016. It can currently be found at the following address:
https://www.vecteezy.com/heraldry/476-vector-crowns

About the Author

Alex David has a Bachelor's Degree in History and Politics, a Master's Degree in Christian Theology, as well as qualifications in journalism and English-language teaching. He has lived in three countries (Italy, the United States and Britain), and speaks English, Italian and French. This is his first book. He lives in London.

Made in the USA
Monee, IL
14 March 2023

29894263R00325